Representations of the Social

P9-CDM-009

To Sam and Robbie

Representations of the Social

Bridging Theoretical Traditions

Edited by

Kay Deaux *and* Gina Philogène

HM
1011
.R46
2001

Copyright © Blackwell Publishers Ltd 2001

First published 2001

2 4 6 8 10 9 7 5 3 1

Blackwell Publishers Ltd
108 Cowley Road
Oxford OX4 1JF
UK

Blackwell Publishers Inc.
350 Main Street
Malden, Massachusetts 02148
USA

IPFW
WITHDRAWN
AUG a 2002
HELMKE LIBRARY

All rights reserved. Except for the quotation of short passages for the purposes of criticism
and review, no part of this publication may be reproduced, stored in a retrieval system, or
transmitted, in any form or by any means, electronic, mechanical, photocopying or
otherwise, without the prior permission of the publisher.

Except in the United States of America, this book is sold subject to the condition that it
shall not, by way of trade or otherwise, be lent, resold, hired out, or otherwise circulated
without the publisher's prior consent in any form of binding or cover other than that in
which it is published and without a similar condition including this condition being
imposed on the subsequent purchaser.

British Library Cataloguing in Publication Data

A CIP catalogue record for this book is available from the British Library.

Library of Congress Cataloging-in-Publication Data

Representations of the social : bridging theoretical traditions / edited
by Kay Deaux and Gina Philogène.
    p.   cm.
   Includes bibliographical references and index.
   ISBN 0–631–21533–6 (hardcover : acid-free paper) — ISBN 0–631–21534–4
(pbk. : acid-free paper)
   1. Social psychology.   2. Social perception.   3. Social interaction.
I. Deaux, Kay.   II. Philogène, Gina, 1961–
HM1011 .R46 2001
302—dc21
    00–010708

Typeset in 10 on 12.5 pt Bembo by Ace Filmsetting Ltd, Frome, Somerset
Printed in Great Britain by MPG Books Ltd., Bodmin, Cornwall

This book is printed on acid-free paper.

Contents

Contents

Part III: Social Representation and Social Construction   129

Part IV: Social Representation and Social Categorization   199

Preface and Acknowledgments

This book is the outgrowth of a conference held at the Graduate Center of the City University of New York on October 9 and 10, 1998, a conference designed to bring together two groups of scholars who do not often meet and to see what intellectual sparks and connections might emerge.

Like most intellectual projects, this one has a number of points of origin. In terms of the collaboration between the two editors, this project began in 1992 in Louvain, Belgium, when the European Association of Experimental Psychology and the U.S.-based Society of Experimental Social Psychology held a joint meeting. On that occasion, the two of us first met and began what has been an ongoing conversation about social psychology and social representations.

In some sense, however, the intellectual history goes further back to the time, before either of us held positions in New York, when Stanley Milgram was a faculty member at the Graduate Center of the City University of New York (CUNY). In an early book about social representations edited by Robert Farr and Serge Moscovici (1984), Milgram contributed a chapter in which he described his studies of mental maps of Paris and New York. The work on social representations of Paris, done in collaboration with Denise Jodelet and aided by Serge Moscovici, had a physical manifestation at the Graduate Center in the form of a very large map of Paris. This map was a central feature of the Social-Personality area's décor until the recent relocation of the Graduate Center. Thus the links between New York and Paris were forged early. The idea of holding a conference at the Graduate Center that would bridge theoretical traditions, bringing the work of social representation researchers to a U.S. audience, seemed a totally appropriate extension of this early alliance.

We are grateful to Steve Breckler and the Social Psychology program at the National Science Foundation for granting funds that helped to support this conference. Financial support was also provided by the CUNY Doctoral Program in Psychology and by Blackwell Publishers. In addition, many faculty, students and staff at the Graduate Center contributed their time and effort to the project, ensuring the success of the conference and the completion of this book. In particular, we want to thank three graduate students in the doctoral program in Social–Personality Psychology – Ellie Buteau, Dana Martin, and Yelena Nemoy – who were with us throughout the project, from the organization of the conference through the review of the chapters in this volume. We also are grateful to Martin Davies, the editor at Blackwell Publishers whose enthusiasm for our project was so important to the development of this book. With Martin's departure from Blackwell, Alison Dunnett took over the project and guided us to its completion. To all of these people, our sincere thanks.

Kay Deaux
Gina Philogène

July 2000

Contributors

JEAN-CLAUDE ABRIC
 Université Aix-en-Provence, France

MARTHA AUGOUSTINOS
 University of Adelaide, Australia

GLYNIS M BREAKWELL
 University of Surrey, England

MARILYNN B. BREWER
 Ohio State University, USA

ALAIN CLÉMENCE
 University of Lausanne, Switzerland

KAY DEAUX
 Graduate Center of the City University of New York, USA

ANNAMARIA SILVANA DE ROSA
 Universita de Roma, Italy

WILLEM DOISE
 Université de Genève, Switzerland

GERARD DUVEEN
 Cambridge University, England

SUSAN T. FISKE
  Princeton University, USA

GEORGE GASKELL
  London School of Economics, England

GABRIEL IGNATOW
  Stanford University, USA

JOHN T. JOST
  Stanford University, USA

SANDRA JOVCHELOVITCH
  London School of Economics, England

NICOLE KRONBERGER
  Universität Linz, Austria

ARIE W. KRUGLANSKI
  University of Maryland, USA

SAADI LAHLOU
  Ecole des Hautes Etudes des Sciences Sociales, Paris, France

FABIO LORENZI-CIOLDI
  Université de Genève, Switzerland

HAZEL ROSE MARKUS
  Stanford University, USA

SERGE MOSCOVICI
  Laboratoire de Psychologie Sociale, Ecole des Hautes Etudes en Sciences
  Sociales, Paris, France

GINA PHILOGÈNE
  Sarah Lawrence College, Broxville, USA

VICTORIA C. PLAUT
  Stanford University, USA

Contributors

WOLFGANG WAGNER
    Universität Linz, Austria

MARISA ZAVALLONI
    Université de Montreal, Canada

Part I

Framing the Issues

1

Introduction

Gina Philogène and Kay Deaux

In offering to bridge theoretical traditions, as the subtitle of this volume promises, we recognize the hybrid nature of social psychology and acknowledge some of the fundamental distinctions that exist within the discipline. One of these distinctions concerns the difference between a sociological orientation and a psychological one. Indeed, from the dual agenda of Wilhelm Wundt at the inception of social psychology to today's lack of contact between social psychologists in psychology departments and those in sociology departments, such segregation has always been present (cf. Stryker, 1989). A second division worth discussing, especially in the context of this volume, concerns the contrast often made between European and American approaches (Farr, 1996; Graumann, 1996). American social psychology has often been praised for setting a standard for empirical research, preferring experimentation to other types of methodology and focusing primarily on quantitative measurements. At the same time, social psychologists in this tradition have been criticized for their narrowness – for creating a discipline that is, in the words of Duveen (2000), "dominated . . . first by behaviourism, and more recently by a no less reductive cognitivism, and throughout this time by a thoroughgoing individualism" (p. 4). In contrast, many investigators emerging from European social psychology have been more concerned with intergroup and societal phenomena. European social psychologists have also characteristically opted for a wider range of methodologies, often using qualitative as well as quantitative techniques in their research.

Although having some historical truth, these bipolar characterizations of the field are undoubtedly too simplistic to describe the contemporary climate. First, it is unreasonable to talk of a single European social psychology. The cultural richness and diversity of Europe's various populations have created many different forms of social psychology, many of which remain unexplored due to linguistic barriers and international access. Further, the climate within the United States is changing as well. Qualitative methods of research have gained a great deal of prominence in recent years, as exemplified by encyclopedic coverage of various qualitative strategies (Denzin & Lincoln, 2000) and two recent well-attended conferences at the CUNY Graduate Center on qualitative methods in psychology. The growth of cultural psychology as a field of interest (e.g., Markus, Kitayama, & Heiman, 1996) poses questions for assumptions of universality and individualism, as well as forces one to look at issues of context and change.

The challenge has been to find a synthesis between the different poles that threaten to fragment the field. By reconnecting two important but often divergent views of social psychology – one from France where the discipline was formally introduced by Durkheim, and the other from the United States where it flourished – we are trying to explore the common ground that may exist in spite of the apparent divergences and dissimilarities. With this introduction of social representation theory to American social psychologists, we hope to generate a dialogue connecting the epistemological dimensions of a sociologically defined theory to those of a more psychological nature. In so doing, we speak to the fundamental questions that social psychologists are called upon to address, namely those that speak to the links between individuals and their social world.

More specifically, the purpose of this book is to introduce the theory of social representations in a manner that contextualizes its presentation within the more dominant and more familiar approaches of American social psychology. Our aim is to show how the social representation approach relates to other perspectives – how it, in fact, creates a rejoinder to the other perspectives currently employed in social psychology research. The strength of social representation theory has been its ability to explain sociocultural phenomena, by being eminently practical in a Lewinian sense. For this reason the conceptual complexity of the theory has been matched by methodological strategies that often combine a variety of empirical techniques. This rich connection between theory and empirical applications, both quantitative and qualitative, has made social representation theory particularly effective in studying modern society.

Social representations, the central element of this approach first introduced by Serge Moscovici, are built on shared knowledge and understanding of common reality. Any interaction, whether between two individuals or two groups of individuals, presupposes shared representations which enable us to name and classify the various aspects of our social reality. It is through those commonly shared and collectively elaborated social representations that we make sense of the world and communicate that sense to each other. As proof of our fundamentally social existence, they originate in daily life quite naturally, in the course of interindividual communication. They allow us to construct a framework of references that facilitates our interpretations of reality and guides our relations to the world around us.

Because we elaborate them together and evoke them frequently, social representations become deeply embedded in our cultural fabric.

The study of social representations involves the study of society in all its dynamic expressions. It focuses on the social nature of thought and the ways in which people change their society. From this perspective the interplay between internal mechanisms and the constantly changing social world is actualized through the interconnectedness of individuals. Far from being a recent interest in the social sciences, this question was one of the principal preoccupations of early European social thinkers. Emile Durkheim, who launched this agenda, made a distinction between individual representations and collective representations. However, he never reached the integrative conception of the two to make a synthesis of them. Others, however, have been more successful, stressing the interconnectedness of the social and the individual. Georg Simmel's concept of "social ideas," Lev Vygotsky's notion of "higher mental functions," and Max Weber's idea of "*Vorstellugen*" are all noteworthy attempts at such an integration. Each managed to complete Durkheim's important contribution without, however, fully extending this effort to a general theory of society.

Social representation theory adds to this quest by introducing a new synthesis between the individual and the social. Here individuals do not form their thoughts in isolation, but by influencing one another and therefore on the basis of collectively shared reifications of objects that make up their reality. These shared representations shape our beliefs, ideas, attitudes, and opinions so as to give meaning to things and help us understand each other. Hence, social representations act as the bridge between the individual and the social world. As a societal construction, socially elaborated and collectively shared, they have a two-fold existence. First, they are the products of social thinking, structuring beliefs, and knowledge about phenomena considered significant for a given community. Second, social representations are the processes by which we construct our reality. As social-psychological mechanisms they shape how we think and talk about events and objects. They are, in other words, products of interconnectedness between people and processes of reference through which we conceive the world around us. It is this dual existence as product and process which gives social representations their omnipresence in our daily lives as the constituent elements of our social world.

The embeddedness of social representations in our cultural fabric rests on two processes through which objects become re-presented in our minds. *Anchoring* categorizes a new object into our preexisting mental systems, thereby rendering a strange and unfamiliar object familiar and recomposing it within ordinary categories (a process that Kashima, 2000, has recently compared to Bartlett's 1967, first published 1932, notion of conventionalization). This ordering activity enables us to classify the object in question and to give it an appropriate name for reference. *Objectification* assures the crystallization of the new object into a figurative core, so as to allow the projection of images. To objectify means to turn something abstract into something almost concrete, relating this to a transfer from the level of idea to the level of existence in the physical world. On the basis of images and related icons an otherwise abstract object is turned into a part of our social reality and becomes perceptibly real (e.g., the image of God as "father," the flag as symbol for nation, the conceptualization of race in terms of skin color). At this point of concretization people can talk about the object, and through communication the object acquires the density of meaning that makes it a "natural" fixture in people's minds.

Social representations exist wherever people engage with one another, giving a structuring context to their otherwise heterogeneous society. Three characteristics help maintain their omnipresence in our social lives. They are above all prescriptive inasmuch as they compose a socially created metasystem that regulates, controls, and directs individual minds. That metasystem is a structure that influences us, often unconsciously, that guides us when we make decisions, and that forces us by means of conventions to take account of what others think about that object. Social representations are also consensual in the sense that they provide a means for calibrating views about an object for comparison and juxtaposition. And this calibration requires a structuring core for the collective conceptualization of an object as one and the same. Finally, once representations are created, they are autonomous to the extent that they lead a life of their own and evolve beyond the reach of individuals.

By its nature, social representation theory is grounded in the operations of the societies in which we live. In its emphasis on consensus and communication, it turns our attention to the lay understandings and the "common sense" of people functioning in a society. Similarly, in grounding itself in the shared belief structure, it is able to address key aspects of contemporary life, directing our attention to those phenomena and events that feature prominently in people's lives (e.g., race, biotechnology, mental illness, and human rights).

Our introduction of social representation theory begins with a theoretical discussion by Serge Moscovici, the acknowledged father of this theoretical perspective, in which he takes us on an intellectual journey through a variety of terrains in attempting to answer the question "why do we need a theory of social representations?" With this discussion as a backdrop, we move in Part II to an introduction of the model via case studies and methods. In her introduction to this section (Chapter 3), Gina Philogène takes note of the interdependence of method and theory in the work of social representation investigators, and the five examples in this section clearly illustrate that interdependence. The contributions of Jean-Claude Abric (Chapter 4) and Alain Clémence (Chapter 6) develop theoretical analyses of social representations, in each case an analysis that has definite implications for methodology. The chapters by Annamaria de Rosa (Chapter 5), Willem Doise (Chapter 7), and Gina Philogène (Chapter 8) each describe a research program in which social representation theory is used to explore a distinctive social phenomenon. Together, these chapters are intended to convey to readers, particularly those previously unfamiliar with work in social representations, the scope and diversity of work in this field.

In Parts III, IV, and V of this volume, we focus on three different social psychological processes – social construction, social categorization, and social identity. In each case, representatives of the social representation school were asked to describe their research programs with an eye to the links that might be made with other theoretical traditions. In turn, two commentators not associated with social representation (SR) theory were asked to offer their thoughts on how theoretical traditions might be bridged. It is through these quasi-dialogues that we hope to discover what bridges are possible, and how research in succeeding generations can take advantage of the mutual contributions that can be established.

The ultimate success of our efforts will, of course, be seen not now but in the future. We hope that investigators in the future will add weight and substance to the bridges that we begin here, and build other bridges as well. If they do, we believe the social psychological enterprise will be richer as a result.

2

Why a Theory of Social Representations?

Serge Moscovici

Lass uns menschlich sein
Ludwig Wittgenstein

In this chapter I will try to explain why I consider this theory a foundation rather than an eccentricity in our field. As soon as I started talking about a theory of social representations, I noticed that the phrase was considered disturbing and in many ways staggering or provocative. And I have met with many more reactions of this kind since. No one, however, has yet asked me the real question: "*Why* a theory of social representations?" I am grateful to Kay Deaux and Gina Philogène for finally putting this question to me and thus giving me an excellent opportunity to answer it.[1]

In 1955, Ann Parsons, the daughter of the well-known American sociologist, was the first from a group of students I had assembled to work on this emerging theory. In her doctoral thesis, which she passed at the Sorbonne, she compared the diffusion of psychoanalysis in France and in the United States. The panel consisted of the psychoanalyst Lagache, the psychopathologist Poirier, and the child psychologist Piaget. Subsequently, the notion of social representation was propagated in France as well as Italy where Ann Parsons went to study the strongly controversial universality of the Oedipal complex. Her study was based on the assumption that this complex is an internalized social representation of brother—sister, father—daughter and mother—son relations (Parsons, 1969). Despite the severe criticism, censorship, or disfavor attached to anything that is not part of mainstream thinking, several generations of researchers have disseminated the theory in most countries and have thus opened new routes for it. In one way, the question why we need a theory of social representations comes too late. The damage is done!

Time gone by, however, has not weakened the freshness of my first intuition. When I started my work the image presented by social psychology was that of a great many unconnected phenomena, a large number of disjointed ideas; in short, such an atomization of things that social psychological unity, as stated in the manuals, was nothing but an academic exercise. Indeed, unity within a research area is not a value in itself. Lack of unity, however, can lead to an impasse. In order to solve this question, I have chosen social knowledge as the focus of social psychology. The different processes – memory, perception, information gathering, dissonance – obviously all work together to provide the actual knowledge within a social context. However, we are all aware that the phenomena and the content of social psychology go further than that, comprising values, standards, histories, myths, conventions, and symbols. These are acquired through direct experience, mainly from relations with our group of friends, our parents, and the culture that is ours.

It is possible to distinguish two sources of social knowledge. We share in the first because we have experienced it directly and are certain of its validity: we know, in the narrowest sense of the word. We know, for instance, with whom we have to shake hands, or that it is necessary to drive on the correct side of the road. The second source of knowledge reveals itself when we state that we know the formula $e = mc^2$, or that smoking causes lung cancer. It goes without saying that in the latter case we believe that others, such as Einstein or medical professors, know the facts, and that we have good reasons to believe in them. This knowledge that we share with others definitely entails a new element: trust. We can therefore state that trust is both at the origin and the limit of social knowledge. And there is not a single form of intellectual activity, including the sciences, in which it does not occur. This explains why, as Newell (1994) writes:

> the content of social knowledge is not given, nor derivable from the basic mechanisms and task features. Such mechanisms are based exclusively on criteria of validity. There is an element of fundamental historical contingency in social situations. The content of knowledge might vary arbitrarily between social groups and cultures, but such body of mores is required. (p. 495)

I would like you to keep in mind this image of social psychology as being the study of social knowledge, which forms the basis of my work.

The next question is obviously: how can we study it? For various reasons I have chosen two important and significant phenomena – social representations and communication (including influence) – as foundations for my work. This choice is supported by arguments that I think are solid (Moscovici, 1976a, first published 1961) so that social psychology can be said to be based on those phenomena. Herein lies the first part of the answer to the question being asked. However, a more complete answer requires that we look at more specific aspects.

The Stuff of Social Psychology

We all would like to understand what social knowledge is, yet everyone approaches the problem in his or her own way. For a person looking at the theory the difficulty lies in selecting the current version of one of the perennial problems of culture and history which appears to express something essential to human life and thought. This may be the reason why we do not always dare tackle them. The perennial problem with regard to social knowledge is: how and why do ways of thinking and their content change in diverging and complementary directions? (Goody, 1977). In ancient days, when philosophy came into being, thinkers had to deal with the problem of moving from myth to logic, from simple opinion to true knowledge (Ortega y Gasset, 1967). For us, since the advent of science and an industrial society, the problem is how to move from philosophy to modern science, from religious beliefs to secular rationality. Every social or psychological science reformulates the problem in its own terms: anthropology sees the problem as that of primitive thinking versus civilized thinking, magic versus science (Horton & Finnegan, 1986; Hollis & Lukes, 1982); sociology sees the problem as one of moving from ideology to science, from nonrational knowledge to rational knowledge (Wilson, 1970; Moscovici, 1988); in psychology and child psychology it is the problem of how the development from the nonrational to the rational occurs. In one sense they are all versions of the fundamental problem of our epistemology relating to the transformation of common sense into science, the transition of preparadigmatic science to paradigmatic science.

What remains is our version of the problem, which few people have tried to tackle and which seems to me to be specific to social psychology. It consists of knowing how science, by spreading throughout society, turns into common knowledge or lay knowledge: in short, how science manages to become part of our cultural heritage, of our thinking, of our language, and daily practices. Or, to put it another way, how and why countless new ideas, strange images, esoteric names relating to the universe, economy, the body, the mind, and history have become accepted ideas by leaving the labs and publications of a small scientific community to penetrate the conversation, the relationships, or the behavior of a large community and to get diffused in its dictionaries and current reading matter. More amazing is the fact that a great variety of theories from the most diverse of sciences, scientific works, and many thinkers, combine and unify in a shared vision, shaped by the intuitions, the interests, and the ordinary experience of each of us. Even if all the illusory and questionable interpretations are taken into account, such a vision manifests a new cultural dimension.

All this shows clearly enough why the theory of social representations appeared while studying the contemporary version of a problem that keeps cropping up within our culture. In view of this problem, what can the theory contribute when, in all other respects, it is ignored or opposed by the dominant perspective? My aim here is less to defend the theory than to take a sober look at some of its crucial implications. It is sufficient to start with looking at what is already suggested by our language, which links the terms common sense and folk science, so that scientific knowledge and vernacular knowledge are closely interrelated. This is confirmed even better by the fact that explanations, ideas, or facts which are no longer current in science, such as Aristotle's physics, part of Newton's mechanical laws, and natural history, are attributed to common sense. In my view, it is not by chance that they coexist with the vernacular ideas on the world surrounding us, the classification systems for diseases, groups of people, or even animal or plant species. We all know what are the first words that a doctor will say to us: "Well, what is the problem?" This question presupposes that we, as patients, are able to give a diagnosis in everyday language. It is then up to the doctor to translate this diagnosis into a medical language. More or less the same thing happens when we are in contact with other experts, whether it is in the area of business matters, family problems, car mechanics, and so on. Our common sense includes a lot of know-how, ways in which to make friends, succeed in life, avoid crises, eat well etc. Everybody agrees that common sense is a genuine encyclopedia of commonplaces relating to psychology: "The grass is always greener on the other side of the fence," or to morals: "Forbidden fruit is sweet," etc., which serve their purpose in many a situation where they appear trustworthy. Even dealers on the stock market, who do not have an exact science at their disposal, rely on a set of commonplaces such as "Trees don't grow sky high," indicating that the value of shares will not increase beyond any limit, or "Buy when you hear canons, sell when you hear violins" to indicate that you should buy when the situation appears worrisome and sell in a favorable period.

It is on the basis of this knowledge that people are mostly aware of their situation or make important decisions; also to a large extent on the basis of folk geography, folk biology, folk medicine, folk economics or folk physics – in retrospect, they all have been rather successful. It would be wrong to say that they are quite erroneous, considering that they are the basis of our modern sciences, and do not conflict with them. Without going into a closer investigation, let me quote Duhem (1903) who wrote: "Our most sublime knowledge is, in the end, based on nothing other than the facts of common sense" (p. 179). But this does not prevent us from noticing the differences between this type of knowledge and scientific knowledge. Firstly, it does not have truth or epistemic error as its only touchstone. Furthermore, common sense is acquired by each of us during the normal course of our life. It is a mother-knowledge which we assimilate, without specific training, at the same time as our mother tongue. It is probably universal, shared by the majority of members in a community and, as James (1978) wrote, "satisfies in an extraordinarily successful way the purpose for which we think" (p. 89).

We are obviously aware of the manner in which common sense develops and changes. To a large extent, it precedes the advent of scientific knowledge and education. It diffuses among what I would like to call folk protosciences, a process comparable to what happens in traditional societies (Jodelet, 1991).

The most spectacular characteristic of modern times could well be, at least here in the West, the commitment made to each and every one to learn how to read and write based on the supposition which has the strength of a conviction that on it depends educational progress, the decline of illiteracy, knowledge in general, and the dissemination of sciences. The arduous learning process is presumably rewarded by "the sweetness of light" it brings to people. It does, however, lead, on the one hand, to the downgrading of folk protosciences and popular knowledge which are considered trivial, superficial, and false. This goes hand in hand with the contempt expressed, for instance, in the currently used phrase "vulgarization of science." On the other hand, there is the solid belief that scientific thought should replace lay thinking and popular lore. In other words, the dissemination and socialization of science aims to replace and eliminate lay knowledge and all common forms of knowledge. This belief also haunts Marxism and liberalism, the current educational practices which appear to be the prerequisite for modern rationality.

I would rather not dwell on the truly discouraging nature of this belief and the general perplexity it causes. I have always believed that the communication and dissemination of science cannot and does not supersede and reduce common sense. Conversely, where they are successful, they enlarge science by transforming it into a new common sense (Moscovici & Hewstone, 1983; Farr 1993). They create, so to speak, *folk postsciences*. They have even generated a considerable industry with its own significance and criteria and employing numerous scientists. While I defend this point of view, I am aware that I have gone against a conception that is deeply rooted in the scientific community and with specialists in the diffusion of scientific information. I do not dispute the comparative merits of the various epistemological schools. What strikes as more worthy of notice is that our contemporary common sense is not produced by thinking individuals but by *thinking societies* in clubs, museums, public libraries, political libraries, cafes, economic or political associations, ecological movements, medical waiting rooms, therapy groups, adult education classes, and so forth. Wherever people chat, cannot but chat, they exchange opinions, information, experiences, listen to "those who know," about health, mind, society, and seek agreement. Through the usual channels of communication new scientific ideas and technical or medical discoveries become part of the normal intellect and language. Even in an extremely simplified and skewed form, such theories and discoveries appear in books on healing, teaching people to enhance their self-esteem or maintain their health, giving clues on "how the mind works." These books prolong and in turn feed the conversations taking place.

Theories and discoveries serve in the end as currencies in the coherent system which consists of heterogeneous knowledge stemming from biology, physics, political sciences, or oriental wisdom. Thus altered, they enter into the astonishing range of folk postsciences which occupy more space in our libraries and bookshops than the science of professional scientists. This result is similar to the transformation of the pidgin spoken on Hawaii at the beginning of the century. Its grammar depended on the mother tongue of the speaker, for instance a Japanese or Filipino. Within two decades, this community had created a new Creole dialect which had its roots in the pidgin, a uniform vocabulary borrowed from the English, and its own grammar which bore no relation to that of English or any other parent language. In the same way we create within our thinking societies, of which the membership fluctuates, a Darwinian Creole, a market economy Creole, a psychoanalysis Creole, etc. The prestige and credibility of these rest on their alleged links with the theories they consist of and their prestigious authors such as Darwin or Freud.

Ironically, it was the works written on the subject by Gustave towards the end of his life that convinced me that my intuitions regarding the problems posed by the transformation of science into common sense were correct. First of all, there is the *Dictionnaire des idées reçues*, so comical and so profound. It illustrates clearly to what extent our dictionaries and encyclopedias are repositories of the common sense of a society or a time. They institutionalize the circulating social representations, shared "spontaneously by most people" (Lahlou, 1998). Flaubert's *Dictionnaire* is accompanied by *Bouvard et Pécuchet*, a novel indeed, but also a historical document of a pattern which emerged towards the end of the nineteenth century, the dissemination of science in modern society. Following the two scriveners launched in a frantic search of scraps of knowledge across agriculture, chemistry, phrenology, etc. gave me the inspiration for my theory. Without any special preparation or discernment they keep reading books by specialists or popularizers that they heard of or on which they can lay their hands. They march forward through the field of science as explorers through time and space. And by letting themselves be dragged into discussion they also carry out experiments within the familiar framework of their environment. When they imitate scientists, it is because of their undiscriminating assumption that reality has to be what science says it is. If Bouvard and Pécuchet founder in their discussions or fail in their experiments, it is because they lack the skill that would allow them to adjust knowledge to the tests one would like to submit it to – a skill that is not acquired from reading books. This exhilarating and pathetic novel paints a convincing picture of the ways in which scientific knowledge is disseminated and communicated. It gives us an image of our thinking societies which cross the various sciences for everyday purposes.

What I found to be even more significant was that Flaubert described the intellectual navigation of these two amateur scientists on the sea of common sense as thinking "in pairs." This is the reason why I have chosen Bouvard and Pécuchet as symbols of the present-day laymen in my theory. It demonstrates that ordinary knowledge, common sense, cannot be produced by the proverbial "man in the street," or the intuitive scientist seeking and thinking alone about existing information. Thinking consists for the larger part of looking for exchange and agreement. It is to procure the pleasure of company. Common knowledge results from countless transactions of thought dialogue. In any case, the novel illustrates my idea of the transition from new sciences to new folk postsciences that our culture appropriates, a process by which the former generates the latter. So there is precious little chance that common sense, which results from this necessary process, will be replaced by what in essence created it and then disappear. This would make the meeting point, or the interface between our culture and our society, disappear, which is impossible.

Well considered, these arguments appear to be pointing towards only one thing with regard to the premise I began with. This is that social psychology, like every science, requires a "stuff" which is not of its own making. This "stuff" is common sense, just as language is the stuff of linguistics, myth that of anthropology, dreams that of psychoanalysis. If I revert to it now, when this premise is no longer in question, it is not out of habit. The reasons that seemed right to me still seem right. It is, above all, in order to make you better understand that people have become familiar with at least their vocabulary.

Right Minds, Mistaken Minds, and Other Minds

Gertrude Stein was once a psychology student. In her memoirs she wrote the following about her professor, William James: "Keep your minds open," he used to say. And someone objected: "But Professor James, this that I say is true." "Yes," said James, "it is abjectly true." (1962, p. 74). I have chosen the recollection of this remarkable woman because I propose to talk about something that could be considered abjectly true, as it means that one can look in different ways at a scientific work. In a classic work we all agree that Heider (1958) claimed à la Borges that he had discovered the theory of interpersonal relations by commenting on the works of philosophers, novelists, playwrights, and psychologists and combining their ideas to form the theory of these relations. This theory is at the same time an illustration of what is common sense and a plea in its favor. And since American psychosociologists have started to become interested in common sense, I figured that they would end up recognizing it as the stuff of social psychology. But that would be forgetting that the literature regarding social knowledge is littered with desperate attempts to define what proper knowledge is and to illustrate that social knowledge is not. It was, rather curiously, the philosophers of the Enlightenment who, while fighting for equality between people, provided the seed for what could be called the *myth of the absurdity* of the beliefs and thoughts of the majority of mankind. Condorcet condemned "public opinion which remains that of the most stupid and miserable group." Diderot confirms that "the opinion of the ignorant and numbed masses in matters of reasoning and philosophy is to be mistrusted, its voice being that of nastiness, of stupidity, of inhumanity, of insanity and of prejudice" (Farge, 1992, p. 71).

This belief – as far as one can generalize – that all that is thought by the common man or the masses is false, all that is said absurd, full of superstition and trivialities, fuels a myth which has persisted until the present day. A model of this myth was drawn up by Hume in his essay *The Natural History of Religion*. The belief in a single god, theism, he thought, remains a precarious ideal: it is not due to the original sin, but to the intellectual and cultural prerequisites that such a conception of the world implies. On the one hand, an enlightened elite with a vision which is sufficiently coherent and rational to allow the existence of a supreme being to be deduced from it. On the other hand, the common herd, that is the rest of humanity with a few exceptions, proves to be incapable of extracting the general principles from their immediate environment to make the necessary abstractions and slides into polytheist ways of thinking.

By trying to get to the heart of Hume's psychology and more or less following his reasoning in the famous *Golden Bough*, Frazer wanted to account for the rich data he had gathered on strange beliefs and rituals of primitive people. He explained them by the erroneous associations they make in a quasi-hypnotic state, which leads them to express strange ideas on magic. This is in contrast to civilized people who, by making correct associations, arrive at conclusions that are no longer magic and become science. By generalizing his observations on savage or childlike thinking, Frazer maintained that this is the same line of thinking as that of the majority of ignorant and lower classes in Europe.

This adds nothing new. Extending the myth of absurdity to the so-called lower civilizations and savages does not take us any further. Be that as it may, the myth was to resurface again unexpectedly as soon as the study of common sense entered into social psychology via the distinction between the expert and the naive layman (even though it is difficult to say what is being understood socially by the one or the other!). All we know is that, as Niels Bohr said, "a specialist is someone well familiar with some of the grossest errors to be made in the field in question, and thus able to avoid them" (Heisenberg, 1975, p. 28). The naive scientist, who is unaware of these gross errors, naively commits them. In a long series of brilliant and really ingenious laboratory experiments it could be shown that novices do not know how to avoid these errors and that most people are nonrational. That is, they do not think in accordance with statistics or logic. They are biased and persistent in their beliefs, their false consensus, or their illusionary correlations (Nisbett & Ross, 1980). All these experiments have become as famous as the celebrated Milgram experiment and we have seen a number of books appear with lurid titles about the fallacy of human thinking in ordinary life, explaining how "The sad story of human folly and prejudices is explained by our ineptness as naive statisticians" (Pinker, 1997, p. 34).

All this is rather sad, because by following closely the road set out by Frazer researchers would have arrived at a similar conclusion. Neglecting the content and specificity of common sense, they ended up turning it into a fabric of absurdities and false ideas. In summary, the principal result of this work in social psychology is to make its subject disappear. Not because of what has been observed not being true, but precisely because no attention was paid to the various aspects (Harman, 1986). In any case, once it was demonstrated that common sense was full of false ideas instead of accepted ideas, one could not but insidiously arrive at the elimina- tive materialism of the philosopher of mind (Churchland, 1992). According to Churchland, folk knowledge is misleading and wrong and must be reduced to and replaced by neuroscience. It would therefore be useless and arbitrary to study it. A number of other authors (Kelley, 1992; Kruglanski, 1989; Legrenzi, 1993) have certainly expressed their reservations with regard to these biases or errors. The study of those was consequently abandoned at the same time as that of common sense for which stereotypes were substituted.

What more can be said? The explanation as to why two out of three people are not good scientists, commit errors, and think in stereotypes was first said to be their limited capacity "to process information" (Nisbett & Wilson, 1977) and, secondly, as cognitive economy. It is possible to challenge the first explanation, as no one seems able to define what these limitations consist of or to provide any independent proof of their existence. The little we know about cognitive economy does not allow us to make any deductions as to what its effects are. According to certain social psychologists it leads to stereotyping. According to Mach, however, who, I think, was the first to lay down its principle, this economy is the motor behind scientific abstraction and generalization. It is impossible to simply admit that the same principle accounts for both stereotypes and their opposite without its own existence being brought into question. Furthermore, we have difficulty in assum- ing that our beliefs and suppositions are by nature irrational. The philosophy of mind and common sense objects to this. Stich (1991) was aware of this difficulty – but he was not alone (Thagard & Nisbett, 1983) – and dissected in a profound book the studies on the so-called biases and the proof they provide of flaws in our normal thought. By questioning their presuppositions and their evidence, the answer was that, when you endeavor to explain the relation between "lay thought" and "scien- tific" or "rational" thought, it was just this explanation that impeded any move forward. They had it ready made. They could not find it in the data themselves, they superposed it on them. And Stich concluded, without mincing his words, "that experimental observations were pursued without any real idea of the research objective, i.e., without comprehension of what was under discussion" (1991, p. 154).

Picking up the still valid argument by Lévy-Bruhl against Frazer, we could assume that the oddities of naive laymen's thought could be due, not to the biases of their reasoning, but to their erroneous social representations leading to conclusions which are incorrect from a scientific point of view. These representations do not depend on the individual, they implicate a social subject distinct from the individual. They present themselves with contents and characteristics that cannot be explained by just considering the individual judgments as such. They may and even do persist in the area of life side by side with other shared representations, let us say scientific ones. This explains, for instance, why students or scientists commit systematic errors. It is because they resort without realizing to Aristotle's physics of common sense in solving trivial problems, even though they are well familiar with Newton's physics (Laurens & Masson, 1996; Pinker 1997).

Let us leave aside the polemic and come to the question whether, within our field, there is not some kind of confusion between the study of lay thinking and that of lay thinkers, in the same way that it is possible to confuse the study of scientific thinking with the thinking of scientists. We all agree on the increase in scientific knowledge and the belief that science is a model of a successful rational undertaking. And yet we know from experience and from studies that how scientists think and what they do is at odds with the characteristics of scientific growth and scientific thinking such as it is presented to us by philosophers and historians on the basis of their theories and experiments. And no one, to my knowledge, has ever suggested assessing the rationality or irrationality of science by submitting scientists to a test of an hour on a theme which is not of vital interest to their passionate mind.

If I am referring to what could possibly be a confusion, it is to avoid another, i.e., believing that the theory of social representations is about folk thinkers whereas it is about folk thinking. This entails a large number of methodical difficulties. As I pursue this discussion, I realize that it has already taken place numerous times and that philosophers and psychologists have long ago made us wary of the tendency to associate the least efficient modes of thinking with "naive" people and the most efficient and spectacular ones with experts. Take for instance Grice: "Part of the trouble," he writes, "may arise from an improperly conceived proposition in the mind of some self-appointed experts between "we" and "they"; between, that is, the privileged and the enlightened on the one hand, and the rabble on the other." (1989, p. 378) This is far from being the only cause of the trouble. The shallow view of human life and thinking is another. In a sober, crystalline style, but in strong words, James stated: "The absurd abstraction of an intellect verbally formulating all its evidence and carefully estimating the probabilities thereof by a vulgar fraction, by the size of whose denominator and numerator alone it is swayed, is ideally inept as it is actually impossible" (1978, p. 92).

Of course, *errare humanum est*, and no one will deny that we may be mistaken in very many ways (Fiske & Taylor, 1994). But if the error signifies a flaw in thought, it can also be an indication of a deviation or a difference. Considered as a whole, common sense does not appear so flawed, platitudinous, or stereotyped as some would have us believe. On the contrary, it presents a richness, a diversity very similar to our language and our daily life (Greenwood, 1990). And should we not acknowledge a type of particular thought, an irreducible alternative to knowledge which is institutionalized by our culture under the guise of religion, philosophy, or science? Albeit for different reasons, what Fodor maintains about folk psychology is also true for folk knowledge in general. It is "the most remarkable fact about the intellectual history of our species" (1992, p. 174). And that is why I very firmly stick to my conviction that it is indeed the stuff of social psychology.[2]

The Primacy of Representation

Despite the time that has gone by, the freshness of that first intuition has not faded; nor has disappeared the question I put to myself: what is the structure of the system underlying this stuff? It was too shallow to consider opinions, attitudes (Moscovici, 1993), or schemes, too misleading to use, as some do, lay theories. Only mature science has theories, and their criteria for true or false cannot be applied to language and ordinary beliefs (Heider, 1958). The only legitimate candidate is therefore a social representation that chooses and combines our shared concepts, links together accepted assertions, decides which aspects from our categories are examples for classifying people and things. It furthermore suggests explanations according to attributes and shared causes (Farr & Moscovici, 1984). It is possible to envisage a social representation by analogy with a paradigm which fashions a certain comprehension of phenomena, prescribed by concepts and legitimate examples as well as procedures for solving puzzles, and which belongs to a scientific community. Such a choice implies the primacy of representations. For many scientists the model of knowledge consists of the immediate perceptive knowledge of an individual – a social perceiver or a social cognizer, as they say. But there are types of knowledge, such as folk psychology and moral knowledge, which to a large extent rely on fictitious or ideal entities – justice, god, money, market, and so on – and which do not offer such perceptual knowledge. We do not "perceive" money by looking at a banknote or cybercash, nor do we notice introversion by observing the behavior of a person. The representation of money or introversion is already there, ready made before we look at the banknote or observe someone's behavior. This is in agreement with something Bentham said a long time ago: "We have access, especially to the "collective fictitious entities" by means of a representation, not a perception." We see them with our mind's eyes, so to speak.

You could ask what our cultures would look like if only perceptions were true and representations illusory? And what would they look like as a set of informations and sensory facts? The answer to these questions is in the beliefs and practices of human beings as the only representation-making species. Humans paint murals, carve statues, invent rituals to imitate rain or hunting, coin pieces of metal and devise words to give and take instead of goods; they conceive alphabets, systems of numerals, and many other systems which stand for things and people, make present what is absent, near what is far. In the words of the philosopher Hacking, in one way or another, constantly, "people represent. That is the part of what it is to be a person" (1989, p. 144). And to be a member of a community.

People can create symbols such as the cross or the Union Jack. Their significance transcends the individual, but certainly not because of their resemblance to the objects they refer to, nor because of a physical link, but simply by virtue of a tradition or convention. Everyone is aware that such symbolic representations last only as long as a group believes in them. Our social and political life (Pitkin, 1967) is based on this mysterious and yet inevitable phenomenon. To quote Simon: "That representation makes a difference is a long-familiar point. We all believe that arithmetic has become easier since Arabic numerals and place notation replaced Roman numerals, although I know of no theoretic explanation why." (1969, p. 77).

Generally speaking, this much is patent and incontestable: changes in representation are accounted for by changes in culture. They are inextricably linked. One of the key differences between the various societies and cultures is the degree to which a representation penetrates their institutions, their beliefs, their relations, their behavior, so as to constitute their true reality. At this level we could, for instance, compare the place occupied by religion in Western culture and in other cultures.

Going further along this line, let us examine what a representation is made of. At once we can notice that it has a conceptual or verbal aspect and an iconic aspect. The former aspect is the one that is usually retained and that is considered in relation to knowledge and language, the latter being considered subordinate to it. Whether this is desirable or not, we can not accept it if we consider the role that images play in communication, scientific knowledge, figurative speech, and even in our own field (Bartlett, 1967). Hebb wrote somewhere: "You can hardly turn around in psychology without bumping into the image." It is certainly possible to turn away from the image and privilege the word, but that does not mean that the image will disappear. When I say to you that Caesar crossed the Rubicon, you grasp a meaning and you "see" an image in your mind. What makes this dual aspect of representation extraordinarily important is the division and the social inequalities expressed by a widespread principle: the lower classes, the masses, primarily have access to the iconic aspect, and the upper classes, the elites, to the more powerful conceptual aspect of the representation. As Pope Gregory the Great said: "Painting can be for the illiterates what writing is for those who can read." So in France and

Italy the magnificent paintings and frescos depicting scenes from the Holy Scriptures were carried out by order of the Church to show off its power and to shape the religious consciousness of the illiterates. The contemporary media follow the same principle: figurative rhetoric is for the masses, linguistic rhetoric for the enlightened minority. To be sure, it can be assumed that the more a representation is widespread, the more it has penetrated the interstices of society, and the more apparent its iconic traits become in the figurative language, and vice versa.

Do not expect me to explain in detail the nature of social representations. I want, however, to bring to light the prevailing tendency to give too much weight to their intellectual and verbal aspect at the expense of their figurative aspect. This tendency is all the more surprising as our tradition has done very little to raise the question of image, of imagination, and of its surprising efficiency. We can now go further and ask ourselves: why do we create social representations? Is it to solve a problem? To achieve what the economy of thought is setting out to achieve? Or, as Bartlett assumed, because we try hard to get a meaning? I myself have suggested a more concrete and observable reason, namely that we create representations in order to make familiar what is strange, disturbing, uncanny. This "principle of familiarity" underpins a large part of psychology and sociology. On the basis of numerous observations, it has become clear that individuals and communities resist the intrusion of strangeness. Obviously, countless novelties among objects and new types of humans seem strange. Different morals, ideas, and languages are at first considered groundless, unreasonable, and inevitably unfamiliar. But then the individuals and groups that cannot avoid contact with the new individuals, objects, or behavior, have to make a representation of them. This allows them to change what is unfamiliar into something familiar, the comparatively esoteric into the customary, so as to feel at ease with it. For instance, in *Death in Venice* Thomas Mann narrates how the severe professor of aesthetics initially feels hostile to the adolescent who appears to him as a stranger whom he has to resist. In the end, however, he compares him to a "divine work of art," that is, to something which is known and familiar to him, and therefore admirable. "Custom makes monsters familiar," an old proverb says.

It appears that metaphors play an important role in the creation of social representations, precisely because they slot ideas and images which are little familiar into others which are already familiar. Remember that during his term in office Reagan proposed the Strategic Defense Initiative. It was not long before this initiative was commonly represented as Star Wars, whereby an incoming missile would be taken out of the sky by an antimissile, as can be seen in children's cartoons. At the same time, the "principle of familiarity" shows us the representation in the light of an activity which follows certain rules and standards in order to achieve an objective. Failing such rules, a culture would have no benefit from creating and sharing a representation. Familiarization necessarily entails being able to identify with the representation of one's group and society. And as one follows from the other, the representation eventually is substituted for the group, such as the national currency or the national flag. To a certain extent, a representation that "stands for" can also "act for" or "act on behalf of" or "instead of" those it represents (Pitkin, 1967). Apart from being symbols, the Union Jack, the Eiffel Tower, the Kremlin, and the cross are also representations of a country, a religion, etc. What they *do* is out of proportion to what they *are*. Take the football team that represented France in the World Cup. This team managed to do what France could not do itself, namely playing football matches. All these examples point to what is achieved by social representations, their goal beautifully expressed by Grice: "Similarly our representations . . . enable objects in the world to do something which they cannot do for themselves, namely govern our actions and behaviours" (1989, p. 291). I have covered all these facets of representation, as symbol and activity, knowledge and practice in view of a goal, because all of them are manifest in our social life.

A Difference that Makes a Difference

By now, if I am not mistaken, you realize that the notion of social representation has appeal, though without a clear idea of what is different about it. I admit that during all these years gone by I have wondered why colleagues talked about it as if it were something simple and self-evident. Of course, everyone knows what representation means and what social means. And if you associate these two meanings and then accentuate their anchorage in society or culture you underline a difference with regard to notions such as social cognition and social perception (Augoustinos & Walker, 1995). But this is not the difference that makes the difference. So let us investigate the matter more closely. The notion of collective or social representation has been deliberately conceived to distinguish social phenomena from the so-called objective, biological, or economic phenomena. It expresses the impossibility of dissociating their real aspect from their mental or symbolic aspect. In this way the representation shared by the members of a group, institution, etc. expresses its identity more fundamentally than its physical means and organization. Indeed, in most institutions – states, churches, universities are cases in point – social representations are far more significant than their status or physical means. Rather than interests and power, it is public representations that play the most important role. They set out the field of activity and inform the members of the social system of their rights and duties, of a sense of belonging.

More precisely, the representation is a notion conceived to explain what, if anything, binds people together in a group, a society, and makes them act together. This is a far less obvious and more highly speculative question. In order to bind themselves, create institutions, and follow common rules, people need a system of beliefs, common representations which are proper to their culture. Mauss summarizes this response in a succinct formula: "Social facts are thus causes, since they are representations or act on representations. At the heart of social life lies a set of representations" (1969, p. 26). Indeed, no other system of interests or forces is as stable, nor is it able to exert on its own sufficient constraint to arrive at the same result. The claim is plausible if you think that we do not know of a society without religion or a set of beliefs, of sacred elements in which members have placed their trust and for which they are ready to sacrifice themselves. Let me clarify this point and insist on its peculiarity.

Such an explanation was certainly plausible before Descartes but not after. Nowadays much is said about the duality he established between body and mind, but precious little about the fact that he transferred this duality to the mind itself. It is in fact a break between the individual mind which acquires knowledge by its own means, and the social mind which acquires it from others, by *example* and *custom*, terms by which Descartes means culture. The truth is discovered by solitary reflection and the subjective evidence of "I think, therefore I am." This is an expression in which "I" cannot be replaced by "we," because errors arise from public authority and public opinion. You can infer from this that private knowledge belongs to the essence of the rational and common knowledge to the essence of the irrational. Whether intentional or not, Descartes thus makes culture the antinomy of reason. This implies that people bound together in a society by beliefs are bound together by fiction, blatant absurdities, and illusory forces that they accept with disturbing complacency.

Hume confirmed this point of view drastically. According to him, religion and beliefs are pure sophistry, empty fictions. Marx too considered them primarily as ideologies and as a sign of our false consciousness. And for Freud religions and beliefs are among the most harmful illusions we have. This is logical, since he defines illusion as an error invested with affect. I could quote many other authors, but it is not necessary to dwell on what has become a commonplace.

Therefore we can certainly say that the notion of collective or social representation is marked by the search for a way out of the antinomy between reason and culture. Durkheim, himself an atheist, maintained strongly the impossibility of imagining that beliefs, which last and according to which we live for such a long time, would be just a bundle of illusions or fallacies. Or that man has invented them to fool himself with an excess of zeal. Beliefs are essential not only to life in practice, but to knowledge in general as well. Furthermore, to Durkheim as to Russell, "believing seems to be the most essential thing we do, the thing most remote from what is done by mere matter. Intellectual life consists entirely of beliefs" (1996, p. 231). For Russell it was the central problem in analyzing knowledge – for Durkheim in analyzing society and culture. Knowledge and belief, this doublet seems like a play on words, similar to "mind and body." Because we cannot separate nor confuse its two elements, it appears to us as somewhat mysterious. Philosophers have used numerous terms (Needham, 1972) to penetrate the crevices of intellectual life described by the words "belief" or "faith." These terms characterize an idea or a concept as vivid, firm, steady, colored. The content is the same as that of knowledge; only the feeling which is in some way attached to it, appears difficult to explain. "I firmly believe" is a strong and positive expression while "I firmly know" is without depth and inappropriate. We notice here a difference in the performative energy of what a person ought or ought not to know.

There is clearly something in this difference, similar to the difference between science and faith, which incites thinkers to separate belief and knowledge. Against this background Durkheim's move seems weird from beginning to end: he wants to introduce knowledge, i.e., representation, into belief and unify the two in rituals and specific practices. Most beliefs, if not all, consist of representations. This becomes apparent in religious cults where sacred or institutional things exist insofar as they are visualized in our minds, but only on condition that they are seen to be shared with other people, either absent or present, in the course of rituals or ceremonies which unite the community. Such rituals and ceremonies endow them with an irresistible energy and force. Mundane objects or emblems have something of a collective representation. By worshipping them, Durkheim assumes, society unwittingly worships itself through interposed divinities, thus binding its members and leading them to act together. In that sense, these representations stand for and act for society.

These few examples of a rich theory are not offered as comprehensive or mandatory. There is no room for interpretation (Allen, Pickering, & Miller, 1989). But whatever the interpretation, it is clear that social representations are supposed to attribute to ideas, as and above all to objects, properties that do not exist in any form or guise. And yet, since it is a question of knowledge and not only belief, one cannot simply satisfy oneself with a *credo quia absurdum*. They do need to have some validity in order not to be completely irrational.

How to test the truth, if I may put it this way, of the power of gods in a piece of stone or wood that is worshipped by believers? When the idolater bows in front of an idol, an image, and offers a sacrifice, does that person bow in front of a fetish that represents nothing else? Is it not irrational to believe in the power of such gods, in their *physical reality*? No, it is not quite irrational, if the believer believes in what they *represent*, what they are the symbol of, i.e., society itself. It is equally rational to pledge allegiance to a piece of cloth or a stick as to die for them, if these stand for the flag, the representation shared by the nation. Their validity is tested, if you like, in relation to their *social reality* and not with regard to their physical reality. "This move," Searle wrote recently, "can exist only if it is represented as existing. The collective representation is public and conventional, and it requires some vehicle" (1995, p. 74) – a vehicle that in religion is material as well as linguistic. The exemplary nature of Durkheim's work lies in the fact that he analyzes the content of simple religious representations to bring to light a coherent knowledge of space, time, causality, or force as they are generated in common. A paradoxical consequence is that scientific representations have their origin in those of religion. In that way he has explained, to borrow a phrase from Gellner, "why all men are rational" (1992, p. 52). A unique and impressive achievement.

Once the antinomy of reason and culture was resolved, the idea of social or collective representation penetrated into anthropology (Lévy-Bruhl), linguistics (de Saussure), the history of philosophy (Cornford), the philosophy of science (Fleck, 1936; Koyré, 1936), and above all in the psychology of thought and child development (Vygotsky, 1962; Piaget, 1965). By studying the representations, these thinkers have demonstrated, for instance, the alternative rationality of the so-called primitive (Lévy-Bruhl) and of language (de Saussure) and shown that certain so-called a priori concepts are built up as the child matures and is socialized (Piaget). I myself became interested in this notion because I wanted to establish the rationality of folk knowledge, not only because I wanted to introduce it into social psychology. Like all my precursors I took my inspiration from Durkheim's notion. I have had to adapt it to my field of research while still retaining, as they did, the implicit axiom common to all versions of collective or social representations: all that is rational is social and all that is social is rational.

To put the matter in a nutshell, this implicit axiom is the difference that makes the difference between the notion of social representations and other notions we know within social psychology and elsewhere. Social representations combine a semantic knowledge and a belief that is rooted in the culture together with the practices that people live by. This is what gives them a character of "reality." In the words of the philosopher of science Koyré: "They have a reality, a reality as hard, as resistant and real – if not more so – as the matter and bodies" (1936, p. 264). The test of time has highlighted the richness of this conception and has made apparent that social phenomena and psychological phenomena have a common texture, seen as they are essentially made out of representations. Therefore it stands to reason that the majority of thinkers I have mentioned have advocated a social psychology focusing on them and elaborating their theories. In fact, a chair was created at the Collège de France in 1943. But Halbwachs, who had been appointed to this chair, died in the Buchenwald concentration camp and was never able to take up his position. It is another use of my nomadic destiny that I have chosen this task without knowing anything about the tradition behind it until recently. It is a task to which Rabbi Tarphon's words may apply: "The task is not yours to finish, but neither are you free to desist from it." My account of it is certainly oversimplified, but I hope that this does not distort the principal argument.

Social Representations: An Empirical or a Theoretical Concept?

What I have just presented relates to the two functions of social representation: communicating and acting. Here lurks the possibility of a misunderstanding of our theory. Until now the term social has been associated with the term "representation" in the same way as it is associated with other terms such as social perception, social cognition, and social discourse. Those may be empirical associations due to observation, due to some ideological tendencies, or mere labeling. Is this empirical association a necessary one? In other words, is it possible to demonstrate that a representation is necessarily social, that it is only produced by social groups and not by individuals? If it is, then we could be certain that our concept is theoretical and not only empirical. By the same token we would have defined what distinguishes individual representations from social representations and what their respective qualities are. To my knowledge, social representation is a rare concept for which such a demonstration exists. I attempted to give one when sketching the theory in light of cybernetics from which it drew its inspiration. According to the latter, the communication of social knowledge is instrumental in the homeostasis (or equilibrium) of a group or community.

Let me start with the observation that each of us has multiple, ambiguous representations. If people want to communicate, they have to adjust to one another. Were this not the case, everyone would have to submit to the controls of different representations and no one would know what the message is, how it is coded. Simply obeying one's solipsistic code makes good communication extremely difficult. This is what quite often happens when a lot of people are together, in a brainstorming group, and so on. No single representation is formed or is stable, and none leads to a consensus. Only the current of a group's pressures and opinions produces a diffuseness and communality which are sufficient for the representation to develop an outline and a structure. Once this is achieved, communication between individuals is possible and regular, because the proliferation of individual representations is limited and their ambiguity appears as deviance. That is, group members know that they are talking about the same thing and talking to one another. We can say that, without a social representation, the existence of individual representations would be uncertain and short-lived (Moscovici & Galam, 1994) and communication quite haphazard.

It is, however, Durkheim's earlier demonstration which made a landmark in the science by solving an important philosophical problem, namely that of Hume's causality and scientific laws in general. Hume observed correctly that individuals could neither conceive the one nor the other on the basis of their perception of the impact between bodies colliding like billiard balls. Their association of ideas and their perceptions are fleeting, do not follow rules, and can lead to any result. In reality, what are seen as causal relations or laws are nothing but simple customs, the anticipation that something which has occurred in the past will occur again in the future. I would not pretend taking up Kant's well-known critique. It forms an answer to Hume's skepticism by stating that causality is one of the a priori categories of reason and thus precedes every experience.

It is clear that Durkheim follows Kant and agrees that a causal representation or a concept cannot be constructed by the free association of ideas or perceptions which are susceptible to change in an individual's mind from minute to minute. However, and here he turns against Kant, neither can they be imposed by a transcendental reason. For Hume the representation appears unstable and lacking in necessity. In Kant, it should be everlasting, which is not corroborated by history. If there is no transcendental reason, the question that remains is: what explains the disciplined, stable, impersonal nature of a shared representation and what exerts such a constraint on the representations of individuals, as is apparent from languages, myths and religions? It is society, Durkheim replies, that produces them and imprints them in the mind through its institutions and rituals. In summary, these achieve in public life what Kant's transcendental "I" achieves in private, beyond the noumenon. Much closer to the time of Durkheim than we are, Piaget formulates the concrete sense of this proof, namely that "left to his own resources, the individual would only know practical intelligence and images, whereas the set of concepts, intellectual categories and rules of thought consist of "collective representations," produced by life within a society as it has occurred since the beginning of mankind . . . From all this Durkheim concludes that reason has a social origin" (1965, p. 145). At the same time we see that differences exist between the two types of representation. Individual representations are recognized by their variability, their dispersion, and their fragmentation. In contrast, social or collective representations are stable, impersonal, and holistic.

This very unusual demonstration surprised me the first time that I read it. It underlined that it is not sufficient to affirm the social nature of thought (or of language). It is also essential to prove that they are necessary, and in particular the holism of collective intellectual life. This means that the significance of a proposition or a belief depends on the relation to other beliefs or propositions that form a whole. It is shocking to us, used as we are to the atomization of beliefs or propositions. Yet holism is one of the characteristics of social representations which captivated, for instance, Evans-Pritchard on hearing of Lévy-Bruhl's studies: "He was one of the first, if not the first, to emphasize that primitive ideas, which seem so strange to us and indeed somewhat idiotic when considered as isolated facts, are meaningful when seen as parts of patterns of ideas and behaviour, each part having an intelligible relationship to the others" (1981, p. 127). I would not like you to say that all these arguments belong to a precomputer age, and that I am presenting to you just a piece of European antique. To show you, however, that these arguments anticipate and can be even better expressed in the light of our contemporary philosophy of mind would take too long (Moscovici, 1998). We would come to a similar conclusion: we think just as we waltz, in triple time. The first step consists of a social representation, the second step of an individual one, and the third step of a real or imaginary referent.

Discursifying Thinking

One of Margaret Thatcher's major contributions to modern thinking is her famous aphorism: "There is no such thing as society, there are only individuals." This is one of those aphorisms in which the speaker denies what he or she affirms, since Thatcher speaks here not about an individual, but about a social representation shared by a tradition, and by at least one group, the British Conservative Party. Obviously the representation has a holistic character. In order to arrive at the notion of the individual, one has to arrive at the notion of a human being, that is, the contrast between a single individual and associated individuals, and so on. All the underlying notions are related to one another, constrain one another so that each word can make a sense in the sentence in which it is used.

Holism, however, is not the index of the arborescence of every notion in our minds, turning into a wild forest. Think of the 40,000 words in James Joyce's *Ulysses*. It is the index of a pattern, of the structure that these notions build up. Holism supposes that relations or a system of relations define elements and that systems are prior to elements. In contrast, atomism assumes that elements are prior to the whole and that it is from them that we understand and construct relations. The obvious differences between these two points of view are very important if we want to grasp the specificity of a social representation as a patterned system of beliefs, ideas, etc. This issue raises, last but not least, two theoretical questions: how do thinking societies create and change such a patterned system of relations? By what kind of process do they do so?

These are questions which I shall now briefly discuss. I would also like to explain why they have moved me away from the classic notion of social representations so that it could become an object of social psychology. In the classic conception, social or collective representations are of a totally different nature from individual representations, as the former are part of the collective consciousness while the latter belong to individual consciousness. One could say that in this conception the collective solipsism of the "we" in the former case has simply been substituted by the individual solipsism of the "I" in the latter case. One wonders how monologues of individual thought can converge towards monologues of collective thought in forming the pattern of a social representation. One could find many reasons why this can happen, the main of them being an attempt to explain the genesis of a representation by institutional practices such as, for example, rituals which exert a constraint on the individual in society. Thus the process of constraint structures individual representations within the context of a collective representation. It means that, from the classic point of view, communication and dialogical thinking play only a secondary role in the genesis of social representations, if they play any role at all. (This view still prevails among social psychologists, and not only as concerns social representations!) Yet one cannot adopt this view if, as I mentioned at the beginning, communication and representation are considered to be the twin phenomenal of social knowledge. You will perhaps ask me in what ways these issues concern holism and the patterning of ideas and beliefs.

If you are patient enough to allow me to go on with my story, let me tell you how I have tackled the idea that social representations are generated and patterned in the process of communication. The question is a difficult one, and in my attempt to answer it satisfactorily my hopes to succeed are modest. I have tried to find a solution depending less on the syntax or semantics of language. Perhaps I can be more explicit when I remind you that, in accordance with my initial hypothesis, social representations are generated and patterned through conversation which, according to Bakhtin, is our primary communication genre. Since then Grice has taught us to associate conversation with communication as a cooperative undertaking. In his view, the intention to express some meaning by an utterance, just as the intention that an utterance means something, causes a particular state of mind in those who partake in the conversation, because they seek to recognize the intention. This is why such talk has a means – ends feature. Its end is to achieve the purpose of conversation, for instance to convince someone that the theory of social representations is a heuristic theory. In that picture, the contribution of the participants will be cooperative and have to follow a set of four now famous maxims. First, quantity: make your contribution as informative as required. Second, quality: make your contribution truthful. Third, relation: be relevant. Fourth, manner: be perspicuous or be orderly. By following these maxims, conversation is more than an exchange of ideas or of words: it imposes a pattern and efficiency on the dialogue between those who are taking part in it.

However, there are important differences between these maxims. One could say that the first three (quantity, quality, and relevance) touch primarily upon the cognitive quality of the information shared by the participants during the conversation (Sperber & Wilson, 1986). The fourth maxim, that of manner, refers more to the social quality, i.e., order or perspicuity – to the art of conversing of the participants. This is why it has to be distinguished "and treated," Gunji writes, "in a wider perspective, where cultural and sociological aspects of language use get proper treatment" (1982, p. 40). I do not mean to say that the other maxims are not social or cultural, only that the fourth one expresses the existence of a specific or an autonomous level of communication. This is why it interests us here, as it concerns the ordering and relating of representations, of beliefs, and so on, in our everyday social dialogue. It is the level of communication at which, as William James anticipated, "All human thinking gets discursified; we exchange ideas; we lend and borrow our verifications; get them from one another by means of social intercourse. . . . Hence we must talk consistently as we must think consistently" (1978, p. 102). And, I add, his maxim of conversation is Socratic.

For social psychologists language is not the top priority. For most of them, cognition or thinking is language-less; for some of them, language is thought-less. Our theory has, however, always presupposed that a social representation is *discursified* thinking, that it is a symbolic cultural system involving language. It has taken me a long time to find out what could be a linguistic feature specific of that autonomous level of communication mentioned above. Perhaps I can illustrate this point if I take the liberty to imagine a solution to the problem Plato mentions in the foreword to his *Republic*: how can one involve a reluctant individual in a dialogue? One can suggest that the dialogue can be made more intriguing by changing the order of the words. You can see the difference between "dog bites man" and "man bites dog." A simple change in the order of the words "dog," "man," and "bites" alters what is uttered and can make the utterance more surprising, raising curiosity. I doubt though that Plato would be satisfied with such a solution which is a commonplace in everyday life and in the mass media.

A genius is someone who transforms a commonplace into an uncommon idea. Such were my thoughts when I discovered Henri Veil's slim thesis (1869), the work of a classical scholar, a refugee in France for racial motive in the middle of the nineteenth century. Veil had a profound insight into language. For him, a sentence is almost a nonexistent, abstract entity. Only when it is communicated does it become something that we call an utterance. This idea forms the point of departure for a number of hypotheses of which I shall refer here only to two. First: the word order in an utterance corresponds to the order of the ideas one intends to communicate. One can ask the question as to how words combine so well in conversation and why they attract one another without appearing to do so. When conversing you start with the words expressing what you would like to say about the topic under discussion, or you present ideas which are already known to both speaker and listener. Then you continue with another part of the utterance conveying to the listener something that he or she knows less well, something of which you, the speaker, try to convince the other participant. Such is the aim of conversation. Second: the ordering of words, corresponding more or less to the ordering of ideas (representations, beliefs) fulfills the fundamental aim of communication. In this respect the differences in the syntactic construction rules of grammar and of meaning do not play any compulsory role. Subject and predicate, verb and adverb, all "assume within the sentence sometimes one role, sometimes another" (p. 16). For

Veil, as for Grice, following the grammatical rules is an "ingredient" of our communication rules; it is a necessary but not sufficient condition of communication. In order to examine this question more fully, Veil has shown in detail that the linear principle of word order overrules the grammatical principles in ancient Greek and Latin as well as in Roman and Germanic languages. More recently it could be shown that this principle also holds true for Slavic languages.

Although Veil's hypotheses generated numerous works, of which the most seminal are those of the Prague school, I cannot dwell on them for too long. Especially in Mathesius's theory (1939), besides the linear principle of word order, both a "grammatical" and a "pathetic" principle are distinguished to account for the formation of sentences in a language. As culture and history are of paramount importance here, the stress laid on each principle also depends on them. Let me offer an example translated from the Ancient Testament. Phrases such as "Walk, you walked" or "Kidnap, I was kidnapped" become in today's English simply "you walked" or "I was kidnapped." Two rabbinical schools have argued about the redundancy of the first word in the ancient version. One school maintained that the first word had an additional meaning because there are no meaningless words in the Bible. In contrast to this, the other school pointed out that the first word did not convey an additional meaning but constituted a communication device for the sake of emphasis because the Bible was written in the language of the people. This appears to be correct. The old Bible followed the linear word order; yet, once translated into English, sentences followed the grammatical principle. This kind of transition from the linear to the grammatical order seems to be a more general case. Firbas (1992), a Czech linguist, has compared a medieval English translation of the New Testament with the modern translation (1957). He found that in the Middle Ages the religious translations followed the linear word order principle while today they follow the grammatical principle. Understandably, this results from the historical evolution of the language and of the rules of communication.

Thus, despite a number of uncertainties that still remain, in communication and in language we can identify, quite autonomously, a social and a cultural layer. What was expressed by the maxim "be ordered," which at first sight seemed to be imprecise, now receives a content that seems to be almost too precise. Perhaps we can simply explore the possibility whether we can uncover the structures of the patterns of social representations that develop during our social intercourse and conversation. There is, of course, a long way to go before we can articulate this aspect of language and communication in a satisfactory way. However, after examining various social representations that have been studied so far, some tentative conclusions can be drawn:

1 Their patterned structure rests on an "initial string of a few themata" (Moscovici & Vignaux, 1994). These are presumed or evident in the culture of a group, so

that its members may not even spell them out in communication. They under-lie the content or they thematize notions, images, and meanings that are just about to become socially shared. These themata appear to have a generative as well as a normative power in the formation of a representation, fitting "new" information to the already existing one. Themata are bits of knowledge or of beliefs shared by people, about which they talk, whether explicitly or implic-itly, and which they take for granted. They can be beliefs (e.g., "the American Dream," "all people are equal"), maxims (e.g., "we are what we eat"), social definitions (e.g., "psychoanalysis is a confession"), categories such as "primi-tive," or symbolic examples such as "Euro-currency." Themata are more or less deeply rooted in a culture. Depending on circumstances, they can enter directly into the public debate or merely be referred to in a social representation. For instance, the contemporary representation of the relations between men and women refers to the themata "all people are equal" and to that of human rights.

2 Themata are specified within a certain domain of social reality and practice. By saying that they are specified, I mean that from these themata people refer or co-refer to beliefs and notions relating to the "object" of the social representa-tion. These are the core notions or core beliefs that pattern other related or new beliefs; they maintain the stability of the network of communicated knowledge and practice. In a series of fine studies Flament, Abric, and their colleagues have shown that equality and friendship are the core notions of the social representa-tion of an ideal group. Moreover, initial themata usually generate several core notions of the same belief which are specific to a social domain. As a familiar example, our arch-theme Nature is specified by different core notions – "race" in the ethnic context, "savage" in the cultural context, "organic food" in the nutrition context, until recently "women" in the sexual context, and so on. The thema ensures a family resemblance between the different social represen-tations. In addition, one thema can sometimes lead to another thema and they both become specified in the nucleus of the emerging social representation. For example, in a study in Central and Eastern Europe two unconnected themata, democracy and market economy, have led to two core notions, responsibility and rights, as an emerging social representation of citizenship.

3 Until now I have chosen very simple examples in order to illustrate more than to prove my point, and I will continue to do so with regard to what I provision-ally call *arguments*. Arguments are beliefs or propositions that relate to the nu-cleus the various notions or propositions associated in a more or less stable way in a representation. We can say that the hundred or so identified complexes (complex of superiority or Sardanapalus, etc.) all relating to the core image of a complex in the social representation of psychoanalysis, are instances of what I mean by arguments. Though they have not been made the object of many studies so far, three kinds of arguments can be distinguished. First, *classifying*

arguments which, to give a basic example, distribute and situate a group or a nation up or down. For example, utterances that refer to reason or to consciousness move them "spatially" upwards, while those referring to emotions or unconsciousness move them "spatially" downwards. Thus we can observe some kind of hierarchy in social representations. We have observed similar hierarchies in the classification of ethnic groups and in minorities studied in France. However, our knowledge in this respect is quite unsatisfactory. We know much more about the classification systems in the so-called "primitive societies" than in the contemporary ones. In social psychology, we must begin to explore how people classify groups and objects, as has been done in child psychology, in the context of their social representations. It is not enough to distinguish them as belonging to in- or out-groups, as kinds of ahistorical and acultural categories. (Rosch & Lloyd, 1978)

Topical arguments replicate the nucleus notions by means of synonymy or denomination in order to give concrete expression to them in conversation. In one way it is possible to maintain that these arguments are at the basis of representations which are more or less individual. This is how, in a study on a social representation of psychoanalysis, I came across a list of approximately one hundred complexes that specify the Oedipal complex in relation to what the individual wants to express (Moscovici, 1976a, first published 1961).

Finally, *performative* arguments set out the "quality," the "strength," or the "charisma" of a social representation. A nonpublished study on Marxism drew my attention to those. I was surprised by the number of arguments referring to its color as gray and dark, and to its emotional tone as expressing sadness, isolation, and inertia. The study of arguments is now at its botanizing stage. We hope that, in the near future, we will be able to better understand how they adjust to a patterned structure and establish the procedure for analyzing themata.

Themata, cores, or nucleuses, arguments are what we find in the patterned structure of social representations. They probably correspond to certain kinds of utterances and to their order in communication. However, we refer here to the work in progress and we should not be blamed that it is not finished. The theory is not born as complete as Athena is from the brain of Zeus. Nonetheless, this privileged relation between communication and social representations allows us to understand better the old and irritating enigma of common sense, i.e., why it affirms one thing as well as its opposite. As examples, think of "Like father, like son" and "Miserly father, prodigal son." Or "Wisdom that comes quick comes in season" opposed by "That wisdom that is ready at hand does not lie deep." To be honest, if the content and the structure of our shared representations are produced according to communicational and not logical rules, it cannot be otherwise. Language, like communication, supposes that when you state something, you are able to abrogate it;

when you affirm something, you can deny it, and vice versa. If an utterance or its opposite does not lead to a contradiction, it is because the group gives greater importance to the one over the other. It is not without an ulterior motive that I make this observation. It shows us that common sense uses to the full this important property of communication. Our social representations occur in pairs, each one having its alternative, such as sacred and profane representations in religion or standard and nonstandard paradigms in science. When we say that a representation is shared, we mean that it is normative, not that it is unique. Therefore, after working for a long time in this field, I conclude that when people say that common sense is platitudinous and stereotyped, it is so in the eyes of a beholder looking at it from a distance.

Why not a Theory of Social Representations?

During the long years of exciting work and doubts, I have wondered: *why not* a theory of social representations? All things considered, many researchers have understood and appreciated what it was about. As one example, I refer to this statement by Michael Billig, one of the most talented social psychologists of the new generation:

> One of the most important recent developments in European social psychology has been the emergence of the concept of "social representations." The emergence of a new concept does not always indicate the formulation of a new idea. Sometimes in social psychology a concept is created to describe a novelty of experimental procedure, and sometimes to accord scientific pretensions to a well-known truism. By contrast, what has characterized the concept of social representations has been the intellectual ambitions of its adherents. They have announced an intellectual revolution to shift social psychology from its roots in Anglo-Saxon individual psychology to the traditions of European social science (Herzlich, 1972). Serge Moscovici, who has been both the Marx and the Lenin of this revolutionary movement, has advocated a fundamental reorientation of social psychology around the concept of social representation. This revolution, if successful, will affect both pure and applied social psychology. In fact, the whole discipline will become more applied in the sense that the emphasis will be shifted from laboratory studies, which seek to isolate variables in the abstract, towards being a social science, which examines socially shared beliefs, or social representations, in their actual social context. (1988, pp. 1–2)

Here I feel inclined to say: "All right, let us leave aside illustrious comparisons and acknowledge that the theory has met with numerous criticisms." Criticisms are like people, in that you have to take them seriously. Yet this is precisely the reason why, to a great number of their originators, I can only say what Evans-Pritchard said of the critics of collective representation in Lévy-Bruhl's time "who were far too easily content to pick holes in the arguments without mastering his main thesis. Too often they merely repeated his views under the impression that they were refuting them" (1981, p. 120). To put the matter in a nutshell, we deal here with a criticism of language more than with a criticism of ideas, which raises the question of respect, of integrity of the dialogue.

Fortunately, I can mention other kinds of criticism, two in particular, that surprised me and require a clear answer. First, that my theory is a so-called European or even French theory. Second, that it is neither experimental nor predictive. What has this to do with science, I would like to ask with respect to the former? Admitting it would be to deny science in general, as far as I am concerned, and the history that is mine. There cannot be an American or European theory any more than there can be a Jewish or an Aryan science. This, however, does not exclude the difference between research styles or intellectual traditions that are typically European, North American, Asian, etc., even in the natural sciences.

As far as the second criticism is concerned, without wanting to compare the theory of social representations to my theory on the influence of minorities, it has given rise to numerous experiments. In any case, we have to acknowledge the diversity of theories: some explain and predict, such as quantum theory; others explain without predicting, for instance natural selection. Mainstream social psychology has lately opted for the former, while my theory belongs to the latter kind. We know that it is illusory to want to make a prediction where a relatively complex theory is required to explain in a meaningful way phenomena which are also relatively complex. This may be why human sciences of which anyone knows the rigor and fecundity – economics, linguistics, anthropology, child psychology – develop theories that explain without predicting. But is this valid for those sciences alone? No, I do not think so. If, despite all the criticism, I proceed as if nothing was wrong, it is because so many generations of researchers did not wonder why or why not a theory of social representations. They have chosen it, as if there were no alternative for a theory which attracted and still attracts them with its scale and fecundity and its general views on culture. But also because it examines current problems, such as health, politics, economics, communication, racism, and diffusion of knowledge. In this wider context, the theory becomes more interesting, it appeals to them and offers them a language that they can use without gratuitous pedantry, thus giving them the possibility of being understood. Essentially, the same goes for those who sought a theory of human thinking completely at variance with the theory of Golem thinking. Here again they reject an abstract construction ideal which hinders understanding the intricacies of social life and experience.

I am still surprised by the energy and fecundity of this theory that diffuses from social psychology to other sciences, can adjust to diverse traditions, and opens itself to them instead of isolating itself from them. Its flexibility, which is sometimes mentioned as a reproach, is normal as long as it is not a Babel. Like any living being that lasts – and knowledge is one of those – it becomes a font of continuous novelty, as varied as reality itself. In addition there is an element unique to this theory that I am keen to preserve and that may explain everything. Husserl has emphasized this magnificently in a letter to Lévy-Bruhl in which he writes that he has found in the latter's work on social representations "a pure psychology which does not treat human beings as objects of nature . . . but which treats them as subjects of consciousness, such as they find themselves thanks to personal pronouns. Saying 'I' and 'we' they find themselves living with one another, like members of families, associations, social ensembles acting within their world and suffering from this world that has for them a meaning . . . out of their experience, their thoughts and their values."

Notes

1 It is proper to note that the theory of social representations was born as a criticism leveled at other theories which were dominant in the human sciences and in social psychology in particular. First, against behaviorism which excluded all intellectual life or "internal" experience. Then against the reduction of social to psychological, of society to an aggregate of individuals, in short against the predominance of individualism in social psychology. Also against the isolation of microsocial phenomena (small groups, influence, etc.) in relation to macrosocial phenomena. And further, against the tendency to see social psychology as a science of "processes," totally losing interest in the problems of society and culture in general. It is true that the idea of social is currently more popular than before. But the other tendencies or theories continue to exist in a renewed form. In fact, the objective of the theory was (and still is, in my opinion) to establish a social psychology not as a special branch of psychology or sociology, but as an autonomous science, such as developmental psychology.

2 Is there anything wrong in criticizing the work on biases and error? Many things, probably, and first and foremost the sheer bulk of information. In any case this is not a criticism of cognitive theory or of social cognition, simply because the real starting point for this work is not scientific. It is the common sense idea of the "irrationality" of the many and the "rationality" of the few. This is one of the oldest ways to distinguish between "we" and "they," legitimate the differences between children and adults, majorities and minorities, higher and lower civilizations, and so on. From time to time the arguments are refreshed, the old wine is poured into new bottles. The question is, however, too serious to be dealt with in a couple of lines.

Part II

Doing Social Representation Research

3

A Theory of Methods

Gina Philogène

The attempt to break the barriers of tradition has enabled social representation theory to clarify some difficult issues that have so far eluded other social psychologists – the tension between the reified universe and the consensual universe comprising modern culture, the relation between language and thought, the interactional dynamics between individuals, and the impact of their social setting, and so forth. In so stressing the multidimensional quality of human thought, social representationists have had to match the complexity of their theory with innovative methodology that typically has combined a variety of empirical approaches to tell the full story (Farr & Moscovici, 1984; Breakwell & Canter, 1993; Doise, Clémence, & Lorenzo-Cioldi, 1993). It is this rich connection between theory and empirical application, both quantitative and qualitative, that has made social representation theory so effective in its efforts to trace the dynamics of change in modern societies.

After Moscovici laid down the framework of social representation theory in 1961, the first generation of scholars to work with him on the theory expanded on its various components. Three scholars in particular contributed to the theory by developing specific theoretical foundations for the empirical application of the theory.

Jean-Claude Abric elaborated a theory of the central core that gives a structure to the representation and endows it with meaning. Surrounding the central core is an organized constellation of peripheric elements that play an important role in concretizing the meaning of the representation. They are at the interface between the central core and the concrete situation within which the representation is elaborated and operates. This double system, comprising the central core and peripheric elements in interaction with each other, enables us to understand some key characteristics of social representations that may otherwise appear as contradictory. These representations are at once stable and rigid, because they are determined by the central core which is profoundly crystallized in the value system shared by the members of a group. At the same time they are dynamic and fluid, because they integrate a wide variety of individual experiences with the social conditions that mark the evolution of the individuals or groups.

In this particular variant of social representation theory the notion of the central core provides an interesting answer to a key epistemological question concerning the link between individual representations and social reality. The central core is the organizing principle that makes the social representation stable, and this stability results from its objectification. That process creates a figurative nucleus, a core of images, which decontextualizes the principal elements of a representation to the point where they assume a life of their own as part of a social context shaping individual minds.

In Chapter 4, Abric presents a brief introduction to his theory of the central core which captures the reification of the representation from the domain of an idea into something we can see and experience – namely, the objectification process. This perspective is reflected in Chapter 5 by Annamaria de Rosa on Benetton, in which she examines the creation of images to crystallize the representation. In this piece she develops her own derivative of Abric's cental core approach.

The second extension of Moscovici's original social representation framework was provided by Willem Doise, who focused on the anchoring process by which the representation is rendered familiar. This process is mediated by the position that the individual occupies. Any object, new or not, gets anchored through a socially created metasystem that regulates, controls, and directs individual minds. That metasystem is a structure which interferes with us beyond our control, guides us when making up our minds about something, and forces us by means of conventions to take account of what others think about that object. How that object is socially represented shapes what we think and how we act towards it.

Because social representations are consensual in nature to consolidate the group, their implications for communication within and between groups are indeed fundamental inasmuch as they provide us with the basis for a shared understanding of objects, people, and events. Such shared understanding gets structured by the implicit and explicit ideas and images accepted within groups. Social representations create a structuring basis for our interactions and communication which serve to define us as interconnected social agents. Individuals may still have very divergent views concerning any given object, but their differences are structured around shared representations of that object. In fact, divergence is necessary for the continued existence of the representations in social life. But these divergences make no sense unless they are compared and juxtaposed to each other, which allows us to understand the common organizing principle, that is, the metasystem.

The theory of methodology for social representation research, which Doise articulated to capture the anchoring process in all of its facets is presented in Chapter 6 by Alain Clémence. Chapter 7 offers a case study by Doise illustrating the application of this approach to the social representation of human rights.

The third extension of Moscovici's original approach to social representation was carried out by Denise Jodelet who argued that a representation always originates from a previous one, having altered mental and social configurations in the process. Jodelet emphasizes that the dynamic nature of a social representation, which is to be capable of continuous change, is rooted in its genesis, that is, in its linkage to preexisting representations. Consequently, the full understanding of a given representation necessarily requires us to start with those from which it was born. It is, of course, precisely this creative quality of self-mutation and transformation that makes the concept of social representation so useful to the study of important phenomena in the modern world. Contemporary society in particular is characterized by a high degree of fluidity and fast-paced change, and in this dynamic "global village" of today people are confronted with a much greater variety of representations.

Studying the genesis of social representations and their embeddedness in our cultural fabric, Jodelet's method uses narratives and qualitative data, while at the same time borrowing from anthropological and ethnographic methodologies. This multilevel approach to empirical investigation, which aims at contextualizing social representations into a sociohistorical framework, is illustrated in the work of Gina Philogène on African Americans (Chapter 8).

Such ecclecticism of empirical methods has made it easier for social representation theory to connect to disciplines other than social psychology. This quality has allowed the theory to be eminently practical in elucidating key social phenomena in contemporary societies. Any complete research would seek to incorporate all three methodological extensions of social representation. In doing so we inevitably make use of a multidimensional approach combining quantitative and qualitative data.

4

A Structural Approach to Social Representations

Jean-Claude Abric

Social Representations Theory

The structural approach to social representations is a direct extension of the theory elaborated in 1961 by Serge Moscovici. What constitutes the point of departure of this theory is the abandonment of the classical distinction – one strongly developed in behaviorist approaches in particular – between the subject and the object. Representations theory assumes, in fact, that "there is no break between the exterior universe and interior universe of the individual (or the group). The subject and the object are not fundamentally distinct" (Moscovici, 1969, p. 9). The object is inscribed in an active context. And the context is at least partially conceived by the person or the group as a continuation of the behavior, the attitudes, and the norms it refers to.

This hypothesis, the abandonment of the distinction between subject and object, leads us to give a new status to what has come to be called the "objective reality," defined by objective components of the situation and the object. We will argue that there is no a priori objective reality, but that all reality is represented. By this we mean to say that reality is appropriated by the individuals (or the group), reconstructed in their cognitive system, and integrated in their value system. These processes in turn depend both on their history as well as on the social and ideological context surrounding the individual or the group.

It is this appropriated and restructured reality which constitutes for the group or the individual the reality itself. Thus, all representations are a form of global and unitary vision of an object as well as of a subject. This representation restructures the reality to permit an integration of objective characteristics of the object, the previous experiences of the subject, and his or her attitudes and norms system. We can therefore define the representation like a functional vision of the world which allows individuals or groups to give a meaning to their conduct, to understand reality through their own system of references, and thus, to adapt to it and to define their place in it.

This is "a form of knowledge, socially elaborated and shared, having a practical aim, and concurring to the construction of a common reality to a social whole" (Jodelet, 1989, p. 36). It is both "the product and the process of a mental activity through which an individual or a group reconstruct the real which he is confronted with and attributes to it a specific meaning" (Abric, 1987, p. 64). Thus, the representation is not a simple reflection of the reality; rather, it is a signifying organization. This signification depends both on contingent factors – nature and constraints of the situation, the immediate context, the finality of the situation – and on more general factors which go beyond the situation itself: the social and ideological context, the place of the individual in the social organization, the history of the individual and the group, social stakes, as well as value systems.

The representation functions like a system for the interpretation of reality which governs the relations individuals have with their physical and social environments. It will determine their behavior or their practices. The representation is a "guide for action," it orients the actions and social relations. It is a system of predecoding reality, because it determines a whole of anticipations and expectations.

Structural Approach

A social representation consists of a body of information, beliefs, opinions, and attitudes about a given object. These elements are organized and structured so as to constitute a particular type of social cognitive system.

In 1976 we proposed the hypothesis of the central core which can be formulated in the following terms: "the organization of a social representation presents a specific characteristic: it is organized around a central core constituted of one or several elements that give the representation its meaning" (Abric, 1976).

The specific structure of social representations

The central core
The central core is determined by the nature of the object represented, by the type of relations that the group maintains with this object, and, finally, also by the system of values and social norms that constitutes the ideological environment of the moment and of the group. The central core – or the structuring core – of a representation ensures two essential functions. One is the generating function through which the signification of other constitutive elements of the representation creates or transforms itself. It is through the central core that these elements acquire a meaning, a

value. The other is an organizing function. The central core determines the nature of the links that unite the elements of the representation to each other. In this sense, it is the unifying and stabilizing element of the representation. In other words, it has a property. It constitutes the most stable element of the representation, the one that ensures the perennial nature of the representation in moving and evolving contexts.

For this reason the central core will be the element in the representation most resistant to change. In fact, all modifications of the central core involve a complete transformation of the representation. Thus, we will suppose that it is the identification of this central core that permits the comparative study of the representations. For two representations to be different, they have to be organized around two different central cores. It is the organization of this content which is essential here. Two representations defined by the same content may be radically different, if the organization of this content, and thus the centrality of certain elements, is different.

In other words, the centrality of an element cannot be conceptualized exclusively in quantitative terms. On the contrary, the central core has, above all, a qualitative dimension. It is not the presence of an important element which defines its centrality, but rather the signification it gives to the representation. It is perfectly possible to conceive of two elements whose quantitative importance is identical and very strong – they both appear, for example, very frequently in the subjects' discourse – but one is in the central core while the other is not.

Peripheral elements

Around the central core, peripheral elements are organized. They constitute the essence of the context of the representation: its most accessible part, but also the most lively and concrete. They respond to three primordial functions – concretization, adaptation, and defense.

Depending directly on the context, peripheral elements result from the anchoring of the representation into the reality. They constitute the interface between the central core and the concrete situation in which the representation elaborates or realizes itself. In that sense they serve a concretizing function, permitting the formulation of the representation in concrete terms to render it immediately comprehensible and transmissible.

Being more flexible than the central elements, peripheral elements also play an essential role in the adaptation of the representation to the evolution of the context. New information or any transformation of the environment can be integrated into the periphery of the representation. Any elements of the representation, which may put into question its very foundations, can in this way be regulated by marginalizing their presence, by reinterpreting them in the sense of the central signification, or by giving them an exceptional character. Compared to the stability of the central core, they constitute the moving and evolving aspect of the representation.

Finally, as we have already said, the central core of a representation resists change, because its transformation would require a complete overthrow. From that perspective we can conceive of the peripheral system as the defense system of the representation (Abric, 1993). In that function of defense the peripheral elements of the representation serve as what Flament (1994c) called its "shock absorber."

Evidence for the central core

The problem of discovering and identifying the central core constitutes arguably an essential preoccupation. By taking into account the three characteristics of the most important central elements, a group of methods emerged which has allowed us to discover and verify the constitutive elements of the core in an incontestable manner.

The first characteristic of a central element of the representation pointing to its core concerns its *symbolic value*. By definition, it is clear beyond dispute that a central element cannot be questioned without affecting the signification of the representation. That is precisely what makes such an element a central one in the first place. In his work on the representation of the ideal group, Moliner (1992) proposed a method for verifying the centrality of representational elements which can be implemented rather easily in field studies as well as experimental situations. He supposed that the constitutive elements of the representation of an object or a situation be known due to a previous study. Based on such a study we can construct a list of elements hypothesized to constitute the central core of the representation. Then the respondent is presented with a short inductor text which is verified to correspond to the representation of the object studied.

At this point we pass to the control-of-centrality phase. This is done by giving the respondent new information which questions the element studied. For example, after having described a good group, the respondent is told that there is a leader, thereby raising doubt about the "absence of hierarchy" which initially constituted a central core element in the representation of the good group. The person is then asked whether, in taking this new information into account, his/her representation of the object has changed or not. By questioning in this way successively the different elements studied, one can identify those elements whose questioning involves a change of the representation. These are the elements of the central core. Those elements whose questioning does not involve a change are the peripheral elements.

In addition, a central element is apparently more characteristic of the representation than any other element. Vergès (1994) has used a specific type of investigation for the study of representations based on questionnaires of characterization. The participant is provided with a list of items whose number is a multiple of three (for example, nine). He/she is asked to choose the three items, which seem to him/her the most characteristic of the object studied, and then to select the three least characteristic ones among the remaining six items. Each item is then assigned a score from one (if it has been chosen as noncharacteristic) to three (if it has been chosen as characteristic). The items of interest to us are those which have an asymmetrical distribution, more precisely those which are chosen by the largest number as "very characteristic." These are the elements we may consider as having a strong probability of belonging to the central core. Their graphical distribution corresponds to a J-curve. The form of the distribution obtained for each item gives us essential information about its possible status in the representation.

The second characteristic of a central element of any representation is its *associative value*. Given that any such central element is directly linked with the signification of the representation, it is necessarily associated with a very large number of constituents of the representation. It relates to many more other elements of the representation than any peripheral element would. It has, in other words, a higher degree of connection.

Finally, we also need to consider *expressive value* as the third characteristic typifying a central element as such. Due to the place it occupies in the representation, a central element has all the chances of being very much present in the discourses and verbalizations concerning the object of the representation. The frequency of appearance of a term – its salience – is an important indicator of centrality, provided that such a measure is complemented with more qualitative information. Vergès (1992) proposed for that purpose to cross two information items, one being salience (i.e., the observed frequency in the free production of a group) and the other being a ranking of the evocation of each term, to permit a first identification of the central core. Such a crossing technique allows us to determine the "zone of the central core" which comprises those elements of high frequency that are given the top rankings. The other zones, comprising either words with high frequency and lower rankings or words given first rankings but appearing with a lower frequency, correspond then to the peripheral elements.

Experimental and Empirical Verifications

The majority of the postulates of the central core theory have been verified to date in a number of experimental research works done in Aix-en-Provence. For a collection of such studies see, for instance, Flament, Abric, and Doise (1998).

An experimental investigation of social representation of artisans had the goal of verifying the stable and organizing character of the central core after disengaging it. In this study participants were first required to learn by heart a list of thirty words associated with artisan. They were then asked to recall this list immediately after having learned it (short-term memory) or after several hours (long-term memory). Two experimental variables were implemented and analyzed, the presence of the central elements in the list and the reference to the object studied (meaning whether the representation is invoked or not). The results obtained (Abric, 1989) showed, on the one hand, that central elements were better memorized than peripheral elements, including a stronger presence in the long-term memory. On the other hand, when participants recalled a list of words associated with artisan (thus evoking the representation) without reference to the central elements, these central elements – though not learned – were recalled anyway. In other words, these elements were reinvented by the respondents. In contrast, when the representation was not invoked, these central words were significantly less reintroduced. Thus, our study managed to verify the role of the central core in generating meaning. By restoring a representation, people were induced to reproduce on their own the central core eliminated by the experimental procedure, for the representation to find its identity and signification.

Research by Moliner (1992) confirmed another important aspect of the central core theory which postulates that an effective transformation of a representation is only possible if the central core itself is questioned. In this study participants were presented – using a short text – with the description of an ideal group whose central core has been well known ever since the work of Flament (1982). Then, at another time, new information was presented that questioned either an element of the central core (absence of hierarchy) or an important but peripheral element of the representation (community of opinions). It was found that, if the central core is questioned, 79% of the respondents considered that the group under consideration did not correspond to their representation of the ideal group. In contrast, when peripheral elements were attacked, only 37% of respondents had such a response. Thus, it is the transformation of the central core which engenders the change of the representation.

In recent years a whole new series of research has been developed with the objective of consolidating this theoretical approach. I am thinking here in particular of Moliner et al. (1995), Rateau (1995), Tafani (1997), Abric (1998), and Guimelli (1998). This research has enabled us to put the notion of the central core into a broader context. For instance, Tafani (2001) has done some research on the relations between social representations and attitudes. The main results of this study can be summarized as follows: attitudes are dependent on and determined by the social representations, but the reverse is not true. Social representations are at best only superficially dependent on attitudes. For example, Tafani found that a change in a social representation produces a change of attitudes, but a change in attitude does not produce a real change in social representations. Attitudes affect only peripheral elements. They have no effect on the central core.

All the studies cited here demonstrate that the structural approach to social representations appears as an important element to take into account when analyzing some of the most important questions posed by the social sciences. That approach is, among other things, particularly useful in helping us to understand the evolution of mentalities, action on attitudes and opinions, social influence (minority or majority), and the internal organization and transformation of rules of social thinking.

5

The King is Naked. Critical Advertisement and Fashion: The Benetton Phenomenon

Annamaria Silvana de Rosa

Introduction: Benetton as a Unique "Social Experiment" for Social Representation and Communication Studies

A big scandal: the advertising campaigns of the Italian clothing company Benetton have all been pronounced scandalous! This judgment occurred again in the case of the Spring/Summer 2000 advertising campaign entitled "*Looking at death in the face*" which showed the faces of prisoners on death row in several American prisons. This campaign on the death penalty (a topical issue already appeared in one of the seven images of the Autumn/Winter 1992–3) was prohibited and its creator, Olivieri Toscani, was heavily criticized, provoking legal action by the State of Missouri and a breach of contract suit against Benetton by Sears Roebuck for distributing Benetton products to their chain of four hundred shops. For many years, neither the company nor its creative director succumbed to the waves of criticism until now, when the explosive effect of the anti–death penalty campaign has rebounded to its creator, finally "dividing" what was so strongly "united" for almost 18 years. On April 29, 2000,[1] it was announced that Benetton—Toscani were "divorcing"; thus breaking up one of the most famous relationships existing between a company owner and a creative director, between commercial and communication leaders.

For several years we have been interested in what can be described as "the Benetton phenomenon" (de Rosa, 1988a; de Rosa & Losito, 1996; de Rosa & Smith, 1997, 1998a , 1998b; Kirchler & de Rosa, 1996). It began as a family business. Founded in 1965 under the name "Maglieria di Ponzano Veneto dei Fratelli Benetton," the Benetton Group was rapidly transformed into an international company whose brand name became both a worldwide financial success and a cultural phenomenon. Subsequent changes in the logo to "Benetton" to "United Colors of Benetton" reflect the progressive change from family firm to national and global company. Luciano Benetton is the "charismatic" figure of the Group[2] and the director of sales since the company was founded, as a company "*born of ideas*" – as he describes. The globalization of the brand name was achieved through centralized planning, marketing, product management, and distribution systems allied to high impact applied information technology. However, it was Benetton's coherent and highly innovative use of advertising that lay at the heart of the repositioning of the Benetton brand image. A rarely used medium, the billboard poster, which cost little compared to television advertising, was revitalized.[3] An implicit invitation to overcome any barrier under the aegis of "the United Colors of Benetton" was blazoned on giant boards in squares and on roadsides worldwide. Communicative strategies have played an extremely important part in the construction of the Benetton economic and cultural phenomenon. The sea change in Benetton's advertising policy was brought about by Oliverio Toscani, a photographer who has worked with Luciano Benetton since 1984. Their successful collaboration is documented in numerous interviews and biographies (Toscani, 1995).

Thus, it was a classic Italian company until they decided to launch to the world a series of advertising campaigns which culminated with the consequences described above. If one takes a look at the campaigns, one is struck by two contrasting aspects. On the one hand there is the contrast between the Benetton products themselves, which are supposed to dress people, being advertised in many instances by posters with the product entirely absent. To underline this aspect, Mr Benetton himself has gone so far as to appear naked on a poster. On the other hand there is the contrast between the major part of the publicity which is conventional, problem free, and the Benetton advertisements that stress the critical problems of western society (racism, deprived children, the death penalty, pollution, Aids, etc.). One could discuss their relevance, but not the underlying "ostensible intention," as the philosophers would have it. It is like the King's new clothes in the well-known fairy tale by Andersen. In that sense, one could say that we are dealing with critical advertisement: we will see this more clearly later on. For the moment it's sufficient to say that Benetton, which sells its products worldwide, has achieved through its communication and marketing strategy a considerable visibility and become an actor in the world of fashion.

It is a strategy that has stirred up professional literature, has provoked a discussion between the public opinion and polarized attitudes, as we will see later. We can say that today there is a discourse "*of*" Benetton about our society, and a discourse of society "*about*" Benetton. In fact, this is a remarkable cultural phenomenon, to the extent that fashion is, as social anthropology and communication studies recognize, a very significant phenomenon in modern society. To better understand the way, we studied the Benetton phenomenon and how the two types of discourses are related, starting with the equation that Moscovici[4] (1988) suggests: $F = f(C, Rs)$, which means that fashion is a function of communication and social representations, in that order. It can be discussed, of course, but at least it has the merit of highlighting the significance of fashion, which at first glance could seem a frivolous topic in the area of social representation studies. It's an appealing possibility that we want to take up with a lot of precautions. One of these precautions concerns what we mean by communication.

Social Representations and Communication

Most of the time we define communication as transmitting information from a source to a target or receiver. It is clear that there is more to it to the extent that this information is iconic and/or linguistic, presupposes a shared code, and so on. We prefer to define communication as "a process of symbolic interaction, in which the possibility of transferring messages occurs on the basis of signs, according to culturally and socially shared rules, i.e., according to codes conventionally defined on the basis of the use of criteria previously selected" (Crespi, 1996, p. 209).

As has often been said, this process is inherent to the theory of social representations. For example, Jodelet (1993) describes the relations between representations and social communications as:

> forms of social thinking used to *communicate*, understand and master the social, material, and intellectual environment. As such, they are analyzed as products and processes of mental activity that are socially marked. This social marking refers to conditions and contexts where representations emerge, to *communication* by which they circulate, and to the functions they serve. This form of knowledge is constructed in the course of social interaction and *communication*. It bears the mark of the subject's social insertion. Collectively shared, it contributes to the construction of a vision or version of reality that is common and specific to a social or cultural entity. This form of knowledge has practical aims and social functions. It operates as a system of interpretation of reality, serving as a guideline in our relation to the surrounding world. Thus it orients and organizes our behavior and *communication*. (p. 184)

In other words, the process of communication has an important role in the *genesis* and in the *functions* of social representations and, of course, in their *transmission* and *diffusion*. They are so mutually interdependent that "any consideration of social representations also means a consideration of communication; social representations originate in communication, they are manifested in it and they influence it" (Sommer, 1998, p. 186). But to seize this communication process, we must take into account the communication systems or genres – conversation, propaganda, etc. – in their reality. Our time has a great diversity in this sense, to the extent that social representations are generated and diffused through multiple communications systems or styles quite simultaneously. It is said to be a multimedia time. It's also a multisystem or multigenres time. Naturally, all this complicates what was relatively simple up to now.

Strangely enough, advertisement, whose importance continues to grow, is a neglected communication system or genre in social psychology in general and in the study of social representations in particular (Farr, 1955; Petrillo & Leonetti, 1996). One reason for this neglect could be a lack of interest in iconic symbols, images, and linguistic symbols. Another reason could be that models tend to focus on the unilateral actions of communication on social representations $\Rightarrow$ (S.R.) or social representations in the form of messages or content on communication $\Leftarrow$ (S.R.). One of the main orientations of our work is to conceive of communications systems as an interactive model of mutually producing or constructing the messages or content $\Leftrightarrow$ (S.R.). This interdependence between what's communicated and who communicates it is primordial in advertising for obvious marketing reason.

Sociocultural dimensions, as referential representational systems common to target and source, involve both target and source profoundly in the active construction, reconstruction, interpretation, and symbolization of the message. This dialogical communicative process occurs within a social sphere that is already organized. This is why one must take into account, whenever possible, this communication process at a level of society (Doise, 1984, 1986). The Benetton phenomenon gives us an opportunity and allows a kind of observation of a "social experiment" due to its original and unique character for the time being.

Social Representations and Corporate Communication: The Benetton Empire

As a commercial enterprise Benetton was dedicated to selling its products worldwide and to marketing its brand image on a global scale, becoming socially visible through its communicative strategies and marketing, as a result of its ability to introduce contrasting options in public opinion and highly polarized attitudes. There is thus a discourse *of* Benetton and a discourse *about* Benetton as a *cultural phenomenon*. The latter is proof of the success of the corporation in its expansion to a national and subsequently global company.

My extensive research program on social representations and Benetton advertising has been focused first on an analysis of the social representations expressed by Benetton through its numerous communication channels – internal company documents,[5] public documents available on the Benetton web site,[6] company publications such as posters, catalogues, *Global Vision*[7] and *Colors*,[8] various forms of sponsorship such as Formula 1 racing, socially directed actions, shop furnishings,

Table 5.1 A History of Benetton

Stages	Messages/Themes	Stylistic Elements	Examples	Communicative Strategies
1. 1966–83	Traditional message: product linked with image and brand name "Magliere Benetton" (Benetton pullovers)	• word + image • *photographic* style	Fig. 1	Association of product with positive social values (Barthes "principle of connotative transfer")
2. 1984–89	Universal harmony: positive social connotations; multi-racial themes "We are different – we are united in the name of the United Colors of Benetton"	• no text • multi-coloured products • *graphic* style (studio photos, collective subjects)	Fig. 2	• Use of multicolored differences as metaphor of universal harmony and of Company • Change of the Logo: "United Color of Benetton"
3. 1989–92	Towards the shock campaigns by means of contrast (transitory phase)	• no more products • forerunner of the shock-photo series • presence of dyad, pair of opposite and contrasting elements	Fig. 3	• Rhetorical use of visual-perceptual, chromatic and metaphorical contrast • Introduction of social issues in advertising • Deviant symbols
4. 1992–93	Indictment of social problems associated with underdevelopment, race, ecology, death penalty,	• real-life photos • photojournalism (*anti*-journalism) • advertising is more shocking than reality	Fig. 4	• Activation of polarized discussion through shock effect • De-familiarisation; de-contextualization; • Debate about advertising methods

5. 1993	Time for a counter-argument: from indictment to action-oriented : social intervention (Clothing distribution campaign)	Fig. 5	• two serial adverts • interrogative form • no colors • image (naked Benetton) plus text	Rhetorical devices: • dialogical structure of the message • abandoning of the color • request for an external legitimation (Red Cross)
6. 1991–95	AIDS as serial topic: 1991 (condoms), 1992 (dying AIDS patient with family), 1993 (part of the body with a HIV stamp), 1994 (hundreds of human faces)	Fig. 6	• Same topic • Different communicative strategies	• Added action value • Rhetorical alternation of soft–hard messages
7. 1996	Against racism: White, Black, Yellow hearts White and Black Horse	Fig. 7	• Image of body part + words • Chromatic contrast	Topic and strategies already used in previous campaigns
8. 1998	Handicap: Down's Syndrome people	Fig. 8	• Product re-appears in the photo • No words	• Added action value • Modulation of communicative tone (tenderness)
9. 2000	Face to the death Real protagonist in the death row of American prisons	Fig. 9	• Photo-journalism • No words	Message shock

and marketing strategies (Nardin, 1987; Kotler, Clark, & Scott, 1992; Righetti, 1993; Semprini, 1994a,1966). Second, I have considered the brand image of the company among its typical target populations, that is, the people who the advertising campaigns are aimed at and who are potential consumers of Benetton products.

Before examining some experimental results concerning these social representations in detail, we must first look at the *social discourse* which the Benetton company has produced.

Social discourse "of" Benetton: advertising and communicative strategies

The expansion of the Benetton company from family enterprise to global company has involved a repositioning of its brand name, in which communicative strategies, particularly advertising, have played an extremely important part (for a history and background information on the Benetton company see Nardin, 1987; Yagi, 1993; Kotler, Clark, & Scott, 1992; Semprini, 1994b, 1996).

A brief history of Benetton advertising campaigns
In order to show how the social discourse "of" Benetton "towards" a social target "about" social issues has developed, it is necessary to show how the communicative strategy in Benetton advertising has changed alongside the development of the brand. We must therefore look first at the company's advertising strategy.

The main stages in the development of Benetton advertising campaigns from 1970 to the present day are summarized in Table 5.1. As the table shows, the first change in Benetton advertising style was in 1984, when Toscani was appointed creative head of Benetton and eliminated the canons of traditional advertising from Benetton's campaigns. The traditional approach of the first stage (1966–83) made associations between the product (pullover) and positive social values (e.g., beauty, richness, landscape), together with conventional seductive allusions and double

Figure 5.1 Traditional approach.

Figure 5.2   We are different – we are united.

meanings, e.g., "only for men" (see Figure 5.1), according to the Barthes model of "connotative transfer" (Barthes, 1964; Semprini, 1996).

This approach was jettisoned in favor of an approach based on a philosophy of universal harmony between different races and cultures using the colors of the rainbow as a metaphorical expression of the philosophy and a representation of the colors of Benetton clothes expanding across the globe (see Figure 5.2). This second stage (1984–9) can be defined by the sentence: "We are different – we are united." Products still appear (pullovers, t-shirts, etc.), but verbal textual elements disappear in the advertising message. The changed brand name *"United Colors of Benetton"* metaphorically emphasizes this strategy: United States of America as a market to conquer in the name of its highly positive civic value; colors as metaphor of races; the aesthetic harmony of the rainbow of colors as metaphor of social harmony, communicating bright and lively feelings. It is explicitly aimed at inducing a need to belong to the great Benetton group (*"all the colors of the world" "all united in the name of Benetton"*). Protagonists of the images are groups of young people or pairs of children and adolescents of different races, in most cases associated with national flags of opposing cultures: America – Russia, America – China etc. Their tender embrace of the globe (see Figure 5.2) suggests an overcoming of current political oppositions.

Toscani summarizes the spirit of Benetton advertising at this stage as follows: "International, homogeneous, and characterized by universal themes, Benetton Group's advertising campaigns have been, since 1984, not only a means of communication but an expression of our time." (O. Toscani, source: Internet Benetton web site, 1998).

The third stage (1989–92) is transitory and can be defined as "Towards the shock campaigns by means of contrast." From 1989 onwards there was a change from advertising the product to advertising the corporation. The poster representing a "new-born white baby being breast-fed by a black woman" is a forerunner of the shock photo series which was to characterize subsequent campaigns. This transitory phase was characterized by the presence of pairs: a dyad, or pair of opposite elements, replaced the group which had dominated the previous stage. Emphasis was on contrast, both in terms of *chromatic* (black and white) and *metaphorical/symbolic*

Rhetorical Devices using Contrast:

- Chromatic
  (Black/White)
- Visual/Perception
  (Detail/Whole)
- Metaphorical
  (Color/Race)
  (Albino girl: Race/Illness)
- Symbolic
  (Devil/Angel)
  (Wolf/Lamb)

Figure 5.3 United colors, divided symbols.

elements (dog and cat in 1990; wolf and lamb in 1990–1; angel and devil in 1991–2, see Figure 5.3). In some cases the contrast is focused on the visual/perceptual opposition between a part, a detail and the whole (e.g., the combined images of a child/adolescent on one side with a part of the body, like a hand, on the other). The chromatic iconic elements focusing on the white/black contrast in the 1990 Spring/Summer campaign were also consistently used in the Winter 1990–1 campaigns.

The transitional nature of this stage is shown by some advertisements which still focus on the "harmony" topic and still use a communicative strategy of collective subjects and multicolors (e.g., mixed race children's choir, bouquet of flowers, painter's table, multicolored balls as a metaphor for the harmony of differences).

From 1991 Benetton advertising changed radically. The positive social message associated with brightly colored products disappeared and several new social topics, all with a strongly "ideological" connotation, emerged. In this transitory phase the topics focusing on social problems prepared the ground for post-1992 photographic realism. However, the advertisements still had an ironic flavor marked by a "graphic" style as used in the advertisements on race (Negro/Aryan/Asiatic children sticking out their tongues, devil/angel black/white children, multicolored wooden children *pinocchi*), sexual transgression (multicolored condoms, toilet paper, black/white priest/nun kissing each other) or the natural world (zebra and parrot; leaves of different colors) in the Autumn/Winter 1991–2 campaign.

Within stage 4, after the Spring/Summer 1992 campaign, Benetton advertising became tougher and more shocking. It can be defined as "The world's woes: advertising is more shocking than reality." Topics were still sometimes focused on the same social problems, like race, but this time they were presented using real-life rather than studio photos and were more strongly connotated in terms of underdevelopment and violence. Examples include a black soldier with a kalashnikov over his shoulder, symbolizing the arms made by white people, holding a thigh bone in his hands; an Indian couple holding their meager belongings, wading through floodwaters; a human cargo boat full of Albanians; and black people climbing over a dividing wall. Other social problems that had never previously appeared in advertising, such as Mafia killings, organized crime, a burning bombed car, and a person dying of AIDS with his family, were also used.

This strategy focused on a message-indictment of various social problems. It contained an implicit request for "for/against" options, aimed at activating polarized discussion in young people (the Benetton target) who are very sensitive to ideologically oriented social problems. The merchandising strategy seemed to be aimed at involving divided segments of the target in animated and conflicting discussions: *"talk about Benetton: it does not matter if you speak well or badly of it as long as you speak of it."* In order to emphasize the focus on social issues, the products disappear from the advertisements which are presented with the realism of photojournalism[9] (or antijournalism, according to Righetti, 1993, p. 109). "Toscani is and is not like the *photojournalists* whose works he uses. Like them he wants to inject the trauma of the real into the era of the lulled. Unlike them, he is a hip-hop sampler, embedding their traumatic image in his so-called advertising" (Blonsky, 1994, p. 58).

Negative reactions were based on the presumed illegitimacy of the intrusion by a commercial company on a discourse space that was traditionally the domain of the medical/scientific, legislative, and political discourse communities (Semprini, 1996). Toscani's response to these criticisms was to claim the right to take a different, more colorful approach to that of traditional commercial advertising, whose image was illusory and which falsified reality. Toscani claimed that his portrayal of worldwide "reality" with its full horror of violence, illness, social and natural disasters (e.g., immigration, racism, terrorism, Mafia, death penalty, ecological disasters), and his use of issues, such as AIDS, which had only been used in nonprofit making advertising was justified not only in terms of an abstract right to "know the truth,"[10] but also in terms of commercial logic – sales figures invariably increased after each campaign. Indeed the success of the advertising campaigns based on the use of universal issues like sex, religion, race, life and death[11] led Benetton not to finance any market research into advertising campaign results.

The Autumn/Winter 1992–3 campaign consisted of seven images all focusing on important social topics, each with a strong indictment of "the world's woes." It was a pessimistic development of the narrative of the previous campaigns, which had been more oriented by the ideology of "fraternity" in the name of "The United Colors of Benetton." The seven images of this campaign once again concerned *race/illness/deviance*, depicted by ambiguous connotations of biological and social differences, such as an Albino in an African tribe (see Figure 5.4). Other images connoted *underdevelopment/violence/exploitation of children*, for example, a poor black girl with a dirty white doll, or children working as laborers on a building site.

Figure 5.4   An Albino in an African tribe.

Ecological subjects included pigs "grazing" in a refuse dump or a cormorant swimming in a black sea of crude oil; *social issues associated with violence* such as the death penalty were illustrated by an electric chair or KGB interrogation.

Stage 5 marked a break with the style of stage 4 because it involved a link between advertising and social action. It can be summarized as "Time for a counter-argument: from indictment to action-oriented message." Communicative acts include social intervention on HIV/AIDS (Benetton campaigns for the distribution of condoms in shops and schools, financing AIDS research, sponsorship publications on AIDS prevention), promoting world peace (distribution of "multicultural notebook-passports" in schools), and relieving poverty (collection and distribution of clothing to Third World countries with the help of the Red Cross). Through this kind of organized social intervention Benetton communicates that the company is able to intervene in areas which have hitherto been the domain of politicians (Ministries of Health, Education, Scientific Research), the church, and humanitarian organizations (Red Cross). On balance, the evidence suggests that the shift from social criticism to action by Benetton was deliberate rather than, as Semprini (1996) claims, a response to accusations of using public and private tragedy for commercial gain.[12] The two serial advertisements, which appeared in the Spring/Summer 1993 campaign are linked to a single message, involving both image and text (see Figures 5 a and b). The style of stage 5 differs from that of previous stages

Figure 5.5   Clothing distribution campaign.

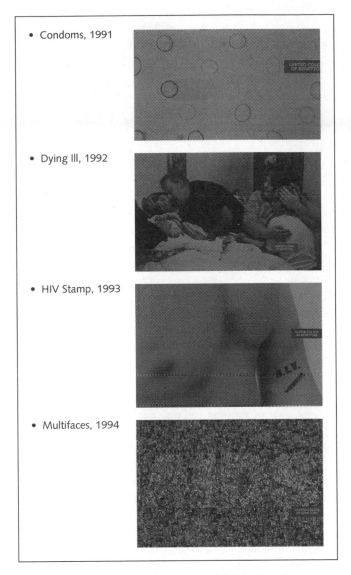

- Condoms, 1991

- Dying Ill, 1992

- HIV Stamp, 1993

- Multifaces, 1994

Figure 5.6 The serial advertising campaigns on AIDS (1991-4).

4 in terms of its use of three rhetorical devices: (a) the interrogative form and the dialogic structure of the message, which directly and imperatively involve the recipients, calling for action; (b) the abandoning of colors, in favor of a more discrete use of black and white; and (c) the request for an external legitimate organization (e.g., the Red Cross) to guarantee the humanitarian nature of the projects.

Figure 5.7 White and black horse.

Stage 6 is defined by a thematic rather than temporal criterion. HIV is a serial topic that has appeared consistently since 1991: "Condoms image" (1991), "dying AIDS patient with family" (1992), different "parts of the body with an HIV stamp" (1993–4), " hundreds of human faces" (1994–5) (see Figure 5.6). Although the topic of the advertisements appeared over several years and the campaigns were the same, the communicative strategies were quite different. Benetton has not simply used the AIDS question in a message/accusation format.

The social issue of racism appeared in the campaign 1996 and is not a new topic. In these advertisement the difference of color, as a metaphor for races, is associated with the words White, Black, and Yellow. In the pair of horses shown in Figure 5.7, the chromatic contrast recalls the previous series of black and white images.

The campaigns of stages 8 and 9 represent an emblematic example of two different ways to look at reality. One is the topic of the handicap represented by a tender mother and her Down's syndrome son (see Figure 5.8) in a photo showing again dressed people communicating tenderness (the product reappears associated with suffering and solidarity). In a second, the topic of the death penalty is represented by the faces of real protagonists who were interviewed by Toscani in the death row of American prisons (see Figure 5.9).

What will be the new stage, after the divorce between Toscani and Benetton, is at the moment an open question. Also, we cannot totally exclude the possibility that they will reconcile at a later stage, transforming this rupture in a phase of modulation of their discourse towards the world.

Figure 5.8 Handicap.

Figure 5.9 Looking at death in the face.

Benetton's communicative strategies
In the light of the social representation paradigm, let us now look at how these different stages reflect different communicative strategies adopted by the company. The main change in strategy between stage 1 and stage 2 came about as the result of the appointment of Oliverio Toscani as creative head of Benetton. At an early stage of these new Toscani-led campaigns, advertisements were still anchored in the product and used a graphic rather than photographic style (Semprini, 1996, p. 36). However, they focused on coexisting multicolored/multiracial elements expressing a positively connotated social message aimed at cultural integration – the forerunner of an advertising strategy aimed at the internationalization of Benetton products and the conquest of the American market.

After stage 2, the strategies of decontextualization and defamiliarization are used to create an effect of "the advertisement being more shocking than reality" (see "two processes – two-strategies" below). At stage 3, for example, the rhetorical use of visual/perceptual, chromatic and metaphorical/symbolic contrasts provokes a semantic short-circuit. Familiarity is destructured by using semantic dissociation and mixing elements from different categories that are conventionally perceived as opposites (see de Rosa & Smith, 1998a). At stage 4, Toscani apparently did not need any such rhetorical strategy. He simply put problematic pieces of the social world in posters and introduced controversial social issues in advertisements – an unfamiliar (defamiliarization) and illegitimate (decontextualization) space for public political discourse. In this way, the controversy about "shock advertising methods" is activated, rather than the social issue itself. What caused outrage was not AIDS, racism, or any of the many other social issues addressed in the Benetton campaigns from 1990–1 but their unfamiliar and decontextualized use by a commercial enterprise. Commerce was not authorized to speak about social issues as other institutions (e.g., medical, political, scientific, religious) were (see Righetti, 1993; Semprini, 1996). Reality is objectified through advertising – it becomes more shocking in advertising than in its natural, culturally legitimate context. Toscani's criticism of conventional advertising as a means of falsifying reality is put into practice in his strategy of showing reality as it is. In "*new-born baby*" Toscani started to break the convention of private/public space division, which assumes birth to be a private, intimate event and not to be shown in a public advertisement by a commercial company. From here there was a progressive escalation in putting the social world on posters as realistically as possible:

> You can see a news photo of the fighting in Sarajevo and it's in context; it conforms to your expectations. Shocking violence in the news is normal. But when you take the same photo out of the news and put a Benetton logo on it, people pause and reflect on their position on the problem. When they can't come to terms with it, they get mad at us. (O. Toscani, source: Internet Benetton web site, 1998)

The two strategies of decontextualization and defamiliarization work alongside the two processes of objectification and anchoring in the representational system and activate a polemical code with strong bipolarization (see Figure 5.10). The theory of minority influence, which will be addressed in the next section, explains how these strategies work in relation to social representations and how this study provides empirical confirmation of their influence. The spirit inherent in all Toscani's campaigns is polemical and avant-garde: "Traditional advertising is cheap songs singing always of the beautiful, telling us how we should consume our life instead of creating it, how we should fail in courage so as never to be disturbed" (O. Toscani, interviewed by Blonsky, 1994).

Communicative strategies adopted at stage 5 are defined by Semprini (1996) as "the cycle of truth." The advertising at this stage had an added "action-value" – the promotion of social activity was a sort of acting-out of advertising itself. One of the best illustrations of the strategic change towards prosocial action is in Benetton's use of the HIV topic. HIV is a serial topic which has appeared consistently since 1991, for example "Condoms image" (1991) and "dying AIDS patient with family" (1992) from stage 3. However, at stage 5, Benetton did not simply use the AIDS question in the message/accusation format. It also supported social work concerning AIDS prevention among the young, for example by distributing condoms in schools, donating money for AIDS research, exhibiting a huge condom monument in public, and devoting a special issue on *Colors* to AIDS.

In attempting to show, through its advertising, that it was not a commercial enterprise which profits from human suffering but was genuinely concerned with social issues, Benetton's strategy at stage 5 was clearly an attempted reply to the increasing criticism that had been provoked by Benetton's previous campaigns. The aim was to re-establish a dialogue with those people who, after the shock campaigns, had become extremely negative towards the company as other recognized humanitarian institutions. It seems that this dialogue, which for many years

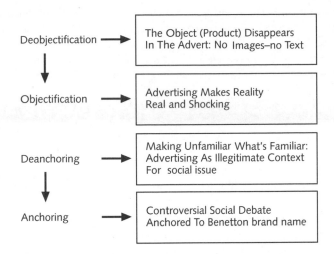

Figure 5.10. Two strategies, two processes.

has been modulated by rhetorical alternating between hard and soft messages, has been definitively broken after the last 2000 campaign "Face to the death."

Social discourse "about" Benetton

> Advertising is the most powerful form of communication in the world. We need to have images that will make people think and arouse discussion. Benetton's intention is to stimulate a critical discussion. It's wonderful to raise doubts rather than sanction certainties by conforming to established rules. (O.Toscani, quoted in T.Yagi, 1993)

> Our advertising is a Rorschach test of what you bring to the image.
> Ad agencies are obsolete, they're out of touch with the times; they're far too comfortable. When the client is happy, they stop trying. They don't want to know what's going on in the world. They create a false reality and want people to believe in it. We show reality and we're criticized for it. (O. Toscani, source: Internet Benetton web site, 1998)

From stage 2 onwards, when Benetton, in its Spring/Summer 1992 campaign, started to use images with a strong social impact, it aroused strongly-held and conflicting opinions (see Landi & Pollini, 1993, for a collection). The following are just a few examples:

> Real reality, not virtual reality. Conscience stimulated to think. (signed letter. Turin, p. 26)

We looked with curiosity and interest at the photo of the young black albino who, because of her illness, was different from others of her race, with the same somatic features as her brothers and sisters . . . It is important that people question themselves, reflect on things which normally are accepted as "different" and are nothing else but "different normality." (letter from two Albinos. Johannesburg, South Africa, p. 66)

If you love life, boycott Benetton. (leaflet distributed in Melbourne, Australia, p. 18)

We'll never buy your blood-stained pullovers again. Does this please you? (signed postcard, London, p. 18)

You are the exploiters of the human race (anonymous letter, Frosinone, p. 20)

As these examples suggest, reactions were both positive and negative. Generally speaking, the social discourse about Benetton generated by this debate can be summarized in the following terms. Firstly, it stirred up debate in a vast cross-section of the community. The role of Benetton advertising has been debated by governments and their lawyers, by social scientists in academic circles, by journalists and opinion makers, as well as by the public. It has involved both experts and nonexperts. Secondly, it has involved debate in a considerable number of social settings. It has been discussed at home, workplaces, clubs, academic conferences, and government buildings as well as in newspapers, magazines, and on TV and radio.

Thirdly, the kind of controversy stirred up by Benetton advertising is polarized. The extracts in Landi and Pollini show opinions that are either clearly favorable or clearly unfavorable, with very few people showing indifference. The favorable opinions claim that Benetton advertising is original, effective, aesthetically pleasing, forward-looking and socially useful, whereas the negative opinions claim that it is cynical, "necrophiliac," and opportunistic. Fourthly, as the above cited examples suggest, the opinions that are held about Benetton are very strongly held; people are either strongly in favor of Benetton advertising or strongly against.

What this social discourse shows is the transformation of a debate about social issues into a debate about Benetton advertising and a debate about advertising into a debate about the company itself. Benetton's strategy of using relevant social problems (discourse "on" the social) is of great interest and curiosity to scholars of mass communication. Indeed the split at the level of public opinion and the resonance obtained in the mass media raise an important question: are the advantages of "visibility" (namely of making the brand name widely known – one of the most traditional markers of an effective advertising campaign) offset by negative reactions to the images? In other words, is not the fact that a large part of the population has a clearly negative reaction to this kind of advertising, accusing it of necrophilia and cynicism, of more relevance than the gains made in terms of notoriety and social visibility? The answer to this question will be grounded on the results of the empirical research described in the next section.

Empirical Results

This section examines some results of an empirical study, aimed to reveal the links between Benetton's global communication strategies and the part played in the construction of the Benetton brand name by the social representation of company-created Benetton discourse (i.e., Benetton as a *cultural phenomenon)*. This examination was based both on media texts about Benetton produced by experts and lay people in publications, interviews, press articles, and letters to magazines and to the company, and on people's conversation within focus groups that had discussed the same media texts.[13]

Social discourse "about" Benetton: the company as perceived by its target

A multimethod approach
The general methodological design behind this project and some of the results of the advertisements used here have been published elsewhere (de Rosa, 1988; de Rosa & Losito, 1996; de Rosa & Smith, 1997, 1998a). Two methodological conditions were used. In one, quasi-experts viewed 11 slides of Benetton images; in a second, "daily use" condition, nonexperts viewed images in magazine advertisements. Advertisements from the controversial 1992–3 Autumn/Winter campaign and the 1991–4 AIDS campaigns were used. Participants in each condition were equally distributed for sex and age. They were tested for message selection strategy, focus of attention, message comprehension, message interpretation, and memory of previous exposure to the same image as well as other familiarization variables. The study was begun in Italy (n = 1257) and extended to other European countries: Austria (n = 232), France (n = 240), and Portugal (n = 120).

The aim of the research was to identify possible connections between the dependent variables linked to the message/advertisement (descriptions of the image; interpretation of the message; interpretation of the meaning attributed to the message by the source; memory reactivation processes; evaluation of the effectiveness of the message; evaluation of the moral acceptability of the message; identification of message topic) and variables outside the message (attitude to message topic; Benetton product buying behavior; sociodemographic data).

With regard to the present discussion, the most significant technique used was the *associative network* (see de Rosa, 1995, for a complete description of these techniques). This projective technique was used first, in order to prevent responses being anchored by information from the questionnaire which might bias word elicitation. It requires participants first to associate words with stimulus words and then to establish connections and branching pattern between the elicited words written around the stimulus word in the center of the page. Thus, it enables respondents to specify the structure of a semantic field themselves. Thus, starting from a free association test, you obtain a textual web. The associative network also gives information about the order in which words come to mind. This order indicates both their saliency and the level of stereotyping of the elicited representations (participants" first words, because of their high level of accessibility, may be both their most salient ones and the most socially shared ones).[14]

The associative network requires people to attribute a particular polarity to each word (positive, neutral, or negative) to describe its connotations. This enables not only the structure and content of a social representation to be revealed, but also the "polarization of the semantic field', that is, the evaluative and attitudinal aspects of the representation. A polarity index calculates the positive, negative, or neutral connotations of the free associations evoked by each of three stimulus words used in this study: image, brand name, and I . This index, which varies from +1 to −1 is calculated by the following formula:

$$\text{polarity index (P)} = \frac{\text{no. of positive words} - \text{no. of negative words}}{\text{total no. of associated words}}$$

A second "neutrality" control index, which also varies between −1 and +1, is calculated. In this way the structure, content, and polarity of particular representations are established.

In terms of data analysis, associative network processing has two objectives: the first is to describe the structure and content of the representational fields associated with image, Benetton and I (achieved by lexical correspondence analysis: SPAD-T; see Lebart, Morineau, and Beçue, 1989), and the second is to reconstruct the discourse dynamics implicit in the structure of the textual web (by applying a content analysis program DISCAN to the corpus of elicited words; see Maranda, 1990). Technical details of these analyses are described elsewhere. The end result is a map of the semantic activity of a particular corpus of the kind shown in Figures 5.15 and 5.16.

The hypotheses of the study were as follows:

1   Alongside highly contrasting reactions to the advertising campaign, the target would have a relatively positive representation of the company and that, paradoxically, the controversy caused by the "provocatory" style of the campaign would be associated with a kind of metacommunication reinforcing positive connotations of the brand name.

2   Within the discourse dynamics of the associative networks (stimulus word "Benetton"), the social representation of the Benetton brand name would mediate between the company's advertisement (and other communicative strategies) and its industrial activity and production (goods and attributes).

Results

As regards the first hypothesis, the polarity indexes of the representational fields associated with the various advertisements of both campaigns (Autumn/Winter 1992–3 and HIV/AIDS serial adverts) were compared with the indexes of the semantic fields activated by the stimulus word "Benetton." Results confirmed the hypothesis regarding the relatively positive representation of the company coupled with the negative, or ambivalent, representation evoked by the advertisements.

Figure 5.11 shows that the average polarity index for individual images tends to be negative for almost all images, particularly the "interview" and "electric chair" photographs. There are less negative reactions to images containing children, such as "tribe" and "child labor," probably evidence of a sympathy effect. Analysis of

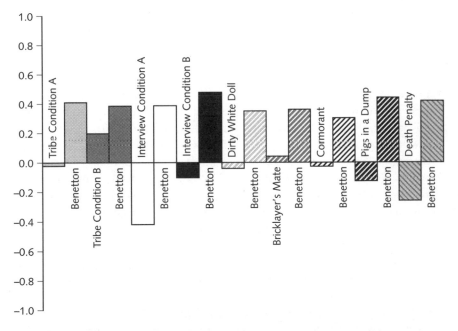

Figure 5.11   Indexes of polarity relating to the 1992-3 campaign and the Benetton brand.
Note   The same graphical pattern identifies the group of subjects who answered both the stimulus "adverts" and "Benetton" brand.

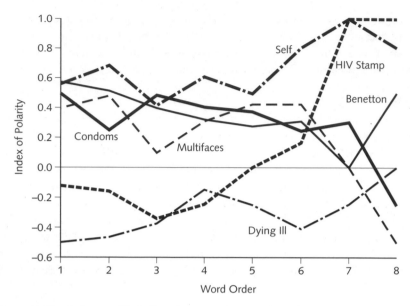

Figure 5.12 Indexes of Polarity relating to the stimulus adverts "condoms," "dying ill," "HIV stamp," and "mutlifaces" (see Figure 5.6) according to the order of elicitation.

variance, using image contents as independent variables and average polarity indexes for each image as dependent variables, shows that evaluation varies significantly in accordance with photograph type (F = 12.58, p < 0.001).

The difference between the largely unfavorable reaction to the seven images of the Autumn/Winter 1992 – 3 campaign and the favorable reaction to the Benetton brand name is shown in the graph, which shows a considerable "disproportion" between the average polarity indexes for individual images (almost always negative) and for the brand name (always positive). These results are confirmed by the significant difference between the average scores represented in the graph, as derived from the t-test.

The same pattern of results emerges from the index of polarity relating to the HIV/AIDS advertisements, compared to that of the brand name. The only difference here is the modulation of the target's reaction in line with the soft/hard rhetorical devices used by Toscani (represented in Figure 5.12, also taking into account the order of a word's elicitation from the first to the eighth evoked words). The AIDS issue is presented softly and positively in "Condom" with a beautiful colored image and in a mass of friendly "smiling faces," but more aggressively in the images of "a person dying of AIDS" or "sexual parts of the body stamped HIV" (for a detailed analysis of the rhetorical devices adopted by Toscani, see de Rosa & Smith, 1998b).

Our findings show that most of the people interviewed considered Benetton advertising to be effective for the purposes of promoting a positive corporate image (54%) and for the purpose of boosting sales (21%), while 18% considered it ineffective and only 6% thought it harmful. Among nonexperts, however, replies to the two questions on the "moral acceptability of Benetton's advertising campaigns"[15] are less favorable and more controversial. Although most of those interviewed (61%) considered Toscani's advertisements to be "morally acceptable because they focus the attention of public opinion on important social questions," only 48.6% of the respondents considered it legitimate to use these issues for commercial ends. This marked fluctuation of opinions reflects the existence, in a non-negligible portion of the target, of an ambiguous attitude, namely a condition of psychological uncertainty (a conflicting condition that is typical of subjects under a minority influence). Thus, Benetton is acknowledged as being able to stimulate (through original images with a powerful emotional impact) reflection on and discussion of social topics such as racial discrimination, marginalization, and violence. At the same time, it is not considered legitimate for these topics to be dealt with by a firm for private business interests (though almost half our respondents thought this was legitimate).

The highly favorable evaluation of the *brand name*, when compared to the less favorable (and often negative) evaluation expressed by the polarity index for the images, seems to show that factors not exclusively and directly linked to the advertising world, but also to the economic and business dimension of the group (a multinational group, whose widely varied interests range from wearing apparel to Formula One, from food to cosmetics) are important in the definition of the social representation of Benetton.

However, this result may be interpreted differently by making reference to Moscovici's theory of active minorities,[16] discussed elsewhere (de Rosa, 1998; de Rosa & Smith, 1997, 1998a). Research (Maass & Clark, 1984; Moscovici & Mugny, 1985; Mucchi Faina, 1995) shows that the characteristics attributed most frequently to "deviant" and "disturbing" groups, that show coherence in defending their positions, are originality, self-assurance, confidence in own ideas, competence and "social visibility." Despite the negative reactions (expressed by the polarity index regarding the images and by replies concerning the moral acceptability of the advertisements), these characteristics could be considered by the target to be indications of success at a communicative and business level, and of a marked distinctiveness from other firms that operate in an anonymous and conventional way on the market (a favorable evaluation expressed, not only by the polarity index relative to the brand name, but also by the responses regarding the efficacy of the communication in corporate image terms).

A minority's power to influence derives, on the one hand, from its style of behavior

Words	Semi-Axis	Absolute contr.
Polemical	–	5.7
Photo	–	3.7
Exploitation	–	3.5
Hypocrite	–	3.1
Wear	–	3.0
Consumer society	–	3.0
Denounce	–	2.2
Toscani	–	2.0
Advertising	–	1.5
Magazine	–	1.5
Sponsor	–	1.5
Success	–	1.2
Fashion	–	1.1
Treviso	–	1.0
Wool	–	0.9

Positioning of Subject's Groups
Sex = Male
Age = 22–25 years
Index of Polarity Related to Benetton: Negative
Index of Polarity Related to Benetton: Indifferent
Index of Neutrality Related to Benetton: Medium
Index of Polarity Related to Oneself: Indifferent
Index of Neutrality Related to Oneself: Medium–High

Words	Semi-Axis	Absolute contr.
Known	+	5.8
Franchising	+	5.4
Work	+	4.7
Condom	+	3.7
Expensive	+	3.6
Adults	+	3.5
Antiracism	+	2.7
Senator	+	2.6
Quality	+	2.4
Contrasts	+	2.3
Young	+	2.2
Interesting	+	1.7
Pain	+	1.4
Union	+	1.3
Peace	+	1.3
Warm	+	1.2
Luciano Benetton	+	1.1

Positioning of Subject's Groups
Sex = Female
Age = Younger Than 22 Years
Index of Polarity Towards Benetton: Positive
Index of Polarity Towards Oneself: Positive
Index of Neutrality Towards Oneself: Low

Figure 5.13 Results from SPAD-T analyzing associative networks related to the Benetton brand name.

(which must be mainly characterized by coherence, but also by a capacity to listen to objections and criticisms) and, on the other hand, from a partial correspondence between the ideas and values which it proposes and the ideas and values which are rooted in the society which is the target of its communications – a notion which is at the heart of the theory of modern communication (Eco, 1976, 1987, 1990). If these conditions are met, minorities often show a capacity to impose their own attitudes and to foster favorable behaviors towards themselves. Flexibility emphasizes the bidirectional nature of the influencing processes, which is based not just on the source's communicative behavior, but also on mutual adjustment between the target's reactions and the source's ability to adjust itself to the characteristics and development of the argumentative context.

Benetton's communication technique is, in fact, clearly marked by the creation and management of conflict. Benetton deliberately creates a conflict in public opinion, while trying to organize it by means of a consistent set of "rhetorical stratagems" (de Rosa & Smith, 1998b) aimed at a greater acceptance of its own positions. Exemplary, in this respect, is the relative modification of strategy, between stages 4 and 5, from "saying" to "doing" (documented by the firm itself and pointed out in the literature by Semprini, 1994b).

Finally, it is noteworthy that the target's representation of the company is split into two poles: one focusing on the advertising hemisphere (polemical, photo, exploitation, hypocrite, consumer society, etc.) and the other on the hemisphere of the production and commercial strategies of the brand name (known, franchising, work, expensive, quality, etc.). The fact that the former is anchored to Toscani and is mainly expressed by men over 22, with a negative index of polarity relating to Benetton, is particularly interesting. The latter is anchored to Luciano Benetton, director of Benetton, and is mainly expressed by women under 22, with a positive index of polarity relating to Benetton (see Figure 5.13). Again it seems that the rhetorical strategy of inducing contrasting representations affects the target, splitting the negative world of Toscani-led advertising ("L'âme damnée de Benetton")[17] and the positive world of the Luciano Benetton-led commercial enterprise.

The results discussed here also support the observation, made by a number of authors (Moscovici, 1980; Moscovici & Mugny, 1987; Mugny, 1991), that the influence exercised by an active minority is mainly indirect. According to them, minorities bring about a cognitive restructuring and a change of attitude which, at a latent level, often corresponds, if not to open and explicit condemnation, at least to clear, partial rejection.

The positive effects achieved by Benetton in the evaluation of its specific brand can also be interpreted on the basis of the "agenda setting" model – a model of the cognitive effects of social visibility (Shaw, 1979). The most important difference between minority influence theory and agenda setting theory is linked to the conflict. Minorities obtain visibility because they infringe upon set concepts, undermining the community's mental schemes and arousing the interest of the media (as a result of their own unorthodox positions). In contrast, according to the theory of agenda setting, social visibility, with its effect at public opinion level, seems to be created directly by the media. According to the agenda setting model, the more an occurrence is spoken about, the more the occurrence is taken into consideration and accorded importance. Paradoxically, therefore, high social visibility could be the cause of the amplification of the perception of the Benetton's economic and business effectiveness. The more Benetton is spoken about (in either a good or bad way), the more it is perceived as a colossus in the communication and business world. Indeed the resonance of Benetton in the media seems to have influenced not only the public (Benetton is one of the five best-known brands in the world) but the media itself, which at times seems to transform itself from mere instrument to unwitting object of influence.

The strong link between the shock advertising campaign and the echo effect in the print media is shown by the distribution of articles published about Benetton in the print media. Figure 5.14 shows that the highest concentration of articles published from 1980–98 in three newspapers (*The Times, New York Times,* and *Los Angeles Times)* falls exactly within the 1991–5 period when the amount of shock advertising was increasing. Computer-aided content analysis (using Alceste) of the whole corpus of articles shows that the *New York Times* focused mainly on Benetton advertising as a source of scandal and controversy during the 1992–3 period, whereas before 1992 and after 1993 it focused mainly on the Benetton business.

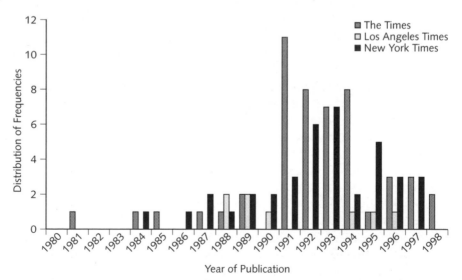

Figure 5.14 Distribution of frequencies of articles about Benetton appearing in *The Times, Los Angeles Times,* and *New York Times.*

This economic representation of the Benetton financial empire also occurs in Benetton's self-representation on its website. The website is organized into three main sections: *Who We Are, What We Say, What We Make*. Analysis of all website texts shows that Benetton's history of scandals appears in *What We Say*, economic questions in *Who We Are* and *What We Make* (associated with product). The company's identity (*Who We Are*) and products (*What We Make*) are attached to the visible, concrete world of Benetton's commercial empire, which is presented as a social alternative to reality and described in *What We Say* in terms of diversity.

Discourse dynamics arising from associative networks produced in answers to the "Benetton" stimulus

As regards the second hypothesis, Figure 5.15 shows the DiscAn[18] results for the associative networks in terms of the discourse dynamics activated by the stimulus word "Benetton." It shows the links between the categories of words elicited from subjects in response to the brand name[19] and illustrates the semantic connections of the "Benetton" representation in terms of all its advertising, marketing, and production activities. This network seems to occur despite the contrasting polarity indexes for the advertising and brand name representations and confirms the effectiveness of the company's communicative strategies.

The most obvious result is the central role of "goods," which seems to act as the organizing nucleus for all the other source/relay elements. As regards "sources," "goods attributes" and "Benetton advertising attributes" have the highest level of activity. "Goods" is the biggest "absorber" with the highest level of activity. The role of "goods" is central: all the other categories on the map (advertising, brand name, economic/commercial aspects) revolve around it.

Associations produced in response to the stimulus "Benetton" refer to different areas. First, the area relating to "production" was described, then the area relating to Benetton advertising, specific Benetton campaign images used in the research, advertising in general, economic/commercial activity, the source and its attributes and the campaign message. This semantic route can be traced on the map via source categories in the upper half and absorber categories in the lower half.

The dual role played by advertising in the semantic dynamics is particularly interesting. It acts as a source (i.e., it is greater than 1) for the Benetton stimulus, particularly for the "message outcome," "emotional correlates" and "message intention" categories, and as an absorber (i.e., it is less than 1) for advertising in general. This highlights the more active part played by Benetton advertising as an activating source for semantic routes compared with advertising in general, which seems to have a more receptive/passive role.

The results for advertisement images show links between the descriptive level

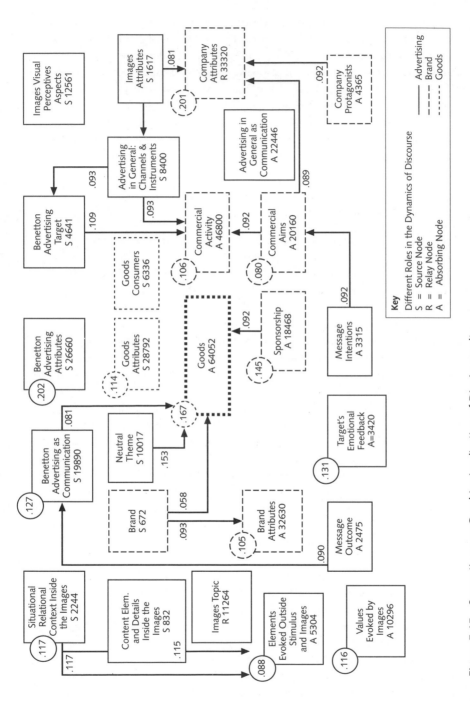

Figure 5.15 Semantic map: Graphic visualization of DiscAn results.

Note Factor Activity > 800; Probability > 0.08; ◯ Loop = probability of one category being preceded or followed by itself.

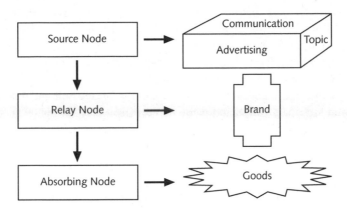

Figure 5.16 Social Representations of Benetton brand. Semantic map derived from DiscAn: different roles in the dynamics of discourse.

("context elements" and "details present in the images" are both source nodes); the interpretative level ("topic" is a mediator and relay); and the evaluative level (values evoked from the images is an absorber node). As regards links between advertising and company production aspects, "Benetton advertising" seems to open up a discourse about the "product" – a surprising result since this discourse had been removed or denied during the advertising campaigns. Benetton advertising seems to play a diffracting role in the associative dynamics as if, starting from the advertising message, the associative discourse was facilitated to act as a source for a number of semantic paths. These are clearly more complex links than those which start from the brand name and its attributes or from "product attributes" and "consumers," all of which tend to revolve around the product.

In conclusion, in the description, interpretation, and evaluation of Benetton advertising, the associative discourse expands in the direction of economic/commercial aspects and source attributes and eventually focuses on the "product" and "protagonist figures" of the Group. Figure 5.16 summarizes the map of the Discan results and highlights how the discourse dynamics move from the world of communication to the world of company and finally on to company production and products. These empirical findings, which link Benetton advertising to Benetton goods, may be the reason for the success of Benetton's communicative strategies and one of the reasons why its advertising is able to deny the product while at the same time placing it in the center of the representational field, and provoke fierce controversy while at the same time increasing company profits.

Moscovici's statement (1976b) that "the original and extreme points of view have much greater probabilities of exercising a strong attraction than of being rejected" seems decidedly appropriate to this study. In fact, despite the criticisms often expressed towards Benetton's strongly transgressive advertising, the representation of the brand name (fueled precisely by this advertising!) is positive in almost all the people interviewed.

This result seems to show that "scandal" pays, not only in terms of fame and social visibility, but also, paradoxically, in terms of image. The relative gap between attitude to the message (highly polarized, i.e., the object of favorable and unfavorable opinions) and attitude to the brand name (almost invariably favorable) is, in fact, coherent with one of the guiding principles of the theory of active minorities: the principle according to which the social influence exercised by heterodox groups which behave coherently in defense of their positions is, though pronounced, mainly indirect.

The self-presentation of the Company as a deviant group within the conformist scenario of advertising is shown in the picture "madmen ready for the straitjacket," which appeared in February/March 1996 in newspapers and posters, and recently on the home page of the Benetton website. In it, the whole Benetton Management team is portrayed with Luciano Benetton in the key position wearing a full straitjacket while all the others are wearing straitjackets over colored trousers. The colors, which break the glacial monotony of the white straitjackets, blend with the smiles on the faces of these "madmen," connoting the "crazy firm's" positive, cheerful, and creative approach.

Conclusion

It's clear that the results of this research are limited to one case and the population we studied. This research confirms the success of Benetton's communicative strategy. Social discourse "by" Benetton "about" social issues sets off a social discourse "about Benetton" which itself sets up a metarepresentation of the brand name: the brand name is expanded and emphasized within self-reflecting circuits which feed off the contrasting forces activated by the source of the message. This process suggests a paradoxical effect (as shown in Figure 5.17): despite powerful resistance to accepting Benetton's communicative style in a large portion of the target, a positive representation of the brand name is still created through communicative strategies capable of arousing controversial attitudes (anchored in polemical social representations) to the advertising campaigns.

But, could we explain it a little bit more completely? What did critical advertisement change? From what we have seen, is it what characterizes it that enables it to have a certain success? A way of answering is suggested by the connection between Benetton's style of advertisement and the behavioral style of an active minority with the fashion world, so to speak. We note its consistent character and the total refusal, until recently, of all that is asked from it to soften its content and/or deny it

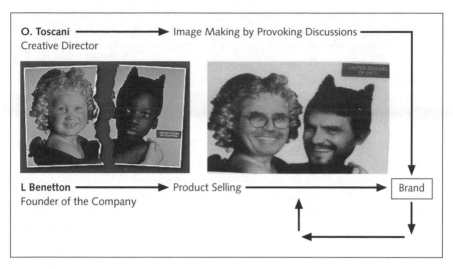

Figure 5.17 F = f (C, Rs): Fashion as function of communication and social representations.

all efficiency. As we know, such consistency creates a conflict through a "virtual" worldwide debate. This conflict or controversy is amplified through the multiple communication genres, including advertisement (icons), interview and press releases (texts), images and texts together (*Global Vision, Colors,* website), and prosocial actions. As we already know, this may be deliberate intention to be sensed as an "active minority," at least in the advertisement community. Achieving social visibility (de Rosa, 1998, de Rosa & Smith 1997, 1998a) is linked to a favorable evaluation of brand. This has also been observed by colleagues saying that Benetton's advertising message has the merit of being noticed and being talked about (Kotler, Clark, & Scott, 1992; Semprini, 1996). We will see what this message is typical of and why it succeeds in its attempt to change the practice established by publicity. In any case, it's a critical practice in the sense that it's normal practice for an "active minority." However, that is just a means towards an end. The end is to innovate, to generate a new social representation of the company that adopts such a strategy. Or, to say it in a commercial way, "the goal is to sell" the brand.

If, in addition, we were to summarize how social representation is shaped during communication, we would say that the two processes (defamiliarization and decontextualization) observed in the Benetton advertisement work along side the processes of anchoring and objectivation. That, by making unfamiliar what is familiar, creates a code for distinguishing and recognizing Benetton's messages as messages that are advertised. Rather than being noise or redundancies, they become events or happenings.

But before coming to a conclusion, let me lightly touch a question of the philosophy of mind suggested to me by Moscovici.[20] A brand name, like Benetton, is usually a proper name. When we speak of social representation, for example, "the social representation of Benetton," we give it a meaning, making Benetton a referent of what is talked about. It is tempting to think that this meaning would express the semantic link, a specific content describing the Italian brand. But Putnam's (1975) analyses have suggested that this semantic link is instituted by a social practice, a "baptism," just as when we call a person Raul or an illness AIDS. Through conventional means we give a person or an illness a name that becomes specific whatever it is, and following that, the changes in the associated representations. This is very important for the theory of social representations and communication (Moscovici, 2000). In fact the process of communication, in particular advertising, could be seen as a baptism process where the family name, afterwards a brand, becomes a referent, one of the referents about what is in the society and the representation which that more or less shares.

In this sense, we could say that publicity does not create a brand image, but a brand to which opinions or behaviors refer in the fashion world in whatever way it is represented at a given moment, or the product (perfume, shoes, etc.) that represents it. It is quite obvious, from our study, that Benetton has become a referent both in the advertising and fashion world. All this complicates what would seem simple in the accepted view of communication. This makes us more sensitive to certain paradoxes. For example the following paradox: the association between social representations and Benetton's name is quite positive. And yet, the messages, their styles face a resistance in a large portion of the public.

But, as we could expect, in all innovations the change achieved by an "active" minority does not exclude a critical judgment of its behavioral style or its qualities. It could be that the resistance is concentrated more on what, as a last analysis, is only a means (behavioral style, tension strategy) and less on what is the veritable end (have people accept an idea, an image, and so on).

It seems that the case was finally closed by the last campaign "Looking at Death in the face" which has symbolically broken the binomium Benetton – Toscani, avoiding the risk of the discourse's inflation and of repercussions caused by redundant rhetorical devices, that is, by the familiarization of defamiliarization. We can see that "death" has paradoxically produced death right within the communicative space conquered by Toscani in the Benetton Company. We will see how Benetton will reposition his brand after the divorce with Toscani, and how, if, and in the name of which "brand" or "patron" Toscani will continue to shock the world. Whatever will be the development of this story (including a remarriage), the communicative genre invented by Toscani will belong to the history of the very special cases within communicative studies.

Notes

The draft version of this chapter was written during my stage at Maison Suger (Sept. – Oct. 1998) as invited *Directeur d'études* at E.H.E.S.S. by kind invitation of Maison de la Science de l'homme. I would like to thank Professor M. Aymard very much for this opportunity. I also would like to express my gratitude to my best friends and colleagues, Serge Moscovici and Rob Farr, who helped me with comments, suggestions, and substantial editing in different phases of the conception and revision of this chapter. In particular – for his fundamental contribution in reshaping the introduction and the conclusion of this chapter, Serge Moscovici should be acknowledged as coauthor.

1 Carlo Brambilla (2000) Benetton e Toscani si lasciano dopo 18 anni. (April, 30). *La Repubblica* p. 25.
2 Luciano Benetton is in charge of sales, Giuliana Benetton of production, Gilberto Benetton of administration and Carlo Benetton of machinery (cf. Kotler, P. Clark, J.G., & Scott, W.G. 1997 4th ed., p. 2)
3 This, in our view, was a strategic company decision aimed at achieving large-scale social visibility at low cost. However, A. Semprini (1996, it. tr. 1997) argues from a sociosemiotic perspective in favor of "ingenuousness," which in his view served to increase the conflictual and controversial social discourse of the Benetton brand name. According to Semprini, this ingenuousness was determined by the poster medium's inability to segment the target. The result was indiscriminate exposure to messages without prior selection by the source of the message:

   Because of its maximum visibility and its position in the public space, posters provide a particularly direct message. It is a form of communication from which there is no protection and which it is impossible not to see. The brand messages thus achieve greater visibility, but also amplify negative aspects in terms of reaction and interpretation. Not only can a poster not be turned off, like a television, or closed, like a magazine, but it is an "indiscriminate" form of communication. Since it is positioned in the public arena, it is addressed to the public in general – of every age, sex or social status. This makes the reception of a poster campaign less controllable and predictable than it would be in a targeted magazine. Although the flow of images and messages circulating in society seems to be chaotic and omnipresent, it is actually channeled, specialized and divided up in order to reach an equally segmented public. From this point of view, the poster is perhaps the least discriminatory advertising medium. Its consequence is the amplification of the controversial effects of communication. (Semprini, A. 1996, Italian trans. 1997, pp. 80–81)

4 Moscovici (personal communication, 1998) during the 4th International Conference on Social Representations, Mexico City.
5 I would like to thank the Communications Sector of the Benetton company, particularly Paolo Landi, for the documents kindly provided by the Company for this research.
6 cf. http://www.benetton.com
7 Global Vision has been defined as "a summary in pictures of the Benetton company; it contains 320 pages with chapters on company philosophy, architecture, product, licensing, advertising." (New projects/ Nuovi progetti, p. 11).

8   *Colors* – "a global magazine about local cultures" – is the Benetton "*manifesto*" pub-
     lished worldwide in seven bilingual editions (English paired with Italian, French, Ger-
     man, Spanish, Croatian, Greek, and Japanese).

9   During this new stage Toscani stopped using his own photos and started to select pho-
     tos among those produced by others.

10   Semprini criticizes what he sees as further ingenuousness by Benetton:

> the communicative arrogance of those who unilaterally break the rules of discourse space,
> ignoring the fact that in saying something one does not only take care about "what to say"
> but also "who to," "in what context," "in what way," "to what end," and "in the name of
> what and who." But there is another aspect that Benetton seems to ignore in its answers to
> criticism, namely that the conditions of interpretation and reception of a message are en-
> shrined in a sociocultural space and cannot be taken out of it. To consider messages as
> absolute objects, with no implications for collaborative interpretation or cognitive proce-
> dures is to ignore one of the foundations of social discourse functions (Debrary, 1994).
> Benetton's arguments seem to forget that every act of communication activates an extremely
> complex actor network.

This leads to a second type of "ingenuousness": just as one cannot make one sector of
the public sensitive to an issue at the expense of another, one cannot ignore that social
discourse is susceptible to a number of receptive phenomena and that the meaning of a
message never completely belongs to the person who is producing it. The justification
that one has been misunderstood and that something else was intended is unacceptable
in a mass communication context. (Semprini, A 1996. Italian trans., 1997, pp. 79–80)

11   Death (represented, for example, in the "*military cemetery*" advertisement, as well as life
     (represented, for example, in the advertisement "*new-born baby*") are collective or pri-
     vate events not to be shown in public commercial adverts, according to the conven-
     tional criteria which regulate this kind of mass communication. "There are just two
     realities: being born and dying. In between is pure fantasy" (Toscani, quoted in M.
     Blonsky, 1994, p. 58).

12   see Semprini's interpretation (1996. Italian trans., 1997 pp. 57–70) of the "*Clothing
     Redistribution Project*" linked to the 1993 "Cycle of truth" campaign. The project – in
     Semprini's view – is clearly a response to the controversy surrounding the previous
     campaigns. It has three clear differences in its communicative style: (a) its explicit inten-
     tion to create a dialogue between the Benetton company leader and any interlocutor
     responding to his appeal for second hand clothes; (b) its abandoning of color in favor of
     the more serious black and white; (c) the provision of legitimacy and external guaran-
     tees through collaboration with nonprofit making organizations such as the Red Cross;
     this is carried out in order to counter criticisms of exploitation.

Although this interpretation is attractive (particularly its idea of the symbolic reap-
propriation of the "product" – clothing – which had not appeared in Benetton advertising for years), these criticisms are put into perspective by the fact that Benetton's
social activism in the area of AIDS had began in 1991 at the same time as its first AIDS
advertisement ("Condoms"), and before the objections by AIDS sufferers and AIDS
organizations to subsequent advertisements ("person dying of AIDS with his family" in
1992 and an HIV stamp on different parts of body, in 1993). In other words the dia-

logue between Benetton and its target was activated earlier and does not follow the linear temporal sequence as described by Semprini.

13 Fifteen focus groups (for a total of 110 subjects) were created ad hoc, each of them discussing a specific media text: for example the issue of *Colors* dedicated to Aids, Religion, Shopping, or the collection of expert opinions collected, for example.

14 With this in mind, some applications of the associative network have introduced a further requirement aimed at identifying the order of importance of each word in the semantic space. This information was then compared with the order of elicitation in order to verify the degree to which the information coincided (cf. de Rosa, 1995: de Rosa, Sinigaglia, & Abric, 1996).

15 To assess the moral acceptability of Benetton advertising two different questions were used, referring to different kinds of explanation (social salience of the topics versus commercial exploitation of social issues):

"According to you, can this advertisement be considered morally acceptable, because it focuses the attention of public opinion on an important social problem?" Answer: YES/NO.

"According to you, can this advertisement be considered morally acceptable because it uses an important social problem for commercial ends?" Answer: YES/NO.

16 This is a theory based on a vast number of experimental tests (for a review of these see Doms, 1983; Maass and Clark, 1984; Papastamou and Mugny, 1985; Nemeth, 1986; Mucchi, Faina, Maass, & Volpato, 1991; Mucchi, Faina, 1995; Perez, Papastamou, & Mugny, 1995). The theory has also attracted the attention of American marketing experts, who are mostly trained in individual-centered social cognition (Folkes and Keisler, 1991).

17 See Horizons: "Oliverio Toscani: l'âme damnée de Benetton." (1998, July, 5–6, p. 8). *Le Monde.*

18 In DiscAn the categories are treated as semantic nodes. For each node of the semantic network DiscAn calculates the contribution of each category to the map (level of activity): a node might therefore generate a wide network of semantic flow, but be relatively inactive, while another might be very active but at the same time hinder semantic flow. DiscAn calculates the probability of transition from one category to a previous or subsequent one (first level Markov chains). In this way probabilistic chains of semantic nodes represented in the thesaurus categories can be constructed; the degree of reception (input) and emission (output) for each of these can also be calculated and their role in the semantic map defined. The degree of reception of a node (d–) is termed "internal semigrade" and the degree of emission (d+) "external semigrade." When the internal semigrade of a node is greater than the external semigrade, we have an attractor or "absorber" node, whose input number is higher than its output. If the internal semigrade is lower than the external semigrade, we have a diffractor or "source" node, whose output number is higher than its input. When the internal semigrade is equal to the external semigrade, we have a transmitter or "relay" node, which neither reduces nor expands the discourse dynamics of the corpus but simply acts as a connector. A high number of relays, however, indicates the presence of stereotypes.

These data enable the semantic "activity" of a corpus to be described. Its internal dynamics depends on the intensity with which each node absorbs, diffracts or transmits. DiscAn the d+/d– score for each node. A score of 1 means that it is a relay node, if it greater than 1 it is a source node and if it is less than 1 it is an absorber node. The total of the internal and external semigrade scores for the respective frequencies (d– f) + (d+ f) shows each node's contribution to the global activity of the corpus and its relevance in terms of discourse as well as semantics. A map of this activity can also be produced from this data (de Rosa & Losito, 1996).

19 Only category nodes with activity factors of over 0.0800 were used for analyzing results, but, due to limitation in the graphical representation, only category nodes with activity factors of over 800 were included in the map.

20 Moscovici (personal communication, Spring 2000) during my stay in Paris at E.H.E.S.S. as Socrates European Teaching Staff.

6

Social Positioning and Social Representations

Alain Clémence

Introduction

The purpose of the social representation approach is to study common sense knowledge about abstract objects or theories. The development of common knowledge starts when these objects or theories become a problem in a given social context. When this happens, more and more people begin to debate around these objects and theories and begin to be involved in the construction of a specific theory.

Social representations are defined as theories of common sense applied to general topics, for example, intelligence, AIDS, violence, computer, gender, health, psychoanalysis, and work, that are discussed in a society. These theories are constructed and used to deal with abstract and complex questions in everyday life. Such questions are, how intelligent is my child? What is the origin of AIDS? Why are some people more violent than others? In answering such questions, we rely on the way intelligence, the origin of AIDS, or violence are defined and discussed in the public sphere. We also rely on the knowledge exchanged and shared around us, among the groups we are involved with. Yet, we can always take a position of our own, which means that we have to refer it to the common points of reference that constitute the normative content network of the social space we are living in. In order to understand this process, it is important not only to know that our reasoning is based on cognitive functioning such as categorizing or doing inferences, but also to know how and why we give specific signification to a given information. This chapter is devoted to the approach of social positioning, i.e., the process by which people take up position about a network of significations. First, I shall present some historical as well as theoretical background of the approach. Secondly, I shall focus on methodological considerations illustrated by a case study.

Historical Background: Thinking in Everyday Life

According to Durkheim (1998, first published 1912), individual representation, as opposed to collective representation, is restricted to internal states that cannot be shared with others. In order to be communicated, such states have to be transformed into things like words, images, and symbols, by the collectivity. When Lévy-Bruhl (1923), an anthropologist, examined materials collected from what he called "primitive" cultures, he used the notion of collective representations in order to make a distinction between *two models of thinking*, a rational model, typical of "civilized" cultures, and a "mystic" model, typical of "primitive" cultures. Piaget used this very distinction when he characterized the child operative thinking and the adult formal thinking. For Piaget (1932), rational thinking is gradually replacing primitive thinking during the cognitive development, while for Moscovici, adults continue to reason like children, even if their thoughts are based on formal, rational or logic principles (Moscovici, 1981, 1994). In everyday life, different kinds of constraints lead us to make a decision or to take a stand without actually following logical prescriptions. For a layman, the *content* becomes central in the organization of knowledge, while formal procedures are followed in scientific thinking (Moscovici & Hewstone, 1983; Clémence & Doise, 1995; see Purkhardt, 1995, for a critical discussion). When we are engaged in contexts requiring technical procedures, we have to follow systematic and logical rules in order to perform efficiently. This is usually the case in the professional area, yet we often reason in the same way when we do "ordinary" things like cooking or doing housework. However, things are very different when we find ourselves in settings in which we are expressing opinions or preferences. Our reasoning often follows a path that appears to be wrong or biased from a cognitive point of view. However, such "mystic" thinking is often well suited to situations in social life such as when we are engaged in convincing or charming people, or interpreting new events or predicting the future. Furthermore, the use of "scientific" reasoning requires too much time and material to be applied in such circumstances.

Common sense and scientific thinking are interconnected. As Moscovici (1976a; Moscovici & Hewstone, 1983) has pointed out, common sense theory is currently more based on knowledge than on experience. More and more people have access to a variety of scientific information, and they use it in their discussions and thoughts. But the diffusion of scientific theories does not imply that scientific thinking is replacing common sense, for common sense as typical everyday thinking transforms scientific theory into another kind of theory. Moscovici showed how this happened for psychoanalysis (see also Herzlich, 1973). Common sense has an influence on scientific knowledge too (Kelley, 1992). The idea at stake here is not to differentiate between experts and novices, rather it is to assess how representational thinking modulates informative thinking because both work in different normative frameworks. The contrast between these two ways of thinking can be illustrated by the kind of transformations that occur when a popular newspaper borrows ideas from a scientific journal. What happens with such newspapers also happens in our daily discussions when they bear on various topics, for in this situation our reasoning is based on images and symbols, and our attention is focused on the content of our topics and our arguments are based on various short cuts and detours. That is the way we try to keep the attention of the person we are speaking to, or to persuade, or seduce him or her. Alternatively, when we act as experts in an office or a laboratory, we have to be specific and use well-defined concepts and follow pre-established logical arguments which actually leads to our being acknowledged as an expert.

The Basic Processes Described by the Theory of Social Representations

The cognitive processes are controlled and oriented by the *normative* meta*system* as Moscovici (1976a) called it. The cognitive system operates by joining, categorizing, etc., different things, but these operations are "reworked" by a metasystem using normative regulations. According to Doise, the theory of social representations is basically "a general theory about a metasystem of social regulations intervening in the system of cognitive functioning" (Doise, 1993a, p. 157; see also Doise, 1993b). The study of social representations answers the question, "Which social regulations engage which cognitive functions in which contexts?" (ibid., p. 58). This controlling operates by means of two sociocognitive dynamics, namely objectification and anchoring.

Objectification refers to the process of transforming abstract information into concrete knowledge through communication (for a detailed discussion of objectification, see Flick, 1995; Jodelet, 1989; Wagner, Elejabarrieta, & Lahnsteiner, 1995). The process ends in figurative, metaphorical, or symbolic meanings, which become *shared, but not consensual, points of reference* during a debating process on a specific topic or issue. Social representation is at this stage a lexicon of meanings drawing from the objectification of the abstract object. By circulating in a social context, the content of this lexicon is used as a map of common points of reference for people. As shared knowledge, this content is organized around some connections between its elements. The content and the structure of these lay theories are actually debated among social psychologists. The structural approach stresses the idea that the content of a social representation is organized around a central nucleus composed of a few consensual meanings (see Abric, 1984, this volume; Augoustinos & Innes, 1990). The dynamic approach maintains that all social representations are composed of different, contrasted kinds of meanings. Knowledge shared by people is precisely this network of variations (see Doise, Clémence, & Lorenzi-Cioldi, 1993).

However, the transformation of information follows different ways depending on the groups in which information is diffused. As Doise quoted, "demands of the metasystem can change according to the social positions in specific networks of relations" (Doise, 1993a, p. 158). Because every social representation is elaborated through debates, different points of view emerge during the transformation of abstract information into concrete meanings. Divergent positions are expressed in public space by individuals belonging to groups who actively attempt to define abstract information from their points of view. Individuals use normative rules (based on ideas, values or beliefs of their groups), for analyzing some ambiguous or unfamiliar aspects of the changing lay theories. To be adopted, figures and meanings have to be anchored in prior knowledge and beliefs. The *anchoring* process results in a specific definition of a theory of common sense by integrating particular figurative meanings of the social representation. A social representation is then constituted by a network of more or less divergent meanings depending of the strength of the discussions around its object. At the same time, these different meanings have to be shared, more or less, in order for the object to be put in the everyday conversations.

Consider, for instance, the social representation of work. The meaning of this notion has evolved a great deal, and is perpetually enriched by new features. As a concept, work appears to be equivocal, and some scientists have suggested that we abandon it for more precise terms (Offe, 1985; Karlsson, 1995). For the same reasons, the notion is still at the center of passionate discussions in the public sphere. Findings of different studies have shown that work is always objectified, at least in European countries, around the figure of a manual and painful activity providing a financial reward (Salmaso & Pombeni, 1986; Grize, Vergès, & Silem, 1987). However, the figure of an intellectual and autonomous professional, like the lawyer or the architect, has enlarged the meaning of work. Work is defined not only as a concrete activity done for earning one's living, but also as an occupation done for self-achievement (Flament, 1994b). Other kinds of figurative meanings begin to emerge in the debate around activities like artistic or sportive occupations long seen as the opposite of work. These different figures shape the network of shared meanings of work in Western societies. The definition people endorse vary according to their working experiences, e.g., self-achievement is more pregnant for intellectual than for manual workers. However, the anchoring process depends also on the diffusion of knowledge and beliefs of different groups in the social world. For instance, the instrumental definition of work has been consolidated these past years by the return of the moral virtues related to labor supported by different political and religious movements (Clémence, 1998).

Social Positioning and Organizing Social Representations

Taking part in a debate around a theory requests of people that they take a stand on common points of reference. Sharing common points of reference does not imply consensual agreement, while a debate implies shared knowledge. *Social positioning* derives from the anchoring of the shared knowledge in different groups. These groups are not only different because they do not have access to the same information, but also because their members share specific beliefs and experiences. Normative principles are developed during a socialization process and they orient positioning on the map of common points of reference. Thus, social positioning is not only the expression of an opinion, it is also a way to process information in order to adapt what we think to what the society thinks. Consequently, it provides the means for articulating the variations between intergroups beliefs and knowledge with the temporary crystallization of a network of meanings in a given public sphere.

In order to take position in the network of meanings, individuals have to know the terms of the debate and to link them to their point of view about social life. Hence, a position is connected to and regulated by more *general principles* of thinking. Depending of the individual involvement in the communicative relationships between social actors, these principles of thinking will be more or less structured and the corresponding positions more or less obvious (McLeod, Pan, & Rusinski, 1995). Moscovici (1976a) presented three modalities of communication depending on three kind of interindividual and intergroup relations. When a new idea is emerging in a social space, a phase of diffusion of information can be observed first. This occurs in a context of relative undifferentiation between social actors and produces a set of common points of reference (see Doise, 1993a). Media with a large audience contribute to the circulation of various thematic elements and multiple opinions. The second phase begins when specific groups intervene by organizing the network according to their knowledge and beliefs. The message is directed towards the members of various groups who look for what to think about the developing debate. Some experts of the group may propagate a principle for weighting the different elements of the network in order to consolidate the well-established doctrine of the group. Other social actors, in particular minorities, develop a stronger perspective with a propaganda based on conflicting social relations. This form of communication is aimed at selecting true and false knowledge and opinions among common knowledge. If the positions resulting in the propagation are expressed as flexible attitudes, those stemming from propaganda appear to be firm and stereotypical.

The work of Devine is a good illustration of social positioning. Devine (1989) based her perspective on social judgment on the conflict occurring between an automatically activated cognition (a stereotype) and a more controlled expression of personal opinions. One could argue that automatic knowledge is in fact common knowledge (a stereotype is more or less known by everybody in a specific social context), and that controlled thinking is social positioning (people express a position against or in favor of a stereotype). It seems difficult to consider a belief as a personal cognitive construction. A stereotype, as shared knowledge acquired during socialization, could be rejected because it is implicated in ongoing social debate. A personal belief is therefore a position that can be taken because individuals have acquired a different kind of knowledge during their socialization (Duveen & Lloyd, 1990).

A personal belief is not merely the result of an individual cognitive activity, but it is anchored in the experiences and values of social groups. Following on Kinder and Sears (1981), Katz and Hass (1988) showed that the racial positions of whites were integrated in more general principles towards social life. A problack position is regulated by a normative principle directed by egalitarian and social justice values while an antiblack position is organized by the Protestant ethic based on meritocracy and discipline. It must also be underlined that some stereotypes appear to be more automatic than others, which is to say, in my view, that they are more shared and discussed than others (see Stangor & Lange, 1994).

Moreover, Devine seems to assert that the dissociation between stereotype and positioning holds true for all stereotypical knowledge. However, it seems that some stereotypes are more easily activated than others. For instance, American students activate stereotypes more easily on the basis of sex rather than race categories (Smith & Zárate, 1990; Stangor & Lange, 1994). Finally, the dissociation appears to be modulated, at least in the case of negative stereotypes, by the position itself. The people against a stereotype do provide positive information, whereas those in favor of a stereotype give only negative information (see Augoustinos & Walker, 1995, pp. 239–244).

Exploring Social Representation: A Methodological Strategy

Following this theoretical framework, a methodological approach of social representations implies three phases. A systematic methodological approach of these three phases including a discussion of the appropriate statistical procedures can be found in Doise, Clémence, and Lorenzi-Cioldi (1993). Therefore, I shall give a short description of the core points of this strategy.

The first point of this strategy is centered on the map of the shared reference points resulting from the objectification process. This implies collecting the elements of the circulating content of a specific object of social representation. One of the most frequently used procedures is the free association between words and objects or closely related terms. It is important to keep in mind that words are treated both as a figurative and a semantic way for defining the object. The results of free association are then analyzed in order to group words together in sets that constitute the network or the map of meanings. In each set some words occupy a central or prototypical place and can therefore be considered as the most prominent figures of the social representation (see Lahlou, this volume). Because only the shared lexicon is of interest at this stage, individuals are momentarily not taken into account. Automatic clustering or multidimensional scaling are statistical techniques well-suited for this kind of analysis.

The second phase deals with social positioning and is centered on the principles that organize the variations between the positions of individuals or groups on the map. Data have to be collected for interindividual or intergroup comparisons. One procedure used to collect these data is standardized questionnaire build on the basis of the sets of meanings detected in the first stage. Responses are examined in two directions: covariations permit one to define the principles of association between meanings held by participants, and levels indicate the stands they take on the shared map. Statistical procedures like factor analysis or multidimensional scaling of individual differences are useful at this stage.

The third phase is centered on the characteristics of individuals and groups. Data on individuals are generally obtained from the same questionnaires used during the second phase. Data on groups can also be collected independently of the research participants (see for instance, Doise, this volume). The analysis links positions and principles to the characteristics of respondents. This can be done in different ways. One way is to base the exploration on specific group membership by evaluating the discriminating power of positions and principles. Another way is based on classical regression models which account for the variance of positions and principles by multiple group memberships.

The study of social positioning is central in this approach of social representations, for it offers a better understanding of the articulation between the shared and debated points of reference and a population of individuals divided into groups supporting different positions in the debate (Elejabarrieta, 1994). In order to illustrate an empirical approach of social positioning, partial results of a study on social representations of solidarity and social welfare are presented.

A Study of Social Positioning: Social Representations of Solidarity and Social Welfare

A currently debated question in Switzerland is the future of social welfare. The terms of the debate are organized around a concrete question of solidarity: who will pay for whom? Everybody agrees that solidarity is a fundamental value of the (Swiss) social welfare system. However, it seems obvious that this value is understood in very different ways. A clear illustration of these divergent positions can be found in the multiple and complicated forms of the welfare institutions. The more important one (AVS) was introduced after World War II and was meant to provide financial support for retired people, and is clearly based on an extensive solidarity.

Everybody has to contribute to this system depending of his or her income, and these contributions are directly distributed to all women (starting at age 62) and men (starting at age 65). The money allocated to each individual is almost the same. In the 1970s, a system of pension funds was installed for wage earners. It is based on a classical principle of individual capitalization. Another important national institution is constituted by a network of private healthcare insurances. Everybody has to contract such an insurance. The insurance companies provide a wide range of benefits, but within a company similar insurances must offer the same benefits. Other institutions partly based on collective solidarity (in areas such as unemployment or political asylum) or on individual insurance (in areas such as unemployment or retirement for craftsmen) are also part of the welfare system.

Two studies were conducted on the topic of solidarity in the context of a national research program on social security (Clémence, Egloff, Gardiol, & Gobet, 1994). A standardized questionnaire was administered to 600 individuals, aged 18 to 20, in 1991, in two French-speaking areas (Geneva and Jura) as well as in two German-speaking areas (Luzern and St Gallen) in Switzerland. One year later, a sample of parents of the research participants were invited to answer a similar questionnaire to which an experimental study was added. In this chapter, only data about the parents, whose age was between 45 and 55 years (129 women and 95 men), are examined.

The questionnaire bore upon the representation and evaluation of different aspects of social welfare such as knowledge about social security, estimation of needs and risks of different social groups, explanations of social problems, personal involvement in social areas, and appraisal of institutional aid.

Common points of reference

Data of a preliminary survey (free word association with the terms solidarity and social welfare and semi-directed interviews) showed that the objectification of solidarity was organized around two meanings. The first one was about *helping behaviors* between persons in close relationships (family, friends); the second one was about the *social welfare* as characterized by mutual aid between unequal groups in different areas (work, health, etc.). Positioning towards social welfare is discussed below.

Social positioning and anchoring

Studies on intergroup relations and on social justice have well documented the fact that individuals are guided by at least two normative principles: a norm of favoritism of oneself and the members of one's own groups, and a norm of fairness based on the respective contributions or needs of every person or every group. This normative metasystem can be affected by different normative principles endorsed by groups. For instance, some of them consider that any kind of resources should be distributed in order to improve social relations, while some others emphasized economic efficiency of goods distribution. Those who were more concerned with the management of social relations than with the efficiency of economic distribution, were also more ready to accept egalitarian strategies in the distribution of resources (Deutsch, 1985; Rasinski, 1987). Individuals who hold a more negative view on social relations could be those who are more in favor of helping deprived groups of people. In other words, positioning towards social welfare could be organized by the principle used to judge social relations. This process does not rule out that attitudes towards aid could also be based on a self-serving principle. If this line of reasoning is correct, positioning towards social welfare (institutional aid) must be more in favor among individuals who evaluate social relations more negatively.

In order to verify this assumption, participants in the "parents study" answered two questions. The first one was about the evaluation of social relations in the Swiss context: participants expressed their perception of *social relations* by means of evaluations of the quality of 12 relationships between dyads of groups using a 5-point scale (from very bad to very good). Examples of such relationships were "employers and employees," "old and young people," "disabled and able-bodied," "unemployed and employed," or "Swiss and foreigners" relationships. The second one was about the position towards the institutional solidarity as applied to different groups: participants indicated their *appraisal of institutional aid* by means of evaluations of the amount of aid in favor of 10 social categories using a 3-point scale (from too high to too low). For instance, they had to judge "aid to elderly," "aid to applicants for asylum," "aid to youths in training," or "aid to drug addicts." For assessing the impact of the self serving principle, participants also estimated the degree of *social health-related risks* of their children in 9 different areas using a 4-point scale (from weak to high). Among other things, participants had to estimate the likelihood of the following risks: "to be victim of a road accident," "to be assaulted on the street," "to have psychiatric problems," or "to have difficulties finding a job." Separate reliability analyses were performed on the items of each domain, and they showed that the interindividual differences can be considered as unidimensional (Cronbach alphas > 0.79).

A multiple regression analysis was carried out on the appraisal of institutional aid by entering the evaluation of relationships and the estimation of risks as independent variables. Two contextual factors were also entered because they could be considered as possible anchored variables of the positioning towards social welfare. The *linguistic group* (Swiss German versus Swiss French) is obviously articulated with economic and cultural differences. The economic context is more favorable in the

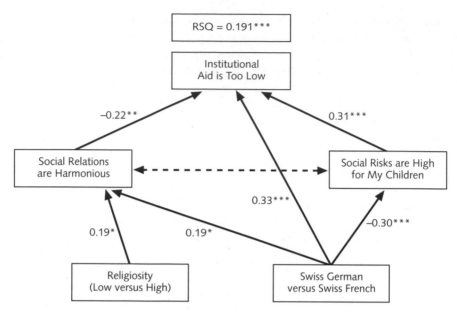

Note   n = 144; Standardized Beta (filled lines) and RSQ: *p<0.05; **p<0.01, ***p<0.001.
          Correlation between *Social Relations* and *Social Risks* (dotted line): R = –0.24, p>0.01.

Figure 6.1   A path diagram of the anchoring of social positioning towards institutional aid.

German than in the French part of Switzerland. Cultural differences are regularly expressed on referendums about social security topics. When most Swiss French voters support collective aid and social institutions, a majority of Swiss German voters support individual self-helping. The *religious observances* (low versus high) was also selected because religious affiliation is historically linked with concrete charity rather than social solidarity. Moreover, religious observances offer a good measure of the degree of integration not only in a specific community but also in the social and cultural context (Isambert, 1982). In order to complete the model, a regression analysis was carried out on each organizing principle separately using both contextual factors as independent variables. Results are presented in Figure 6.1.

The results show that positioning towards social welfare is organized by a self-serving principle (estimation of risks for children) and the evaluation of social harmony. These positionings are directly anchored in the linguistic division: Swiss French exhibited a more favorable position than Swiss German. However, the position of Swiss German appeared to be more positive than the position of Swiss French if we consider indirect effects: Swiss German evaluated more negatively the social relations and estimated that the risks are higher than the Swiss French did.

Taken together, the results showed that the adhesion of Swiss German, but not of Swiss French, to social welfare depended of the evaluations of insecurity and social harmony. An indirect effect of the religiosity is also observed: high religious observances imply a more harmonious perception of the social relations and a more negative position towards social welfare.

Organizing principles and positioning in an experimental context

An experimental investigation was added to the parents' study in order to test the effect of the perception of social relations, as organizing principle, on positions towards the contributions to social institutions. A design was drawn in order to manipulate the degree of perceived tensions between the privileged and the underprivileged. Harmony in these relations was presented as needing either to be improved or to be kept identical. At the beginning of this section, we saw that the evaluation of social relations is an organizing principle of the positions towards the institutional aid. By the same token, this principle should organize the positions towards the contributions to social welfare institutions. It was predicted that participants would accept a proposal of contributions more readily if social relations were to be improved rather than kept identical. The design of the experiment was based on the discourses held by different political movements, some of them claiming that solidarity in social welfare has to be developed in order to restore social harmony, while other movements claiming that solidarity, in order to be preserved, had to be maintained at the current level.

The experimental part of the study was presented in the form of "*a proposal submitted by experts for solving problems in financing social welfare.*" Participants were invited to state their degree of agreement with the proposal and to evaluate its consequences in different areas of society: financing of two social security systems, solidarity in society, struggle against poverty, economic growth, and personal freedom.

Two independent variables were introduced. The first one was about the type of argumentation produced by the experts. In one condition, arguments aimed at producing a perception of *harmonious* relations in society stressed the fact that the "*solution of social problems depended on the maintenance of good relations among all.*" In the other condition, arguments aimed at illustrating the existence of *inequality* stated that "*the solution of social problems depended on the increase of support by the richest in favor of the poorest.*" The second independent variable was about the content of the proposal submitted to the participants that either respected the *status quo* or argued in favor of an *increase* of contributions to two social institutions.

Preliminary analyses showed that gender, social status, and linguistic group membership did not affect the answers of the participants. Analysis of variance of the degree of agreement with the proposal submitted to the participants revealed a main effect for Type of argumentation (F (1,174) = 7.07; $p < 0.01$). Agreement with the proposal was on the average higher when the basis of the arguments was *inequality* (M = 2.73) rather than *harmony* in social relations (M = 2.39). The model explains 5% of the variance (F (3,174) = 2.97; $p < 0.04$).

Evaluation of social relations was then entered as an independent variable with scores reduced to three degrees (*negative, neutral,* and *positive*). It was therefore possible to control whether the effects of perception of social relations were comparable in allocations and contributions in the realm of social welfare. Agreement with the increase proposal should be higher when participants had previously evaluated social relations negatively rather than positively.

The analysis of the results revealed a significant interaction between Content of proposal and Evaluation of social relationships (F (2,174) = 4.35; $p < 0.02$). Participants who considered that the social relations were *negative* were less in favor of the *status quo* than in favor of the *increase* proposal (Ms = 2.41 versus 2.85) (F (1,174) = 4.48; $p < 0.05$). On the contrary, participants who considered social relations *positively* were more in favor of the *status quo* than in favor of the *increase* proposal (Ms = 2.67 versus 2.24; F (1,174)= 3.84; p = 0.052). For the middle of the scale participants, the difference was not statistically significant (Ms = 2.46 versus 2.69). The main effect of Type of argumentation remains stable (F (1,174) = 5.87; $p < 0.02$). The model explains more than 15% of the variance (F (11,174) = 2.67; $p < 0.005$).

Conclusion

Social positioning towards social welfare is oriented by the principle that individuals use when they evaluate the social relations. When they consider that the social relations are harmonious, they adopt a restrictive point of view in the domain of institutional aid. When they consider that the social relations are damaged, they are in favor of more mutual aid. Experimental results showed that this principle plays an important role at a general normative level: participants expressed a higher agreement with a proposal of experts when the experts' arguments were centered on damaged rather than on harmonious relations. Furthermore, the results showed that their own evaluation of social relations oriented their positioning towards the type of proposal. Therefore, evaluation of social relations appears to be one of the principles organizing the social representation of solidarity and social welfare.

The theory of social representations still appears for some social psychologists as too abstract and vague. In a sense, they typically encounter the problem of objectifying and anchoring the network of concepts. It could be that the normative metasystem of the field of social psychology implies theoretical and methodological principles that explain such a social positioning. Nevertheless, the strength of the theory resides in the innovative proposals for analyzing and understanding how we ordinarily think in the context of social life. The difficulty of such a program is that results have to be perpetually updated, for theories of common sense keep evolving.

Note

Thanks to Francois Rochat for his helpful suggestions during the editing of the final version of the text. The reported study was supported by the Swiss National Science Foundation (Grant NR. 4029–28206).

7

Human Rights Studied as Normative Social Representations

Willem Doise

The Social Psychological Study of Human Rights

In the spring of 1986, I was invited to present the contribution of social psychology to an interdisciplinary study group on social sciences and human rights (HR). The work on obedience to authority (Meeus & Raaijmakers, 1987; Milgram, 1974) and on the justice motive (Lerner, 1977) led me to the conclusion that in the name of authority or in the name of justice itself, individuals easily admit and even perpetrate violations of other individuals' fundamental rights. But the research on the development of moral judgment (Kohlberg, 1981, 1983; Piaget, 1932) which I also presented made me develop the idea that normative representations of social reality play a role in societal functioning and that they are not sufficiently investigated by social psychologists.

Hence, a research program was initiated to further the social psychological study of HR. A guiding idea of that research is that mutual interactions and communications between humans generate normative social representations. While interacting with each other, individuals know that their fate will be affected by that interaction, at least in certain domains, to a certain extent, at a certain cost. Normative representations exist about what these mutual effects should be. As there are many kinds of interactions, characterized by all sorts of differences in status, purpose, forms of interdependence, and degree of formality (see, for instance, Deutsch, 1985), we dispose of different models of acceptable relationships, of explicit or implicit models of contracts that should govern these relationships, of prototypes of fair and just relationships. These guiding principles for evaluating relationships are part of human cultures.

HR are considered to be part of such principles. They should, at least by intention, organize our social interactions. For historical (i.e., economical, political, military, religious, and also scientific) reasons, Western societies were led to organize relationships not only within national and cultural boundaries, but also across such boundaries. Resulting prototypes of social contracts considered to be valid across national and cultural boundaries are indeed complex even though they have been elaborated by official institutions as was the case for the Universal Declaration of Human Rights (UDHR) adopted by the General Assembly of the UNO in 1948.

According to René Cassin, who co-chaired the drafting commission with Eleanor Roosevelt, the Declaration is made up of six groups of articles (see Agi, 1980). The first group of articles enunciates the basic principles, such as equality, freedom, dignity. The second group focuses on rights of the individual (such as security of the person, equal protection by the law), and the third concerns the rights relative to interindividual relations (amongst them freedom of movement, right to found a family). The fourth group of articles involves public rights (e.g., freedom of expression, equal access to public service); the fifth group deals with economic and social rights (e.g., social security, right to rest and leisure); and the sixth covers the rights relative to international law and order, also mentioning duties to the community.

In 1948, it was not obvious that all groups of rights contained in the Universal Declaration would meet the agreement of the General Assembly (see Agi, 1980; Lauren, 1999; Humphrey, 1984; Renteln, 1990), given the opposition between members favoring an exclusive declaration of individual judicial rights and members furthering a more socioeconomic view. Such oppositions still exist today, even among nonspecialists, as was shown in a recent study by Doise and Herrera (1994). They found that persons who invoke judicial rights are usually not the same as those who invoke socioeconomic rights in their answers to open questions about HR. This study was limited in relying on a small number of respondents residing in Geneva. Therefore an objective of other investigations on which I will report here was to investigate the extent to which institutional definitions of HR are traceable in social representations underlying opinions, attitudes, and beliefs of individuals in various countries.

Human Rights Studied as Normative Social Representations

The study of HR as normative social representations benefited greatly from the systematic investigation by Doise, Clémence, and Lorenzi-Cioldi (1993) in *The Quantitative Analysis of Social Representations*. In this book, social representations (SR) are defined as organizing principles of symbolic relationships between individuals and groups. A first assumption on which this definition is grounded is that various members of a population under study share common views about a given social issue. SR are generated in systems of communication that necessitate common frames of reference for individuals and groups participating in these communications. An important phase in each study of SR therefore is the search for a common map or common cognitive organization of the issues at stake in a given system of communication.

However, SR theory does not imply that individuals sharing common references necessarily hold the same positions. A second assumption of the SR theory is that differences in individual positioning are organized. Individuals may differ according to the strength of their adherence to various opinions, attitudes, or stereotypes. Hence, researchers on SR have to search for the organizing principles of individual differences in a representational field.

A third assumption of SR theory is that such systematic variations are anchored in other collective symbolic realities, in social psychological experiences shared to different extents by individuals, and in their beliefs about other aspects of social reality (Doise, 1992–3). An exhaustive study of individual positioning in representational fields entails an analysis of the anchoring of SR in shared group memberships.

In the process of research on HR it gradually became evident to me that these three assumptions of SR theory, outlined by Doise, Clémence, and Lorenzi-Cioldi (1993), were highly relevant for the social psychological study of HR. A question that was addressed more directly in my investigations on the social representations of HR after the writing of that book was to what extent the UDHR, or other institutional definitions of these rights, offered common references to the populations under study for organizing their beliefs about HR.

Another question bore on the nature of individual positioning in the field of HR. In line with findings of previous research it was hypothesized, for instance, that important modulators of individual positioning would be beliefs about individual efficacy and the efficacy of institutions, (e.g., the government) in having HR respected.

Thirdly, it was assumed that individual positioning toward HR could not be exhaustively studied without analyzing positioning in other systems of symbolic relationships. Anchoring of HR positioning was studied by analyzing relationships with value choices and representations concerning conflicts between social groups and categories, or relationships between individuals and institutions. Other analyses of the anchoring of SR investigated how national and cultural group memberships held by individuals influenced their SR. In this case, the general hypothesis was that shared social placement leads to specific interactions and experiences that also modulate SR in the field of HR.

Three Investigations of HR as Normative SR

Social representations of HR violations

In this questionnaire study by Clémence, Doise, De Rosa, and Gonzales (1995), pupils and students aged 13 to 20 years and living in four different countries (Costa Rica, France, Italy, and Switzerland) were invited to answer 21 items presenting various situations involving violations or limitations of individual rights. Some of these situations (e.g., situations of racial discrimination, imprisonment without trials or legal assistance, starvation) can easily be referred to classical definitions of HR contained in the Universal Declaration. Other situations, dealing with the rights of children or with family affairs are less explicitly related to Articles of the Universal Declaration. Lastly, some situations dealing with economic inequality or health matters (e.g., prohibition of smoking, hospitalization in case of contagious illness) are apparently not covered by official definitions of HR. Results of this study, as indicated in Table 7.1, were very clear. For the various situations, the order of frequencies of relating them to HR violations shows a convergence in the application of criteria across countries. In this sense we can speak of a significant amount of common understanding.

Complete consensus about HR is far from being reached. However, when consensus is defined as a majority view, it is reached for 17 situations. Opinions are divided about parents who oblige their children to attend church services; only minorities consider that enforcing hospitalization upon contiguously ill people, unequal salaries, or prohibition of smoking may be, or are, violations of SR.

Other questions were answered in a rather convergent way across countries. These questions were related to governments' infringements in the domain of civic liberties (e.g., suppressing elections or demonstrations), to the protection of privacy in relation to inquiries of government and business management, to various social regulations in favor of common wellbeing (e.g., vaccinations, wearing helmets on motorcycles), to more or less immoral individual actions (e.g., bribery, cheating), and to general attitudes of fatalism (such as there will always be rich and poor, good and evil people, superior nations).

How were variations between individuals in these various domains structured? In each domain, factor analyses show the high importance of a first factor; alpha coefficients on additive scores for each domain are also high. Therefore, a straightforward method for investigating the organizing principles of differences in individual positioning was to factor analyze the six additive scores obtained by each individual, that is, the number of situations considered with certainty as violations of HR, the number of governmental actions considered unacceptable, the number of queries made by the government and business firms considered to be abnormal, the number of official regulations interpreted as infringements upon individual

Table 7.1 Graphical Representation of Proportion of Respondents Answering "Yes Certainly" or "Yes Probably" to the Questions about Human Rights Violations in the Study by Clémence, Doise, De Rosa, & Gonzales (1995)

	% Total	France	Switzerland	Italy	Costa-Rica
1. Imprisonment without lawyer's defense	86.1				
2. Parental child-beating	82.0				
3. Men and women left to die of hunger	81.3				
4. Prisoner condemned after riot without lawyer's defense	79.3				
5. Obliging children to work in factories	79.3				
6. Whites prevent Blacks from renting a flat	78.9				
7. Neighbors prevent construction of AIDS center	78.4				
8. Imprisonment due to protest against government	78.1				
9. Divorce pronounced without informing children aged 10–14 years of future caretaker	76.9				
10. Pronouncing someone insane followed by confinement without hearing	75.1				
11. Obliging children to abandon their studies	75.0				
12. Women obliged by government to veil their faces	73.0				
13. Mayor prohibiting gypsies from settling	64.2				
14. Husband preventing wife from going out alone	63.9				
15. Refugee suspected of murder expelled without hearing	60.5				
16. Wife preventing husband from going out alone	57.9				
17. Killing a burglar who broke into one's home	55.6				
18. Obliging children to attend mass	49.3				
19. Contagiously ill people forcibly confined in hospital	42.7				
20. Higher salaries for some people	41.8				
21. Prohibiting smoking in a meeting	30.5				
	n = 989	n = 255	n = 250	n = 234	n = 250

Note: >80% ■ >60% ■ >50% ■ <50% □

freedoms, the number of individual actions reported as unacceptable, and the number of agreements with fatalistic assertions. A principal component analysis was carried out on these six individual scores, and three factors with an eigenvalue of above 1 accounted for 59.8% of explained variance.

The first factor obtained high loading on these scores of unacceptable governmental actions, of HR violations, and of abnormal queries on the part of government and business firms. A second factor opposed scores of fatalism and the number of unacceptable individual actions to the number of government and management queries considered to be abnormal. Numbers of regulations considered to be infringements upon individual freedoms almost exclusively orientated the third factor.

Organizing principles of individual positioning in the SR of HR violations are therefore clearly related to the defense of individual rights against political and economic authorities (factor 1) or to a fatalistic world view repudiating a higher amount of individual initiatives but accepting more willingly managerial and state control (factor 2). The third organizing principle can be termed anomic, as it merely involves rejection of social regulations that favor common wellbeing.

Various analyses were carried out in order to check the links of the above described individual variations with sociological characteristics and with relevant opinions about politics and about the judicial system. The main results of these analyses were that those with a more extended conception of HR violations manifest a preference for the political left, are without religion, are older, and agree with the idea of a recourse to an international court. Refusal of social regulations is more often found among respondents without religion and in favor of the left, and also for those who affirm that they would not denounce a culprit when they are falsely accused themselves. In contrast, a conception more favorable toward social control is more characteristic of religious practitioners, sympathizers of the political right, and those who would denounce a culprit.

Another result has to do with the responses to questions about trust or distrust in the judicial system of one's own country. People who distrusted their own judicial systems consistently broadened the domain of situations that were considered to be violations of HR and were more often certain in their judgments about what is a violation of HR or what is not. In their important study on youth and law, Percheron, Chiche, and Muxel-Douaire (1988) drew attention to the importance of trust or distrust in the judicial system as an organizing factor of more general attitudes in the domain of law and order.

The main conclusion to be drawn from this study is that respondents in different countries approach HR issues in similar ways. Such a convergence does not preclude differences in individual positioning that are anchored in related symbolic systems.

An International Study with the Articles of the Universal Declaration

In this research (see Doise, Spini, & Clémence, 1999), the complete text of the UDHR was presented to students in 35 countries. The samples of respondents were university students in psychology, law, science, social work, and various other fields from the five continents. In a first part of the questionnaire, participants were asked to answer eight questions about personal involvement and agreement, personal efficacy, and governmental efficacy for each of the 30 articles of the UDHR. In a second part they answered questions about value choices, perception and experience of social discrimination and interpersonal conflict, and explanations of social justice.

In the first analysis, a hierarchical cluster analysis designed to accentuate intraclass homogeneity was run on indices of the Euclidean distances between articles based on the sums of responses to the eight scales for each article. The aim of this analysis was to study respondents' organization of the field of HR as defined by the Universal Declaration.

This analysis resulted in the division of the articles into two main classes that, in turn, divided into two subclasses. A close inspection of these subclasses of groups of rights shows an almost complete correspondence with the categories described by René Cassin (1951). The first main cluster groups the whole of the more social rights (Cassin's classes of social economic, public, and interindividual rights) and the basic individual rights (protection from torture and slavery and the right to life). The second main cluster is composed of individual judicial rights, fundamental principles and the three articles concerning societal order. Additional analyses show that in each national group respondents manifest significantly greater adherence to the basic and social rights than to the rest of the rights. These results clearly support the idea of a common organization of responses in relation to the different groups of rights in countries from all over the world, especially concerning the opposition between basic and social rights on one hand and the other rights on the other. However, the more specific oppositions between basic and social rights are also very common. We can conclude that the hypothesis of a common organization of the articles across countries is corroborated by our findings.

To extract the organizing principles of differences between individual attitudes or positions in our crossnational study with the Universal Declaration, the responses to the 30 articles were submitted to various analyses. Some of these analyses can be considered "pancultural" according to Leung and Bond's (1989) definition: statistical operations were realized across all the respondents of the 35 countries, ignoring their country of origin. Other analyses aimed at removing the country effects from individual scores by subtracting the country mean from each individual's score. These analyses are "individual level" analyses in the sense of Kenny and La Voie (1985), but we called them "acultural."

For both kinds of analyses we retained the solution in four groups of respondents. As results for both analyses were highly convergent, they can be commented on together. Members of the first group had the highest scores on all types of scales. They can be considered *advocates* of the idea of HR. Another group felt that they were personally concerned with HR but that it was not very easy for governments to do something. This response pattern could be typical of *personalists*. A third group may be called pessimists or *skeptics*. These people had the lowest scores on all scales. A last group considered that they were rather powerless in having the rights respected but found the government more efficient in doing so. This response pattern is typical of *governmentalists*.

Most participants in this study also answered questions about their value priorities, their perception and experience of social conflict, and their experience and explanations of social injustice. Using a pancultural and acultural approach once again, factor scores were used to assess individual positioning in these realms.

Inspection of the first functions of the discriminant function analyses (see Tables 7.2 and 7.3) with the pancultural as well as with the acultural scores leads us to the conclusion that, in general, strong support for the values of universalism and social harmony and agreement with a societal explanation of social injustice were systematically related to more favorable human rights attitudes as expressed by advocates and governmentalists. Opposed value choices resulted in skepticism or more governmentalist attitudes. This function may be interpreted as referring to a universalistic positioning in a search for social harmony and happiness, although conscious of threats coming from societal dysfunctioning.

All kinds of felt injustice are positively correlated with the second function, as well as the perceptions of tensions and explanations in terms of economic system and human nature. Correlations are more systematic for the pancultural analyses as is also the case for the negative correlation with concern for personal happiness. These results manifest a positioning shaped by the personal experience of, and concern about, various forms of discrimination and injustice considered as inevitable products of human nature and economic relations, and linked with less concern about happiness. Such positioning is characteristic of personalists, and to a lesser extent of skeptics. In contrast, those who are relatively more concerned about happiness are often to be found amongst governmentalists and advocates.

Other analyses of anchoring concerned links with nationality. Skeptics were relatively more numerous in Japan and India, whereas personalists were more often found in countries with serious HR problems (according to the ratings by Humana, 1992) and human development problems (according to the ratings of the United Nations Development Program, 1996). Governmentalists were more common in more developed countries or in countries that had recently changed to a democratic regime.

There are clearly organized differences in SR of HR within countries, and one

Table 7.2 Correlations of Variables for Two Discriminant Functions in the Study by Doise, Spini, & Clémence (1999)

| | Function Correlations | | | |
| | Pancultural Analyses | | Acultural Analyses | |
Factors	1	2	I	II
Universalism (values)	0.68	0.13	0.74	0.08
Social harmony (values)	0.48	0.15	0.42	0.24
Societal dysfunction (explanations)	0.40	0.09	0.36	0.15
Hedonism (values)	0.15	−0.11	0.08	−0.16
Interpersonal injustice (experiences)	−0.09	0.63	−0.20	0.40
Ideological discrimination (experiences)	0.08	0.51	0.00	0.53
Happiness (values)	0.19	−0.42	0.21	−0.18
Ethnic discrimination (experiences)	−0.06	0.41	−0.04	0.17
Social discrimination (experiences)	−0.07	0.41	−0.05	0.16
Social tensions (perceptions)	−0.16	0.32	−0.08	0.36
Economic system (explanations)	0.14	0.31	0.09	0.37
Human nature (explanations)	−0.14	0.28	−0.04	0.24
Aggressive assertiveness (explanations)	0.05	−0.08	−0.02	0.06
Natural antagonism (explanations)	−0.10	−0.04	−0.16	0.24
Ethnic tensions (perceptions)	0.12	0.04	−0.08	0.47
Socialization (explanations)	0.16	0.13	0.16	0.20
Ideological tensions (perceptions)	0.29	0.18	0.09	0.32
Traditionalism (values)	−0.05	0.17	0.12	0.00

Table 7.3 Centroids of Four Groups Observed for Two Discriminant Functions in the Study by Doise, Spini, & Clémence (1999)

| | Functions | | | |
| | Pancultural Analyses | | Acultural Analyses | |
Groups	1	2	I	II
Advocates	0.39	−0.12	0.31	−0.13
Skeptics	−1.11	0.18	−1.00	0.12
Governmentalists	−0.36	−0.21	−0.54	−0.09
Personalists	0.25	0.27	0.12	0.26

of the aims of our transcultural research was to investigate the extent to which such within-country and between-country variations are organized in homologous ways. To an important extent the answer to this question is affirmative, as the acultural study of different anchoring patterns again highly converged with the pancultural one.

Between-individual variations and between-nation variations in anchoring seem to modulate HR positioning in the same way. For instance, respondents who strongly favor universalistic values have more favorable HR positioning independently of national group membership. But it is also true that in countries in which adhesion to universalistic values is higher, global attitudes toward HR will be more favorable. *Mutatis mutandis,* the same reasoning holds for the links involving other value choices, felt injustice, and perceptions of tensions.

A Developmental Study of SR of HR

Research by Doise, Staerklé, Clémence, and Savory (1998) more specifically aimed to study the development of adolescents' SR of HR. Two main hypotheses were at the origin of this questionnaire study carried out in Geneva with 849 youths of different age, school streams and pre-professional training.

The main hypothesis was that institutionalized definitions of HR should become more salient as a function of progress in age and scholastic experience. However, such a regularity in development should not necessarily imply an absence of variations in individual positioning which can privilege different kinds of rights more or less related to individual wellbeing or to societal functioning.

The questionnaire was composed of two sections. The first question consisted of open-ended questions, such as the following: "For a number of years now, Human Rights have been a frequent topic of discussion. In your opinion, what are these rights?" The second section of the questionnaire was composed of questions with rating scales. A list of 30 rights was presented to the respondents. For each right respondents used a 4-point scale to express their opinion that the right was to be considered "a bad, a rather bad, a rather good or a good example of a Human Right." Other sets of questions dealt with confidence in various institutions and with political values.

In order to prepare an automatic textual analysis, a database was prepared with all answers to the open-ended questions. A list of different answers to the first question, alphabetically ordered, and without references to characteristics of respondents, was presented to five members of the research team. They had to indicate for each listed right whether or not it was related to one of the 30 Articles of the Universal Declaration. Table 7.4 presents the average numbers of rights that in each degree were related to the same Article by a majority of judges. The link with progress in schooling is straightforward, just as is the inverse link for the number of

Table 7.4 Mean Frequency of Expressed Human Rights and other Rights by Educational Level (number of years in full-time education) in the Study by Doise, Staerklé, Clémence, & Savory (1998)

Educational level	7	8/9	10	11	12/13	T*
$n =$	246	190	107	126	136	
Age (years/months)	13/4	14/0	17/4	18/4	19/10	
Mean frequency of HR	1.85	2.02	2.25	2.66	2.79	7.02**
Mean frequency of non-HR	1.70	1.33	1.07	1.12	1.14	−5.21**

Note. *T-values from linear contrast analysis. ** $p < 0.001$

rights not so clearly related to the Articles. A more detailed analysis shows that the evocation of the category of public rights particularly increases with age. Rights belonging to this category were also most frequently mentioned by Genevan adults in the investigation of Doise and Herrera (1994).

Three dimensions were retained at the automatic textual factorial correspondence analysis. The first dimension clearly opposes a negative to a positive pole. Towards the first pole are interdictions and human rights violations, whereas the second pole attracts various rights to be respected, such as rights to accommodation, food, life, and voting. The dimension therefore opposes negative and positive assertions. The second dimension opposes words related to concrete and individual rights (e.g., home, family, school, food) to terms relating to more public rights (e.g., freedom, belief, voting). The third dimension is based on a contrast between a more subjective positioning (will, go, make, love, believe) as opposed to a more categorical one (gender, racism, difference, woman, child). The projection of two illustrative variables (degree and school section) shows that positions evolve from negative to positive (first dimension), and from concrete to public (second dimension) with the advancement in educational degree.

Other methods allowed investigation of the intervention of social developmental variables in individual positioning. Regression analyses on factorial scores of the variables of academic degree, gender, academic stream, religious affiliation and practice evidenced an effect of higher degree (p < 0.0001), and more prestigious academic stream (p < 0.002) in furthering a positive conception. In contrast, more regular attendance at religious services is negatively linked to such positioning (p < 0.002). For positioning on the second dimension, only degree has an effect in the direction of favoring more public rights (p < 0.0001.) Positioning on the third dimension is a function of degree (p < 0.0001), belonging to a more prestigious stream (p < 0.0002), male gender (p < 0.04) and Swiss citizenship (p < 0.005), all variables that promote a more categorical interpretation of rights.

Another procedure of checking intervention of social developmental variables made us first realize a hierarchical clarification analysis of individuals as a function of their coordinates on the three dimensions. Four classes of individuals could be distinguished and an investigation of the most typical answers of each class of each class (see Table 7.5) shows the relevance of a classification in categories of public (190 respondents), libertarian (117), concrete (293), and egalitarian (208) positioning. Links with advancement in degree are particularly salient for public positioning, increasing in proportion from 13% to 44%, while libertarian (from 24% to 3%) and to a lesser extent egalitarian (from 24% to 17%) positions decrease with advancement in degree.

In a second part of the study, 30 rights, some of them corresponding to Articles of the Universal declaration of Human Rights, were rated according to their prototypicality as human rights. Eight of these rights were considered highly prototypical by all participants and were therefore not taken into consideration for this analysis of differences in positioning. A hierarchical cluster analysis was carried out in order to classify respondents according to their responses for the remaining 22 items. A classification into four groups was retained.

To summarize descriptions of the four groups, one can say that the first group is generally reserved about the right to dissent, and the second avoids definitions in terms of concrete rights and those linked to school situation. The third group and fourth group, respectively, consider positive rights and rights to dissent as more typical. Progress in degree is significantly linked to an increase of definitions in less concrete and more positive terms, and to a very significant decrease of the reserved attitude towards dissent.

Other patterns of anchoring were also assessed in this developmental study. Beliefs about the usefulness of institutions and political values were important anchoring variables in prototypicality ratings. A discriminant function analysis shows the variety of anchoring patterns. Advancement in degree, left-wing and communitarian orientation, together with doubts about the usefulness of some public organizations for the individual and general attitudes which are less favorable towards family, religion, and sport clubs, further more principled and enlarged HR definitions and inhibit more restricted and concrete definitions.

Putting Things in Perspective

The three phase model of studying SR quantitatively (see Doise, Clémence, & Lorenzi-Cioldi, 1993) proved to be useful for the social psychological study of HR. The quantitative study of shared meanings, of patterns of individual positioning,

Table 7.5 English Translation of Typical Responses by Typology based on an Open-Ended Question in the Study by Doise, Staerklé, Clémence, & Savory (1998)

The Public n = 190 23.5%	The Libertarian n = 117 14.5%	The Concrete n = 293 36.3%	The Egalitarian n = 208 25.7%
• Freedom of worship	• To think as one wishes	• Right to housing	• Everyone should have the same rights
• Freedom of belief and religion	• To go where one wants	• Right to own property	• All men are born and die equal
• Freedom of expression	• To go out when one wants	• Right to have a motorbike	• Man and woman must be treated equally
• Freedom of opinion	• To do what one likes with one's own body	• Right to have clothing	• An old man has the same rights as a young man
• Freedom of movement	• To have the relationships	• Right to eat and drink	• There is no race between all types of men
• Freedom of action	• To eat what one wants	• Right not to sleep outside	• Nobody should be racist
• Freedom of trade and business	• Not to feel compelled to do certain things	• Right to express oneself and to think	• Treat all men in the same way, be they white or black
• Physical liberty	• To do what one wants (play sport, watch TV)	• Right to write	• Every man has freedom in his civil and religious beliefs
• Moral liberty	• To dress as one wants	• Right to work and to have one's place in society	• No one has the right to kill
• Freedom of press	• To go to bed when one wants	• Right to have days off	• Not to beat a man if he has committed a crime
• Right to vote	• Have the right to become a police officer	• Right to love and be happy	• It is forbidden to massacre people

- Equality of rights

- To live in freedom

- Right to be tried by a due process
- Right to be a member of an ethnic group
- Right to demonstrate

- Right to privacy

- Not to oblige a pupil to go to a circus when he is 15
- To be safe all over the world

- Not to harm the other

- To do what the others do

- Right to medical care

- Right to have children

- Right to have a family and a name
- Right to go to school

- Right to a nationality

- Right to say yes or no

- It is forbidden to torture

- No man shall be a slave, he shall be free
- Every man shall be respected

- One must be protected when travelling in another country
- Right for foreigners to bring their family into the country
- Right to refuse to go to war

and of their anchoring in related meaning systems has shown its relevance for the analysis of adolescents' beliefs about HR violations, for planning and analyzing a crossnational study with the UDHR and for studying the growth of HR awareness in Genevan youth.

Differences between the three-phase model approach and other social psychological approaches in HR studies are difficult to assess as very few social psychologists have researched SR. Among them are Diaz-Veizades, Widaman, Little, and Gibbs (1995) and Stainton Rogers and Kitzinger (1995). Both studies have focused on differences in common understanding of HR.

Stainton Rogers and Kitzinger (1995, p. 102) concluded from their study that "10 representations were identified and profiled" and that "No common bedrock, in terms of a consensual endorsement or rejection of propositions, was found to ground the manifold. We take this as saying that the expressed representations form a set of free-standing, alternative understandings. Rights, in public discourse, we deduce, are best taken as a manifold of integral discourses that stand in mutual complementarity one to another." However, they did not look for a common understanding or an anchoring of these differences. "We take the view that the Q methodological approach we have employed results in a form of presentation in which the 10 accounts can and do 'speak for themselves' in all their diversity." (1995, p. 102) Although the sorting task was carried out on very rich material by 57 respondents chosen for their specific involvement or noninvolvement in HR groups, they limited their study to a description of different discourses about HR.

Diaz-Veizades, Widaman, Little, and Gibbs (1994) shared more of our concerns as they also used the UHDR to study what we call organization of individual positioning as well as anchoring of this positioning in the construction of their questionnaire. However, they made significant changes in the original document, reformulating the 30 articles of the UDHR into 116 more concrete items, such as: "If a person does not make enough money to support his or her family adequately, the family should be aided by the government"; "There are times when people should be kept from expressing their opinion"; "Men and women should have equal rights in a marriage"; or "A person's home is his or her 'castle' and should not be interfered with by others."

For each item their respondents (mainly North American college students) expressed their degree of agreement on a 7-point scale. However, many items "had very low variance because of high rates of endorsement, so they could not correlate highly with other items. After these low-loading items were deleted, 38 items were reanalyzed using an iterated principle factor analysis" (Diaz-Veizades, Widaman, Little, & Gibbs, 1995, p. 317). Clearly, we are confronted here with a logic different from the one that we have adopted. Diaz-Veizades and colleagues favored the study of systematic interindividual variation to the detriment of analyzing the common meaning aspect of SR. When eliminating about two thirds of the items from their questionnaire, they could retain four factors. A first factor, called Social Security, concerned access or entitlement to an adequate standard of living (e.g., food, housing, medical care). A second factor, labeled Civilian Constraint, dealt with the acceptability of limiting individual civil and political rights. The theme tying items together for the third factor was that of Equality, evidenced most clearly by items dealing with equal access to basic rights for all individuals regardless of race, gender, or beliefs. Finally, items with the highest loading on the fourth factor involved Privacy issues (Diaz-Veizades et al., 1995, pp. 317 – 321). They also analyzed anchoring (without using the term) in showing, for instance, that respondents adhering more to a Civilian Constraint conception of HR were also those who obtained higher scores on a Nationalism scale and lower scores on Internationalism and Civil Liberties scales. Their political preferences were also more likely to favor Republicans over Democrats, as opposed to the preferences of adherents to a Social Security conception who favored Democrats and had higher scores on Internationalism.

Colleagues from anthropology and cultural psychology are very concerned about the problem of the universality of HR, whereas political scientists discuss the danger of HR being used as a tool for furthering Western imperialism. At different phases of the reported investigations, the issue of an ethnocentric or imperialistic use of HR was raised: while discussing with colleagues the advisability and feasibility of such studies, while inviting colleagues to participate in them, while interpreting results such as those concerning cross-national variations in HR positioning, and while presenting data to diverse audiences. The least one can say is that while doing and reporting HR research one should be aware that ethnocentric interpretations of HR abound.

Such ethnocentrism was experimentally studied by Moghaddam and Vuksanovic (1990) without using the theoretical framework of SR. They asked undergraduate students to answer a questionnaire about HR issues. The questionnaire is identical in three conditions except for the fact that in a first condition the context referred to was Canada, in a second condition the Soviet Union, and in a third condition the Third World. Typical items were: "All forms of censorship should be done away with in (Canada/Soviet Union/Third World societies)" or "everyone in (. . .) should have access to free health care." Overall support for HR was stronger in the context of the Soviet Union and the Third World than in the Canadian context. In a second study, three scenarios were used concerning a television news anchor woman who was fired from her job, a tortured member of a terrorist group, and a female shoplifter, again presented in three different contexts. As in the first study, support for HR was stronger in the conditions of the Soviet Union and Third World than in the condition of Canada.

Such results tend to confirm the opinion of critics who consider HR as a Western export article, useful for others but less so for ourselves. Staerklé, Clémence and Doise (1998) therefore continued the line of research initiated by Moghaddam and

Vuksanovic (1990). We also found asymmetries in SR of HR and in explanations for HR violations when they are presented across different national contexts.

Interindividual relations, intergroup and institutional dynamics, and value priorities modulate representations of rights' universality, inalienability, and indivisibility (see Clémence & Doise, 1995). This contextual modulation is also the case for other SR. Studying HR as SR is a challenging undertaking, even more so as it involves integrating findings from other research traditions.

8

From Race to Culture: The Emergence of African American

Gina Philogène

When adjusting to change, people must go beyond reflecting upon actual circumstances and consider alternative courses of action, new solutions to conflict. In that respect they must take account of others. The choices we make, which come to determine our social actions, depend on the social representations we share. These are the driving force carrying us through processes of change in our society. They impose a structure on our social world, provide us with some collective basis for a consensual interpretation of social objects, direct our thoughts towards possible scenarios that correspond to our immediate interests, and orient our sequence of actions.

I have always thought that one of the advantages of social representation theory is its capacity to provide a framework for the analysis of societal change. Social representations are vectors of change, because they are the medium by which we communicate new situations and adjust to them. In this paper I shall focus on one such manifestation of social representations as vectors of change, looking at how a new group denomination engenders a reconceptualization of the group thus renamed. In this context I wish to introduce a special category of social representation, one that I termed anticipatory representation in light of its forward-looking nature as a vehicle for collective projections of a redefined future.

Making a New Object with a Name

Since social representations are created through interaction, they crystallize around language, in the formation of a terminology for things that we share. By naming a new and unfamiliar object, we crystallize its representation in a word or words as shared thought constructs. This allows for an eventual classification of the new object into preexisting mental systems.

Even though naming plays a crucial role in the anchoring of new objects (Moscovici, 1984b), social psychologists have paid relatively little attention to the strategic significance of names. In contrast, this topic has been explored by a number of influential linguists, anthropologists, and philosophers whose combined insights on that subject provide us with a rich framework for the inclusion of names and naming processes in social representation theory.

To name someone or something is to make a reference by which a causal or conventional relation is established between the object and the symbol; that is the name. When we choose a name for an object, we place the thing so named in a system of conceptual relations and conditions, as well as factual beliefs. Indeed, in the act of naming we denote the class of all particular things to which the name applies. Names, and here we might include group designations as proper names, serve as identifying markers which by the application of a rule associate the object being named to a preordained class. In that sense the French anthropologist Claude Lévi-Strauss (1966) has referred to the naming process as an "enterprise of classification." The name chosen makes reference to a meaningful system of commonly shared and understood characteristics that define a class of objects thus named.

Once a thing has been determined as namable, the name chosen for it assigns that thing to a defining structure of functions and properties. Our commonly shared factual beliefs, what Chomsky (1975) termed "common-sense expectations," automatically assume these functions and properties to exist whenever the name is used. The stipulation that a thing be given a specific name thus carries with it certain commonly shared presumptions about concepts and categories. These in turn determine what the name does in the minds of individuals and shape how its meaning is communicated between them.

Names thus are meaningful. But the meaning of a name, by which it connects to the object it represents, is not there a priori. That meaning has to be established by the act of naming the thing, it has to be contextualized in a system of language, and it has to be maintained by consistent use of that name. In other words, as part of our language names have to be elaborated, and this elaboration of their meaning is a fundamentally social activity (Wittgenstein, 1958). The meaning of a name thus lies entirely in how it is used in interactions. People are able to communicate what is on their minds, because they share a language for describing what occurs outside their minds. They can therefore agree about the meaning of a word and maintain this agreement in their applications of it.

Such meaning is not a product of individual mental activity, but instead the result of collective creation. Both Saul Kripke (1972, 1980) and Hilary Putnam (1975, 1983) emphasized the importance of the origin and history of names in determining how they function and what they come to mean. For Kripke the naming process commences with an "initial baptism" in which the object gets named or the reference of the name is fixed by description, and the name gets passed, as Kripke put it, "from link to link." In this "historic chain of transmission," a phrase coined by Putnam, the reference fixed originally in the naming process is preserved and refined to the extent that it is commonly understood.

The Emergence of African American

Names given to groups play an important role in a multicultural and multiethnic society such as the United States. They must be analyzed in their historical evolution, within their specific cultural setting, and as a product of struggles over their meaning (Dauzat, 1956). When an established group denomination gets replaced by a new one, we can surmise that broader changes are under way. Names, after all, are a filter for group identity as well as intergroup relations. I have tried to illustrate this point in a study focusing on the recent switch in names applied to Americans of African descent, from "Black" to "African American" (Philogène, 1999).

Any exploration of the deeper meaning underlying this particular switch in names must start with a clear understanding of race as a defining issue in the evolution of the United States – from slavery and Civil War to segregation and the Civil Rights struggles of the 1950s and 1960s. Today, thirty-five years after Civil Rights legislation abolished outright segregation in the United States, the issue of race still dominates public discourse in this "diverse nation" (Bell, 1992; Terkel, 1992; West, 1994). Of course, its presence has changed over time as the result of efforts to reconcile a dissonance between the democratic ideals of this society and its race-based discriminatory practices (King, 1964). It so happens that changes concerning race have usually come about during periods of social unrest and often culminated in a switch of the denomination applied to Americans of African ancestry ("Slave," "Colored," "Negro," "Black," and "African American").

In the case of African American, Kripke's "initial baptism" occurred in December 1989 at a reunion of Civil Rights leaders in New Orleans when Ramona Edelin, then president of the National Urban Coalition, proposed that term as the new official designation for Americans of African descent in lieu of Black. Her suggestion was enthusiastically endorsed by the participants of the meeting and followed up by a nationwide campaign to propagate the new term. This effort proved successful. Use of the term grew rapidly, helped by its widespread adoption among public-opinion makers (television, newspapers, politicians) and its endorsement by a subgroup identifying themselves as African Americans.

The switch from Black to African American in fact introduces a new dimension in the conceptualization of Americans of African ancestry. While it is true that the sequence of different names ("Colored," "Negro," "Black," and "African American") used to identify black Americans reflects incessant attempts to change perceptions and attitudes concerning the group, it is only in the latest manifestation,

switching from Black to African American, that renaming the group indeed coincides with its reconceptualization. Such change in names corresponds to a shift
from a racial dichotomization to a cultural multiplicity. This new name is consistent
with the designation of everyone else, juxtaposing a cultural specificity to "America,"
a semantic structure adopted by other groups such as Italian Americans, Irish Americans, etc. (Banton, 1988; Walzer, 1990; Smith, 1992). As Jesse Jackson phrased it in
1989: "There are Armenian Americans and Jewish Americans and Arab Americans
and Italian Americans. And with a degree of accepted and reasonable pride, they
connect their heritage to their mother country and where they are now. . . . To be
called African American has cultural integrity" (see Smith, 1992).

By focusing away from race onto culture, the new term has the potential of
achieving precisely what the term Black could not do in the mid-sixties, namely to
change the underlying social representation of the group. Switching from Negro to
Black created a sense of pride in Blackness ("Black Power," "Black is Beautiful").
This effort succeeded at first because of the unity of the group in its struggle against
racial intolerance in America. But as the term gained acceptance in mainstream
America, it lost its initial political context and, with that, its negative connotations
as a racial term resurfaced. In the case of African American, however, the elaboration of meaning is not confined to the ingroup alone. Instead this recent "positivation"
of the group is a broad-based cultural phenomenon. The term, transcending group
boundaries by reflecting the pluralistic visions of America, engages black as well as
non-black Americans alike. This collective redefinition of America, embedded in
the new social representation of black Americans, is what sustains the projective
qualities of African American. Precisely these qualities have also been actively diffused by public opinion makers and normalized by the "political correctness" movement.

Such broad-based diffusion has created a consensus of meaning around the use of
African American which has allowed the new name to become itself a new social
representation capable of redefining the object. While still in the making, this social
representation gradually transforms perceptions about the group and its relations
with the rest of society. As the term circulates more widely in public discourse and
becomes familiar, it gains its capacity of re-presenting black Americans by projecting a different future for all. It is precisely through those anticipations, whose collective elaboration endows them with normative force, that a group can be redefined
and repositioned with the help of a new name.

Conducting an onomastic study, which focuses on the name and the naming
process, provides us with a useful methodological tool. This approach makes it
possible to examine how the introduction of African American transforms group
identities and intergroup relations by engendering collective anticipations of a different future. Those anticipations are positive and get validated in a symbolic world.
Such an onomastic study has the added advantage of showing how the various

denominations used to identify Americans of African descent have evolved in time and what people ultimately think of them today.

Study 1: Name Preferences

Method

To measure the extent to which African American signals a transformation in the representation of black American, a study was conducted in New York on the basis of questionnaires given to 139 black Americans and 143 non-black Americans, mostly college students and professionals. Participants were asked to rank six denominations that have, throughout history, been commonly used to refer to Black Americans (i.e., African American, Afro American, Black, Colored, Negro, and People of Color). The questions centered on which name is used, which ought to be used, which is best to use, and which will be used for Americans of African descent.

Results and discussion

Table 8.1 shows the percentage distributions of responses for the black American sample. African American is used by a third, but only one in seven report being called as such by non-black Americans. Already nearly one in two picked African American as the most preferred name for themselves. Fifty-eight percent considered the term to be the most positive when used by the ingroup, while nearly two-thirds thought of it as the most positive when used by outgroup. Finally, slightly more than half of the participants anticipated the term to be used more in the future.

Table 8.1 Choice of Name (African American versus Black) for Black American Sample

Name	Used by		Preferred	Positive		Used in Future
	Ingroup	Outgroup	Preferred	Ingroup	Outgroup	Future
African American	33.8	14.6	44.1	58.2	64.7	55.0
Afro American	4.6	6.9	10.2	9.0	10.1	10.8
Black	50.0	63.1	30.7	17.2	15.1	19.2
Colored	2.3	6.9	3.1	3.3	3.4	3.3
Negro	2.3	4.6	3.3	1.7		4.2
People of color	6.9	3.8	11.8	9.0	5.0	7.5

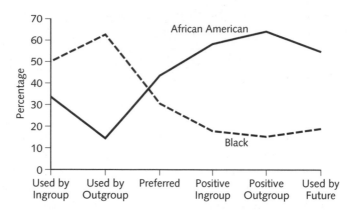

Figure 8.1 Choice of name (African American versus Black) for black American sample.

Among the six denominations the two dominant terms are evidently Black and African American even though the terms Afro American and People of Color have a consistent presence in public discourse. Figure 8.1 shows their respective response distributions across the different levels to be exact mirror images of each other. While African American is only used by one out of three black Americans and is projected to be used even less so by non-black Americans, its overall evaluation is much more favorable. The tendential convergence of both terms concerning their future use (also observed among non-black subjects in Figure 8.2 below) indicates a degree of uncertainty about the continuing evolution of the naming process compared to how positively African American is already evaluated.

Non-black American participants were asked in similar fashion which of those six names they most frequently use to refer to black Americans, which one they prefer, which one they judge as the most positive, and which term they thought would be more used in the future. Table 8.2 shows the percentage distributions of their answers. Over two-thirds used the term Black. Even though only one out of five non-black respondents used African American, slightly more than what black respondents in our first sample reported to be called by non-black Americans, their evaluation of the new term was much more favorable than indicated by its limited usage. Already there is a remarkable increase in favor of African American when people were asked to indicate their preference, while for the term Black that number decreased to 40%. Over three-quarters of the respondents thought that the new denomination projected the most positive images whereas only 6% picked Black. Finally, two-thirds of the sample thought that African American will be used more in the future, compared to 10% who opted for Black.

Table 8.2 Choice of Name (African American versus Black) for Non-Black American Sample

Name	Used	Preferred	Positive	Used in Future
African American	19.1	33.6	76.9	66.4
Afro American	6.4	20.4	13.4	17.6
Black	67.4	40.1	6.0	9.9
Colored	2.8	2.9	–	–
Negro	2.8	0.7	0.7	1.5
People of color	1.4	2.2	3.0	4.6

In Figure 8.2 I compared the percentage distribution of the two dominant terms, Black and African American, for each of the four questions posed in this sample. Once again, as was the case in our first sample, the curves appear as mirror images of one another.

This study of name preferences indicates quite clearly the tenuous and complex coexistence of Black and African American as competing denominations for Americans of African descent. In terms of current usage Black is still the dominant term which, given the recency of African American, is no surprise. Nonetheless, already one in three black Americans prefers to be called African American. At the same time only one of six reports being called that way by non-black Americans, an

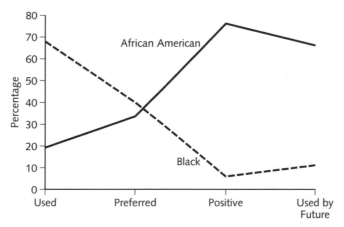

Figure 8.2 Choice of name (African American versus Black) for non-black American sample.

estimate that seems confirmed by the outgroup's own response. Although non-black Americans still show a somewhat greater preference for Black than African American, that difference is significantly less than the usage gap between the two terms.

The particular pattern of tension found throughout our study, namely using Black while at the same time showing a greater preference and more positive attitude toward African American, illustrates the emergence of a new social representation, still in the making, which competes with a well-established representation of the same object. Despite its novelty, the term African American is already anchored as an essentially positive representation of the group. Both black Americans and non-black Americans consider African American as the term most likely to evoke positive images. Also noteworthy is the term's orientation toward the future, with majorities in both samples believing African American to dominate in years to come.

It is precisely the combination of positive and future-oriented qualities demonstrated in this study that characterizes African American as an anticipatory representation. That kind of representation is a locus of projections and as such a vehicle for innovation. In our case the innovation involves a collective effort to re-present a group hitherto excluded on the basis of race for possible integration on the basis of culture. Such an anticipatory re-presentation is by definition less concerned with what was or what is than with what will be or should be. Hence the new group designation can coexist with others, in particular Black, even to the point of being interchangeable with one another as these competing names evoke different, alternative, even complementary contexts of images and associations. This is why many people can think of African American as the most positive term and prefer it for that reason, yet at the same time still use Black more often than not in everyday conversation.

This convergence of meaning concerning African American is fundamental to the argument presented in this paper. Its emergence as an anticipatory representation driven by future-oriented projections seems to have already impacted on the ways contemporary America views black Americans. This social representation, while still in the making, provides us with an opportunity to examine how a previously established representation gets transformed to fit interests newly defined by the collectivity. Such an examination requires us to identify first the key components which have organized our established representation of the group in question. On the basis of those components we can then delineate the field of the representation and find its common ground among various groups.

Study 2: The Social Representation of Black Americans

Method

An analysis of the social representation of black Americans was conducted to take a closer look at the representational field of the group in order to understand how the names Black and African American coexist in contradistinction with each other. An inventory of questions related to race in America was given to two samples, composed of black and non-black participants respectively, to assess their attitudes and opinions about black Americans as well as their perceptions of the relation this group has to the rest of America. The questionnaires used in this study, similar for both samples, measured attitudes concerning racial discrimination, the destiny of black Americans in America, their separation from the American culture, a sense of Afrocentrism, different attributes derived for the most part from the Katz and Braly (1933) questionnaire, cross categorization of race and gender, and responses to racism.

Results and discussion

The factor analysis of responses to the two questionnaires yielded in both cases a variety of factors of scale-like quality which reflect the ambivalence between race and culture in contemporary America very clearly. Together they comprise the central topoi of our culture in the United States – its optimism, the belief in a "just world," a strong emphasis on integration based on equality, the American dream of a safe and prosperous middle-class life, but also the lasting and troubling legacy of race. For lack of space I will only discuss one topos, a recurrent theme that has been associated with black Americans throughout the course of this country's short history – from the days of Thomas Jefferson and early psychologists studying race (Bache, 1895; Ferguson, 1916) through Katz and Braly (1933) as well as Gilbert (1951) all the way to Dovidio and Gaertner (1986). That topos is a scale composed of seven items which I have called the *Negative Images* scale. In two separate samples, one composed of black participants and the other of non-black participants, I found exactly the same scale with a strikingly similar pattern (see Table 8.3). Not only did both samples yield essentially the same composition of items, but in both instances the scale has the same reliability (alpha = 0.86). For black Americans, the scale accounted for 15.7% of the total variance in subjects' answers while for non-black Americans it accounted for nearly twenty percent.

These congruencies crystallize the fact that the items composing the scale are not only consensually shared, but correspond to how we all have come to understand the group to a point where members of the group, that is, Americans of African descent, are themselves only taking position against the scale. Black Americans had

Table 8.3 Comparison of "Negative Images" Scales for Black and Non-Black Subjects

Black Americans		Non-Black Americans	
Black Americans are often rude	3.23	Black Americans are often rude	4.13
Black Americans are loud	3.91	Black Americans are loud	4.40
Black Americans are talkative	4.14	Black Americans are quick-tempered	4.44
Black Americans are quick-tempered	4.02	Black Americans are lazy	3.43
Black Americans neglect their family	2.67	Black Americans are talkative	4.48
Black Americans are lazy	2.59	Black Americans are arrogant	3.79
Black Americans are arrogant	3.08	Black Americans neglect their family	3.48
X:	3.38	X:	4.02

Note Midpoint for mean value is at 4

a general inclination towards disagreeing with the scale (M = 3.38), while non-black Americans were basically neutral with a slight tendency towards agreement with the scale (M = 4.02). Figure 8.3 presents some of those differences.

The similarity of the two curves is striking. The most interesting aspect of this concordance is the fact that the *Negative Images* scales result from two separate factor analyses, one derived from the black American sample and the other from the non-black sample. In each case the first two items to load on their respective factors were "rude" and "loud." While the curves in Figure 8.3 were based on the pattern of answers for black Americans, they are similar to those of non-black subjects who, however, tended to agree more with these depictions.

The consistently strong presence of *Negative Images* in both samples confirms the negative prevalence of race in the American culture. The seven items composing that scale are cultural markers which organize everyone's thinking about black Americans around a racial paradigm. They comprise what Joyner (1989) called a "deep structure" that helps generate our specific cultural patterns.

Changes concerning race are as important as the underlying issue itself, since they indicate broader transformations in society. After all, slavery ended in a civil war; its successor, segregation, was overcome a century later by an unprecedented wave of social agitation across the entire nation. America underwent major convulsions each time it had to rid itself of anachronistic paradigms of racial hegemony, and in every instance that struggle reorganized the common ground from which people living in this society have derived their meaning as Americans. If race has defined America like no other issue, then it stands to reason that any change concerning its status will inevitably reverberate through the many facets of this society.

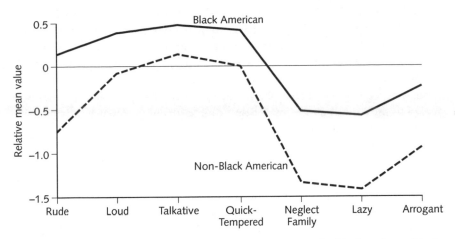

Figure 8.3 Relative mean responses of "negative images" for black and non-black subjects.
Note Midpoint at 0.

That is precisely what we face today with the emergence of African American as a new group designation in lieu of Black. This new social representation marks the first time a group, which until now had been defined on the basis of race alone, is being redefined on the basis of culture and thus in correspondence with America's idealistic self-definition as a multicultural society of equals.

Race and the American Creed – central topoi of American culture in the Aristotelian sense of common ground – thus interact with each other today in novel ways. The society-transforming dynamics of their interaction center not least on the coexistence of African American and Black as competing social representations of the same object. My final study seeks to examine precisely this tension between the two alternative social representations. Its purpose is to identify that common ground in the American culture concerning race, which defines what people belonging to different groups think about black Americans, and to see how that issue is being transformed today with the introduction of African American into our social life.

Study 3: African American's Decentralization of Race

Method

This study examined the extent to which the choice of denomination between Black and African American has indeed influenced perceptions and evaluations of black Americans. Toward this objective I controlled for a "context effect" by giving half the subjects in each sample a questionnaire, which referred to Americans of African descent only as Blacks, and the other half of each sample a questionnaire which only used African Americans when referring to the group. In addition, I split the samples of black American and non-black American respondents each into two groups, depending on whether the person chose Black or African American with regard to the various dimensions of that sample's name preference questionnaire. Then I compared the respective mean values of those subgroups for the *Negative Images* scale, the dominant factor emerging from my Study 2.

Among the dozen or so factors originally identified in Study 2 (see Philogène, 1999), the *Negative Images* scale was selected as the dependent measure for three key reasons. First, it appears in both samples with the same item composition. Second, it has by far the largest percentage of variance among all factors analyzed in either sample (15.7% for black Americans and 19.4% for non-black Americans). And finally, this scale is also characterized by the same high reliability for both samples (Cronbach's alpha = 0.86). For all these reasons the scale best crystallizes the common ground concerning perceptions and attitudes about Africans of American descent.

Results and Discussion

The particular approach described here enables us to identify differences in the scale value as a result of the denomination chosen by the participant. In other words, as independent variables, the denominations African American and Black are expected to yield some significant differences between their respective scale values. This proposition is based on our theoretical understanding of African American as an anticipatory representation redefining the group away from race to culture. Apart from the obvious fact that the black American sample should score lower *Negative Images* values than the non-black sample, we would generally expect those who choose African American, on any of the dimensions investigated and in either sample, to have lower mean values and thus agree less with the scale than those preferring Black. Tables 8.4 and 8.5 summarize our findings by listing the relevant scale values of both samples pertaining to the *Negative Images* scale for each applicable dimension of name preference.

Response means and *t* values for the black American sample are presented in Table 8.4. Although African American scored consistently lower mean values than Black, only three dimensions were significantly different. Indeed, our analysis revealed the choice of denomination to have had significant effects in terms of the name used by outgroup members, $t (96) = 3.72$, $p < 0.05$, the name respondents themselves preferred to use, $t (91) = 6.60$, $p < 0.01$, and the name they thought projected the most positive images, $t (88) = 7.00$, $p < 0.01$.

Table 8.4 Mean Scores of the Name Used with Respect to Various Scales

| | Name Used | | |
	African American	Black	F
Black Sample			
Ingroup			
Cultural inclusion	5.85	6.21	4.60*
Dual consciousness	5.44	5.75	6.46**
Outgroup			
Negative images	**2.51**	**3.34**	**4.60***
Non-Black Sample			
Images of black women	5.56	5.03	4.22*

Note *$p < 0.05$ **$p < 0.01$ ***$p < 0.001$

These findings indicate that the choice of denomination in a specific context makes a difference. First, when asked about the term used, the responses of the black American participants seem to indicate a difference only pertaining to the term used by the outgroup, and not by the ingroup. Second, the preferred term (i.e., what ought to be used) also yielded significantly different means between the two subgroups. Finally, the denomination projecting in their own opinion the most positive images (i.e., best to use) made a strong difference whereas what respondents thought the outgroup judged as projecting positive images made little difference in their responses. Together these findings lend support to the claim that African American and Black may in fact be perceived as two separate representations by our black American sample.

Concerning the non–black sample we see a less pronounced impact of the choice of denomination. While those choosing African American tended to have lower scale values and thus seemed to agree less with the *Negative Images* scale than those opting for Black, their differences were by and large not statistically significant. The summary of results presented in Table 8.5 shows, however, two differences in response means worth mentioning. Non-black participants preferring Black tended to agree with the *Negative Images* scale (with a mean above neutrality level of 4) while they were more inclined to show disagreement when they picked African American as the preferred denomination. The same kind of difference, namely one subgroup showing a propensity to agree while the other subgroup shows an inclination to disagree, was also evident between those responding to a questionnaire using "Blacks" and those in the non–black sample using a questionnaire in which the group was consistently referred to as "African Americans."

When comparing the two samples, we see our hypotheses clearly borne out. In

Table 8.5 Mean Scores of the Name that Ought to be Used with Respect to Various Scales

| | Name that Ought to be used | | |
	African American	Black	F
Black Sample			
Negative images	**3.00**	**3.81**	**7.95***
Cultural participation	4.84	5.33	5.54**
Dual consciousness	5.82	5.17	8.70***
Non-Black Sample			
Negative images	**3.70**	**4.28**	**4.26***
Images of black women	5.52	4.60	13.56***
Permanence of discrimination	3.91	4.71	6.36*
Myrdal's dilemma	4.46	5.23	4.97*

Note $*p < 0.05$ $**p < 0.01$ $***p < 0.001$

every instance, across both samples, those choosing African American scored consistently lower values on our scale than those opting for Black. The new name thus seems already to have had a significant impact on how the group is being perceived. In addition, black respondents scored consistently lower mean values than non-black respondents.

Conclusion: The Emergence of an Anticipatory Representation

As clearly indicated by the empirical analysis presented here, the term African American is already well anchored in contemporary American society as a new and distinct social representation of an object hitherto referred to as Blacks. In the onomastic study of names and naming processes (Study 1) we saw a convergence of reference among black as well as non-black Americans with regard to this new group denomination. Even though the term is not yet used as often as Black in day-to-day conversation, it is endowed with strongly positive and future-oriented meaning by both groups. Obviously, the term coexists with Black as an alternative denomination that evokes different, generally more favorable associations about the group it represents.

When we examined this duality of representations about Americans of African descent by clarifying the representational field of the object (in Study 2), we found that the term African American, while already well anchored as an alternative group designation, has not yet been fully objectified. The dominant presence of an *Negative Images* scale, which we obtained in both samples from different questionnaires, clearly indicates that Americans still organize their thoughts about the group to a compelling degree around negative characterizations of boisterousness and irresponsibility that have pervaded this racially divided society ever since its inception. This continued race-based categorization of the group has so far prevented African American from becoming a fully developed alternative social representation that is clearly disassociated from race.

While the term African American has not yet managed to get so objectified as to redefine the object in question completely away from race, it nevertheless has already impacted in terms of reshaping attitudes and opinions about black Americans. We must therefore understand that group designation as a social representation in the making which gets personified, and thus made concrete, by a subgroup claiming the name for itself. By becoming in this context the carrier for a new social identity, the term allows the ingroup to redefine its dual consciousness of being part African and part American in a more constructive way towards inclusion as an equal, yet culturally distinct group in a multicultural society. For non-black Americans the new term embodies their vision of America as an egalitarian society strengthened by the diversity of its population and symbolizes in this way the possibility of leaving a painful past behind at last. Both groups therefore have an active self-interest in propagating the new term. The collective effort of its elaboration centers on widely shared projections of a different future in which Blacks have been redefined more positively into African Americans and racial discrimination will have given way to cultural inclusion.

It is precisely this projective force and the consensus behind it which prompts us to categorize African American as an *anticipatory representation* (Philogène, 1994). This kind of social representation plays a crucial role when social actors reconstitute a common understanding of the world they share. While a social representation refers to a consensual world of collectively elaborated meanings allowing us "to classify persons and objects, to compare and explain behaviors, and to objectify them as parts of our social setting" (Moscovici, 1988), an anticipatory representation remains still in the making and is therefore not yet fully capable of such objectification. Its strategic relevance for social-psychological inquiry is that, as a carrier of innovation, it is nourished by presuppositions which point to a network of interconnectedness orienting individual thoughts and actions towards a different future. By exploring the dynamic properties of African American as anticipatory representation, we can see how individuals collectively rethink the social object.

Anticipatory representations, which are after all new social representations in the making, become real gradually and at first only in a symbolic sense, as carriers for projections of a different future. In other words, the new representation – here the term African American – gets naturalized before it gets objectified, requiring us to separate these two processes which social representation theory generally treats as aspects of the same process (Moscovici, 1984b). Based on our empirical findings it seems fair to conclude that the new term is already well anchored and becoming rapidly naturalized on the basis of positive and future-oriented projections while not yet having managed its objectification to re-present the group devoid of traditional race-based categorizations.

Anticipatory representations, such as the name African American, emerge in our midst when new circumstances force us, as a group or a community, to rethink the present and imagine the future as part of adjusting to a changing reality. These representations, essential to processes of change and innovation, are a catalyst for collective efforts to project a future together in the sense of Weber's "*Vorstellungen*" (Weber, 1925). For that reason, they are a particularly challenging and interesting object of analysis, because they highlight the dynamic qualities and the normative force of such a collective effort aimed at changing our reality (see the Y2K bug, the stock market, the single-currency project of the European Union as examples).

Part III

Social Representation and Social Construction

9

Functional Aspects of Social Representation

Saadi Lahlou

A Patchwork of Theories

Each scientific approach usually has a good degree of validity for the specific phenomena upon which it was originally designed; alas, its explanatory power decreases with distance from that original niche. This we all know: it would be crazy to explain air resistance with psychoanalysis. Therefore our scientific description of the world has to be a patchwork of theories.

Still, domains overlap, phenomena are intricate, and we quickly drift away when we try to encompass our object of study. Furthermore, as any specialist is naturally inclined to explain everything with the model he or she masters (cf. Gould, 1980), crazy attempts where theories try to encompass phenomena out of their range are not so rare: Marxism and language, economics and government, biology and intelligence, etc. One sign that disciplines have gone past the limits of their natural niche is often the all-critical style of their approach and their limited use of empirical data.

This problem is especially salient for phenomena at the crossroads of several academic domains, because each domain tries to colonize its margin. And this is unfortunately the case for the phenomena addressed by social representations (SR) theory. SR theory specialized on a crossroads, at the articulation between individual and social, and between symbolic and real (Moscovici, 1982).

So, in the patchwork of social science, what is the SR theory's specific domain of validity? SR theory, developed for the study of lay knowledge (Moscovici, 1976a, first published 1961), addresses problems which are also of concern to other theoretical framework and research traditions. *Culture, rules, conventions, mediating structures, common sense, common knowledge, habitus, shared cognition, mental models, prototypes, pensée sauvage, archetypes, schemata, scripts, concepts* . . . are some of the categories with which the phenomena we call "social representations" have something in common. But the theory invented by Moscovici is especially relevant for describing and understanding "hot" social issues – social objects in the making or in rapid change. Why? Because its constructionist perspective and concern with social function (Herzlich, 1972) are apt to take into account the feedback loop between social construction and individual thought and practice.

This concern for studying social objects "in the making," and not as static constructs, draws the limits of SR theory's domain of excellence. Still, SR theory is more than a scientific crossroads between social and individual on one way, and thought and action on another. Social representations exist with a function of their own. I shall argue here that *cooperation* is the key problem, and I shall present social representations as solutions to this problem.

To clarify this question, this paper attempts a glimpse at the *functional* aspects of social representation, taking the cooperation problem as a starting point. First, the ecological value of cooperation among groups will be highlighted (section 2). Then, I'll argue that cooperation needs to be supported by some social objects, for which the main specifications will be given (section 3). I shall then illustrate with the example of *eating* the type of results an SR approach can bring (section 4).

Cooperation as an Organic Behavior?

"Unaquaeque res, quantium in se est, in suo esse perseverare conatur"[1]
[Spinoza, Ethics, III: VI]

"il y a un point singulier où la société se substitue à la nature, où l'évolution sociale prend le pas sur l'évolution bionaturelle. A cet endroit, les deux chaînes de réalité se séparent tout en se continuant."[2]
[Moscovici, 1974, p. 290]

Entities cannot survive without some effort. We may call *things* the objects that survive by a passive effort of resistance to change, e.g., material objects like rocks or chairs; and *beings* those which *act* upon their environment to ensure their survival and development. Living organisms such as plants or animals, but also supraorganisms, like groups or organizations, are of this second kind.

Survival is, for all beings, a matter of linking perception of their environment to action, in order to perform relevant, efficient behavior. Beings that survive act in relevant ways: they adapt their action to the context. The link between context and action, seen from the being's perspective, is a perception/action loop, where the "meaning" of what is perceived depends on "what may be done" to or with it, what the environment "affords" (Gibson, 1986). In other words, this loop includes an *interpretation* of the environment by the being.

This interpretation can be more or less complex. Simple organisms without memory exhibit rather stereotyped responses. The tick (*Tixus Ixodes*) standing on a branch will let itself fall if it smells butyric acid. This is an adapted action, since butyric acid is contained in the sweat of mammals, which are the tick's prey. The tick is therefore likely to fall on a mammal's hairy back, where it will dig its head in the hot skin, and pump nourishing blood, as well described by Uexküll (1934). Here, interpretation is "hardwired" in the tick's biological organization; so is the coordination between its internal parts that produce the tick's behavior from the subject's interpretation of the phenomenal flow. Beings with memory may interpret signs in the world as signals triggering useful actions, based on their experience (Pavlov, 1927). For instance, pigeons may pick a lever that supplied them with food in previous training.

Above this first level of selecting relevant perception/action loops and repeating the successful ones, some animals, especially among higher vertebrates, are able to plan and perform new behaviors on the basis of *representations* of objects (Griffith, 1984). Chimpanzees will pile up crates to reach bananas (Köhler, 1917), dolphins will invent new behaviors to obtain fish (Bateson, 1979), and so forth. They probably intentionally chunk internal "simuli" (Minski, 1986) into simulated action chains, linking present situation to expected outcome. Whatever the process actually is here, interpretation and coordination are "software," but remain mostly at the individual level. Still, these individual representations bring an ecological advantage for those animals, inasmuch as they enable them to cope adequately with new objects and situations.

The existence of mental representations among lower animals in the *scala naturae* remains controversial; still their existence among the most common and most extensively studied species of primates, *Homo Sapiens*, is generally accepted, and recognized as a decisive ecological advantage in everyday behavior. Here, individual coordination between sensory and action organs is mediated by individual representations.

Let us now look at the most complex organisms we know: human groups in the wild, self-constructed through evolution and history as composite sets of beings and artifacts: "people with culture." Like other organisms, these groups are subject to the rules of survival. One peculiarity of groups is that action is distributed among participants, but that, unlike in individual beings, there is no physical nervous system which links these participants together to coordinate perception and action. Still, groups survive in time, and they have grown the functional equivalent of the reflex loops of microorganisms or of the individual mental representations of vertebrates. What are these social equivalents of individual representations? I argue: social representations.

Social groups turn out to achieve outstanding results when coordinating their action, surpassing individual performance. Pyramids, space shuttles, but also every action and artifact of our societies (e.g., ice creams cones, television, conferences) are the product of complex social coordination, aiming at common goals and distributing action among thousands of beings and things. Intentions and plans, building on previous acquaintance, are communicated; actions are executed locally by individuals or small groups and contribute to the emergence or maintenance of larger social patterns. Here, interpretation and coordination rely on mnemonic systems or objects that transcend the individual. Those *social constructs* are, through culture and education, projected or transcribed in symbolic forms, and reified in artifacts (e.g., tools, plans, monuments, documents, institutions).

In doing so, groups make available to individuals these symbolic representation systems which are the products of collective cultural development.[3] Therefore, individual humans benefit of complex symbolic *thought* and reasoning, and may produce, as individuals, amazingly sophisticated behaviors involving even objects absent from the local context. Symbolic thought proved efficient, as it brought us to the top of the ecological chain. As we see, those social constructs are the same as those that individuals use in their everyday life in their relation with the beings and things which constitute their social world.

These social objects, the constructs used by these groups and individuals to cope with their world collectively, communicating their intentions, negotiating and co-ordinating their actions, are what SR theory studies. They are socially constructed, but used by individuals also. So these constructs link the individual with the group, on one hand, and perception with action, on the other hand. Moreover, as we have seen, because their function is adaptive they are versatile and ever changing by nature.

To sum up, social representations are cultural organs shaped by social evolution; they have a pragmatic function of supporting group cooperation for a better survival. They are mediating structures (Hutchins, 1995) facilitating coordination of activity between humans, and between humans and things. Individuals inherit these organs from their group and use them in everyday life. When we talk about a social representation of something (say "X") by a group, we point at the mediating structure for coordinating action between group members for constructing and/or coping with "X."

Social representation research, as a branch of social psychology, emphasizes two aspects: articulation between the individual and the group in the *construction* of social objects; and articulation between the individual and the group in the *use* of social objects.[4] Social construction and communication are the main concerns for SR theory. The key figure is Moscovici's (1971, 1984a) psychosocial triangle: Ego, Alter, Object. No object can be conceived without social perspective, in the eye of the Other, the Socius ("Alter"); conversely, relations with the socius are mediated by objects. The psychosocial triangle provides framework for analysis of phenomena by resituating "objects" in their social setting (look for the Socius!), and also by reminding the researcher that there are objects at stake in the relationship.

Thus, one of the main distinctive traits of SR theory is that it knows that the phenomena it studies stand at a crossroads, and that they are not given nor static, but are socially constructed and in continuous evolution.

The Coconstruction of Groups and their Objects

Let us now consider the problem of efficient coordination within a social group. Its members try to act together with a common intention. Cooperation has two aspects. The first is the pragmatic aspect: "what do we do." Individuals must use a reference system that contains the objects they perceive (the context) or try to construct (the intentions). The second aspect of cooperation is the social: "who are *we*." The fact that the group exists as such, does indeed share general frameworks, and is willing to cooperate, is a trivial but essential prerequisite to collective action.

Pragmatic aspect

The *pragmatic* (or cognitive) aspect covers technical coordination and labor distribution. It includes general frameworks such as time, space, and taxonomies of objects; but also symbolic systems (e.g., language) which may describe possible arrangements of the objects in those frameworks and specify action. This pragmatic aspect links information to action.

A good cooperation tool should provide the individuals with guidelines for their own action, but in such a way that all those local parts indeed contribute to a single global, coherent process. It should, still, appear flexible enough to adapt to variable local contexts. We shall see that social representations meet these contradictory requirements.

Social aspect

The *social* aspect covers the existence of the group as such, and links the individuals to the group. It involves notions such as trust, motivation, identity, and individual interests. Try to organize a bank robbery with a random sample of 10 individuals, and you will see that it is not so trivial: sharing the pragmatic reference system and understanding the language is not enough for cooperation. This social precondition has strong implications for the *construction* of social objects and coordination modes. It accounts for many traits of the social constructs that we may call metapragmatic: that is, not specified by the instantaneous necessities of efficient action, but rather by the conditions of possibility of this action in a collective framework. This is where the theory of social representations becomes necessary, while pragmatic aspects could be more or less dealt with by classical cognitive theories.

Coconstruction

The two aspects are not independent. Their interaction during history construes both groups and objects as cultural entities, and interweaves them. Empirically, the group becomes defined by the possibility of communication between its members, and concerted action based on its internal social labor division. It is a chicken and egg problem. People who cooperate often become a group;[5] and it is easier for a group to cooperate. This link between action and identity is well expressed by the subjective notion of "participation" (Lévy-Bruhl, 1985) which encompasses both aspects.

But within the group, and towards the object, people occupy different positions. Cooperation may include negotiation or conflict. A given state of things at one moment (e.g., social rules, distribution of property, ethics, production processes, political system) is the result and reification of compromise and "rapports de force." The construction of the social representation of an object is a series of fights and influences, a mixture of propaganda, propagation, and diffusion, and also of contrasted practices, as Moscovici (1976a, first published 1961) demonstrated for psychoanalysis. What appears *ex-post facto* as static tradition may hide a dynamic equilibrium between conflicting interests. Change one thing, and you jeopardize the arrangement of many other beings and things. The structure of social objects is often a subtle compromise that enables each user to see it as acceptable, although users' interpretations may differ from one another.

Any object will be a stake, an issue, or a concern for some sets of individuals whose activity or interests are involved with this object. There is no neutral object, for its shape and properties will matter in different ways to different populations, and might generate conflicts and negotiations. An adequate approach to the problem must consider the various positions of actors in respect to the organizing principle of their relation (Doise, 1985, 1989; Palmonari & Pombeni, 1984; Clèmence, Doise, & Lorenzi-Cioldi 1994). SR theory faces this problem, and accepts that object construction is a result of interaction between actors with different social, historical, and cognitive perspectives: this is why they are essentially dynamic objects.

Eating for Example

I shall not enter further into theoretical and epistemological discussions. These aspects have been discussed with talent by my colleagues, in the course of internal critiques and discussions with researchers from other academic traditions (see Jodelet, 1984 for a global picture; Moscovici, 1989 for a history; Jodelet, 1997, for a bibliography). Although I believe that SR theory presents unique and immensely interesting epistemic properties, I found that one major interest of this theory is its ability to deal with *real* societal issues. As the proof of the pudding, here is an example, the SR of "eating," upon which I shall try to give a "taste" of how SR approach can accommodate phenomena.

Eating is a basic need (Maslow, 1943). It is also a societal one, although the terms of the problem may vary between cultures. It is an everyday behavior, and it is also deeply invested with economic stakes. Specifications of the food industry and service rely on what industry knows of consumer's needs and representations. Finally, it is one of the seminal objects of social psychology (Lewin, 1943). Considering the immense literature on food, can SR theory bring something relevant and new?

Method

Our study first evidenced the structure of the representation by analyzing the content of two different sources of empirical data. The first material is of an usual type in SR research (e.g., de Rosa, 1988b): free word association on the word "eating" ("manger") of 2000 French adults (a representative sample of continental France) in face-to-face at-home interviews.

The other is extracted from a cultural source, a classical reference dictionary (*Le Grand Robert*, French equivalent to the *Webster*). This dictionary provides, with each entry, a list of associated terms (such as synonyms and analogs). The associated terms of "manger" were cropped, and then the associates of these associates, yielding 588 associates of "manger" in the French language. The extensive definitions of the 588 entries obtained were then copied, yielding a corpus of about 500 pages.

We therefore obtained two corpuses of text: *associations by live human respondents, and associations by a cultural source.* The principle of the method is identical for both sources: the source is stimulated with the name of the object, and induced to produce statements relating to that object.

Both corpuses were submitted to statistical analysis of textual data for segmentation and content analysis. We used ALCESTE (Reinert, 1986, 1993), a sophisticated segmentation software which cuts the corpuses into small text units (answers, or sentences) and then clusters together text units with similar lexical content into classes. Classes are constructed on purely statistical criteria based on word stem cooccurrence in text units. Each class therefore gathers text units with similar lexical content. The software provides the researcher with the typical words and sentences of each class, for interpretation (see Table 9.1). Each class was considered as a basic element of the SR, following validated interpretation procedures (Lahlou, 1996a).

Results

Interestingly, both sources (humans and Robert) yield a similar structure of six elements: *Desire, Take, Food, Meal, Filling up,* and *Living.* Individuals indeed

Table 9.1 Classes from Dictionary Analysis

DESIRE

désir+, faim, appétit+, soif, satisfaire., envie+, convoit+, assouvi+, rassasi+, avidité, apais+, dévor+, avide+, affame+, cupid+, content+, besoin+, mourir., arde+, curiosité+, excit+, yeux, passion<, regard+, tendance+, attrait+, glouton+, éprouve+, amour, sexuel+, instinct+, honneur+, avoir, brul+, moder+, dévorer, soul+, être, aval+, inclination+, creve+, apéritif+, goulu+, creus+, proie+, colère, extrêm+, recherche+, aspir+, abstin+, friand+, sensation+, presser., sentiment+, vouloir., inf+, claque+, argent+, sa, physique+, joi+, viv+, ivre+, naturel+, force+, porte<, ses, plaisir<.

(desire, hunger, appetite, thirst, satisfy, envy, lust, assuage, satiate, greed, etc.)

TAKE

touch+, attrape+, prendre., main+, nez, attaqu+, embrass+, baise+, joue<, mordre., ventr+, gonfl+, qqn, saisir., parole+, battre., lèvre+, ouverture+, doigt+, bras+, ball+, navire+, pied+, serre+, sur, fondre., entrer., avec, ouvrir., se, tirer., claque+, coup<, aspir+, tomb+, lui, langue<, visage, jeter., partie<, tenir., passer., laiss+, dent+, mouvement+, bouche+, voir., devant, ferme+, arme+, porte<, bout<, contre, arrêt+, gueul+.

(touch, catch, take, hand, nose, attack, embrace, kiss, cheek, bite, stomach, bulge, smbdy, seize, speech, fight, lip, orifice, finger, arm, etc.)

FOOD

viande+, pain+, aliment+, fruit+, pat+, légum+, animal<, cuire., tranch+, bouill+, plant+, couper., salad+, lait+, dent+, morceau+, coût+, conserv+, rat+, digest+, porc, mange+, poisson+, sec+, fromage+, gras, végétal+, soup+, boeuf+, nourrit+, sucre+, comestible+, suc+, beurre+, tartine+, liquide+, herb+, boîte+, saucisson+, trempe+, nourr+, bouche+, maigre+, épaiss+, boire., gibier+, fourr+, rumin+, oiseau+, frais+, grain+, grill+, chair+, vert+, chien+, petit+, boul+, prépar+, cuiss+, feuill+, gâteau+, croût+, potage, aval+, croqu+, fleur+, fine+, boisson+, chaud+, seche+, substance+, froid+, garni+, oeuf+, orifice+, taille+, point+, gros, produit+, arbre+.

(meat, bread, food, fruit, pasta, vegetable, animal, cook, slice, boil, plant, cut, salad, milk, tooth, piece, cost, canned etc.)

MEAL

repas+, table+, restaur+, plat+, dîne+, cuisin+, déjeuner, invit+, serv+, buffet+, vaissel+, servir., cantin+, festin+, couvert<, fête+, café+, menu+, noce+, nappe+, hosti+, gastronom+, soir+, heure<, assiette+, communi+, coll+, mange+, ensemble, thé+, convive+, soup+, tasse+, gala+, récept+, jour+, entrée+, dessert+, offic+, serviette+, cher+, spécial+, paye<, prépar+, léger+, carte+, pièce+, on, frugal+, général+, nuit, mettre., boisson+, région<, cours, verre+, hôte+, milieu+, ou, grand+, après, chez, récipient+.

(meal, table, restaurant, dish, diner, cook (kitchen), lunch, guest, serve, etc.)

LIVING

connaître., bon+, sentir., aim+, agréable+, emploi+, goût+, possed+, vivre., est, je, vie, éducation, appréci+, ne, idée+, joui<, femme+, esprit+, juge<, il, beau+, âme+, amer, apprendre., suivre., moral+, riche+, social+, vit, pas, caracter+, que, ressentir., savoir, société+, cet, charmant+, corromp+, accueil, dieu+, exquis+, coeur, ouvrage+, valeur<, sentiment+, c'est, vous, assimil+, adopt+, passion<, affect+, ai, musique, sens, ador+, habit+, intére<, nature, instinct+, homme+, qualité+, travail+, verbe, inf+, fill<, ce, humain+, recevoir., enfant+, me, chose+...

(know, good, feel, love, nice, use, taste, possess, live, be, I, life, education, appreciate, no, idea, enjoy, woman, mind, judgement, he (it), beauty, soul, bitter, learn, follow, moral, rich, social, etc.)

FILLING UP

rempl+, épuise+, encombr+, ronge+, sature+, consum+, détruire., approvisionn+, sujet+, absorb+, empli+, imbibe+, vide+, feu, plein+, farci+, bourr+, chose+, complet+, abreuv+, fatigue+, fortifi+, imprégn+, voiture+, dévorer, consomm+, n, placer., garni+, occup+, eau, entier+, gonfl+, rendre., fonction+, brûl+, pron+, jusque, gorge+, discours, temps, user., article+, accompli+, trop, air, abstrait+, ses, marchand+, soul+, pass+, dissip+, compl+, son, force+, sang+, truffe+, dépenser, vill+, entam+, quantité+, se, fer, dévor+, muni+, dépense+, perdre., tout, tête, désign+, coeur, fort+, livre+, marche+, racine+, ravitaille+, charge+, bouff+, anal.

(fill up, exhaust, congest, gnaw, saturate, consume, destroy, load, subject, absorb, fill, soak, empty, fire, full, cram, stuff, etc.)

Note. English translation of the first lexical items of each class is provided in bold font. Raw listings of typical French lexical roots are listed, and most are truncated, which is indicated by the sign "+" or "<" at the end, while verbs are written at the infinite (ending with ".").

---

refer to a single, cultural, paradigm. We shall come back later to this important point.

The difference is that one of the elements (*Take*) is almost absent in the humans' associations, and another (*Filling up*) takes different connotations (*quantitative* equilibrium in Robert, *qualitative* in humans). Others stay very much the same, including their respective size.

Classes from the dictionary analysis are shown in Table 9.1. The top list of the classes' typical lexical roots are presented, straight as they come from the statistics

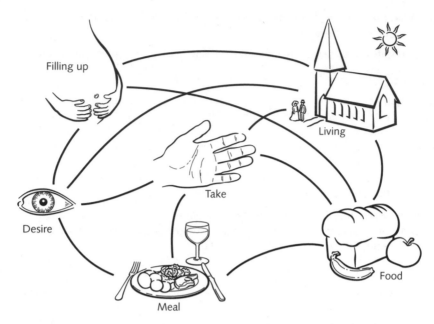

Filling up

Living

Take

Desire

Meal

Food

Figure 9.1 A subjective view of the elements of the social representation of "eating" in France.

listing. A lexical root is typical of a class if it appears significantly more frequently in the textual units of that class. Units may be truncated, since the software considers together the lexical variants of each root (e.g., *désir+* stands for *désirer, désir, désirant, désirs, désireras, désiré*, etc.). More loosely said, each class is characterized by the words that are typical of the discourse it contains. By analyzing those words one can interpret the content of that class: for example, class "DESIRE" is made of desire, hunger, appetite, thirst, etc.

As one may notice, this social representation contains obvious common sense (the behavioral sequence of food ingestion). But it also contains social (*Meal*) and ethical elements (*Living*). Social representations always exhibit this "obvious *ex post*" characteristic, for they *are* common sense. Still, the actual number of elements, their nature and organization are not necessarily trivial and may even differ from explicit didactic sources as dictionaries or manuals. Therefore the SR approach, using the natives' psychological material, provides us with a description at a level of granularity appropriate for human thought description: no neurons, no scientific constructs; just plain natural thought, common sense. SR theory has no hegemonic claim to give *the* right description of how people think or act,[6] but it strives to express it at a level as close as possible to the subjective perspective of lay persons.

Of course, this is only a *lexical* projection of the social representation, limited by our linguistic investigation method. To remind the reader that the elements have emotional, motor, and proprioceptive dimensions, I prefer to represent the elements of the social representation "non verbally" as shown in Figure 9.1.

Discussion

Now that the framework is set, let us look at some interesting points. I shall focus on the following questions: (a) representation and action, (b) social and individual representations, and (c) social values in representation. More details can be found in Lahlou (1998).

Representation and action: from structure to process

What is the link between representation and behavior? Some of the SR elements may be motor (e.g., *Take*), enabling the representation to unfold as a pragmatic script, in context. Let us examine a human subject, inhabited by the social representation we just described. Remember its elements are associated in the mind, as our free association experiment just showed. In a context where hunger (*Desire*) is present, if acceptable *Foods* are present, by the virtue of association the other elements of the representation will emerge. The representation may then naturally unfold into the trivial biological script (*Hunger / Take / Food* (until) *Filling up*); but this will respect the formal behavior syntax of the relevant *Meal* according to local context (e.g., breakfast, snack, etc.). This script may be acted in context, since the Take is a motor element and will be applied to the actual *Foods* present in the context. The domain of application of social representations is not only the mind, but also the everyday world.

Note that a relevant script was produced here by an individual subject using the elements of the *social* representation itself, as empirically determined (and this is what makes this discussion nontrivial). Relevance in context is ensured by the fact that each element of the SR is a paradigm in itself. For example Food is a paradigm of edible objects which may be encountered (with avatars[7] from "Apple" to "Zest"). The various avatars of each paradigm enable one to perform adequately by adapting the general schema to the local context. With the same social representation of eating, a given person is able to perform an adapted yet efficient sequence in very diverse situations, by choosing the relevant avatars of the required elements in the local context. Hence, a local application of the SR might be:

faim / grignoter / fruit / buffet / santé
hunger / nibble / fruit /buffet /health

which accounts for the sequence "nibbling a fruit in a cocktail party because it's the only healthy food available on the buffet";

soif / aspire / boisson / abreuve
thirst / sip / drink / quench

which may be described as "taking a drink to quench one's thirst." Elements in the context may be recognized as local instances ("avatars") of the paradigm, and/or arguments in performing the script.[8]

Those scripts depend not only upon circumstances, but also upon groups. Free association on "eating well," a prompt designed to elicit pragmatic association, was asked to another sample of 1600 French adults. We obtained eight typical scripts or action principles. Some groups favor certain scripts. The scripts obtained are only combinations of some elements of the SR of eating. Here are 3 examples: "To eat what I like" is made of *Desire/Take*, while "To eat one's fill" is *Take/Filling up*. "(To eat) balanced and healthy" is made of *Take/Filling up/Living*. This last script is more frequently attested in women of our sample, while "To eat one's fill" was more found in younger respondents.

Social representations often display this amazing versatility: people can act in opposite ways while still using the same SR framework, by focusing on some aspects only. As we can see, natural evolution shaped social representation with unexpected properties, yet functional.[9] Their versatility enables communication, compromise, and cooperation between parties with different attitudes ("What you see is what you fancy" effect), but also flexibility in individual use ("Swiss knife" effect), although not *anything* is possible. All subjects possess all the elements in their individual representation, even if they do not use them on an everyday basis at a given period. Still, the other "blades" might be useful at another period of life, or in unusual conditions, e.g., adult married persons report coming back to the single person's minimal cooking practices when their mate and children are away.

Notice how the empirical structure of the SR of eating performs the contradictory requirements of coordination mentioned in the earlier discussion of pragmatic aspects: providing individual guidelines for behavior, adaptable to local contexts, and still that can be aggregated with others to coproduce social events (meals).

Individual and social representation
We assume that social representation is a species of individual representations, in the biological sense. Social representations are to individual, mental, representations what a species (e.g., Dogs) are to a specific individual (e.g., *this* dog, "Rex"). A social representation is a population of individual representations, which are scattered over a population of humans.[10] Which comes first, the social representation or the mental representation? That's a chicken and egg problem: what comes first, the dog, or the dog species? They are coconstructed, and hence codependent. There is no *tabula rasa* in cultural issues, and the social representation is such an issue.

What we (observers) call the pattern of the SR is the set of elements *we* perceive as common to the population of individual avatars (say, like a Dog – the species – has four legs, one tail etc.). In a sense, the SR is a construct of the observer, scientist or naïve layman of the street. But it is more than just an arbitrary set, because individual representations of the same object do have genetic and functional relations with one another: they are reproduced (by learning) from one another, and they crossbreed in the process of communication.

This population of representations is distributed over the population of people. To use Moscovici's expression, representations "inhabit populations." This enables coordination. When two people, Ego and Alter, want to coordinate upon object X in a specific situation, they can communicate by referring to the social representation of X, through their own individual representations of X. As members of a same group, they assume to share the same social representation. And as we saw, they indeed do share at least the general framework, if not details.

Defining social representations as a *population* of avatars is more than a metaphor. As said earlier, individual representations are actually generated by the reproductive propagation of other avatars of the same representation, as in biological species (Lahlou, 1996b). Avatars may undergo adaptive mutations, which will be diffused over the population when they bring a selective advantage; slightly different phenotypes may develop in some subpopulations to adapt to local conditions. In other words, it is because social representations are populations of avatars confronted with local pragmatics that they are fit for pragmatic purposes; it is because the local avatars of SR are individual representations that social representations are a tool for coordination of action in human groups.

Now, let us look at "eating" again. First, consider the great similarity between what is obtained from a cultural source and from individuals, and between individuals. Individuals indeed refer to a single, cultural, paradigm. This was predicted by the theory, but empirical evidence is always welcome.

But individual representations vary slightly from group to group, according to local specificity. In another survey, we asked a representative sample of the French population (2000 adults, face to face interviews at home) for free association on "eating well," and found marginal differences by age and gender. High intake of energy and social content of the meal are more salient in people under 30, while those 60 and over make more associations on health and food limitation. Women insist on balanced and light food, while men mention rich food more often (Lahlou, 1998) (see Table 9.2).

Respondents hereby reveal how they have internalized some widespread sociological norms and constraints (seniors should restrain on food, women should take care of their body, men should be "bons vivants" etc.). This link between practice involving some specific elements of the social representation and the salience of those elements in the representation of the population involved has been shown

Table 9.2 Items Significantly Over-Represented in Free Association for "Eating Well" Among Inhabitants of France

Younger: bouffe (grub) copains (pals), restaurant, couscous, dessert, gâteau (cake)

Elder: peu (few), sans (without), excès (excess), modérément (moderately), raisonnable (reasonable), cholesterol

Women: équilibré (balanced), légumes (vegetables), sain (healthy), laitages (dairy products), vitamines (vitamins), kilos, lait (milk), varié (varied)

Men: bon (good), foie gras (pâté), qualité (quality), banquet (feast), vin (wine), pomme de terre (potato), français (French); choucroute (sauerkraut), sauce, frites (French fries), charcuterie (delicatessen), copains (pals), steak, canard (duck), restaurant, boeuf (beef)

---

many times (e.g., Guimelli, 1994). Here, representation appears as a biological organ, of which certain parts would grow more salient with use, like a tennis player may grow a larger right arm.

Social values
Another function of the social representation is to ensure the existence and maintenance of the group (see previous discussion of the social aspect). Structural research showed that social representation can be described as an organized set of basic elements of two kinds, with a hierarchy (Abric, 1984, 1994a, & 1994b). The "noyau central" (kernel) contains essential elements; in their absence the subjects cannot recognize the object (Moliner, 1996). For instance, a "company" must make profit (Flament, 1994a), and members of an "ideal group" must be friends. Abric highlights that some elements of the kernel are values, and insists that what makes the group is the sharing of those values. By their very nature, social representations refer to some organizing elements that characterize the group. Note that attitudes towards these values may vary in the group, but still they stand as landmarks structuring the communication framework.

In our example, "eating," some elements will carry values that are fundamental for the group. Here, just the right satisfaction, without excess, as balance between not enough and too much, which constitute the *Filling up* element, is one of the basis of good social behavior, greed or undue asceticism being equally stigmatized in French society (Charuty, 1991). Another element, "*Living*" is made almost only of moral values, as assessed by the typical terms: *good, love, nice, taste, live, be, life, education, idea, enjoy, judgment, beauty, soul, moral, social, etc.* (the full list includes *God* and other strong values). Ethnographic studies show how much eating practice is linked with social cohesion; even outside France, there are few social events without public food ingestion. Social identity includes eating habits. The role of "eating" as a social cement has been integrated in the very structure of the SR of "eating." This ensures that every individual or group practicing "eating" will regenerate and maintain the group as such with those in-built guidelines. More generally, every social representation includes social dimensions that make the object a "fait social total."

As usual, structure sustains function, and function shapes structure; this makes no epistemological problem in SR theory.

Conclusion

The SR domain is an agitated crossroads: the social interaction between beings and things, and it is pretty uncomfortable to dwell in a crossroads. I have tried to show how the two interfaces which social representations contain (perception/action and individual/social) are connected by the very function of social representations as a cooperation instrument for social groups.

This functional approach complements the structural approach widely developed in our community. It also opens research perspectives. Most objects studied previously by SR theory are societal issues, and, as we have seen, this is where the theory is most efficient. But considering social representations as cooperation tools suggests that SR theory might also be quite effective for studying collaboration at the scale of smaller communities, for instance in professional settings.

Notes

1 "Every entity, so far as it lies in itself, strives to persist in its own being."
2 "There is a singular point where society substitutes for nature, where social evolution takes the step to bio-natural evolution. At this point, the two chains of reality part but still continue one another."
3 It may not be superfluous to state here that, as already noted by Freud (1921), there is no thought but social thought. Symbolic ability and the categories of mental life are, for each individual, basically social and learned through socialization. The other part of the loop, where individuals contribute to global culture, is essential in a historical perspective, but comes afterwards: cultural contributions are usually made by educated adults, not by preverbal children. There is no such thing as a nonsocialized "person." Even the more basic functions, such as eating, embed cultural aspects in their representation kernel: for instance, the meal (Lahlou, 1998) and the cultural and moral determination (Douglas, 1966; Rozin, 1982, 1990; Fischler, 1990) of what is edible (e.g., frogs, dogs, larvae).
4 The epistemic aspect (link between construction and use at individual level) and the historical aspect (construction and use at social level) have been less developed; ex-

changes with cognitive psychology and cognitive science for the first, and with sociology and history for the last would certainly be fruitful.

5 Cooperating, even on accidental basis, contributes to create a group. This is empirical evidence, of which the reasons are many. One may be that group identity builds on common history. Also, for individuals within the group, there is often a positive feedback between membership and activity, which is mediated by identity. Social psychology has shown how role and status, which are identity constituents, are linked with the labor division. The role of an individual is the set of behaviors others expect from him or her; and his or her status is the set of behaviors this individual can legitimately expect from others (Stoetzel, 1963). In other words, social identity is linked with the individual's position in the social labor division. Individuals depend upon objects and upon the group for their own definition.

Alternatively, it is obvious that objects depend on the group for their definition. Even objects, which have an identical name, will be in fact different between groups: we already mentioned "food," an apparently unambiguous functional category, which still may differ from one group to another. The differences may even be more striking with objects or categories like gender, kin, god, health, etc.

6 Neurological, economic, or behaviorist descriptions may be more relevant for other purposes.

7 We call "avatar" a local instantiation of the social representation, as encountered in the world or in discourse. E.g., "this professor, Moscovici" is an avatar of the social representation of "the professor." In Hindu religion, avatars were the forms of embodiment of Vishnu on earth. Although avatars may differ, they are all considered incarnations of the same entity. As a set of all its possible avatars, the social representation is a paradigm.

8 I use the term "script" here in the vague sense of "action program," and not in specific reference to one of the many specialized meanings given to this term by various authors in the psychological or cognitive science literature.

9 Not every actualization of SR is efficient. The magic thought about food, including the incorporation principle (Rozin, Millman, & Nemerorff 1989; Fischler, 1990), seems to be an inappropriate, but frequent, application of the social representation of eating (Lahlou, 1998).

10 And, as we saw with the example of the dictionary, representations may inhabit other media than human beings.

10

Killer Tomatoes! Collective Symbolic Coping with Biotechnology

Wolfgang Wagner and Nicole Kronberger

Introduction

Some decades ago a promising director made a movie called "Killer Tomatoes" which was later awarded a prize for being one of the worst movies ever produced. The gist of the plot is that innocent looking tomatoes turn into aggressive beings attacking horrified shoppers. Though not attributing the full spectrum of such human behavior to tomatoes, a significant proportion of the European public maintain a menacing image when it comes to genetically modified organisms.

When a new technology enters the marketplace of everyday life, it frequently creates ambivalent feelings in the public. On the one hand, technologies are meant to make everyday chores easier and to make life more comfortable. On the other hand, many technologies, specifically radically new ones, involve operations that are based on complex scientific achievements. This was the case with satellite related space technology in the Fifties, with nuclear energy technology in the Sixties, and it is the case in the Nineties with biotechnology that uses genetic manipulation to tailor the properties of living organisms.

While lacking an understanding of the scientific bases of modern technologies, people nevertheless attempt to understand what it is and what the scientists do to form an opinion about it. Specific examples are technologies that are proximal to our everyday life, either by becoming part of the household, such as information technology, or by their products, such as food and medical treatments. Modern biotechnology may lead to crops and foodstuff, which are or will be offered on supermarket shelves to the very same ordinary people who have scant understanding of industrial genetics. Their own body might eventually be subjected to genetic tests and cures, and there are self-proclaimed "experts" who – for whatever reason – talk of producing clones of humans who some day could be their closest relatives.

This struggle for understanding may occur at different levels. Some people, such as the more scientifically literate ones, might read the relevant columns in newspapers or buy and consult professional literature on the topic. This is the straightforward way. However, the proportion of people who have the necessary educational resources or the time necessary for such study at their disposal is probably not too high. Hence, many people need to resort to other means of understanding that are governed by common sense.

Collective Symbolic Coping

In a cross-national study on the perception of genetically modified organisms in Europe it was found that fantastic images of genetically modified organisms play a significant role in people's understanding of what biotechnology is about. Such images or representations are the product of a collective process of symbolic coping with new phenomena and a crucial component of everyday thinking and common sense. The image of the "gene-less" natural versus the "gene-enriched" bioengineered tomato, which is simultaneously perceived as contagious and monstrous, is not simply a wrong cognition or fairy tale, but a naturally occurring way of understanding new and complex phenomena. It will be argued that representations are socially constructed, culturally correct in their own sense and functional in everyday social life.

Biotechnology and genetic engineering are relatively new technologies in Europe and especially in Austria. They were not known to a significant proportion of Austrians until the middle of this decade. Meeting a largely unprepared public, genetic engineering was experienced as an unfamiliar technology with unknown procedures and consequences. It was certainly not just a minor novelty but a highly relevant application with its products threatening to penetrate everyday life.

Such new technology needs to be coped with materially as well as symbolically. "*Material coping*" comprises activities by scientists, engineers, and politicians to reduce health hazards and to control ecological risks by technical means and to a certain extent also through political decisions and legislation. The process of "*symbolic coping*" is at the heart of social representation theory and explains how representations are formed by a collectivity. By the term "symbolic coping" we mean the process of appropriating the novel and unfamiliar in order to make it intelligible and communicable. If the members of a group lack a shared representation of some relevant phenomenon, they engage in a sense-making activity. This involves naming the novel and attributing characteristics, which allow the phenomenon to be talked about. In this understanding symbolic coping is the collective activity of a group struggling to maintain the integrity of its worldview which is also crucial for social identity.

The collective activity emerges, of course, from the sum of individual responses to the challenge of the novel. Individual coping involves attempts to render the unfamiliar familiar by suggesting a name and by alluding to a known and similar phenomenon. Among individuals united by the canopy of a shared language and common understandings, individual responses will not be arbitrary, but rather are located within the frame of a shared culture. Therefore, the number of solutions attempting to render the new intelligible, which are suggested by individual members of a group, will converge towards a few ways of understanding (Sperber, 1990). Finally, when a qualified majority of group members as well as mass media reporting agrees in discourse on a shared understanding, it can be said that the group attained a new social representation.[1] In total, however, a group's qualified agreement on a representation can not be reduced to the sum of individual activities but is a collective event in its own right.

Nowadays, the discourse guiding collective symbolic coping is dominated by media communication. However, it would not suffice if the media discourse were not accompanied by personal conversations. In general, personal communication and media consumption follow a tendency of homogamy. *Homogamic communication* means that people prefer to converse with others of similar opinions and to read newspapers which are likely to confirm one's own beliefs instead of presenting opposite opinions. It was shown for example that people who were enclosed in a location for an extended period of time talked significantly more with like-minded others and that the closest relations developed between persons with similar opinions (Griffitt & Veitch, 1974). Homogamic communication further enhances converging solutions in the process of symbolic coping.

Initially, symbolic coping involves a class of responses, which are called "anchoring." Similar to the process of categorization existing representations that are deemed applicable come to the fore and are used for naming and understanding. When AIDS first hit the marketplace of public opinion approximately two decades ago, for example, it was understood in terms of venereal diseases like syphilis or, by the more religiously minded, as God's punishment. It was only later that a specific representation called AIDS developed which allowed this illness to be distinguished from venereal diseases in everyday discourse (Marková & Wilkie, 1987).

Bartlett already described the process of anchoring (1932), although in different terms. What he called "conventionalization" is well illustrated by his often-quoted experiment on the serial reproduction of the story "War of the Ghosts." For Westerners this story has a rather unusual plot involving ghosts and black things (the soul?) coming out of the mouth of a dead man. He noticed that this story, after having been serially reproduced by several generations of subjects, contained many new elements, which were more typical for Western culture at the expense of the original foreign elements. Bartlett explained this finding as showing conventionalization at work that makes people understand strange words or ideas in terms of more familiar schemata. Using serial reproduction as well, this process was shown to exist for individual (Bangerter & Lehmann, 1997; Kashima, 2000) as well as for group recall (Stephenson, Brandstätter, & Wagner, 1983).

Another step in the collective process of symbolic coping is called *objectification*. Objectification means to construct an icon, metaphor, or trope, which comes to stand for the new phenomenon or idea. It has an image structure that visibly reproduces a complex of ideas and weaves it into the fabric of the group's common sense (Lorenzi-Cioldi, 1997; Moscovici, 1984b, p. 38).

Jodelet (1991) observed images of "decay," "curdling" like butter, "fall," "souring," and "turning off" like milk, when her French lay subjects talked about mental illness. With these metaphors they likened "the phenomena of organic transformation [that is falling mentally ill] with processes of a more or less material nature" (pp. 209ff). This study shows that the choice of the image or trope is not arbitrary. Being farmers and village dwellers Jodelet's respondents used the image of souring milk to characterize mental illness because it is closer to their everyday experience than it would be, for example, to the inhabitants of large cities. Close experience of these source domains allowed them to "explain" the threatening, unfamiliar, and "strange" phenomenon of madness. Hence, objectification depends upon the characteristics of the social unit where a social representation is elaborated. The specific social conditions of a certain group favor specific kinds of tropes to be used for objectification by which an unfamiliar phenomenon is represented and made intelligible. Such differences in social conditions between groups may be sociostructural, historical, cultural, or subcultural, intergeneration, or differences in educational level. Differences in living conditions of groups delimit the space of experiences of their members, which in turn delimits the universe of available tropes. Whether an image is accepted or not by a group is neither a problem of truth nor an arbitrary choice, but determined by the group's experiential world and the negotiated consensus of the group members (Moscovici, 1988; Wagner, Elejabarrieta, & Lahnsteiner, 1995; Wagner, 1996). The resulting trope does not need to be "correct" or "accurate" in the sense of scientific truth. It just needs to be *good to think*. A trope is good to think if its meaning is well embedded in the group's local world of experience, if it is simple, and if its symbolism appeals to the group's dominant aesthetic sentiments. If images and associated beliefs are good to think they are also socially true, meaning that they are *warranted assertible* (Habermas, 1973, pp. 239ff). Warranted assertibility of an image or belief X means that whenever a person enters into discourse with another a justified consensus about X can be reached given the right condition. This consensus-creating condition bears neither upon logical consistency of X nor upon empirical evidence for X, but upon the force of the argument implied by the people's shared cultural assumptions.

It is not always easy to discriminate anchoring from objectification. In fact it seems that they are two poles of one more or less continuously evolving process of symbolic coping. In broad terms the structure of this continuous process can be likened to the model of metaphorical understanding suggested by Lakoff (1987). Wagner, Elejabarrieta, and Lahnsteiner (1995) used this model to show that popular thinking about conception is based on a sexual role metaphor. People liken the activities and characteristics of sperms and ova (the target domain to be understood) to the sex role – stereotypically active behavior of men respectively to the passive behavior of women (the source domain in terms of which the target is understood). The effect is stronger with sex role conservative than with sex role liberal respondents. This metaphor, hence, renders the process of fertilization and the division of labor among biological cells intelligible in terms of the people's living conditions and the therefrom derived experience: that is, whether they live in sex role conservative or in more sex role liberal relationships, determines the preference for the metaphorical comparison.

The Study

The introduction of biotechnology in Europe occurred in many countries at varying speed during the last decade and it was accompanied by country-specific social and political processes. There are countries, for example UK, where genetically engineered food was readily available in the supermarkets for many years, where political actors have dealt with health and safety regulation and where the media maintained an ongoing discourse about the topic for more than a decade. There are other countries, for example Greece, Spain, and Portugal, where genetic engineering rarely if ever was a political and media issue before 1996. Finally there are countries like Austria where genetic engineering started to be an issue approximately at the end of 1995. Therefore, in 1996, the Austrian population, media, and political actors stood right at the beginning of having to cope with this new technology.

In an extensive research study (scheduled from 1996 to 1998) many aspects of the public perception of biotechnology in Europe were assessed. These were the political and media history about biotechnology in a series of countries, an all-European survey including open-ended questions about biotechnology, a series of focus group and interview studies, and detailed press analyses for crucial time periods in selected countries.

The fortunate timing of this study allowed analyzing the Austrian data in comparison to those of other European countries. We think that this "natural experiment" can give some indication of the process of collective symbolic coping with biotechnology at work in Austria at the time of the survey in 1996 and to reveal the contours of an emerging social representation.

The present research uses the longitudinal media data and the survey data from Austria and compares them with data from other European countries. The survey provides data about attitudes, beliefs, and images related to genetic engineering held by Europeans in the fall of 1996. The media history highlights the intensity of public debate that preceded the snapshot survey data.

A representative random sample of approximately 1000 respondents in each of the 15 member countries of the European Union was presented a survey questionnaire by professional survey contractors. The questionnaire was presented to the respondents according to standard survey procedures. Data were collected in all countries during October and November 1996.

The questionnaire contained a series of questions concerning knowledge, beliefs and attitudes towards modern biotechnology. Of these items the following were used in the present study:

1   The following six items compose a scale of textbook knowledge about general biological facts. By textbook knowledge we mean the kind of knowledge that is normally acquired through formal education in school or later in adult life. The answers to these questions can directly be found in appropriate textbooks:
    (a)   There are bacteria which live from waste water.
    (b)   The cloning of living things produces exactly identical offspring.
    (c)   Viruses can be contaminated by bacteria.
    (d)   Yeast for brewing beer consists of living organisms.
    (e)   It is possible to find out in the first few months of pregnancy whether a child will have Down's Syndrome.
    (f)   More than half of the human genes are identical to those of the chimpanzee.

    A score of textbook knowledge was the sum of correctly answered textbook items. It ranges from "0" for no correct answer to "6" for all items answered correctly.

2   The following three items target imaginary beliefs about genes and genetically modified organisms. These were found to be relevant bits of beliefs in pilot interviews and focus group studies. Although there are correct textbook answers to the imaginary items, they constitute a way of reasoning that is sufficiently separate from textbook knowledge to warrant separate treatment.
    (a)   Ordinary tomatoes do not contain genes while genetically modified tomatoes do.
    (b)   By eating a genetically modified fruit, a person's genes could also become modified.

(c)   Genetically modified animals are always bigger than ordinary ones.

All the items in both lists above allowed for "don't know" responses.

In an open-ended question the respondents were asked to list the newspapers and magazines they read. The data from Austria and Greece were used to divide the sample into readers of the so-called tabloid press (low media quality)[2] and the quality press (high media quality).[3] It should be noted that the term "tabloid newspaper," originally used to describe sectors of the British press, fits much better for part of the Austrian press than for the Greek. Local informants provided the categorizations.

For the longitudinal media data a sample of the opinion leading press was randomly selected between the years 1973 and 1996 in several countries. Each sampled issue was scanned in its entirety for articles reporting about biotechnology, genetic engineering, or related issues.

Politics, Media, and Images

For Austrians, the year 1996 for the first time meant a massive publicity of modern biotechnology. In this year several biotechnology firms aired their plans to release genetically modified crop under normal agricultural conditions. This publicity was brought about by somewhat confused political reactions and societal resistance, which was extensively covered, and sometimes whipped up by the media. On average, Austrians indicate the highest score of having recently heard or read about

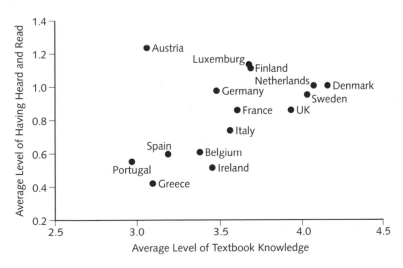

Figure 10.1   Scatterplot: EU countries, average level of textbook knowledge by average level of having heard or read about biotechnology.

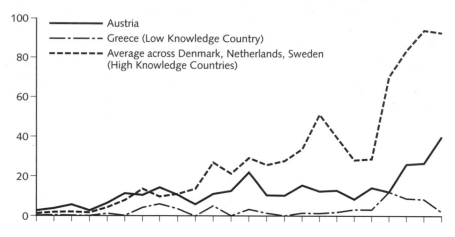

Figure 10.2 Media intensity data (N of counts) adapted from Durant, Bauer, & Gaskell (1998, p. 291).

biotechnology. Figure 10.1 plots the 15 EU countries on the two dimensions "Having read or heard about biotechnology" and "Average level of textbook knowledge.

Figure 10.1 also shows that, on average, Austrians are among the European nations with a low level of textbook knowledge. Taken together, this finding indicates that Austrians were massively confronted with a new technology for which they were widely unprepared due to a low level of media reporting in the preceding years. Given the extent of public awareness, it can be safely stated that biotechnology represented a highly relevant topic in 1996, which is one of the first criteria to expect a social representation to exist as shown by Wagner, Valencia, and Elejabarrieta (1996).

Figure 10.2 contrasts the intensity of media reporting in Austria with Greece representing the three *low knowledge countries* in the lower left corner and with the three *high knowledge countries* assembled in the upper right corner of Figure 10.1. Unfortunately, from the cluster of the three low knowledge countries, Greece, Portugal, and Spain, Greece is the only country from which suitable media data were available.

Figure 10.2 clearly shows that the onset of massive media reporting was different in the three groups of countries. Denmark, Netherlands, and Sweden have had a high level of media intensity years before the onset of media discourse in Austria. In Greece biotechnology gained no significant publicity until 1998. The graph in Figure 10.2 depicts all articles scanned to contain biotechnology. For articles specifically reporting about genetic engineering the differences are even more striking (Seifert & Wagner, 1998, p. 251).

The intensity of media reporting is suggestively correlated with the time of onset and intensity of governmental, legal, and NGO policy activity. Until recently, Greece (Marouda-Chatjoulis, Stathopoulou, & Sakellaris, 1998) and Austria (Wagner, Torgersen, Seifert, Grabner, & Lehner, 1998) had by far the lowest level of political activity in comparison to the high levels and early onset in Denmark (Jelsøe et al., 1998), Sweden (Fjæstad, Olsson, Olofsson, & v. Bergmann-Winberg, 1998) and the Netherlands (Midden, Hamstra, Gutteling, & Smink, 1998).

Austria, hence, assumes a particular position in Europe. In the year 1996 it had intense political debate, at times heated media coverage about biotechnology and therefore a high level of contact with the topic, a generally low level of textbook knowledge about biology, and additionally the highest level of resistance to the products of biotechnology, specifically crops, food and other nonmedical applications (Wagner et al., 1998b).

In psychological terms the majority of Austrians was confronted massively but late with issues of safety, risk, and technical details related to genetic engineering. The average person was not prepared to understand what this flood of media reporting was about and had little access to the scientific complexities in genetic manipulations and the potential risks involved.

Accordingly, a rather high proportion of respondents to the questionnaire, that is 29% of opponents and 13% of nonopponents, directly or indirectly express fear about biotechnology in the open-ended question of the survey questionnaire. They justify their fear with their ignorance. They fear the unfamiliar new technology and the artificial food it will produce that eventually will be part of their everyday diet whether they want it or not.

In this situation people are likely to develop their own understanding of how biotechnology works and what its products are likely to be. The public will symbolically cope with this frightening situation in order to reduce insecurity and to settle on a shared understanding that allows communication about the unfamiliar technology. Collective coping in this case involves creating and converging on images, which symbolically represent the basics of how biotechnology works on a mundane and everyday level.

Three elements of such a relatively shared image were part of the questionnaire:

1 The belief in genes being something artificial and extraneous to natural beings which are brought into living beings only by biotechnological means (belief in natural tomatoes not containing genes, "tomato image"),

2 The belief that these genes, once introduced into foodstuff, can infect a person ingesting such food ("contagion" or "infection image"), and

3 The belief that genes introduced into living beings makes them bigger or monstruous ("monster image").

Figure 10.3 The "media image" of biotechnology. (Reprinted from SALZBURGER NACHRICHTEN, March 19, 1997. © Erwin Johann Wodicka.)

In modern society images rarely become shared if they do not also share a common cultural basis and if there are no mass media which take on this image and which provide for its necessary widespread publicity. Particularly the press plays a crucial role in this "epidemic" process (Sperber, 1990). The "tomato image," being the core of all further imagery, is nicely illustrated by photographs which rather frequently appeared in several newspapers and magazines at the beginning of the year 1997 in Austria. They all depict red "healthy looking" tomatoes that receive an injection by what looks like a scientist or physician (Figure 10.3). When facing the people's initiative "Against applying genetic engineering in Austria" (*Anti-Gentechnik-Volksbegehren*) in the first half of 1997, primarily the tabloid press – being partisan in favor of this initiative – used such photographs as well as headlines such as "For a gene-free Austria," "Against gene-tomatoes," etc. These headlines resonate with the public's representations we found in the survey conducted a few months earlier. Collective symbolic coping, hence, presupposes intense media activity whose images, however, would not become widely shared if there were not the same or similar thoughts and images already widely held by the individuals. Specific susceptibility of the individuals is a prerequisite for images and beliefs to catch on widely.

Textbook Knowledge and Images

Across all 15 EU member countries 30.7% of respondents believe that natural tomatoes do not possess genes whereas genetically modified ones do, 23.7% believe that eating genetically modified food may infect one's organism, and 35.4% maintain that genetically modified organisms are always bigger than natural ones. Hence, a substantial proportion of the European population believes in images that we think pertain to a social representation of biotechnology.

If these beliefs and images were part of a social representation, a significant portion of respondents should hold either two or even all three images jointly. This should be significantly more pronounced in Austria where people were confronting biotechnology as a topic in media discourse only very recently. Furthermore, if the belief in those images results from recent symbolic coping processes, they should be relatively independent from textbook knowledge that was acquired in school and later formal and informal education. Figure 10.4 depicts the percentage of people at each level of textbook knowledge in Austria, in low knowledge countries and in high knowledge countries.

A 3 x 6 ANOVA cross-cutting the three groups of countries (Austria versus low versus high knowledge countries) by level of textbook knowledge (1 through 6) for the relationships depicted in the three graphs shows a significant main effect for country on each of the three measures of belief. More Austrians simultaneously believe in all three images ($F(2,6643) = 16.14$, $p < 0.001$), fewer Austrians explicitly reject them ($F(2,6643) = 45.79$, $p < 0.001$), and fewer Austrians admit ignorance than respondents in high as well as low knowledge countries ($F(2,6643) = 13.24$, $p < 0.001$). This is true across virtually all levels of textbook knowledge. The high level of factually incorrect acceptance at low and high levels of textbook knowledge, the low level of admitted ignorance and the low level of people who correctly reject the three images in Austria can be taken to indicate the pressures to try to understand what biotechnology and its products are about. They are challenged by the new perspectives this technology offers and try hard to cope with it on a symbolic level. They are more subjectively confident to know whether the images are true or not as expressed by their low level of admitted ignorance.

It must be noted that the present analysis checking for beliefs in three images simultaneously uses a rather strict criterion. Therefore the 10 % rate of endorsement by Austrians does not look very impressively and one may question whether it is legitimate to speak of a shared representation. However, a much higher proportion of people in Austria (about 35 to 40%) and in other countries believe in at least two of the three images simultaneously. The reported effects remain virtually the same if the criterion is set to simultaneously believing in two or three images.

It is somewhat surprising that the received wisdom of textbook knowledge does

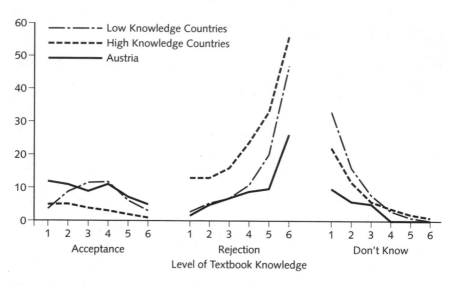

Figure 10.4 Percentage of respondents in each of six levels of textbook knowledge who simultaneously accept or reject three images, or who admit ignorance, in Austria, in low knowledge countries, and in high knowledge countries. *Note* Respondents with acquiescence response patterns were excluded.

not seem to be of much help in scientifically veridical understanding. Although the popular beliefs are far from being veridical images of what genetic engineering is about, that is, they are outspokenly wrong in scientific terms, respondents do not seem to connect to their textbook knowledge base, particularly if they possess higher than average knowledge levels. Fewer of the more knowledgeable Austrians admit ignorance in this matter (scoring "don't know"), fewer Austrians correctly reject these images (scoring "false"), and relatively more Austrians accept these images at face value (scoring "true") than respondents from either high or low knowledge countries.

Media Consumption and Beliefs in Images

It has been shown that media, specifically tabloid style newspapers, explicitly transport bits and pieces of this representation in their coverage of biotechnological issues. Consequently, readers of tabloid style newspapers should be more likely to share in the tomato – infection – monster image than readers of quality newspapers. Figure 10.5 presents the data.

A 2 x 2 x 2 ANOVA cross-cutting media quality (low versus high) by level of

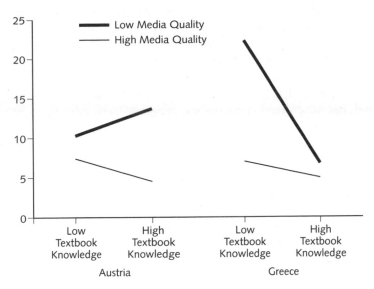

Figure 10.5 Relative frequency of respondents simultaneously holding three images by quality of consumed newspapers, level of textbook knowledge (dichotomized), and Austria versus Greece (low knowledge countries).

textbook knowledge (low versus high) by country (Austria versus Greece as a representative of the group of low knowledge countries) shows the interaction between country, level of textbook knowledge, and media quality ($F(1,1129) = 5.54$, $p < 0.05$), a simple interaction between country and level of textbook knowledge ($F(1,1129) = 4.68$), $p < 0.05$), and main effect for level of textbook knowledge ($F(1,1129) = 4.21$, $p < 0.05$) and for media quality ($F(1,1129) = 14.63$, $p < 0.0005$) to be significant.

Overall, a higher proportion of readers of the low quality press (13.3%(unweighted)) than readers of the high quality press (5.9%(unweighted)) and a higher proportion of respondents with a higher than average level of textbook knowledge (11.6%(unweighted)) than respondents with a lower than average level of textbook knowledge (7.6%(unweighted)) believes in three images. However, the interactions between media quality and level of textbook knowledge run opposite in the two countries (Figure 10.5). While more readers of the low quality press in Austria tend to believe in three images if they have a higher than average level of textbook knowledge (13.6%) than if they have a lower than average knowledge (10.4%), the effect is opposite in Greece. Readers of the low quality press believe less in three images the more knowledgeable they are (21.6% (low knowledge) versus 7.5% (low knowledge)).

We interpret the finding that consumed press quality reverses the expected effect of knowledge in Austria to be a consequence of symbolic coping during an intense political and media debate. It connects to the finding that subjects tend to be the more confident and the more extreme in their opinion the more imminent a transaction based on this opinion is and the more similar in opinion others are perceived (Gerard & Orive, 1987; Gerard & Wagner, 1981; Holtz & Miller, 1985). During 1996 and later the situation in Austria was radically different from the situation in other European countries. Symbolic coping was triggered by the sudden appearance of genetically engineered products accompanied by a political debate which made it mandatory for the average man and woman on the street to take sides. The tabloid section of the press became partisan of the anti-gene-technology movement, thereby creating a feeling of group cohesiveness and of a common cause. At the same time the press – either implicitly or explicitly – offered ready-made iconic representations of the technology. Consequently, the societal pressures to take a position on a political issue raised the people's confidence in their beliefs and imaginations, be they scientifically veridical or not. This was particularly the case, when they already possessed higher than average levels of textbook knowledge about biology, which for the majority of respondents is probably only superficial. Knowledge, even if it is superficial, additionally bolsters confidence in new interpretations of challenging facts such as biotechnology. This was shown already by the virtually zero level of admitted ignorance, that is, "don't know" responses by more than average knowledgeable respondents in the foregoing section (Figure 10.4).

Photographs like the one in Figure 10.3 did virtually not appear in the press before the survey was fielded in fall 1996. They were extensively used in several newspapers before and after the people's initiative in spring 1997. The convergence of people's imagination and the press's use of such photographs as metaphors of biotechnology in a political matter can probably be explained at the more fundamental level of a shared cultural background. It is this background, which determines a more general aesthetic consensus about which images are good to think and which are not.

The Representation of "Killer Tomatoes" as a Social Construction

Social representations are a result of collective symbolic coping processes. A group confronts a new and therefore unfamiliar phenomenon such as biotechnology and its products which promises to penetrate people's everyday life. However, the novel offers not only a promise but also a potential threat. The media discourse develops rapidly, and there is also considerable public debate about the legitimacy of crop release experiments. The debate finally culminates in a people's initiative and the associated exchange of arguments. Missing the necessary cognitive means of understanding this technology, people are nevertheless called upon to take positions and express opinions. In order to do this, people need a symbolic handle for the new phenomenon, that is, the members of the group form a representation . The way to do this at an early stage of a representation's sociogenesis is to anchor it in preexisting knowledge.

Being a product of collective symbolic coping, the present representation is a collectively elaborated construct. Whereas scientific knowledge is produced under strict and explicit methodological guidelines, common sense and representations are formed informally. Scientific knowledge is a means for material coping with some outside world and its truth condition "is that condition which guarantees that actions based on that [knowledge] will succeed" (Papineau, 1990, p. 27). Material coping with brute facts, however, is different from symbolic coping (Wagner, 1998). Representations allow people who are not in the possession of the theoretical and methodological assets of scientists to understand otherwise inaccessible phenomena.

What the public elaborates has to fit an aesthetic consensus. This means that representations, to make the unfamiliar familiar, connect to everyday experience and established beliefs. This is achieved through objectification by metaphor where an unfamiliar phenomenon is structurally linked to a familiar one. In the present example we observe a series of metaphorical relationships being reflected in the images.

The manipulation of organisms is familiar from medicine and chemistry. People generally know that foreign substances can be injected into organisms, for example in inoculations, and it is not far-fetched to anchor one's understanding of genetic manipulation in this experience. Consequently, genes, in this imagination, are something foreign to the manipulated organism and hence genetically engineered tomatoes should possess them, while naturally grown ones should not. The associated belief in infection follows straightforwardly. Foreign substances, like for example bacteria, are known to pass from one organism to another. Hence, genes might very well do the same. Finally the belief in the monstrosity of genetically engineered organisms is also related. "Frankenstein" is not far from these imaginations and in fact often appears in interviews.

A video spot launched by an Austrian tabloid paper in 1998 vividly illustrates this complex of interdependent images. It shows a scientific laboratory where some men in white coats inject a substance into an apparently natural tomato. Subsequently this tomato grows to a monstrous red globe until it explodes and injures the men. Although the producers of this spot certainly know that this can just be a metaphoric image, they perfectly mimic what a large portion of the public believes and what we observed as the interrelated beliefs in gene-tomatoes, infection and monstrosity. These images capture the "What is it" and the "How does it work" part of the social representation "genetic engineering." We know from other studies that the representation in its entirety is actually much richer and also embraces moral aspects as well as other areas of knowledge which do not concern us here (Gaskell, this volume; Wagner et al. 1998a).

By giving shape to the public's understanding, the representation defines the characteristics of the social object "biotechnology." Although the term and associated scientific practices existed in laboratories the world over even before it became a matter of interest to the majority of people, biotechnology as a public phenomenon did not exist prior to its being represented. What is or was known in the scientific laboratories under the label of biotechnology is not the same as its public perception. In the social representations approach the public's images are not interpreted as a false or biased representation of the scientists' understanding, but as a reality of its own. Being more concerned with its symbolic than with instrumental value, this representation determines and is determined by the ways and forms of discourse in public and political arenas. The representation of biotechnology is not only socially constructed in the discursive movement of a collectivity, but is itself constructive by giving birth to social objects. The representation is a shared way of talking and thinking about a target phenomenon. Therefore a representation logically precedes the social object "biotechnology" while temporally they are coexistent.

At least immediately before and after our data were collected, the images were a true representation of biotechnology for a considerable fraction of the Austrian population due to their being conventional. The people's beliefs in gene-tomatoes, infection, and monstrosity are confirmed and warranted assertible by newspaper headlines and the fact that thousands of others share in the rejection of genetically engineered crops and food. Although the opponents of biotechnology in Austria (with the exception of diverse NGOs and the Green Party) do not form a well-defined social group, they recognize each other in communication, just as they recognize the newspapers to read for maintaining homogamic discourse. Social representations are confirmed by fulfilling their function as a means for affiliating and communication.

We think that the findings from the present study on the one hand replicate some results reported in Moscovici's (1976a) study on the image and public of psychoanalysis in France in the 1950s. Both Moscovici's and the present study are concerned with a new scientific approach becoming widely popularized. Both illustrate the people's use of experientially proximal source domains for anchoring, the objectification of common-sense thinking about the science in figurative structures, and different styles of media reporting such as "diffusion" used by the quality press and "propaganda" by the tabloid press. Alternatively, the present study transcends and complements the study of psychoanalysis by focusing on a phenomenon with intense proximal relevance for the average consumer. While the political left's resistance against psychoanalysis in France was part of an ideological war, the resistance of wide fractions of the European public to genetically engineered organisms results from concerns for health, ecology, the make-up of everyday food, and the morally tolerable (Wagner et al., 1998a). Further, the advent of psychoanalysis had neither legal nor policy implications in France, while biotechnology and its products do have such implications in all countries. Third, in the present research we could study the public's symbolic coping with biotechnology at a cross-national, or, if you so want, cross-cultural level. Such comparison adds new perspectives to social representation research.

This comparative perspective as well as the diachronic data allows a closer look at the evolution and the changes a representation can undergo with time. We expect that certain elements of the Austrian's representation found in 1996 will evolve and approximate those that already exist in countries with a longer history of contact with the technology. We also expect that in countries with low contact and awareness of biotechnology's challenges in 1996, such as Greece, Italy, Portugal, and Spain, a collective symbolic coping process and representation will emerge in the near future. We dare to predict that the course and structure of this process will probably be similar to the Austrian, but due to cultural and historical divergences the potential source domains of images will differ.

Conclusion

The argument put forward in the present research is based on a wide variety of data and methods ranging from recent political and media history to a survey at a specific point in time. It is pure coincidence that Austria had its first serious encounter with genetic engineering at the time when the European-wide survey was fielded. Collective symbolic coping and the resulting social representations are always historically relative processes and can usually not be studied under the controlled conditions of a laboratory. Therefore the findings and interpretations offered here do not strictly prove a well-derived hypothesis; nor does this research imply that symbolic coping processes and sociogenesis of representations always follow the lines presented here. As lamentable these restrictions are for a social psychologist, so true it is that social reality rarely does us the favor to comply to our methodological desires for control and replicability. Suffice it to say that the theory of collective symbolic coping and social representations opens a wide and fruitful field of research to the societally interested psychologist.

Notes

This chapter reports research that was conducted as part of the EU Concerted Action, contract #BIO4–CT95–0043 (DG12-SSMA) granted to John Durant, Museum of Science and Industry, London. The Austrian research was funded by the Austrian Fonds zur Forderung der wissenschaftlichen Forschung, #P11849-SOZ, granted to the first author.

The authors gratefully acknowledge the help of Angela Stathopoulou in categorizing the Greek newspapers and thank all participants of the national teams participating in the EU Concerted Action without whose direct or indirect contribution to the data collection the present study would not have been possible. We also thank Sofia Daimonakou for helpful comments on an earlier draft of this chapter.

1   Note that innovative processes that involve relatively new interpretations of phenomona may occur as well. In everyday life, however, this plays a marginal role.

2   The newspapers of the low quality group in Austria were "Kronenzeitung", "Kleine Zeitung," "Täglich Alles," and "die Ganze Woche"; in Greece they were "Adesmeytos Typos," "Ethnos," and "Eleytheros."

3   The newspapers of the high quality group in Austria were: "Kurier," "Salzburger Nachrichten," "Der Standard," and "Die Presse"; in Greece they were "Apogeymatini," "Bima," "Eleytherotypia," "Kathimerini," "NEA," and "Risospastes."

11

Social Representations, Public Life, and Social Construction

Sandra Jovchelovitch

Introduction

In this chapter I want to advance some ideas that are concentrated around one main proposition: social representations are a form of symbolic knowledge intrinsic to public life. Public life, I argue, is the place in which they are generated, develop, meet other representations, change and, if the social and historical conditions so determine, die. In order to develop this argument, I shall proceed in two steps. First, I shall address the links between social representations, as a specific type of social knowledge, and the public sphere, as a specific type of social space. There are various types of social knowledge and not all are social representations – think, for instance, of science and collective representations. In the same manner social spaces vary in form and configuration and not all of them can be described as a public sphere – think, for instance, of the family. By addressing what is specific to the public sphere I hope to show what is specific to social representations and how they differ from Durkheim's notion of collective representations. This first step should make clear the conception I wish to advance about the ontological status of representations, and provide the basis for the second part of my discussion where I address the problem of construction, and more specifically, the limits of construction.

I argue that construction in social representations theory is directly related to the symbolic function of representations. It is through a careful assessment of the symbolic register that we can best understand the constructivism of social representations. At the same time, and paradoxically to some, I argue that precisely because symbolic knowledges such as social representations are social, cultural, and historical they cannot fully construct reality. It is, I argue, in the properties of a socially constructed knowledge, dependent on history and culture, that we find the reasons which explain why symbolic knowledge cannot be taken as the measure of all reality. In short, it is because knowledge itself is socially constructed that it does not fully construct reality. It constructs partial realities, it constructs human reality, but these are not, and should not, be understood as the whole of reality. While advocating the constructed character of all human experience, I argue that a strong constructivist perspective recognizes that reality goes far beyond what we can make of it.

Traditional and Detraditionalized Public Spheres: From Collective to Social Representations

Under which conditions can a type of knowledge such as social representations emerge? This question directs us to two essential, and interrelated, dimensions of the production of social knowledge: the problem of genesis and the problem of context of production. In more than one way, this question can be answered through a consideration of Moscovici's original work on psychoanalysis (Moscovici, 1976a) and his earlier accounts of why the Durkheimian concept of collective representations was transformed into the social psychological concept of social representations (Moscovici, 1988, 1989).

For Moscovici, as for Durkheim before him, the genesis of social knowledge is to be found in the social context. The link between knowledge and the social context of its production is a problem that permeates the theory of social representations from its inception. Moscovici's *oeuvre* is, in many ways, an attempt to provide an answer to the most fundamental assumption established by the work of Durkheim and his followers, even the most reticent ones: when societal conditions change so does social knowledge. This assertion is crucial to the theoretical edifice of the theory of social representations and to all those traditions of thought in psychology, sociology and anthropology which, deeply influenced by phenomenological traditions, sought to establish that knowledge – any form of knowledge, from science to common sense – is bound to the social context of its production.

From this perspective, the usage of "social context" is more than an abstraction or an added variable in a research program. Indeed, the link between social knowledge and social context demands an understanding of what gives form to a social context, what makes one social context different from another and how these differences produce variety in social psychological phenomena. It poses the need to unravel theoretically and empirically how the structural features of a social context are decisive in accounting for the genesis, development, and transformation of any type of social knowledge. Thus once we accept that social knowledge is shaped by social context, we face two new requirements. The first is to inquire in depth, and conceptualize, the features of a social context, and the second is to ask what happens to knowledge when a social context undergoes change.

The difference between collective representations, as described by Durkheim, and social representations, as proposed by Moscovici, can be explained precisely by a careful assessment of the social contexts which Durkheim and Moscovici studied and sought to understand. From collective to social representations the change is clearly related to transformations in social context. Moscovici himself provides an illuminating statement in this regard in his reply to Jahoda in the pages of the *European Journal of Social Psychology* (Moscovici, 1988). There he makes clear why the concept moved from collective to social representations. He writes:

> In our days, therefore, collective representations as it used to be defined no longer is a general category but a special kind of representations among many with different characteristics. It seems an aberration, in any case, to consider representations as homogenous and shared as such by a whole society. What we wished to emphasize by giving up the word collective was this plurality of representations and their diversity within a group. . . . In effect, what we had in mind were representations that were always in the making, in the context of interrelations and actions that were themselves always in the making. (p. 219)

More recently, Moscovici has also stated:

> I prefer to use only "social" because it seems to me that a cultural belief or a ritual in modern times is secularized and embedded or constituted in the society, a society in which conversations and communications between individuals become historically more important than in more traditional societies. (Moscovici & Marková, 1998, p. 400)

In both quotations Moscovici refers to the more fluid dynamic of modern societies, where worldviews and practices are contested and negotiated, and the space for a homogenous, unquestioned, and single view of the world is very limited indeed. In opting for "social" and dropping "collective" Moscovici is acutely guided by the problem of plurality and the renewed importance of communication in modern societies. As he points out, it would be an "aberration" to think today of representations consensually shared by a whole society. Societies have changed and very few, if any, remain traditional in the sense described by Durkheim.

What has changed then in the social contexts considered by Durkheim and Moscovici? It is my contention that the crucial difference between the social contexts considered by Durkheim and Moscovici's refers to changes in the public sphere, and more specifically, to the issue of tradition versus detraditionalization in public spaces. Indeed, to understand the societal features which are key to the production of social representations and, at the same time, undermine collective representations we need to examine the process of detraditionalization in the public sphere. This process can be better understood through the concept of the public sphere, as developed by Habermas (1989, 1992) in his seminal work on the topic.

Habermas has described in detail the concept and phenomenon of the public sphere (1989). His account remains to this date the most comprehensive analysis of this new category of capitalist society. In it, Habermas extensively discusses the emergence, development, and transformation of the bourgeois public sphere in Europe and defines it as a space where citizens meet and talk to each other in a fashion that guarantees access to all. It is a social space where:

1   All members, at least ideally or in the word of the law, meet as peers and discuss and decide in conditions of equality (the first article of any bourgeois constitution refers to the equality of all men before the law);
2   Where the arguments of authority are replaced by the authority of arguments;
3   Where access is open to all and visibility guides the procedures and;
4   Where rational dialogue and nothing else establishes the legitimacy and subsequent authority of a proposition.

According to Habermas this set of assumptions is ushered in by the achievements of an age that gradually freed itself from tradition and unquestioned historical orderings and sought in rational debate and democratic dialogue the response for matters of common concern. Historically, this can be located around the set of ideas and events, which stemming out of the European Enlightenment, came to define what is called Modernity. Centralized sources of authority, expressed by the power of both Church and State, gradually lost ground to the emergence of an informed public of citizens who together construct a *public sphere*. The public sphere and its principles are produced by – and in turn, help to produce – a social space where argumentation and rational dialogue are the key entry points to deal with difference in perspectives. In it, participants are recognized by the quality of what they have to say and not by the authority or wealth of their position.

It is obvious that these assumptions have never been fully realized. Habermas has been extensively criticized for failing to realize that the liberal model of the public sphere rested, in fact, in a number of important exclusions, of which women and workers were the most flagrant (Landes, 1988; Eley, 1992). Other commentators on Habermas work have noted, however, that the principles under which the public sphere sought to function remain normative ideals, which can help us to question and challenge the quality of public (Holub, 1991; Calhoun, 1992).

Another stream of criticism has pointed out, correctly in my view, that other public spheres need to be recognized, even if they are not guided by the principles described by Habermas (Fraser, 1990). While agreeing with the importance of the principles of the Habermasian concept of the public sphere as normative ideals, I believe that it is important to recognize that there are public spheres that do not conform to them. There are other "publics" that also need to be recognized. It would be incorrect, in my view, to call a public space "public sphere" only if it is guided by the mostly unrealized principles described by Habermas.[1] Think, for instance, of a market place in traditional societies or of ritualized ceremonies, such as carnivals, and other types of religious celebration. They are certainly different from the liberal model dominant in the West. They are, nonetheless, public spaces in so far as they constitute a space that (a) is shared by all members of the community and (b) is the stage for issues related to the common life of the community. The principles that organize the sharing of that space and the location of people in it are just *other* than the ones adopted by the liberal model of the public sphere.

It is here, I suggest, that we need to introduce the problem of tradition and detraditionalization. By considering traditional and detraditionalized public spheres, it is possible to do justice to the fundamental differences in the knowledge they produce while retaining the nonetheless fundamental proposition that all social knowledge is produced in a public space. These differences become clear when considering the set of assumptions underlying public spaces in traditional societies. The principles of detraditionalized public spheres stand in clear opposition to the basic rules of so-called traditional societies where:

1   The authority of some few sacred people defines the legitimacy of worldviews and constrains the access of members;
2   Where secrecy guarantees the sacred and;
3   Where inequalities in status structure the display of views by some members and the silencing of others.

In this type of traditional society what kind of social knowledge is possible? As Durkeim (1996, first published 1898) and Durkheim & Mauss (1963) showed, what emerges from this type of social context are collective representations.[2] They are a type of everyday knowledge which all members share and which operates as a full binding force; they are produced through conditions of strong asymmetry between participants; they are strongly bound to, and dependent upon, ritual, and the conditions for their change are minimal. Collective representations are a type of knowledge resistant to experience, argumentation, and logical proof, which relies mainly, if not purely, on the social bond and its subjective value. They have the force of a social fact in the Durkheimian sense and fulfill functions of social integration and reproduction while guaranteeing a strong solidarity between those who share them.

To advance slightly the second part of this chapter, which will tackle the problem of construction, in this type of knowledge reality *is* its representation. Here, the social knowledge constructed by a community in the form of collective representations constructs, in the sense of fully defining for participants, all reality. It is the social world that shapes and circumscribes all that exists, and the community, with its peculiar hierarchy, is the fundamental source of authority. In this type of society the *subjective of the social* (i.e., everything related to the power of the social bond and the feelings of allegiance and obedience it entails) has primacy over the objective (what happens to be the case) and there is very little scope for individual variation.

We still find instances of this primacy in the way some young people find they "need" to conform to what is considered to be the "right thing to do" by their communities. Individual aspirations, which are shaped by today's multitude of options circulating in public spaces, clash with the rules of more traditional communities, where members are expected to live by, and comply to, the rules established traditionally in ritualized practices and collective representations. Here one can understand why Durkheim has been criticized for his tendency to speak of society as a homogenous unity (Giddens, 1971; Moscovici, 1988). The claustrophobic nature of his overtotalizing conception of the social is evident, for social conflict in Durkheim is always related to the oppositions between the individual and the collective. The notion that society can also be conceptualized as a system where there is tension and contradiction between different groups, or collectives, is quite absent from his sociology (Giddens, 1978).

Before I proceed any further it is important to note that the descriptions above correspond more or less to ideal types and that neither traditional societies nor detraditionalized public spheres are fully immune to the influence of their opposite. Traditional public spheres, however, are much more resistant to the introduction of novelty/difference and, indeed, the predominant form of everyday knowledge (collective representations) that they produce is especially apt to fulfill the function of resisting novelty and the transformations it may entail. Traditional societies call upon the power and emotional dimension of the social bond to reproduce the knowledge they believe to be right and needed to perpetuate their way of life. In detraditionalized public spheres, on the contrary, both strong elements of tradition and strong challenge to tradition exist side by side. These diverse tendencies meet, clash and are constantly negotiated in the public sphere (Beck, Giddens, & Lash, 1994; Heelas, Lash, & Morris, 1996; Thompson, 1995).

This dynamics was particularly clear in my own research on the health beliefs of the Chinese community in England (Jovchelovitch & Gervais, 1999; Gervais & Jovchelovitch, 1998). We found that the older generation of Chinese people holds on to the collective representations which express the culture, the traditions and the identity of the Chinese people. They also expect their offspring to follow on their values and representations and rely heavily on the power of family hierarchy and community bonds to see this through. The youngsters, in their turn, are torn between the expectations of their traditional community and the reality of a detraditionalized, Western, public sphere where they were born and grew up. Accordingly, they expressed a mixed representational field made of the clashes and negotiations resulting from their experience as *BBCs* (British Born Chinese).

The experience of the Chinese, as that of so many other diasporic communities, sharply exemplifies the antinomies of detraditionalized public spheres, where fluidity and multiplicity in knowledge constitute the dominant way of life. It is in this type of detraditionalized public sphere, I suggest, that we find the conditions under which social representations emerge. They are a form of social knowledge that comes into being in a social arena characterized by the mobility, and even more important, the diversity of social groups, a high degree of reflexivity propitiated by the multiple encounters of different traditions, the massive and widespread circulation of information through the development of the mass media (and more recently, the World Wide Web) and last, but not least, the liberal principles of equal access to, and full visibility in, the public sphere. If social knowledge in all its forms is bound to the social world in which it is produced then, *per force*, social representations cannot be equated to collective representations. Social representations at times encompass, at times reject, and most of the time derive from, collective representations, but they cannot be immediately equated to them. A new public sphere calls for, and produces, a new type of social knowledge.

Social Representations and the Appropriation of the New

As stated above, contrary to collective representations, which tend to appear as the dominant form of social knowledge in traditional public spheres, social representations are symbolic forms typical of more contemporary, detraditionalized public spheres. They are a new type of social knowledge: a social knowledge particularly suitable to cope with the new, and ontologically and epistemologically bound to the macrosocial developments of our time. These developments have lead to, among other phenomena, a clouding in the processes of making sense of the world, to a complexification in the "nesting of representations" to use an image proposed by Rommetveit (personal communication, 1997). This means that communities of people now must handle the diversity of realities that constitutes their life horizons and find new symbolic strategies to make sense of them (Jovchelovitch, 1997, Gervais & Jovchelovitch, 1998). Some of these realities are utterly new, some are grounded in well-established traditions, and some belong to the merging of realities that takes place in highly mediated societies. In any case, sense is attained, sustained, and transformed in a manner that transcends the limitations traditionally imposed by context.

Context today goes beyond place and depends on a number of spatial and temporal displacements that upset our traditional dependence on locale. This, of course, does not erase the importance of locales in the production of sense; it can, in fact, provoke a recrudescence in the importance conferred upon the local (as in the revival of local identities vis-à-vis the threat of globalization). However, locale alone is no longer sufficient to explain the formation of knowledge and how human life is coping with the increasing otherness embedded in the various knowledges that shape local experience and ways of life. This otherness derives from a new regime of objects in the social arena; an arena that has enlarged and shrunk at once, and brings the interplay between near and remote, familiar and unfamiliar, same and other to new degrees of radicalization.

It is by taking into account these transformations in the public sphere that we can fully appreciate the innovative character of Moscovici's theory of social representations and what, in my view, constitutes its breaking ground as a social psychological theory. When Moscovici formulated the initial postulates of the theory, the signs of a detraditionalized, late modern, public sphere were still in an incipient form. However, his empirical study on the transformations psychoanalysis underwent as it moved from one social group to another, provided the evidence to ground the production and transformation of social knowledge in the vivid dynamics of the social milieu.

La psychanalyse, son image et son public (Moscovici, 1976a) can also be read as a study about the manner in which psychoanalysis is appropriated and resignified as it moves from one social group to another and penetrates different lifeworlds, different horizons, different identities, and different projects. In short, what happens with psychoanalysis when it leaves the enclosed walls of clinical practice, the narrow circles of training and expert societies, and falls, as it were, in the real world of everyday life? What type of process is at stake when a specific type of knowledge – in this case scientific knowledge[3] – circulates through the social fabric far beyond the source of its production? The answer was clear to Moscovici: this knowledge changes. It changes in the same way it changes the people who have changed it in the first place. Thus, psychoanalysis was not only what its "owners" would make of it, but it became a different phenomenon as it penetrated the lifeworlds of urban – liberal professionals, catholics, and communists, the social groups Moscovici studied.

This difference, or internal disjunction in the representation of a social object, can only occur because it takes place in a society where worldviews are removed from one single source of authority and legitimization and confront each other in more or less equal terms in the public sphere. Think, for instance, what would happen if the psychoanalytic institution could determine what every single social group should think of it? As in a photocopying line, social knowledge would be a mere reproduction (although not even a copy is a perfect reproduction). However, there is no one single institution in a detraditionalized public sphere capable of imposing its authority without some form of contest. The process of institutionalizing specific representations in these societies is entangled in a complex network of competing interests, representations, and powers. Diversity of worldviews engenders representational systems that express variety and reminds us that the phenomenon of social representations is as much about shared and consensual symbolic codes as it is about contradictory and unresolved ones.

The diversity and plurality of the public sphere produces a great deal of unfamiliarity, or strangeness. In fact, it is the strangeness introduced by differences and contradictions that sets into motion the processes of anchoring and objectification, through which the unfamiliar is tamed and made familiar. Anchoring is nothing but the attempt to settle a new, and therefore strange, meaning into the established geography of symbols of a community. Objectification, in its turn, gives to novelty a concrete, almost "natural," face. Anchoring and objectification are triggered to "settle accounts," as it were, with new meaning, to make it known, to reduce its threat or the fears it generates, to make it a part of the "us" of a community of people (Gaskell, this volume; Philogène, 1999). Or, as Moscovici has put it, to make the unfamiliar familiar (Moscovici, 1984b). In this sense it is crucial to acknowledge that social representations are forms of knowledge dependent on the introduction of the "strangeness" of the other and its novelty/difference (Jovchelovitch, 1998c). Note that this other can be any empirical other, from a different social group in the same community, to a "stranger" in Schutz's sense (Schutz, 1944), who comes from far away and upholds different cultural values. The other, by its sheer condition of being other, upsets one's way of thinking and conceiving of the world and disrupts the familiarity of the taken-for-granted.

It is in order to tame the strangeness of this unfamiliarity that a new social production of knowledge starts, leading to the formation of social representations. Since they draw on the unfamiliarity produced by the other as a condition for their formation, we can say that social representations are as much about constructing meaning as they are about constructing bridges that link the diversity of perspectives constitutive of public life. In this sense, social representations are forms of knowledge structured to handle difference and have close links to the quality of public spaces. Indeed, they are themselves indicators of this quality. Public spaces that allow difference and dissent to coexist, be negotiated and reworked through dialogue and equality of access are, *par excellence*, the space in which social representations are produced. Totalitarian societies,[4] alternatively, militate against the production of everyday knowledges such as social representations. Representations produced in the bubble of social life, where different worldviews are allowed to propose their project and sustain the claims they make about reality and what the future should be, are potentially dangerous to whoever wants to sustain the supremacy of a single worldview, sure of itself and of the "truth" it proposes.

Thus what accounts for the actuality of Moscovici's study on representations of psychoanalysis, some 40 years after its publication, is precisely the contemporary character of the very questions Moscovici posed then. These questions have not aged. What happens with knowledge – any form of social knowledge – as it moves context and penetrates the lives of different social groups and is reworked by a variety of modes of communication and interaction, remains one of the most pertinent and challenging questions opened to the social sciences. It is a question as much related to the possibility of communication between different worldviews, different ways of knowing, thinking, and living, as it is to the potentials embedded in this communication and the quality of our public spaces. In my view, it also binds the theory of social representations to a theory of modernity, insofar as the distinctive phenomenon it theorizes – social representations – are bound to a modern, detraditionalized, public sphere.

This argument could be taken even further if one considers Moscovici's notion of cognitive polyphasia, something I have discussed in more detail elsewhere (Jovchelovitch, 1998b). Moscovici introduced the concept in his study about the reception of psychoanalysis in France. He found strong evidence that different types of rationality were involved in the construction of psychoanalysis in France; these rationalities were dependent on the context of their production and intended to respond to different aims. The striking finding, however, was that contrary to well-established interpretations of cognitive phenomena, the different rationalities did not correspond to different groups, in different contexts; on the contrary, they were capable of coexisting side by side in the same context, social group, and *mutatis mutantis,* the same individual. I do not have the space to expand on this notion here, but it suffices to say that social representations are described by Moscovici as sociocognitive structures guided by cognitive polyphasia, capable of encompassing different logics, which social actors draw on as a function of different contexts and practical demands. Further evidence has been gathered by a number of empirical studies in the field of social representations (see Gervais & Jovchelovitch, 1998; Wagner, Duveen, Themel, & Verma, 1999). The notion of cognitive polyphasia, which corresponds both to the polysemic nature of meaning and to the contradictory demands of a detraditionalized public sphere, consolidates the critical stance of social representations theory towards the view of a rationality identical to itself, a view dear to most theoretical developments in the history of social psychology (see Farr, 1996).

In the foregoing I have argued that social representations are forms of social knowledge bound to the public sphere. Moreover, I have shown that the type of public sphere in which social representations emerge stands in opposition to traditional public spheres such as those studied by Durkheim. In both cases, there is the underlying assumption that social knowledge is organically linked to the social context of its production. The issue posed to the theory and to the development of its empirical program is to qualify this proposition. It can do so by investigating more precisely the ways in which transformation in the structure and form of public life entails transformation in the structure and form of the social knowledge which is there produced.

I hope I have shown that, in the study in which the theory of social representations originated, Moscovici was already grappling with a form of public sphere fundamentally different from the traditional societies Durkheim sought to understand. Durkheim's collective representations possess the status of a social fact in its "hard" sense: even though they are produced by social actors, they acquire a character that is external to human action and condition all individuals of the societies in which they are present to think according to the categories they propose. Contrary to traditional societies that keep their knowledges firmly controlled by sacred individuals, sacred rituals, and sacred objects, modern societies are characterized by the reflexivity associated with social representations. Nothing is "naturally accepted," everything is under question, or as Marx would say, "all that is solid melts into the air."

Thus my analysis, starting from the question I put at the beginning of this section, has in a sense come full circle. Under which conditions can a type of knowledge such as social representations emerge? The tentative answer I provide is that they can only emerge under societal conditions which have escaped from unquestionable historical orders, where the belief in a pregiven order of things has declined or, at least, lost some of its authority, and where voices of authority become decentered, resting either on a variety of voices or, as in the case of most industrialized western societies, on self. Social representations therefore need the bubble of conversation, conflict between social groups and encounters between different perspectives to come into being. They need the process of decentration of worldviews (Habermas, 1991), a process which challenges the status of traditions and sets into motion new forms of social knowledge. These social representations, while struggling to come to terms with the provisional unfamiliarity of the new, also provide the means through which communication and action can be established.

Social Representations, Social Construction, and Reality

Let me now turn to the problem of construction. There has been much debate about what is "construction," and what construction entails in social psychology and in the social sciences in general. It is not my intention here to trace the various shades of this debate, something which has been effectively done by Danzinger (1997) in a recent review. My intention is rather to relate the problem to the issues I addressed in the first part of this chapter and to state what I believe to be the constructivist character of the theory of social representations.

In the avant-propos to the second edition *of La Psychanalyse, son image et son public* (1976a), Moscovici stressed that his original ambition with that work was to redefine the concepts and problems of social psychology, taking the phenomenon of social representations as a starting point and *reaffirming its symbolic function and power to construct reality*. It is, I argue, the careful analysis of the symbolic function that clarifies the constructivist nature of the theory of social representations. The analysis of the symbolic function also elucidates the public, cultural and historical dimensions of knowledge.

Traditional empiricist notions consider the central function of cognitive systems to submit to an a priori reality, a reality that both precedes and ignores the labors of cognition. By copying the features of this pregiven reality as closely as possible, mental representations may produce a reproduction that differs as little as possible from it. This type of conceptualization defines representation as an individual process of mentally copying the outside world. The symbolic function of representational activity, that is, the fact that a representation is a medium for investing the outside world with *meaning*, is mainly ignored. Ignoring the symbolic function has thrown subjects of research into a state of perpetual error (usually called "bias") where, from the perspective of the researcher, subjects do not remember correctly, do not perceive correctly or correctly know what they are talking about. It is a conceptualization so deeply rooted in psychology that it became mixed with the *phenomenon* of representation and contributed to produce the neobehaviorism expressed by some extreme forms of discursive psychology (for an example, see Ibañez, 1994). Ironically, in being reluctant to theorize representation or cognition, critical psychologists allow traditional cognitivism to have the ultimate say about these phenomena (Jovchelovitch, 1996).

Now it is precisely the symbolic dimension of representations that inspires researchers in the field of social representations and demarcates its difference from traditional cognitivism. The analytic focus is on what people *mean* as they engage in the task of making sense of the world in which they live and communicate with others about it. The analysis of meaning is not primarily concerned with whether a meaning is "right" or "wrong" in relation to any given reality. On the contrary, the analysis of meaning is concerned with the expressiveness of utterances, images, rituals, or any other representational act: it is concerned with the symbolic function of the representational act and its power to construct what is real to a group of people. It is through the symbolic function that we can make sense of the fact that the same social object acquires different shades of meaning to different people in different contexts and times. It is also the symbolic function that allows "errors" and "biases" to be considered as expressive symbols worth of analysis and interpretation. Moreover, the insertion of temporal and spatial considerations, which correspond to the vital problems of historical and contextualized understandings, is directly derived from the acknowledgment of the symbolic register. This has firmly established the theory of social representations in what Geertz (1993b) calls the interpretative turn in the social sciences. Inspired by Moscovici in *La Psychanalyse, son image et son public* (1976a, first published 1961) and Jodelet in *Madness and Social Representations* (1991), researchers in the field continue to pursue the symbolic dimension.

Following the constructivism opened up by the work of developmental psychologists such as Piaget (1954) and Vygotsky (1978, 1994), the theory understands that reality, and knowledge of reality in whichever form it takes, are not immediately given to us; that between the world standing out there, in itself, and any possible knowledge we can have of it, there must be a process of bridging, of mediation, of active symbolic construction. Things in themselves mean nothing; people must *represent* them and make them signify, that is, they must give them a meaning using a symbol. Through the work of representations our social world becomes a multitude of symbols which define what is real for us and allow the world of things to come into existence, as it were. It is the triangulation between people (in plural because human reality is made of a multitude of perspectives; it is not an individual person who constitutes human life), objects and the work of representations that produces the symbolic register in which we live. Humans need to construct in self and cognitive development, in work, in institutions, in culture, the conditions which make them human, and define, to a large degree, the worlds in which they live.

Social construction accounts for the complex and difficult, painful but liberating, process of producing culture and all that culture entails, that is, a cultured human being, cultured societies, cultured knowledges, and cultural artifacts. Such is the power of symbols: to construct realities, to institute them, to prescribe what should be and what should not be accepted, and to produce extremely concrete and real consequences in people's lives. This, however, does not mean that the material world or our biological make up is not important. We are both cultural and natural creatures, and our cultural being is deeply intertwined with the sorts of bodies we have and the kind of world to which they belong. Culture transforms nature, but does not do away with it and, in fact, it could not itself exist without it. Processes of cultural production, or processes of social construction, are dependent on an outside, objective and natural world, from which they draw the materials without which nothing can be constructed. To understand this substantive materiality of social life – expressed both in natural elements and in objects, machines, rooms, walls, other people, etc. – permits us to understand how the material world offers resistance to one, and the degree to which it frames and encloses the possibilities of human action and construction.

In this sense, reality is, in itself, much larger than what we socially construct. It not only contains dimensions which continually escape the knowledge we have of it, but it also contains dimensions which, even though constructed by humans, confront them as objective matter. Symbolic knowledge, as perhaps the most crucial process of cultural production, plays a pivotal role in what we can know of reality and in shaping the meaning we invest in it. But knowledge, as a representational system, as a symbolic system, cannot be equated with reality because this is analogous with saying that reality *is* our representation. Symbols, however, represent reality and reshape it; they produce meaning out of it. They are not it.

Between knowledge and its object, or between representations of reality, and reality itself, there is a difference, a disjunction, which can be clearly identified and explained if one takes seriously the historical, cultural, public, and symbolic dimensions of knowledge. I believe that a clear appreciation of these dimensions can contribute both to dissipating some problematic views in the field of social representations itself (see Wagner, 1996, for an example of what I believe is a problematic view; see also Wagner, 1998 for an interesting elaboration of his previous position) and to replying to the excesses of some streams of post-modern psychology.

The historical dimension of knowledge

Knowledge cannot be immediately equated with reality because knowledge is historical. To understand the historicity of knowledge we just need to observe how it changes over time. This can be observed both in biographies and in cultural history. It can also be observed through historical empirical evidence, both in relation to the history of sciences (Canguilhem, 1991; Lakatos & Musgrave, 1970) and to the history of mentalities (Ariés, 1960; Blumenfeld-Kosinski, 1990; Camporesi, 1995, Young, 1995). Should we have thought that knowledge is reality, the sciences would not have evolved and forms of lay thinking about, and knowing of, reality would not have changed. Take, for instance, representations of black people, of women, and of colonial peoples. These three groups of people have been historically represented as inferior and these representations have, to a large degree, defined their identity and conditions of being. These representations are real enough, but to say that black people, women, and colonial peoples are *really* inferior means to acknowledge that they can only be what the eye of a dominant beholder makes of them. This is certainly not the case, *vide* the social movements and struggles of so many excluded peoples. Knowledge therefore suffers the transformations of history and remains bound to temporal displacements that give to it a provisional character.

The cultural dimension of knowledge

Knowledge cannot be equated with reality because knowledge is cultural. To understand the cultural dimension of knowledge we just need to observe how it compares across contexts. Human societies are not homogenous and they produce different cultural assumptions that frame reality in different ways. This means to say that what is said here is different from what is said there, that there is a number of "taken-for-granteds" which vary across place, and that people in the plural, and not just one person, inhabit the world (Arendt, 1958). Should we advocate the coincidence between knowledge and reality, reality would be either pure fragmentation or pure isolation, since every culture has the right to advocate its reality as the "real one." There is a wealth of evidence coming from the social sciences that shows how different cultures produce different knowledges and operate under different assumptions concerning reality (Bhabha, 1994; Geertz, 1993a; Lévy-Bhrul, 1910/ 1985; Said, 1993, 1995; Todorov, 1992). Knowledge therefore is open to cultural variation and remains bound to the spatial displacements that give to it a limited character.[5]

The public dimension of knowledge

Knowledge cannot be equated with reality because knowledge is public. To understand the public dimension of knowledge we just need to observe how it changes in relation to the different interests and projects associated with different social groups. Society is a public field of tensions and differences, where social groups struggle to propose their views and the projects they hold for the future. Plurality in the social field coupled with power differentials in access to resources shape the knowledge formation of both individual people and social groups. The public sphere is an arena where knowledges compete, clash, and are renegotiated, making clear the distinction between knowledge and its object. In societies with decentered conditions of legitimation, that is to say, where not only one, but diverse centers of power claim authority and legitimacy to construct knowledge about reality, it becomes clear that knowledge cannot be immediately equated to the object it intends to capture. In fact, it is in the guiding principles of detraditionalized public spheres, where plurality can be fully expressed, that we see more clearly the clear distinction between representations and reality.

The acknowledgment of the historical, cultural, and public dimensions of knowledge entails, therefore, the understanding that knowledge is a limited and incomplete enterprise, and that for us, the real will always be an unfinished business. It is precisely this precarious nature of knowledge that propels the knower towards the as yet unknown dimensions of reality and therefore sustains the very possibility of development in knowledge and expansion of what is real to us. As much as knowledge constructs what is real for us, it does not apprehend the whole of reality, a domain ever open to our tentative efforts to capture it. In many respects, this position coincides, albeit in a different wording, with Wagner's (1998) discussion of the differences between a domesticated world and "somethings," i.e., things that do not deserve to be called objects. The "something," although phenomenally there, is not yet named, or symbolically "domesticated" by the representational labor of a group of people. It "has to do with what Searle (1995) calls 'brute facts,' and it is useful as a reminder that there are many things beyond socially constructed worlds" (Wagner, 1998: 306). This is something Durkheim has also shown convincingly in his attack on pragmatism (Durkheim, 1983, first published 1955).

To recognize that the unknown is constitutive of our efforts to know goes hand in hand with the human struggle for accuracy in cognition, since it is not true that "everything goes." There is an almost obvious problem in stating that "reality is what I, or we, know," in the same way that there is an obvious problem in stating that if reality is what each of us can make of it, every representation of reality is as good as any other. As much as social representations theory struggles to rehabilitate lay knowledge and bring into focus its power to signify, it also needs to keep an acute awareness of its limitations, because no knowledge is completely immune to distortion, to misunderstanding, to barbarities. Knowledges can reveal and mislead, emancipate and oppress, and we need to distinguish between a symbolically structured order and the order referred to, as the only condition of critique.

Thus we need to recognize that not every story can be accepted as history and not every representation is accurate towards its object. Conceptions that defend the "everything goes" deny the arduous and painful struggle of so many human groups to reach a precise knowledge and to overcome the various distortions which entangle it. To say that truth and falsity are socially constructed does not mean to say that we can just throw away the idea of truth, and even less, the idea of falsity. For centuries, to go back to the example I used above, humans have constructed representations of others which are a clear expression of the necessity of truth. Although the consequences of these representations are extremely real to all those involved in the set of practices they originate, it is only the notion of truth which can put them where they belong, which is the realm of falsity.

Concluding Remarks

In this chapter I have expanded the discussion which I initiated some time ago about the link between social representations and the public sphere (Jovchelovitch, 1995, 1998a, 2000). Drawing on one of the most fundamental premises of the theory of social representations, i.e., that social knowledge is bound to the social context of its production, I have discussed the discontinuities between Durkheim's concept of collective representations and Moscovici's concept of social representations. I have shown that social representations are forms of knowledge bound to detraditionalized public spheres, where novelty plays a crucial role and worldviews compete in more or less equal terms in the social arena.

Having established the differences between social and collective representations in relation to a transformed public sphere, I addressed the issue of social construction. I argued that, although we construct knowledge, we do it *in relation* to a reality which permanently escapes from our making. Knowledge constructs what is real for us, which is not necessarily real for other people and other historical periods. Thus knowledge is limited, incomplete, and unfinished; it can never grasp the wholeness of reality. There is always an unknown dimension in reality to be explored and known. I explained this apparent contradiction between knowledge of reality and reality itself through a discussion of the historical, cultural, and public dimensions of knowledge. Finally, I argued that the distinction between representations and reality needs to be understood and preserved as fundamental to sustain the very idea of critique.

These issues are not final and certainly there is much more to consider in the study of social representations. They are important, however, and I believe they grow in importance if we take into account the globalizing tendencies of late modernity. Meanings, knowledges, and ways of life travel today freed from the spatial and temporal restrictions which traditionally have characterized our relations to times and places. This freedom, which we owe especially to the development of the mass media of communication, produces a new reflexivity which allows social representations to clash, to compete, to intermingle, and to appropriate new sense. But it also brings to the center of our discussion what happens in those communities which lack the material, cognitive, and symbolic resources to propose and to defend their representations and way of life.

It is not a matter of denying the increasing processes of communication and circulation of information; here there is no return and the world the twenty-first century will see will have expanded and shrunk in a dimension without precedents. But this process puts into sharp focus concern and solidarity with the diversity of the peoples on our planet and the hard realization of the invisibility of so many peripheral communities. Different and distant lives are not unconnected lives, and the history of all cultures is also the history of cultural borrowings. Sometimes the emphasis on our differences obscures the fact that what we have in common – and "we" here means anybody, wherever they come from – is precisely the multiple contexts that make each human experience unique in its own right. Defending this diversity needs to be today, just as it has been for almost 300 years, central to the project of an enlightened universalism.

Notes

Research for this paper was conducted while I was a Directeur d'Études Associé at the École des Hautes Études en Sciences Sociales in Paris. I would like to thank M. Maurice Aymard, at the Maisons des Sciences de l'Homme, for providing such a hospitable and congenial environment in which to work. This paper has benefited greatly from discussions I have had over the years with Martin Bauer, Gerard Duveen, George Gaskell, Robert Farr, Pedrinho Guareschi, and Wolfgang Wagner. I am also grateful to Kay Deaux and Gina Philogène for their very helpful comments in a previous version of this paper. I am indebted to Professor Serge Moscovici, who has patiently listened to my ideas and concerns and generously gave me his time and knowledge while I was conducting research on these issues.

1   It is important to note, however, that unrealized principles are not necessarily unrealisable

principles. Normative principles have precisely the function of guiding and constraining action and historical change.

2 To acknowledge that collective representations are not the only form of social knowledge which exists in detraditionalized societies, would require of Durkheim to conceive of the social as a field of tensions, malleable to the impact of novelty and the transformations made possible even by minorities. This conception is absent from Durkheim's sociology and present in Moscovici's social psychology. This is all the more clear in the context of Moscovici's theory of active minorities, and in his proposition that the function of social representations is to deal with novelty and familiarize us with the strange.

3 It is interesting to note that psychoanalysis in France has always been treated as a scientific theory. This is not the case in Britain where psychoanalysis has struggled to prove its epistemological credentials as a scientific theory. In this discrepancy we have yet another case of how cultural traditions are deeply intertwined with the production and acceptability of what comes to constitute scientific knowledge.

4 It is important to make a clear distinction between authority and totalitarianism. Totalitarian regimes try to prevent the production of everyday knowledges by *force*, whereas traditional societies operate by the *authority* and *power* of the social bond itself. The latter derives its power from the fact that it is recognized; the former needs force and, frequently, state violence to exert its effects.

5 Please note that I am not referring here to scientific knowledge, which is a type of social knowledge which intends to transcend the limitations imposed by time and space. Sometimes it manages to do so, sometimes it does not, whereas everyday knowledges such as social representations are *always* bound to time and space. The theory of gravity applies independently of time and context (on Earth), whereas social representations of women, biotechnology, or health are always bound to time and context.

12

Social Representations: Catching a Good Idea

Hazel Rose Markus and Victoria C. Plaut

As self-appointed representatives of that imagined community dubbed the American social psychological mainstream, we found the papers by Lahlou, Wagner and Kronberger, and Jovchelovitch to be generative and illuminating. In previous years, the theory of social representations elaborated here often seemed to us, and we believe to many other American colleagues as well, provocative, important, but in the end a bit difficult to grasp fully. Social representations was the type of theory that if you forgot your lecture notes on the day you intended to cover this material, you were in trouble. But in these papers and in the volume in general the picture seems focused and the ideas American user-friendly. No doubt this impression can be traced to the carefully drawn insights of these specific papers and to Moscovici's remarkably straightforward presentation of the theory that precedes them, but it may also reflect a change in the condition of the American social psychological audience.

Cognition Goes Public

Recently in many circles, there is a growing need to talk about cognition not just as internal and private, but also as somehow external, public, and shareable, and suddenly, just as social representations theory might predict, the theory is clear, compelling, even obvious in some respects. It appears that after a long period of time in which this might have happened but didn't, the general idea of social representations is catching on; the concept of social representations has begun, as they say in this literature, to inhabit the population of American social psychologists. It now seems that there is much to be appreciated in this theoretical approach and many ways to put it to work.

Social representations theory as formulated by Moscovici (1976a, first published

1961) can be used for examining and analyzing the function of everyday knowledge. Social representations have been defined by Jodelet (1991) as "a kind of knowledge, socially constructed and shared, having pragmatic purpose and contributing to build a common reality for the community." This theory has often seemed the square peg, something that doesn't quite fit American theoretical purposes because it has not respected "traditional" conceptual boundaries and has insisted on interweaving ideas and constructs that are typically kept separate from one another – content and process, the individual and the collective, perception and action, representation and communication. Yet now when Lahlou (Chapter 9, this volume) asserts that the social representations are "a cooperation instrument for social groups," are "socially constructed, but used by individuals also," and "link the individual with the group, on one hand, and perception with action, on the other hand," and then underscores the need for social representations in group cooperation by inviting us to imagine trying to organize a bank robbery with a random sample of 10 individuals, it all begins to make sense.

Similarly when Wagner and Kronberger note that social representations are the product of "a collective process of symbolic coping" and "a crucial component of everyday thinking and common sense" (Chapter 10, this volume), it is possible to glean something of the coordinating and functional aspects of social knowledge, and have some insight into the idea that the focus in social representations theory is not just on the content of social knowledge but also on the dynamic meaning-making process which binds people together. And when Jovchelovitch (Chapter 11, this volume) describes social representations as cognitive structures "capable of encompassing different logics, which social actors draw on as a function of different contexts and practical demands," we begin to have a feel for the ways in which all of these papers are casting everyday knowledge in a larger, even a starring role in human behavior. From a social representations perspective, knowledge doesn't just sit there inside the head waiting quietly to be called on in the right situation by the internal director, but instead gets a job and takes on a life of its own.

The theme of the understanding that emerges from these papers then is that while social knowledge can be an individual creation, as it is communicated and shared, it becomes an integral part of the social context and in the process comes to structure and regulate individual behavior. As Jovchelovitch describes it, social representations move "from one social group to another and penetrate different life worlds, different horizons, different identities and different projects." All of these papers serve to make the argument that the role of the representing process in creating and maintaining the social world should be the object of more intense scientific scrutiny. And we begin to have an incipient appreciation of Moscovici's report (Chapter 2, this volume) of the excitement he experienced with the intuition that representations "express something essential to human life and thought." Humans' capacity for making meaning with others and for building worlds according to these meanings is not just an accidental feature of our nature; it may be a central feature of human nature. Representations come with being human. Cognition and knowledge creation have a practical social function and are shaped by social life. This could be seen as a problem and as a source of bias and fallacy, or instead as the very phenomenon to be understood.

Social psychologists working in the American context have always examined variation in the nature and composition of the immediate social context (e.g., was the participant working alone or next to another, were there three other people witnessing the event or was the actor alone, was the person giving the instructions an authority in a white lab coat or another participant) and have noted the powerful influence of even seemingly minor situational or contextual variation on social behavior. Although they have focused on the attitudes and schemas that distinguish individuals in a given context, social psychologists have paid only scant attention to those meaning systems, models, scripts, or representations that are likely to be shared as a result of being similarly positioned in the social world and that bind people together so that they can communicate and act together. For the most part, meanings or social knowledge have not been acknowledged or investigated as significant aspects of the social context.

Networks of Meaning

That people everywhere live within and through powerful webs of meanings is becoming apparent from findings and theories in three flourishing areas of social psychology – social cognition, stereotyping, and culture. Research in all of these areas points to the existence and the significance of pervasively distributed social knowledge that is durably salient and easily accessible for use in evaluating and communicating. For example, the burgeoning priming literature leads us to ask why is it that with only a gentle nudge – experimentally with only the exposure of a few words – a whole package of attitudes and actions can be set in motion? Why is it that priming a person with terms such as jazz or ghetto invokes racial stereotyping in all people, regardless of whether they score high or low on a scale of prejudice (Devine, 1989)? Why is it that the IAT – the implicit association test (Greenwald, McGhee, and Schwartz, 1998) – which measures the differential association of two target concepts with an attribute can reveal negative attitudes that respondents claim they do not hold (e.g., negative attitudes to ethnic or racial group members)? Why is it that simply requiring African-American students to note their race before taking a difficult test impairs performance relative to the situation when race is not activated (Steele & Aronson, 1995)? Or why is it that priming a person with concepts related to secure attachment (e.g., secure, trust, etc.) reduce expressions of outgroup hostility (Shaver, 2000)? How can it be that requiring a person to unscramble sentences containing words associated with the elderly stereotype (e.g., gray, senti- mental, Florida) walk more slowly when they leave the laboratory situation (Bargh, Chen, & Burrows, 1996)? The answer to all of these questions appears to implicate what Greenwald, McGhee, and Schwartz (1998) call "socially significant associa- tive structures" (p. 1464), but the source of these structures and the diversity of ways they can shape behavior remains to be understood. What Bargh, Chen, and Burrows (1996) refer to as "growing evidence of automaticity in social psychological phe- nomena" suggests a powerful role of social representations in coordinating indi- vidual social behavior and locates the source of this behavior not only in the preconscious, but very importantly in the distribution and concentration of social representations in a given context.

The fact that various bundles of social knowledge can be so easily activated and that the consequences of this knowledge activation are so seemingly significant for action suggests that the networks of ideas and images hypothesized by social repre- sentations theory, perception–action loops as Lahlou describes them, do indeed exist and that these networks have had and continue to have important social func- tions in individuals lives. Moreover, the type of knowledge that can be activated in these studies seems to be the type of "hot" knowledge (i.e., knowledge that is dense and multifold and that has been a part of many previous communications) that is, as Lahlou points out, continually "in the making" or in rapid re-making or change. Attention to the kind of knowledge that is most charged in a given community – for example, knowledge about the self, about race, about freedom and independ- ence, about God, about age – should allow researchers insight into what types of evaluations and actions can be most easily primed and also to theorize about why some reactions and actions can be primed for some people and not others, about what types of primes (experiential, conceptual) would be impactful in particular situations, and about what should follow.

Culture and Meanings

That networks of meanings don't just float free waiting to be activated but instead have an ongoing role in social integration is revealed most clearly in studies in the area of cultural psychology. It is here that we are beginning to see again that hu- mans create and live within worlds of their own making. There is structure and stability in our conceptions and understandings of the world and these create and maintain a solidarity among those who share them. This social representational glue is typically invisible and taken for granted, becoming evident only in the process of trying to make sense of actions that cannot be made sense of with one's own reper- toire of representations. As social psychologists have expanded their attention to include not just the study of people who are highly similar with respect to sociocultural positioning and thus make use of many overlapping social representations (e.g., young, middle-class, European-Americans), the conditions that highlight social representations are increasingly common. For example, they have begun to pay systematic attention to the differences in behavior that are associated with a wide variety of sociocultural contexts defined by gender, ethnicity, race, region of origin, age, religion, social class, occupation, birth cohort, and so on.

Often the differences among cultural contexts are not subtle. Worlds that are separated by education or race or class, for example, are often strikingly different from one another. Consequently, there is now a need to more fully and systematically characterize and delineate these sociocultural contexts. These contexts vary not only in their structural features – size, complexity, status arrangements – but very importantly in their content, nature, prevalence, concentration, and distribution of their defining images, meanings, and symbolic behaviors that are habitually engaged by people in these contexts. Social psychologists are beginning to ask what is it about these meanings that makes a difference for various aspects of psychological functioning and how do they do so, or what are the mechanisms by which these networks of images and meanings influence behavior.

We predict then that American mainstream social psychology appears poised to develop a theory of context and also a theory of how the sociocultural context constrains and affords or constitutes behavior. With greater attention to a variety of sociocultural contexts, it no longer seems sufficient to claim that psychological processes are just "influenced" by the context or to define social psychology simply as the study of social influence. There is a need to specify the nature of this influence. A sociocultural context does not give rise to a stable or group essence, something that can be controlled or held constant, or something that is overlaid on "basic" experience. Rather a context is defined by a complex of meanings – a semiotic space – and also a set of practices that represent and foster these meanings. Being a person, any kind of person, requires engagement of specific meanings and practices; all experience requires sociocultural participation. And it is in developing a theory of how experience is socioculturally grounded that a theory of social representations can be extremely useful. Social representations can be regarded as specific mediators of sociocultural influence.

According to social representations theory, some of the most important differences among people reflect their engagement with different meaningfully patterned worlds – and these differential patterns of engagement lead to a difference in the content and distribution of social representations. Social representations theory provides a set of perspectives and answers for how social knowledge comes into everyday thinking and contours common sense. Moreover, it is a theory that transcends the view of culture as a static and bounded entity, and in principle it could handle the diversity of meanings and practices that come with communities with more interfaces, connections, and relations between groups.

Cultural contexts can be described in part in terms of the nature and form of the social representations that can be chronically accessible or easily activated. Wagner and Kronberger, for example, discuss a variety of European contexts where "killer tomatoes" functions as a symbol that makes biotechnology intelligible for lay people and that weaves it into the fabric of the group's common sense. Similarly, according to Lahlou, social representation is a "population of individual representations which are scattered over a population of humans . . . [the social and the mental representation] are coconstructed and hence codependent" (Chapter 9, this volume). Focusing in a particular social representation, Lahlou contends that French cultural contexts can be characterized in part by the particular nature of social representational space that is associated with eating. Lahlou points out that seemingly basic and ordinary acts are saturated with meanings that must be understood to understand behavior. As an extension of his work, it would be useful to compare the social representational space of the French with that of Americans. In America which has many Calvinist roots, eating is often cast as almost sinful, and if eating is pleasurable, it is certainly so. In general there is a widespread worry among Americans that one should not do too much eating, and since the social representational space of eating serves different social functions in America, it should take an importantly different form than it does in France.

To take another example, European-American middle-class contexts are characterized by social representations that conceptualize the person as a free and atomistic entity who chooses, who decides, who is in control, and who pursues goals on the basis of a set of internal attributes, preferences, and abilities (Markus, Mullally, & Kitayama, 1997). These representations structure both lay and scientific thinking, and as a consequence Americans often resist the idea that they are influenced, let alone constrained by their social contexts or by other people. Indeed this is one of the reasons that the idea of social representations has been slow to spread. As Wagner and Kronberger note, a specific susceptibility of the individual is a prerequisite for images and beliefs to widely catch on. The American notion that individuals are agentically in charge and in control of their actions prevents effective communication about the ways in which this view of the person reflects a incorporation of an individualist ideology rather than an empirically-based analysis of the how the mind functions. In other words, the core of American's social representations about themselves is that they are free from social constraint and that they live outside social representations.

World-making

Recent empirical studies which indicate, for example, that people living in East Asian contexts or working-class contexts in the United States behave differently than people engaged in mainstream American contexts provide evidence that social representations do more than reflect the social world, they are also involved in world-making – creating and maintaining the social world. Studies in a variety of cultural contexts suggest that many well-known psychological principles, for example, that self-determination is the most powerful motivator for children (Iyengar & Lepper, 1999) or that inconsistency between thought and action creates conflict and dissonance (Heine & Lehman, 1997) may not be human universals. Instead they may be generalizations about worlds that are organized by and that have instituted particular social representations about the individual.

Social representations theory holds out the promise of understanding the various relations that may exist between the sociocultural and the individual, and further of analyzing the person as a cultural participant who is simultaneously a social construction and a social constructor of experience. These three papers share and foster the increasingly common sense idea that we live through and within and by our social representations. Together in various communities we make our worlds and we think and feel and live within them. What emerges across the three papers is some insight into this ongoing cycle of mutual constitution. People and their social worlds make each other up (Shweder, 1991; Fiske, Kitayama, Markus, & Nisbett, 1998). This is a start but still the questions of why this kind of information, where it comes from and how it influences behavior remain to be understood.

From a social representations perspective, the unit of social life or of social being is not only an actor "acting" under the mediation of a set of motives or knowledge structures. The unit of social being can be seen more comprehensively as a circuit defined both by representation of some features of the social context and by some communication of these features, or phrased another way, representation and through one's actions – re-presentation. Very significantly, however, Jovchelovitch (Chapter 11, this volume) makes clear that the process of mutual constitution is not seamless and she argues that "symbolic knowledge cannot be taken as the measure of all reality." Addressing the inescapable relativism point, she argues that knowledge constructs partial realities but that "these are not, and should not, be understood as the whole of reality." While assuming a constructivist point of view, she suggests that "reality goes far beyond what we can make of it."

In sum, judging by the title of many new edited volumes, the goals of many recent conferences and networks, and the discussion sections of a growing number of journal articles, all at once there is a need for a psychology that is content-full, relational, historically-conditioned, culturally grounded, and contextually contingent. These papers together with others collected in the volume provide an outline of how the theory of social representations may be instrumental in developing just such a social and dynamic psychology.

13

What We Do and Don't Know about the Functions of Social Representations

John T. Jost and Gabriel Ignatow

The theory of social representations, as articulated by Moscovici (1981, 1984b, 1988) and an ever-increasing number of fellow enthusiasts, is surely one of the most exciting intellectual developments to occur within social psychology over the past four or five decades. By focusing explicit attention on the reciprocal interaction between the individual and society, Moscovici has dared to engage theoretical issues that have generally been reserved for the likes of Marx, Weber, Durkheim, and their followers. By stressing the symbolic and meaning-making aspects of shared thought, Moscovici has done for psychology what Berger and Luckmann (1967) did for sociology, what Geertz (1993b, first published 1973) has done for anthropology, and what Weick (1979) has done for organizational behavior. All of these theorists adopt a cognitive perspective, but they do it in a way that captures rather than expunges the rich sociality of mental life. The theory of social representations is unusually ambitious and far-reaching for a discipline that is traditionally as reserved as social psychology. This is probably the theory's great strength and its weakness.

It is all the more impressive that the theory of social representations has spread its influence during the very same years that social cognition has claimed the almost singular attention of experimental social psychologists. While many researchers have gone deeper and deeper into intrapsychic investigations of on-line cognitive processing (e.g., Higgins & Bargh, 1987), a central and explicit aim of research on social representations has always been to provide an account of human cognition that is deeply social and that does not reduce the act of thinking to an internal mental process (Moscovici, 1981, 1984b, 1988). At its best, the theory of social representations provides empirically viable accounts of social and cultural dynamics by which human beings form and spread *shared* beliefs about the nature of reality; these are the very dynamics that have been most neglected during the ascendancy of social cognition.

From our perspective, merely demonstrating the existence of shared social representations is far less interesting than providing evidence that social representations serve specific social and psychological motives or functions for their adherents. This means that, in the end, social representational theorists must go beyond mere description, which they are sometimes reluctant to do. In part because of an affinity for social constructionist metatheory (e.g., Jovchelovitch, this volume; Lahlou, 1996b; Wagner, 1996, 1998), researchers of social representations seldom conduct experimental studies, and they generally refrain from making causal claims or explaining the origins of specific representations. Our view is that the theory of social representations would be well-served by adopting some of the complementary strengths of the social cognitive movement, which has used experimental methods to produce the most direct causal evidence available concerning structures, functions, and processes having to do with mental representations of the social world.

A relatively strong commitment to the social constructionist epistemological position has resulted not only in an aversion to experimental methodologies but also in a reluctance to examine issues of accuracy and bias with regard to social representations. Thus, Wagner and Kronberger (this volume) assert that "representations are socially constructed, culturally correct in their own sense and functional in everyday social life" (Chapter 10), without acknowledging that variations in the degree of accuracy may provide important insights into the functions served by social representations. Again, a comparison with research in social cognition is instructive. Theories of social cognition have advanced immensely over the past twenty years or so, largely as a result of focusing on errors, biases, and distortions (Fiske & Taylor, 1994; Greenwald & Banaji, 1995; Kahneman, Slovic, & Tversky, 1982; Nisbett & Ross, 1980). To show that people depart from some objective standard (such as a standard that is established under experimental conditions) is a very powerful way of demonstrating that people are seeking to satisfy some social or psychological motivation or goal. Thus, we learn a great deal about the functions of thinking when we attend to the dysfunctional aspects of thought.

In what follows, we consider the current state of theory and evidence pertaining to five functions that social representations may be said to serve. All five of these are related, either directly or indirectly, to the concerns of Lahlou, Wagner and Kronberger, and Jovchelovitch in their valuable contributions to the present volume. These are the functions of: (a) group coordination, (b) rational argumentation, (c) symbolic coping, (d) environmental compensation, and (e) system justification. Although each of these functions is plausible, there will be little direct evidence in support of functional claims until we develop experimental paradigms and related methodologies which allow us to measure or manipulate the emergence and transmission of social representations and to observe their effects on other social and psychological variables. Following a discussion of the need for experimental approaches to social representations and their functions, we close by considering some of the limitations and possibilities of functionalism in general with regard to the study of social representations.

The Coordination Function of Social Representations

Building on an earlier analysis, Lahlou (1996b, Chapter 9, this volume) argues that social representations serve the function of coordinating group activities and facilitating cooperation among individuals. He mentions both "pragmatic" aspects having to do with technical coordination and the division of labor and "social" aspects having to do with affiliation and group life. Lahlou notes that many of the most important human achievements (including ice cream cones, ancient pyramids, and space shuttles) may be ascribed to our capacity for developing socially shared representations and to act collectively in pursuit of a common image.

While we agree that efficient coordination is, in principle, an extremely important function that social representations could serve, the issue has not yet been framed in an empirically tractable way. Because social representations are defined as shared symbolic products, it must be true by definition that they involve coordination and cooperation among individuals. What needs to be shown is that the creation or adoption of a social representation facilitates group performance. But it is not clear that the concept of a social representation is well specified enough to be operationalized in such a way that it is distinct from other forms of communication. In other words, if Lahlou is merely saying that communication facilitates coordination, then he is not saying much; the special contribution of social representations (apart from shared communication in general) to group activity has yet to be articulated.

Lahlou (1996b) has also hypothesized that even though the different elements of a given social representation may be present in the environment, a person will not possess an *explicit* representation in which these elements are brought together until he or she interacts with someone else who possesses the representation. So, the uninitiated may start to drink out of the finger-bowl and eat the lemon that is on the dinner table, until someone explains that these items are for washing one's fingers after eating seafood. Lahlou's arguments here are fascinating, but there is no empirical research that actually demonstrates the transmission of a social representation from one person to the next, unless one counts the vast literature on persuasion and social influence (e.g., Eagly & Chaiken, 1993), which was in full swing long before Moscovici developed the concept of a social representation.

The research that Lahlou does present, on the subject of social representations of "eating," is purely descriptive in nature and does not provide any direct support for his notion that social representations serve a coordination function. On the basis of an impressively thorough and large-scale attempt to catalogue the semantic relations among food-related concepts, Lahlou finds, among other things, that men and women have somewhat different associations to eating, such that men stress pleasure while women stress health. There are age differences, too, with respect to the "moral" aspects of eating. But these age and gender group differences are merely described; they are not explained, although a passing reference is made to "widespread sociological norms and constraints." There is no discussion of how these different representations might serve to coordinate pragmatic activities or to facilitate group identification. And so, while it seems plausible that social representations do assist with tasks of cooperation and coordination in both life and work, this idea has not yet been subjected to direct empirical confrontation.

The Rational Argumentation Function of Social Representations

Closely related to issues of cooperation and communication, Jovchelovitch (1995, Chapter 11, this volume) proposes, provocatively, that social representations are relatively recent phenomena that are made possible by the advent of a "detraditionalized public sphere," by which she means an open, liberal, and democratic society, as opposed to a primitive world in which authority is derived exclusively from status and power distinctions. Jovchelovitch draws heavily on the writings of Habermas in outlining the criteria for the "public sphere," which include: equality among citizens, the authority of rational argumentation, equal access to and public visibility of justice procedures, and the achievement of legitimacy through dialogue and mutual agreement. The social representations that emerge under these circumstances are said to be autonomous, reflexive, creative, public, and possibly even liberating. Jovchelovitch (this volume) writes that, "Nothing is 'naturally accepted,' everything is under question, or as Marx would say, 'all that is solid melts into the air.'"

But it is important to remember that Habermas was describing an *ideal* state of affairs in which rationality and freedom trump power and status. In actuality, we do not question authority so readily, we do not challenge all forms of inequality, and we do not typically engage in free and open debate, because the "ideal speech situation" described by Habermas seldom (if ever) exists in practice today. This means that it is an empirical issue as to how homogeneous and how widely diffused certain social representations are and how much knowledge systems actually "compete, clash, and are renegotiated" (Jovchelovitch, Chapter 11). To anticipate the arguments below, it is an empirical issue as to how much our social representations serve a system justifying function and how much they serve to challenge the system.

Still, Jovchelovitch's ideas suggest that social representations might serve an important function in liberal society, namely the function of facilitating rational argumentation. Unfortunately, there is no direct evidence linking the presence or absence of shared social representations to the quality of argumentation or the likelihood of persuasion. Close attention to the contents and dynamics of social representations reveals that, in many cases, they are relatively unenlightened and even downright misleading. Stereotypes, for example, are social representations that probably do not further the causes of tolerance, freedom, and rationality. And, although contagion sensitivity may be an adaptation that functions well for the avoidance of pathogens in the physical environment (Rozin, Haidt, & McCauley, 1993), Wagner and Kronberger (this volume) demonstrate that exaggerated sensitivity is incorporated into social representations of biotechnology, leading to increasingly irrational beliefs about disease contagion caused by genetically altered plants and vegetables. The social conditions that are likely to increase or decrease the rationality and flexibility of social representations have yet to be explored empirically, but Jovchelovitch's contributions steer us in that worthwhile direction.

The Symbolic Coping Function of Social Representations

At the heart of Wagner and Kronberger's (this volume) captivating account of "killer tomatoes" is the hypothesis, implicit in Moscovici's (1981, 1984b) writings about the "anchoring" and "objectification" functions of social representations, that novel and unfamiliar things are psychologically threatening. With regard to recent advances in genetic alterations in fruits and vegetables, Wagner and Kronberger argue that people form social representations of biotechnology as a collective way of symbolically coping with their fear. Thus, shared representations of genetically altered produce as spreading disease and germs emerge as a way of assimilating the unfamiliar technologies with familiar bodily experiences. One problem with Wagner and Kronberger's analysis is that such social representations do not seem to satisfy needs for coping very well, insofar as fear seems to be increased rather than decreased by representing biotechnology in this way.

A related but more methodological problem, not at all unique to Wagner and Kronberger's interesting work, is that the "threat" is merely assumed, and it is not measured or manipulated. In order to demonstrate that social representations serve a "symbolic coping" function, one would have to gauge perceived threat before and after the development or application of a social representation, in order to show that the social representation reduces fear or motivational threat. This is implicit in the functionalist logic that Wagner and Kronberger apply, but it is not investigated directly by the descriptive research that is presented.

Wagner and Kronberger's argument, like Moscovici's work on anchoring and objectification, assumes that social representations serve to make the unfamiliar seem more familiar by representing new or foreign elements in terms of old or common experiences. This is a highly plausible and yet untested hypothesis. Our research also suggests, somewhat tentatively, that the opposite may also be true: in certain communities, people may develop social representations that invoke concepts and processes that are notably absent from their local environments.

The Environmental Compensation Function of Social Representations

We have conducted content analyses of professional lexicons in which the jargon of computer industry workers in California's Silicon Valley is collected and defined (Ignatow & Jost, 2000). Our qualitative research suggests that social representations in Silicon Valley emerge precisely because they incorporate concepts and experiences that are missing or taboo. Thus, we propose that social representations might also serve a "compensation" function in addition to the much-discussed "anchoring" function. In the relatively antiseptic settings of computer workspaces and on-line environments, people seem to bring into the intellectual environment stirring and taboo topics such as the human body, mortality salience, and animal life, which are otherwise conspicuously absent from the communal discourse.

For example, such metaphorical terms as "assmosis," "bloatware," "braindump," "dogfood," "idea hamsters," and the "bleeding edge" serve to inject the environment with vitalistic imagery that has little to do with the familiar and mundane nature of computer workspaces. In short, people seem to be engaging in a form of linguistic play that draws on human and animal themes of life and death that are rather foreign to the hygienic workplace. Our analyses also indicate that there are more social representations involving disgusting human and animal bodily imagery than in other comparable professions, and that there has been a steady increase in such imagery over the thirty year period in which the computer industry has grown (see Ignatow & Jost, 2000).

The System Justification Function of Social Representations

The functional perspective, so admirably adopted by Lahlou, Jovchelovitch, and Wagner and Kronberger, has been part of the theory of social representations for some time. Moscovici (1988) discussed the social functions of social representations, and he proposed a distinction among "hegemonic representations," which he hypothesized would be uniform, coercive, homogeneous, and stable, "emancipated representations," which he proposed would be autonomous, group-specific, interpretive, and coordinated, and "polemical representations," which he argued would be conflictual, controversial, antagonistic, and oppositional. These themes are addressed also by Jovchelovitch, who stresses the conflictual and dissensual nature of public discourse. Unfortunately, there is only one study that attempts to examine these notions empirically, and the results are profoundly inconclusive (Canter & Monteiro, 1993).

Nevertheless, the notion that groups develop social representations and attempt to influence others to adopt those representations as a way of achieving social and political goals strikes us as one of the most fascinating and unique aspects of the theory of social representations. But it is not enough to simply assert, as some proponents of rhetorical and discourse-analytic approaches do, that these dynamics exist. Cognitive hegemony and cognitive emancipation should be demonstrated empirically. This is, in fact, the goal of the theory of "system justification" (Jost & Banaji, 1994), but our research is admittedly at a very modest stage of development.

We have shown, recently, that stereotypes of Northerners and Southerners in the U.S. and Italy tend to justify perceived economic differences between these groups. People in these countries believe, for example, that Northerners are more intelligent, more hard-working, more refined, less violent, and so on, than people from the South. What is more, people from the South seem to accept these representations, showing a good deal of *out*group favoritism. But how do we know that these representations serve a system justifying function? One piece of evidence is that the mere act of thinking about stereotypical social representations while completing the stereotyping measures makes respondents believe that the socioeconomic differences between Northerners and Southerners in the U.S. are greater in magnitude, higher in legitimacy, and less likely to change in the future, compared to a control condition (see Jost, Burgess, & Mosso, in press). By varying the order in which people are asked to form or access specific representations, it is possible to observe the effects of one cluster of beliefs on another.

We also find that respondents' political ideology moderates the expression of ingroup and outgroup favoritism, increasing the gap between Northerners and Southerners in terms of ingroup favoritism as one moves across the political spectrum from left-wing to right-wing (Jost, Burgess, & Mosso, in press). These examples go beyond mere description of social representations of Northerners and Southerners. By linking geographical stereotypes to chronic and temporary ideological variables, the case is strengthened that these stereotypical social representations are serving a "hegemonic" or system justifying function.

On the Need for Experimental Studies of Social Representations

By rejecting or simply avoiding an experimental approach to the study of social representations, researchers make it more difficult for themselves to demonstrate the *operation* of social *processes* and *functions* such as objectification, anchoring, coordination, argumentation, coping, compensation, and the like. Think how much stronger the contributions of Lahlou, Jovchelovitch, and Wagner and Kronberger would be if they provided direct empirical evidence that representing the world in a certain way changed the functional or motivational state of an individual or group. At present, the most interesting functional claims are untested. This is true also of our own work on the compensation function of social representations in Silicon Valley (Ignatow & Jost, 2000). Work on the system justifying function of stereotypical social representations is a bit farther along (Jost, Burgess, & Mosso, in press), but clearer evidence of causal mechanisms is required there as well.

We are not suggesting that researchers of social representations should do experiments just like social cognition researchers; we are proposing that they should do different kinds of experiments, ones that shed light on the collectively shared formation and transmission of "ways of seeing" or "ways of representing," and to show how these processes account for phenomena that are not captured by experiments that address more individual cases of information integration. It should be possible, for instance, to manipulate the presence or absence of a given social representation, in order to assess Wagner and Kronberger's hypothesis that social representations serve to reduce fear and Lahlou's hypothesis that social representations help to coordinate activities among work groups and teams. These concerns should not be inconsequential to the next generation of social representational theorists. Lahlou, Jovchelovitch, and Wagner and Kronberger have each advanced *empirical hypotheses* in elaboration of a functional theory of social representations, but progress on assessing these hypotheses may be inhibited by commitments to social constructionist epistemology and methodological descriptivism.

Limitations of the Functionalist Perspective

Although we find the functionalist strand of theorizing about social representations exemplified by Lahlou, Jovchelovitch, and Wagner and Kronberger to be very promising and exciting, some *caveats* are in order. Unless one develops research paradigms in which independent variables are clearly distinct from dependent variables (see McGuire, 1989), then functional claims are largely circular or tautologous. The researcher simply concludes that if a social representation exists, then it must serve some function for its adherents, but the only evidence for the function comes from the existence of the social representation. Future research must produce ways of independently measuring or manipulating functional or motivational states, if work is to progress.

A second issue has to do with the potential neglect of *dys*functional aspects of social representations. By assuming (rather than demonstrating) that social representations are functional, as Lahlou, Jovchelovitch, and Wagner and Kronberger do, one runs the risk of missing the ways in which social representations fail us or constrain us or even do us harm (cf. Jost, 1995). By attending to the dysfunctional quality of some social representations, we may encounter evidence that we are using social representations to serve nonrational ends, whether it is to defend against fear of the unknown or to justify the status quo, even at our own expense. In social cognition, for example, evidence that people perceive illusory correlations, misuse statistical base rates, rely on predictively invalid stereotypes, and opt for mental shortcuts and heuristics has contributed to an understanding of some of the functions served by cognitive operations, namely conservation of effort, reduction of informational complexity, confirmation of prior beliefs, and so on (e.g., Fiske & Taylor, 1994; Kahneman, Slovic, & Tversky, 1982; Nisbett & Ross, 1980). Future research on social representations should similarly document the ways in which our (normally adaptive) processes for developing social representations lead us astray, so we can better understand why they take the forms they do.

In the meantime, the current assembly of authors deserves credit for identifying several important functions that social representations might plausibly serve. Aggregating across their work and ours, we propose five likely candidates, in addition to the oft-cited functions of anchoring and objectification. The five we have in mind are: group coordination, rational argumentation, symbolic coping, environmental compensation, and system justification. We look forward, with great anticipation, to the next wave of research, in which the causal and functional roles of these variables and others are illustrated with the kind of rich and subtle detail that we have come to expect of accomplished theorists of social representations.

Part IV

Social Representation and Social Categorization

14

Social Categorization: Towards Theoretical Integration

Martha Augoustinos

Social Categorization

A central and fundamental process common to most, if not all approaches in social psychology, is social categorization. Indeed, it could be argued that social categorization is the unifying concept within contemporary social psychology. Categorization has long been considered a universal cognitive tendency which serves to either simplify an overly complex world, or to render it more intelligible (Lakoff, 1987). Borrowed from cognitive psychology and the pioneering work of Eleanor Rosch on natural object taxonomies, categorization refers to the process of identifying stimuli as members of one category, similar to others in that category and different from members of other categories (Rosch, 1975; 1978; Rosch, Mervis, Gray, Johnson, & Boyes-Braem, 1976). Categories impose order on the stimulus world, and by doing so allow us to communicate about the world effectively and efficiently. Categorization is thus fundamental to perception, thought, language, and action (Lakoff, 1987).

As with natural objects, social objects such as people, events, and actions also need to be identified and categorized. Like nonsocial categories, members of a social category share common features. Thus the human tendency to categorize people into their respective social group memberships according to gender, class, race, ethnicity, sexual orientation, etc. Categorizing people and events allows us to organize and structure the social world in a meaningful way. Again, such categorizations are viewed as highly functional and, indeed, necessarily adaptive in orienting us and allowing us to communicate effectively about the social world. Social categorization, however, is assumed to be a more complex process because social objects are variable, dynamic, and interactive. Category inclusion in the social world is thus shaped and influenced by a multitude of factors.

While social categorization is a key concept in social psychology, not all theories share the same assumptions regarding the nature of this process. Indeed, there exist considerable theoretical tensions over why, when and how we categorize. This chapter contrasts the way in which social categories and the process of social categorization has been theorized by four distinct theoretical approaches within the discipline: social cognition, self-categorization theory, social representations theory, and discursive psychology. In particular I will contrast the dominant approach to social categorization as embodied in social cognition with that of social representations theory which emphasizes the shared, collective, and ideological nature of social categories. Current empirical work will be discussed on the social and ideological construction of social categories and their contextual and functional use in everyday talk. This work challenges traditional views that categories are preformed cognitive constructs "in the head" waiting to be activated. While the practice of reconciling distinct theoretical and epistemological approaches is fraught with problems (Doise, 1986), this practice has the capacity to identify and articulate points of convergence between different traditions of research in social psychology. The possibility of reconciling these different theoretical approaches therefore will be considered.

Social Cognition

Contemporary social cognition regards social categorization as emerging and developing from a fundamental cognitive need to simplify an overly complex social world. By categorizing individuals into their respective group memberships we are able to simplify reality and thus render it more intelligible. Moreover, it is argued that the functional cognitive need to categorize is inextricably linked to stereotyping. As generalized descriptions of a group and its members, stereotypes emerge inevitably and automatically from the categorization process. Indeed stereotyping is the cognitive activity of treating individual elements in terms of higher-level categorical properties (Hamilton & Sherman, 1994; Stangor & Lange, 1994). Together, social categorization and stereotyping lead to ingroup favoritism and outgroup bias (Tajfel, 1981b), as well as the tendency to perceive an outgroup and its members as more homogeneous than ingroup members (Linville & Jones, 1980). Stereotypes are therefore inextricably linked to discrimination and prejudice.

From a social cognitive perspective social categorization is primarily based on salient and identifiable features of a person such as age, gender, and race. Fiske (1998) refers to these categories as "the top three" because they are "central, visually conveyed, automatically accessed categories" (p. 375). There may, however, be cultural and contextual specificities that determine which categories are the most salient to perceivers. For example, in Britain, social class may have the same degree of salience as race and gender. In some parts of the world, and in certain historical periods, religious affiliation may have considerable salience and utility in social perception.

Social cognitive research has clearly demonstrated that social categorization is cognitively pragmatic and useful. However, the nature and content of social categories are rarely problematized within this tradition of work. While stereotypes are regarded as distorted and biased descriptions of social groups, the social categories themselves are regarded as reflecting real and valid group entities in the social world. Categories such as man – woman, black – white, young – old, rich – poor, are treated as uncontested and nonproblematic social objects that are perceived directly through identifiable physical and social features.

The current "renaissance" of research into categorization and stereotyping is primarily motivated by the view that categories as cognitive representations, and categorization as a mental activity, both reflect fundamental features of our "cognitive architecture." Moreover, the research on the automatic priming of categories and their associated stereotypes (Bargh, 1994; Devine, 1989) reinforces and augments this cognitive perspective. Categories and their automatically activated stereotypic associations are viewed as "energy-saving devices," freeing up valuable attentional resources elsewhere (Macrae, Milne, & Bodenhausen, 1994). Category activation is therefore conceptualized as fast, automatic, and often beyond conscious control (Fiske, 1998).

While social psychologists occasionally make overtures about the need to link this cognitivist account of categorization and stereotyping to more sociocultural perspectives, the motivational, symbolic, and ideological nature of categorization has been relatively neglected. Most contemporary work in social categorization remains overwhelmingly cognitive. Thus, the social origins, and the contextual functions of particular categorizations have been largely neglected and supplanted by an account that sees their origin and function almost entirely within the normal, day-to-day routine of cognitive life. While experimental studies in the laboratory quite readily demonstrate the automatic and stereotypic activation of social categories upon the presentation of verbal primes, in the everyday world of social interaction and communication, interactional goals and psychological motivations become contextually important (Fiske, 1998). Categorization may be inevitable, but as I hope to demonstrate later, there is nothing inevitable about the particular categories, or the content of those categories, which are relied upon in any instance.

Self-categorization Theory

In contrast to the predominantly individualistic approach to social categorization in the social cognition tradition, Oakes, Haslam, and Turner (1994) provide a more social analysis of categorization based on the social identity tradition founded by Henri Tajfel (1981a) and its more recent theoretical derivative, self-categorization theory (Turner, Hogg, Oakes, Reicher, & Wetherell, 1987). In contrast to social cognition research that is not articulated by a single integrative theory, but rather an associated set of methodologies, self-categorization theory is a specific theoretical framework. Self-categorization theory begins with the premise that we are first and foremost social beings and that cognitive and psychological processes such as categorization, are motivated and shaped by social group memberships and identities.

A central thesis in this approach is that perceiving people as members of groups (group-based perception) has the same cognitive and psychological validity as perceiving people as individuals (individual-based perception). While social cognition assumes that individual person-based perception is more accurate than perception based on social group membership, self-categorization theory argues that in many everyday social contexts and interactions, group-based perception is more psychologically valid, meaningful, and useful. Indeed, such group-based perception is viewed as reflecting the material and social reality that groups exist in power and status relations to each other and that social identities are furnished by these social group memberships. For example, the fact that individuals are categorized according to gender and that this can trigger gender-stereotypic perceptions is grounded in and reflected by the nature of power and status relations that exist between men and women in most societies.

While social-cognitive accounts conceptualize categories as rigid stored mental schemas with fixed and invariable content, waiting to be "activated," self-categorization theory predicts that the process of categorization itself and the content of categories are fluid and dynamic and depend on the social context. The group is always defined in terms of a particular social relational context. This context determines the nature of self – other comparisons that are made and reflects the relative relations between a particular ingroup and outgroup.

Oakes, Haslam, and Turner (1994) argue that all perception, including group-based, person-based, and self-based perception, involves the dual cognitive processes of categorization and stereotyping. The material and social intergroup relations existing within society at any particular point in time are "apprehended" through both categorization and stereotyping. Rather than simplifying reality, categorization elaborates and enriches social perception. Oakes, Haslam, and Turner (1994) argue:

> Categorization itself elaborates rather than reduces the information available in a stimulus. It is the crucial process which brings together our general understanding of and theories about the world on the one hand, and the material reality in which we live on the other. (Oakes, Haslam, & Turner, 1994, p. 113)

Stereotyping is associated with the perception of social categories that can range in their degree of inclusivity from self, through interpersonal categories, to larger social aggregates. Given the social and psychological "reality" of group life, the process of stereotyping is regarded as psychologically valid and veridical rather than biased or distorted.

In a similar vein, Leyens, Yzerbyt, and Schadron (1994: see also Yzerbyt, Rocher, & Schadron, 1997) advance a social pragmatic view of perception, arguing for the interactional, motivational, and goal-oriented nature of thinking, that "thinking is for doing" (Fiske, 1992). Like Oakes, Haslam, and Turner (1994), they stress that social perception is flexible and context-dependent. Depending on the interactional and accuracy goals of the perceiver, people will rely on either categorical or more individuated information to make judgments about others. Categorical judgment is not always the rule, nor is it considered to be less accurate than individuated perception. Rather than being "abstracted simplifications", categories are viewed as rich and elaborate "reservoirs of meanings" (Leyens, Yzerbyt, & Schadron, 1994, p. 205).

Social Representations Theory

While the analyses provided by Oakes, Haslam, and Turner (1994) and Leyens, Yzerbyt, and Schadron (1994) both emphasize the psychological and motivational nature of categorization, like the social cognition tradition they too are predominantly cognitive approaches to categorization and social perception. More specifically, self-categorization theory rarely problematizes realist assumptions about the nature of social categories. All approaches thus far view categorization primarily as a cognitive process that does "good" and essential cognitive work. Relatively scant attention has been paid to the symbolic, political, and ideological nature and functions of social categories. Social categories and their associated stereotypes are more than just cognitive schemas or psychologically rational (albeit flexible) constructions. Categories are social representations, possessing all the features that Moscovici (1981, 1984b, 1988) has attributed to representations: they are symbolic, affective, and ideological representations of social groups within society which are extensively shared and which emerge and proliferate within the particular social and political milieu of a given historical moment. But categories do not simply exist in individuals' heads waiting to be activated. They are socially and discursively constructed in the course of everyday communication. Categories are flexible and dynamic representations that are constructed *in situ*, within a specific relational context at a particular point in time. Moreover, such group representations are viewed as emerging and developing from the social identities that are grounded in group life itself. Here we can see the links between the theory of social representations and self-categorization theory, both of which emphasize a social functional analysis of group perception based on social identity.

Consistent with the self-categorization view, categories are rich symbolic meaning systems that often function to elaborate an impoverished "social reality" as much as they simplify an overwhelming one. Social representations theory insists on the shared, symbolic, and collective qualities of social categories. The shared, consensual, and collective nature of stereotypes and the social categories upon which they are based were once central and defining features (e.g., Katz & Braly, 1933; Tajfel, 1981b). As Haslam (1997) has recently argued, this tradition is being eroded by recent cognitive accounts which define stereotypes as individual cognitive constructs residing "in the minds of individuals" (Hamilton, Stroessner, & Driscoll, 1994, p. 298), and "which need not be consensually shared" (Judd & Park, 1993, p. 110).

The extent to which representations are shared or consensual in nature has attracted considerable critical debate within social representations theory. This is of particular importance since individual variation will always exist within a group's "shared" perspective. Notwithstanding diversity, social representations theory suggests that with increased social communication and interaction, representations of the social world become more consensual in nature. Several multidimensional scaling studies investigating the development of young people's representations of Australian society confirmed that with increased age, individual variation in these representations decreased considerably (Augoustinos, 1991). Thus although there was not complete consensus, as socialization proceeded from adolescence to early adulthood, societal representations became more consensual and shared. Unlike some empirical studies in the social representations literature, consensus was not assumed but was measured and confirmed by analyses sensitive to individual differences. In a similar vein, Hraba, Hagendoorn, and Hagendoorn (1989) found that, while there was considerable agreement among respondents regarding the content of the ethnic hierarchy in The Netherlands, suggesting the existence of a shared representation, the form of the hierarchy varied across domains and different contexts of use. Together, these studies suggest that shared representations are not necessarily static structures, but are used in dynamic and flexible ways by different people across different contexts of use. Indeed, the dynamic and contextual nature of social representations is something that Moscovici has emphasized in his writings. Moscovici does not deny that diversity exists within a consensual framework. "We can be sure that this consensus does not reduce to uniformity; nor, on the other hand does it preclude diversity . . . There is a consensual universe, but there is not a precise consensus on every element at each level" (Moscovici, 1985, p. 92). The research by Doise, Clémence, and Lorenzi-Cioldi (1993), for example, has demonstrated that individuals orient themselves differently in relation to consensual meaning systems. Thus, while at the collective level social representations function as shared objectified structures, at an individual level there is variability as to how the elements of the representation are framed and articulated.

In social representations theory, anchoring is the process by which novel or strange social objects are rendered familiar by comparison to culturally accessible categories. This process is akin to categorization, but unlike the social cognitive tradition that regards categorization as an individual cognitive process, anchoring is a collective and ideological activity shaped by the power and social relations within a particular historical moment. The categories of comparison and classification come from the social and cultural life of the individual, whose own experience is embedded in the traditions of a collectivity. Within social representations theory, anchoring or categorization does not merely contextualize social stimuli, social objects are epistemologically located by the process of allocating names and labels (Augoustinos & Walker, 1995).

Specific social categories through constant everyday use and consensual validation can become objectified symbolic meaning systems. As Moscovici (1981, 1984b) so clearly describes, once objectified, such constructions can assume an independent, and almost material and prescriptive reality. Even so, these objectified meaning systems are subject to change depending on the functional purposes to which categories are put. The centrality and significance of particular social categories and their associated representations depend on one's subject position and a group's relational standing to the category in question. This in turn is subject to shifting psychological, social, political, and economic factors. This raises two related questions: what functions do certain categorizations serve and what consequences do they have?

Discursive Psychology

These two questions are at the heart of discursive approaches to categorization. Discursive psychology (Edwards & Potter, 1992; Potter & Wetherell, 1987; Wetherell & Potter, 1992) introduces a contextual and functional analysis to social categorization which does not treat social categories as rigid internal cognitive phenomena located in people's heads: that is, as preformed static structures which are organized around prototypical representations of the category. Rather, discursive psychology is concerned with how people discursively constitute categories to do certain things. As Potter & Wetherell (1987) argue:

> Instead of seeing categorization as a natural phenomenon – something which just happens, automatically – it is regarded as a complex and subtle social accomplishment . . . [that] . . . emphasizes the action orientation of categorization in discourse. It asks how categories are flexibly articulated in the course of certain sorts of talk and writing to accomplish particular goals, such as blamings or justifications. (p. 116)

From this perspective, categorization is not simply a cognitive, internal process based on direct and veridical perception, but a "discursive action" which is "actively constructed in discourse for rhetorical ends" (p. 77). This approach emphasizes what people are trying to do, and what effects they are trying to produce, with their talk at different times. Social categories used in talk are expected to be variable, flexible, shifting, and even contradictory depending on the functional and contextual use of the category.

Edwards (1991, p. 517, original emphasis) for example, describes categorization as "*something we do, in talk*, in order to accomplish social actions (persuasions, blamings, denial, refutations, accusations, etc)." The strength of discursive approaches is that they are able to empirically demonstrate the active construction and use of categories in discourse, and the ideological effects and consequences some uses and constructions have. This is different from the usual social-cognitive approach which treats categories as fixed social entities "out there" in the real world which, in turn, are represented as discrete cognitive entities in people's minds. It emphasizes the social-constructionist nature of social categories and identities. Consistent with their views on the variability and fluidity of discourse, discursive psychologists emphasize the dynamic, contextual, and functional way in which categories are constructed in discourse. Categorization and stereotyping are viewed as situated discursive practices (Edwards, 1991) rather than cognitive processes.

Social Categories in Racial Politics

In this section I want to combine social representations theory with a discursive approach to demonstrate the historically-constituted nature of social categories that take their shape and content from the social and cultural history of a collectivity. That is, social categories derive their meaning and substance from the pervasively held shared social representations of a group, or, in this specific case, "a nation." In particular, I want to examine the specific deployment and everyday use of social categories that have been central to what has been invariably referred to in Australia as the "race debate." The aim of the analysis is to demonstrate that far from being nonproblematic social objects that are directly and readily perceived, the constitutional boundaries of social and demographic categories are variously constructed and contested in everyday talk (Sacks, 1992) and in political rhetoric.

Since the election of the conservative Liberal-National Party Coalition in 1996 "race" has assumed an extraordinarily salient position in Australian politics. Central to debate in the Australian polity has been the nature of the relationship between indigenous, or Aboriginal-Australians[1] and the rest of the nonindigenous population, in particular over the issue of land rights for indigenous people. Adding fuel to the debate has been the emergence and proliferation of a right wing political party called "One Nation." The controversial and contentious views of the leader of this party, Ms Pauline Hanson, has ensured that "race" and "identity" have remained salient and prominent issues in Australian politics since 1996.

The discourse of a unifying national collective identity has been a central platform of One Nation. This nationalist sentiment was used by Pauline Hanson and her supporters to question the legitimacy of Aboriginal rights to land and self-determination, and indeed, the legitimacy of Aboriginal people to self-categorize and identify as "Aboriginal." Specifically, One Nation challenged and contested both the legitimacy and constitutional boundaries of this social category in a number of ways.

One specific way in which Hanson and her supporters challenged the legitimacy of the category "Aboriginal" was to question the adoption of an Aboriginal identity. This was achieved by the deployment of a unifying superordinate category and identity, "Australian." Hanson argued that a continued emphasis on "small minority groups" or other cultural identities operates at the expense of acknowledging one's Australian identity. Being Australian was represented by One Nation as having unifying properties that serve to collectively unite everyone living within the nation state. "Other" identities, it was argued, functioned divisively in differentiating between numerous subcultural groups.

The primacy afforded to a collective Australian national identity and the moral necessity of self-categorizing as Australian to the exclusion of other identities functioned to undermine the political and moral legitimacy of Aboriginal people to have their indigenous and cultural identities recognized and affirmed. In this way, existing differences in culture, sociopolitical history, and psychology were subsumed (even negated) by appealing to the moral imperative for all people living within the nation state to adopt a superordinate national identity.

Another way in which One Nation contested the constitutional boundaries of the social category "Aboriginal" was to question whether individuals of mixed descent, who lead urban, nontraditional lifestyles, could legitimately identify and self-categorize as Aboriginal. For example, a One Nation candidate standing for the recently held national election (October 1998) argued that only people who had undergone traditional Aboriginal initiation rites should be regarded as Aboriginal. Mr Ted Hagger was quoted as saying "If a person wants to become an Aboriginal they should go through the ceremony and be an Aboriginal and live in an Aboriginal situation and not have the best of both worlds." Asked what he meant by "Aboriginal situation," he said "Well hunter-gatherers and people who live out there, say Lajamanu or in the Tanami desert." Furthermore, Mr Hagger who has a part-Aboriginal son-in-law said he was "darker" than his son-in-law, whom he said should be called a "part-coloured person or whatever *but not an Aboriginal*" (1998, July 27, *The Advertiser*, emphasis added).

Of more significance to the argument regarding the contested nature of social categories is the way in which Pauline Hanson has appropriated the category "indigenous" by declaring herself and all people born in Australia to be "indigenous Australians." Again here we see how the definitional and constitutional boundaries of a social category are being challenged and contested in everyday social life. Of particular interest is whether the appropriation of the category "indigenous" by political conservatives who want to constrain and limit the political and social aspirations of Aboriginal people will necessitate the creation of a new label or category around which Aboriginal people can collectively identify and mobilize. Gina Philogène's research on the emergence and development of the social category "African American" is instructive here, for it illuminates how changing social and political conditions shape and determine the representations associated with different category labels (1994, Chapter 8, this volume). Since the British colonization of Australia a variety of categories have been used to refer to Australia's indigenous people. Original social categorizations such as "savages" and "natives," which reflected the imperial and colonial interests of the day, were supplanted later with categories such as "blacks," "Aborigines," and "Aboriginal Australians." More recently, these predominantly racial categories have been replaced with the category "indigenous." Thus we have witnessed a shift away from the use of categories which emphasize color and racial group membership, to a category which emphasizes Aboriginal people's original presence and occupancy of Australia prior to British "settlement." This is consistent with other minority groups in the world, like African-Americans, who have moved away from the use of self-categories which emphasize color and race.

Reicher and Hopkins (1996a, 1996b) note that the construction of specific categories of membership and the nature of entitlements associated with these memberships may be a central feature of persuasion in political rhetoric. The final example demonstrating the socially situated and strategic deployment of social categories comes from an "Address to the Nation" by the Prime Minister of Australia (Mr John Howard) that was publicly broadcast on national television on December 5, 1997. The political speech concerned the highly controversial nature of a piece of legislation his Government introduced in order to limit land claims made by Indigenous Australians on pastoral leaseholds on Crown land.[2] The High Court ruled, in 1996, that native title can survive or, rather, be held to coexist, on pastoral leaseholds. Various interest groups including the rural lobby, mining industries, and the Federal Government itself, argued that this new ruling threatened the economic interests of pastoralists and miners. It was this judgment, the so-called "Wik decision," which was the direct precursor to the explosion of the current "race debate" in Australia. After a period of consultation with the "interested" parties, John Howard's Coalition Government issued what was described as a "10-point plan" to amend the existing Native Title Act.

Of particular theoretical relevance to work on social categorization is the specific and strategic deployment by Howard of what may, on first glance, appear to be routinely nonproblematic demographic or occupational categories – "Aborigines," "farmers" and "miners". Rather than being such, these social categories are revealed to be situationally crafted to achieve very specific local ends. The rhetorical project of Howard's address is to present the native-title issue as a conflict of interest between two main groups: the Aboriginal people of Australia, on the one hand, and Australia's "farmers," on the other. The extract below presents the opening paragraphs of the Prime Minister's speech.

The Prime Minister, Mr John Howard:
01   Good evening. Tonight I would like to talk to you about striking a fair
02   and decent balance in this very difficult debate about Wik, or Native
03   Title. You all know there has been a lot of debate and a lot of
04   differences of opinion but I think we all agree on one thing and that is
05   the sooner we get this debate over and get the whole issue behind us
06   the better for all of us.
07   I think we probably also agree on some other things – for example,
08   the Aboriginal and Torres Strait Islander people of Australia have
09   been very badly treated in the past and we must continue our efforts
10   to improve their health, their housing, their employment and their
11   educational opportunities. And in doing that we should always
12   remember that the Aboriginal people of Australia have a very special
13   affinity with their land.
14   I think we would also agree on how important the rural and mining
15   industries are to the future of our country. Between them they
16   contribute 63 per cent of Australia's export income and that helps
17   generate a lot of wealth, which in turn enables us to help the less
18   fortunate within our community.
19   Australia's farmers, of course, have always occupied a very special
20   place in our heart. They often endure the heartbreak of drought, the
21   disappointment of bad international prices after a hard worked season
22   and, quite frankly, I find it impossible to imagine the Australia I love
23   without a strong and vibrant farming sector.

While there are several features of the speech worthy of comment, the analysis here will focus primarily on the specific category selections deployed by Howard (Aboriginal people and farmers) and how these categories are contrastively constructed and represented (see LeCouteur, Rapley, & Augoustinos, 2000). Although itemized as protagonists here, "mining industries" are mentioned only once again, in passing, at the very end of the address. For the remainder of Howard's speech, the category "rural and mining industries" is telescoped to "Australia's farmers" and, subsequently, in a contrast pair, to "Aboriginal people" and "farmers."

Of significance is the strategic lexical selection of the categories "farmers" and "farming properties," which are deployed instead of the legal categories at issue: "pastoralists" and "pastoral lease holdings." It is no accident that Howard specifically deploys these categories for they are able to invoke culturally salient symbolic representations historically associated with the Australian farmer: the quintessential "Aussie battler," iconic of Australian national identity (Alomes & Jones, 1991; Ward, 1958). Howard's highly emotive and romanticized construction of this social category rests upon a widely shared collective narrative – a social representation – regarding the trials and tribulations of Australia's farmers. Howard uses romanticized representations of "the bush" in his (explicitly disavowed) advocacy for the interests of this group. All that is good and positive about Australia is embodied by this sector of the community. Threats to a "strong and vibrant farming sector" (l. 23) are represented as threats to the nation as a whole. "Farmers" are represented as the symbolic expression of Australianness: they are important to the future of the country (l. 15), they contribute export income (ll. 15–16), they generate wealth (l. 17), they endure heartbreak and disappointment (ll. 20–1), they work hard (l. 21), they are strong and vibrant (l. 23). Farmers are constructed and represented in ways that emphasize an enduring and nationally profitable relationship with the land, a relationship in which they are active agents.

These particular symbolic representations could not have been invoked if Howard had used the very specific legal categories at issue in the Wik controversy: "pastoral leaseholds" and "pastoralists." The most dominant and culturally accessible representation associated with pastoralists in Australia has been that of wealthy landowners. Indeed, Bachelard (1997) documents that those pastoralists who would benefit most from the Government's amendments to Wik were among Australia's richest individuals and companies. This wealth stands in sharp contrast to small agricultural farmers, many of whom were forced to sell their land and personal assets during severe economic hardship in the late 1980s and early 1990s. Thus Howard's strategic use of the category "farmer" accomplished rhetorical work that the category "pastoralist" could not have achieved.

Howard's romantic construction of "farmers" also stands in stark contrast to the construction of Aboriginal Australians. While Howard acknowledges that Aboriginal people "have been very badly treated in the past" (l. 09), the emphasis is on the past and not on any present-day injustices. Billig (1991) argues that what is not said reflects the parameters within which ideology operates perhaps more clearly than what is. There is no mention of the "heartbreak" and "disappointment" that Indigenous Australians may have "endured" over 200 years. The Aboriginal people of Australia are constructed, not as occupying a "very special place in our hearts," but merely as having "a very special affinity with their land" (ll. 12-13). Throughout Howard's speech "Aboriginal people" are delineated as a distinct social category, separate to and different from other Australians. His talk is replete with "we/their" contrasts: "*we* must continue *our* efforts to improve *their* health, *their* employment and *their* educational opportunities" (ll. 9–11, emphases added). Aboriginality is not, then, normatively bound to active agency but, rather, to passivity; to waiting for others to act on problems, problems which do not include dispossession of their land. In contrast, "the rural and mining industries" are constructed as valuable and active contributory parts of the future of the Australian nation (l. 15). The "lot of wealth" generated by these industries is constructed as the necessary prerequisite for the ability "to help the less fortunate within our community" (ll.17–18): a general and nonspecific social category (presumably those in need of health, housing, employment, and education) into which, by implication, "Aboriginal people" fall.

Like Howard's representation of "farmers," his construction of Aboriginal people as passive (waiting on others to improve their life conditions) and unproductive (they have a special affinity with the land whereas farmers produce wealth), also rests on a pervasively shared social representation. In analyzing everyday talk on race relations in Australia, Augoustinos, Tuffin, and Rapley (1999) found descriptions of Aboriginal people as passive, inactive, and unproductive to be very pervasive. Participants used three recurring and interrelated metaphors to structure their representations of Aboriginal people. These metaphors were those of "hierarchy," "mobility," and "fit." Throughout our participants' talk Aboriginal people and their culture was described as "primitive" and "backward" compared to European culture which was described as "technologically advanced" and "superior." Aboriginal people, it was argued, had "failed to adapt" to the superior culture that had been introduced by British "settlement" and this accounted for their present disadvantaged social status in Australian society. While Aboriginal people as a group were not constructed as biologically inferior, they were constructed as culturally inferior. Aboriginal problems were represented largely in Social Darwinist terms as problems of fit and adaptation to a culturally advanced and superior culture. Moreover, their failure to fit or adapt to this dominant culture was viewed primarily as preventing Aboriginal people from improving their social status through upward social mobility. As Essed (1991) has emphasized, the replacement of the metaphor of a biological hierarchy of groups with that of a cultural hierarchy is central to the covert and subtle nature of contemporary racism. As Moscovici and Hewstone (1983) describe, the use of graphic metaphors is a central process by which abstract notions are transformed into culturally accessible everyday knowledge or common sense. The complex domain of race relations in Australia, in particular the relations between an indigenous minority and nonindigenous majority, is one where issues of social identity, history, and nationhood are also at stake. The metaphors of hierarchy, fit, and mobility conceptually articulate a coherent Social Darwinist representation: a representation that is not only central to constructions and representations of Aboriginal people, but also commonly used to understand and make sense of race relations and race politics in Australian society. Howard's construction of Aboriginal people as passive and unproductive rests on this Social Darwinist representation, which while may not be endorsed by all Australians, is a highly available and culturally accessible representation.

Thus Howard's management of the identities of the protagonists clearly establishes the relative status and the scope of the moral claims that are normatively bound to the two categories. By virtue of their agency, their suffering and contribution to the "less fortunate," "farmers" have a legitimate entitlement not only to lobby Government but also to have their wishes respected by Government. Aborigines, in contrast, with a mere "affinity" to land (ll. 12–13) and a passive dependency on the largesse of others, have no such entitlement. Central to the success of Howard's project here – the acceptance by the audience of the inevitability and appropriateness of his proposed legislative amendments – is that his address is built upon the construction of the categories of persons with an interest in the debate. By establishing the superordinate category of "farmers" as contributory, sentimentalized, battlers in the bush, in direct contrast to the dependent and unproductive Aborigines, the rhetorical project of Howard's address functions to establish what these categories of actors may legitimately expect as their entitlements (Sacks, 1992). Indeed, after protracted debate in the Federal Parliament, the Government's proposed legislation to limit Indigenous claims on pastoral leaseholds was eventually passed in the Senate in 1998.

The above analysis which combines both social representations and discursive approaches allows us to empirically demonstrate the active construction and use of categories in discourse, and the ideological effects and consequences some uses and constructions have. This is different from the usual social-cognitive approach that treats categories as fixed social entities "out there" in the real world which, in turn, are represented as discrete cognitive entities in people's minds. It emphasizes the socially constructed, contested, and rhetorical nature of social categories and identities.

Towards an Integrative Theory of Social Categorization?

In reviewing the contrasting ways in which social categories as representations of groups and categorization as an activity have been theorized and constructed within social psychology, it is clear that an integrative metatheory of categorization is required. While the practice of reconciling distinct theoretical and epistemological approaches is fraught with problems (Doise, 1986), bringing different approaches together can help identify and articulate not only the distinct differences between them, but also possible commonalities. For example, all of the approaches to categorization reviewed, whether it is social cognitive research, self-categorization theory, social representations, or discursive psychology, emphasize the centrality and importance of categorization in social perception. Whether one construes categorization as an automatic cognitive process or a situated discursive activity used for rhetorical ends, we know that the use of social categories has the capacity to define reality; to define parameters of inclusion and exclusion, to position the self and one's identity in relation to the category, to generalize features to a whole group, and importantly, to evaluate.

To date, there is little theoretical consensus as to why we categorize. Social cognitivists argue that it is driven by our need to simplify reality, self-categorization theorists suggest that it elaborates upon and enriches social reality, discursive psychologists argue that categories allow us to do things, and social representations theorists believe that categorization is a symbolic and ideological activity which explains and rationalizes the way the world is. What I'd like to suggest is that these various explanations are not necessarily mutually exclusive. Whatever our theoretical and epistemological preferences, it may be more theoretically and empirically challenging to acknowledge that categorization may serve all or any of these functions, depending on the context. An integrated metatheory would have as its goal the specification of the situations and conditions under which particular categorizations may be relied upon over others and in what ways these are linked to individual cognitive (cognitive economy), group-based (enriching social information) and/or system-serving (ideological) motivations (Stangor & Jost, 1997). By conceptualizing categorization as a situated, contextual practice we are perhaps more likely to specify the conditions and situations in which specific categorizations are used. This is in keeping with Fiske's (1998) increasing emphasis on the socially pragmatic and psychologically motivated nature of social categorization. Whilst category activation can be automatic and spontaneous with little conscious thought and effort, in everyday life, categorization is shaped by the interaction goals and psychological motives of the perceiver. The categories that are used in any specific context can shift from general overarching categories to subtypes and subgroups, depending on the perceiver's needs and interests. People are "motivated tacticians" (Fiske, 1998) who may categorize someone as a "woman," a "black woman," a "feminist," an "American," depending on the social and relational context. Rather than being an automatic and relatively thoughtless process, categorization is motivated and strategic. There are a number of category choices that can be made, and it is in everyday talk and interaction that such strategic selections become evident. Categorization may be inevitable, but there is nothing inevitable about the particular categories, or the content of those categories, which are strategically relied upon in any instance. It is more instructive to look at how particular categories function ideologically by justifying and legitimating the social, economic, and political positions of certain groups in society (Jost & Banaji, 1994), than it is to look at the reliance of thinking on categories.

Leyens, Yzerbyt, and Schadron (1994) also remind us that currently, in most western societies at least, it is socially and culturally undesirable to judge others solely on the basis of their group membership. This social norm acts as a constraint on how a person is categorized, and what categorizations may be relied upon in any instance. A situated approach to categorization, in naturalistic settings, where much more is personally and socially at stake than in the "safe" confines of judgments made in laboratories, has the potential for specifying how wider collective and ideological values are shaping and influencing individual and group-based practices, practices which have traditionally been assumed to be cognitively inevitable and automatic. The analysis of everyday talk and conversation is an important site for examining how categories are deployed *in situ* and what consequences specific categorizations and group constructions have. As Billig (1996) argues, such an approach also allows us to look for contradictory and dialectical devices in everyday argumentation concerning social category entitlements. The constitutional boundaries of any category are never set in cognitive templates but can be argued over and contested. However, it is important to ground such an analysis in the social, cultural, and historical context. As social representations theory suggests, categories are not created anew every time they are used. All categories are socially constructed representations that have a prior history. Social psychology must move beyond the narrow cognitive information processing models that have dominated categorization research thus far. Social categories are more than just pictures in the head, they are part and parcel of our collective and ideological lives.

Notes

1   This social category refers to the indigenous people of Australia who occupied the Australian continent before the arrival of the British. Aboriginal Australians are also referred to as "Aborigines," "Aboriginal people," and "indigenous Australians" amongst other category identifiers. As will become evident later in the chapter, the category label that is actually deployed in any instance to refer to this social category varies depending on the strategic goals of a particular user. Moreover, such category labels have varied historically, and are associated with different representations.

2   Pastoral leaseholds refer to expanses of Crown land (owned by the Government) that have been leased to pastoralists for a 99-year term specifically, but not exclusively, for the grazing of livestock. "Pastoralists" are people who raise livestock – the American equivalent would be "ranchers." Governments introduced pastoral leases in the nineteenth century as a way of regulating the holdings and activities of squatters who had occupied and appropriated large expanses of Australia's so-called "wastelands." "They became seen as Australia's version of the frontiersmen" (Bachelard, 1997, p. 23), many of whom amassed enormous wealth and in time, exercized considerable political influence.

15

The When and the Why of How: From Mental Representations to Social Representations

Fabio Lorenzi-Cioldi

Social cognition approaches offer many useful models of how individuals organize information about people and elaborate mental representations of groups. However, these mental representations are held by a generic, socially unspecified individual. By pointing to factors that determine the content of these mental representations, facilitate their emergence, activation, and use, social representations theory draws attention to the social context in which individuals live and interact. Hence, the social representations approach shifts the theoretical focus from formal properties of the individual's mental representations to the properties of the surrounding social context. This chapter provides illustrations of how, by introducing the larger social context, mental representations turn into social representations. Broadly speaking, the notion of social context will encompass two different aspects of an individual's background: proximal variables, which refer to parameters characterizing the social interaction, and distal variables, which refer to positioning of the individual's membership groups in the social structure.

Gendered Self-Representations

Social cognition approaches to gender stereotypes quite often emphasize individual differences in the use of a single defined process (e.g., the gender-schema). Status differentials between the sexes are usually not systematically called into attention.

The research examples I will present in this section show that the application of cognitive principles can be traced back to the differential positioning of gender groups in the social structure.

Individualism, collectivism, and the gender groups

It is a widely shared assumption among sociologists, anthropologists, and social psychologists, that Western societies value conceptions of the individual which stress "individualism," that is, an individual's autonomy, freedom, and separateness with respect to other people (e.g., Fiske, Kitayama, Markus, & Nisbett, 1998; Lee & Ottati, 1993; Markus & Kitayama, 1991; Triandis, 1994). Although individualistic beliefs sustain an image of a classless society, of a society of loosely related individuals who are striving for mobility along lines of individual competence and personal adherence to moral values (e.g., DeMott, 1990), those with power and status have been found to personify independence and autonomy more closely (Guillaumin, 1992; see also Apfelbaum, 1979; Deschamps, 1982; Sampson, 1977). Specifically, the dominants' self-representations match to a larger extent the shared representation of an autonomous individual than the subordinates' self-representations (Crocker, Major, & Steele, 1998). This reasoning leads to the following hypothesis: the dominants come to define themselves mainly as "persons," whose group membership makes only a minor contribution to their self-concept. Conversely, the subordinates' relative distance from this shared representation forces them on most occasions to frame their self on the attributes which are associated with their group-label as a whole (Lorenzi-Cioldi, 1998).

There is some support for this hypothesis in the social-psychological literature. For instance, research on sex-role stereotypes has documented that descriptions of "men in general" match closely those of "adult healthy persons" – sex unspecified – whereas descriptions of women comprise more group-specific characteristics (i.e., more relational and expressive characteristics; cf. Broverman, Vogel, Broverman, Clarkson, & Rosenkrantz, 1972; Hamilton, 1991; Lorenzi-Cioldi, 1988).

Furthermore, correlational research has shown that such differences are not specific to the gender domain. Questionnaire data gathered by Jackman and Senters (1980), for instance, showed a common tendency for women, African Americans, and low socioeconomic status group members to perceive the social structure in categorical terms, and a tendency for the corresponding outgroup members to perceive it in more personalistic terms.

Lorenzi-Cioldi and Joye (1988), using unobtrusive procedures, demonstrated an analogous tendency for individuals low in socioeconomic status and in educational background to organize a vast array of occupational labels along homogeneous classes which uncover status oppositions (e.g., blue collar versus white collar, low-paid and female occupations versus well-paid and male occupations).

Finally, research on spontaneous self-perception (e.g., using the *Who-am-I?* test) has repeatedly shown that less privileged group members are more likely than the corresponding outgroup members to describe themselves using holistic and depersonalizing features, especially the relevant group labels (e.g., McGuire, 1984). This trend has been observed using a variety of asymmetrical group memberships, such as the level of education and the prestige of the institution that people have attended (Deschamps, Lorenzi-Cioldi, & Meyer, 1982), ethnic membership (Lorenzi-Cioldi & Meyer, 1984), and gender (Hurtig & Pichevin, 1990; Lorenzi-Cioldi, 1994).

In more general terms, this literature suggests that a shared social representation of the autonomous person is differently activated among groups of people. By taking into account properties of the social structure, one can anticipate a tendency of subordinate group members to attenuate their uniqueness and to emphasize collective identity, and a contrasting tendency of dominant groups to stress their personal distinctiveness and to attenuate collective identity.

This conjecture can be examined by using gender as an instance of asymmetrical group membership. The assumption that men have higher status and greater power than women is central to many social psychological analyses of gender stereotypes and behavioral differences between the sexes (e.g., Eagly, 1987; Fiske, 1993a; Ridgeway & Diekema, 1992). Accordingly, although people in Western societies value self-conceptions in terms of what makes them different and distinguished, women have concurrently been portrayed as propounding a more relational, communal, and connected self and ingroup representation than men (Gilligan, 1982; Harding, 1986; Markus & Oyserman, 1988). Following these premises, one can speculate that men and women differ as groups depending on the degree of proximity of their ingroup representations to the shared cultural representation of the individual as the basic unit of social perception: men match it more closely than women (Eagly & Mladinic, 1989; Kashima et al., 1995). It can thus be predicted that traits which denote autonomy and independence should be firmly endorsed to describe a superordinate category (the Western culture more than the Eastern culture), and to describe men, as well as "persons in general," more than women. Descriptions of female targets should embody average levels of both the shared individualistic traits (e.g., independent, individualistic) and the ingroup collectivistic traits (e.g., conformist, follower).

Ratings and free descriptions of the relevant targets (superordinate: cultures; and subordinate: gender groups, people in general, and the self) on various traits representing individualistic and collectivistic contents were collected in a series of studies (Lorenzi-Cioldi & Dafflon, 1998). Put together, the results of these studies demonstrated that the target "Occidentals in general," representing the superordinate ingroup, was typically described in terms of the individualistic traits, and the target "Orientals in general," representing the superordinate outgroup, was typically described in terms of the collectivistic traits. However, the participants, whatever their gender membership, endorsed at least to a moderate extent traits relating, on the one hand, to a shared representation of an individual's autonomy and uniqueness, and, on the other hand, to more specific ingroup representations (i.e., individualistic for men, and collectivistic for women). "People in general," "Occidentals," and "men in general" were thus described similarly, and attributed traits related to individualism. Hence, male targets were perceived in the same way as were the superordinate ingroup and the generic person. Female targets, on the contrary, were attributed intermediate levels of both individualistic and collectivistic traits.

These results give preliminary support for the idea that in Western cultures, where the dominant social representation of individuality refers to a self-contained person, only those who are likely to have more power and status, that is, men, are fully identified with this content. This shared social representation is attributed to a lesser extent to female targets.

Enactment of the gender-schema

I will now consider the manner in which self-representations of men and women differ in terms of the intergroup context in which individuals are located. As a consequence of the compelling salience of the collective and group's features for subordinate in comparison to dominant group members, it is likely that self-representations of women are more deeply embedded in an ingroup–outgroup comparison than self-representations of men, which are more likely to display interpersonal comparisons.

Bem's (1981, 1993) gender-schema theory provides a nice test of this conjecture. According to Bem, gender-schematic individuals display a readiness to organize information about themselves and other people in terms of the male–female (ingroup–outgroup) dichotomous categorization. In this respect, masculine and feminine attributes (i.e., culturally shared social representations of masculinity and femininity) face one another as opposing ends of a single continuum. Gender-schema theory predicts individual differences in the use of gender to organize incoming information. According to social representations theory, I alternatively predict a social positioning effect, that is, group differences in the use of this schema. Specifically, by virtue of their differential placement in the social structure, women should display more gender-schematic perceptions than men.

Support for this hypothesis was obtained in a series of experiments using unobtrusive or indirect measures, such as reaction times, clustering of the information in free recall, and errors in name-matching paradigms (Lorenzi-Cioldi, 1991, 1993). These measures may be an important advantage over direct measures when the procedure involves groups with unequal status and makes the participants' task especially reactive (e.g., Wittenbrink, Judd, & Park, 1997). In one of these experiments, men's and women's self-descriptions on a series of masculine, feminine, and neutral attributes were elicited and response-times were measured. Following Bem's (1981) gender-schema theory, these self-descriptions were examined by comparing the average latencies of responses on schema-consistent information (i.e., acceptance of ingroup attributes and rejection of outgroup attributes) to the average latencies of responses on schema-inconsistent information (acceptance of outgroup attributes and rejection of ingroup attributes). Gender-schema theory predicts that individuals make use of the gender categorization insofar as they process consistent information faster than inconsistent information. The results showed that women overall processed consistent information faster than inconsistent information, providing clear support for gender-schema theory. Men, however, did not, showing a trend in the opposite direction.

Evidence of this differential salience of the ingroup–outgroup categorization also comes from other experiments using a variety of procedures. For instance, Hurtig and Pichevin (1990; Pichevin & Hurtig, 1996) demonstrated how effectively various moderators (numerical ratio of the sex groups, dimensions of intergroup comparisons, and primes) alter the perceptual salience of the male but not the female sex-membership. The latter remained highly accessible and thus readily available for use to all participants irrespective of their sex and of the context's characteristics. For instance, Pichevin and Hurtig (1996) manipulated the numerical distinctiveness of the male and female categories in mixed-sex groups. Consistent with distinctiveness theory (McGuire, McGuire, Child, & Fujioka, 1978), the authors found that the salience of a person's sex increased as his or her sex category was in the minority. However, the results also showed that this effect was confined solely to men. Women displayed a readiness to categorize themselves in terms of gender, regardless of the situation. Pichevin and Hurtig maintained that the sex category may be an *identity marker* for women, that is, a chronically or automatically accessible self-defining attribute, while it may be a mere *social marker* for men, that is, an attribute that becomes self-defining only for some individuals and in specified circumstances, like any other self-defining attribute.

Social Representations of Groups

The preceding illustrations using gender groups suggest that dominant group members, but not subordinates, perceive themselves – and are perceived by outgroup members – as a gathering of individuals with more or less diverse characteristics. Analogous modalities of group perception have been dealt with in the social cognition literature.

Models of how individuals cognitively represent information about self and others, and more specifically, information about group membership, are often referred to as "mental representations of groups." Three such models have been successively elaborated and have been extensively applied in the social cognition literature: the Aristotelian, the prototypical, and the exemplar models.

Inaugural models have been rooted in an *Aristotelian* approach to classification. According to this approach, membership in a category results from a partitioning of the social world into discrete, mutually exclusive, exhaustive, and homogeneous categories. In each category, all the members share the same basic properties, which become the "essence" of the group.

Modern conceptions of category structure depart resolutely from this "all-or-none" conception of the organization of group information. The most prominent idea is the *prototypical* approach (e.g., Rosch, 1975). A cluster of modal or salient attributes determines inclusion in a group. The group's members distribute around these typical features. Because each individual's characteristics match to a differing extent the category features, a certain amount of within-group heterogeneity or variability arises from comparisons between group members: not all the category members consider themselves, or are entitled to be, members of the category to the same degree. Group membership expresses itself in degrees of discrepancy between the prototype – an ideal and not necessarily real member – and the various group members, who are also potential members of other neighboring categories.

Even more within-category heterogeneity is promoted in *exemplar-based* models (e.g., Smith, 1998). These models, which were elaborated more recently, posit that a mental representation of a group need not include abstract features or summary judgments about the group members' shared or modal characteristics. Social categories consist of a number of particular instances or exemplars drawn from personal contacts, learned from the media, and so on. Group membership is not abstracted on-line, at the time group members are encountered; rather, it is computed later on by taking into account the whole set of known group members.

As I have suggested, these mental representations of category membership have various psychological implications. The most important one, for the present purpose, is that exemplar-based mental representations of groups carry more internal variability compared to prototypically-based groups, which, in turn, carry more variability compared to Aristotelian-based groups (Linville & Fischer, 1993; Park & Hastie, 1987; Park, Judd, & Ryan, 1991). Whereas the Aristotelian approach advocates the group members' homogeneity and interchangeability within the group, the prototypical approach, and even more so the exemplar approach, allows for more interpersonal heterogeneity.

The social cognition literature is replete with empirical attempts to corroborate one or the other model of group representations (see Smith, 1998). From the standpoint of social representations theory, however, these models are not mutually exclusive. Social representations theory helps to discover how the social context regulates the process by which one and the other type of group representations are actualized in everyday thinking. As I have extensively shown elsewhere, a crucial moderator is the perceived social status of the target individual (either oneself or another person) to whom the category applies (Lorenzi-Cioldi, 1998).

Indeed, recent empirical findings suggest that various conceptions of a group apply to individuals differentiated by their relative social status. As I have already suggested when discussing the previous examples, experimental and correlational data show that people elaborate different images of a group (either an ingroup or an outgroup) according to the positioning of the target group in the social hierarchy. The subordinates often conceive of themselves and of their ingroup members as interchangeable persons, that is, as *aggregates*. Their personal features derive to a large extent from features that are ascribed to their group as a whole. In contrast, the dominants indulge in displaying an identity that appears to be gained outside their membership. They conceive of themselves as *collections*, that is, as a gathering of individuals endowed with a fair amount of uniqueness and interpersonal distinctiveness. Hence, collections epitomize a modality of group membership that is most adequately represented in the exemplar view of the organization of social information, whereas aggregates epitomize a group which is most adequately represented in the Aristotelian, or prototypical, view. Hence, Aristotelian, prototypical, and exemplar mental representations of a group describe the way images of oneself and other group members emerge among people differentially located in the social hierarchy.

As a group and in most situations, collections are often described as "vague collectivities" (Millett, 1981, p. 68). The group members' personality, to borrow Guiot's terms, emerges as a "closed system which society 'impinges upon' but does not structure" (1977, p. 694). Conversely, aggregates are described as "invisible" individuals (Apfelbaum, 1979, p. 196), a marker which encompasses lack of recognition of the subordinates' personal distinctiveness. On the dominants' side, Dahrendorf (1964, p. 262) maintained that "*Enumeration* is often one of the best methods of avoiding the wearisome business of defining terms like 'elite' or 'upper class.'" Clearly, enumeration refers to a conception of a group as a loose collection of individuals and subgroups (a sort of *Who's who* group, quite the opposite of a holistic conception). But why should the task of defining the upper class be a more "wearisome business" than that of defining the lower class? This is possibly because lower classes and, more generally, underprivileged groups, are assigned more entitativity and substance (see Bauman, 1982). The group's name then becomes a "label of primary potency" (Allport, 1954, p. 179) which prevents the perceivers from making finer differentiations within the group. As Glass pointed out (1964, pp. 142–43), "members of minority groups are socially placed primarily not on grounds of their individual origins, conditions and aptitudes – but in their capacities as members of a group to which particular roles and locations in society are assigned, explicitly or implicitly."

Let me further illustrate the novel idea of a collection group by advocating a metaphorical description of a group of "artists," or "managers," or else "chief executives," as reported by Bourdieu and de Saint Martin (1978):

> The distinctive feature of the "elites" of "democratic" societies is to define themselves statistically and therefore to be delimited by statistical boundaries that never take the shape of *strict demarcation lines*: . . . not all members of the group possess all the properties that define the group per se and, as for the contour of a cloud or a forest, the contour of a group is an imaginary line (or surface) such as the density of individuals (droplets of condensed vapor, trees or chief executives) is on one side higher, on the other side lower than a certain value. [. . . The] fact that the different group members are such that they *cannot be substituted*, if not compared, that is they can never be identified between themselves in all respects and exceptions can always be opposed to any definition, produces the subjective illusion of the mystery of the indefinable "person" and of the group, founded as it is on the miracle of the election, that is nothing more than a sum of "exceptional" individuals or "personalities." (pp. 33–34, original emphasis)

This portrayal of chief executives departs altogether from an Aristotelian and even from a prototypical conception of the group. The group is left aside and appears, at best, molded on a gathering of individuals as a function of their prominent and distinctive characteristics, or as a function of their social standing. Let me note that in an experiment manipulating status differentials between groups, Thibaut (1950) was depersonalizing low-status group members by just allocating a code number to them, whereas he was designating high-status group members with their first name. Hence, the dominants were represented as being distinct, heterogeneous, "non-interchangeable," whereas the subordinates were simply denied of a mark of personalization and interpersonal distinctiveness.

These speculations about mental and social representations of a group lead to clear hypotheses for the study of the internal variability of groups. Specifically, the prediction of a divergence between heterogeneous dominant groups and homogeneous subordinate groups has recently received some empirical support (Lorenzi-Cioldi, 1998; see also Lorenzi-Cioldi, 1993, 1995; Lorenzi-Cioldi & Doise, 1990; Lorenzi-Cioldi, Eagly, & Stewart, 1995; Mullen, 1991). A program of research using both natural and experimentally created groups demonstrated that high-status and low-status groups correspond, at a more formal level, with opposing models of category representations in the social cognition literature. In a low-status or aggregate group, the emerging categorization model is of Aristotelian (at best, of prototypical) inspiration: the group members tend to possess all of the attributes that define this group at an abstract level. In a high-status or collection group, the model is exemplar-based, sometimes a mixture of exemplars and prototypes: members endorse more or less strongly a subset of their group's attributes, or else, the group is made up of a juxtaposition of prominent instances. The group's features are then occasionally abstracted from consideration of the whole set of the group members.

By taking into account properties of the social structure, particularly the social hierarchy, seemingly universal, antagonistic, and mutually exclusive mental representations of a group, such as those called up, in turn, by the Aristotelian, prototypical, and exemplar-based advocates in social cognition, become concurrent and compatible. The social representations approach therefore obliges us to move beyond notions of a generic information processor, to take into account the anchoring of the individuals' social representations in the social structure, and, more specifically, the social positioning of the perceivers and the target group members.

From Mental Representations to Social Representations

Social cognition perspectives on individuals' mental representations clarify how individuals – whose location in the social structure remains unspecified – think and act in a variety of circumstances. These thoughts and actions are formalized in abstract models of cognitive functioning, for instance by the gender-schema, and by the contrasting structural properties of various mental representations of groups. Social representations theory further explains *why* and *when* such general cognitive principles are activated and applied in social reality. In this respect, molecular approaches to social cognition and more comprehensive approaches to social representations complement one another.

Social cognition approaches to the ways in which individuals organize social information may be right, yet they are not enough. Because of their lack of concern about supraindividual dynamics (that is, cultural, social, and ideological dynamics), purely cognitive models venture to reify an individual's cognitive functioning. This reification has accompanied the elaboration of "good" models, that is, efficient, heuristic, and predictive models. Important as it may be, however, this task has distracted researchers from the study of the conditions that facilitate, hinder, or moderate the implementation of a plurality of cognitive principles. The individual appears to be an information processor according to certain formal rules. As soon as they are formalized, cognitive principles are assumed to be evenly spread (at least in a given culture) and mechanical in their effects. Researchers engage in disputes about formal properties of such cognitive principles. The dispute between Bem (1982), who propounded the notion of a gender-schema, and Markus and her colleagues (Markus, Crane, Bernstein, & Siladi, 1982), who propounded the notion of a self-schema, is a nice illustration. Let me briefly outline this dispute.

Bem advocates the idea of a *bipolarity* of the gender-schema, whereas Markus emphasizes the *unipolarity* of her notion of self-schema. I have already suggested that, in Bem's view, sex-typed men and women are concerned with the domain of gender as a whole, that is with the masculine and feminine traits and behaviors as opposing ends of a single continuum. Conversely, in Markus's view and according to her competing notion of self-schema, people become "experts" in the processing of information related to a particular domain, either the feminine or the masculine domain. In contrast with gender-schema theory, self-schema theory posits that "one who develops a self-schema with respect to femininity becomes an expert in femininity, but there is little reason to assume that this person simultaneously becomes an expert in masculinity – no more reason, in fact than to assume that a thin person will have a well-developed sense of obesity or that an extrovert will have a well-developed understanding of introversion" (Markus et al., 1982, p. 49). Thus, masculine and feminine traits and behaviors are organized as two independent domains, and self-schematic people become expert users of either one or the other domain. In sum, these models differ with respect to their structural or formal properties. Bem's model is theoretically holistic and empirically bipolar, and Markus's model is particularistic and unipolar. The dispute between these authors revolves around demonstrating from each side the pervasiveness of the individuals' use of a single defined schematic process, either the gender-schema or the self-schema. However, as I have suggested in the preceding section on the gender-schema, social representations theory remains more open to the possibility that individuals may use, according to their social positioning and the contexts in which they interact, different kinds of schemas in their processing of the social information.

The following comments by Shweder and Sullivan apply well to this situation:

> The basic idea of a central processing mechanism is that deep within all human beings is an inherent processing device, which enables us to think (classify, remember, infer, imagine), experience (feel, need, desire), act (strive, choose, evaluate), and learn. Not only is the central processing mechanism presumed to be an abstract, fixed, and universal property of human mental life; it is also presumed that this abstract, fixed, and universal form transcends and is sealed off from all the concrete, variable, and particular stuff, substance, or content upon which it operates. . . . One quick and dirty (and striking) indicator of the influence of [the central processing mechanism heuristics] on personality research is the strong inclination among social-psychological researchers to move very quickly – indeed, to rush – from the discovery of some local, context-specific, meaning-saturated regularity (e.g., an audience facilitation effect or a dissonance reduction effect) to the representation of it in the literature as a fundamental law or basic process. We suspect that this "presumption of basic process" is so commonplace because of the hegemony of the central processing mechanism *as an idea.* . . . It then takes about a decade for the latest "fundamental" or "basic" process to be unmasked as a "mere" local regularity. (1990, pp. 407–408)

Moving beyond formal properties of the individuals' cognitive functioning, social representations theory draws attention to a variety of moderating factors in the way cognitions are enacted. In the examples I have presented in this chapter, social representations theory helps to explain why and when some people – not people in general – endorse individualistic and/or collectivistic traits, conceive of themselves as interchangeable group members or as unique individuals in a collection of people, and display or do not display a gender-schema. In the latter case, for instance, the theory demonstrates that gender-schematic processing of the information arises not solely because of the match between the gender stereotypes and the male and female categories. Other factors, such as the social positioning of men and women in the social structure, intervene to shape the individuals' self-representations. As Kihlstrom and Cantor pointed out, "We have treated the self as an object of knowledge – as a mental representation of a thing that exists in the physical and social world. . . . We have nothing to say about the self as knower, except, obviously, to identify it with the cognitive system that encodes, retrieves, and transforms information. But the matter of the self-as-knower is not simply a matter of information processing" (1984, p. 40). This is possibly because comprehension of the self-as-knower is also a matter of perceiving, judging, and acting from the point of view of an ingroup which can best be described as a specific location in the social structure.

16

Attitudes, Social Representations, and Beyond

George Gaskell

Introduction

At first sight a discussion of research on attitudes and social representations invites an evaluative comparison. For here, it might be considered, are two long-standing programs of research competing for the explanation of common phenomena. In the first part of this chapter an outline of the two programs shows such striking divergences to suggest that a comparison between them is a category mistake. Essentially, the phenomenon of attitudes, as currently conceived, is not the same as the phenomenon of social representations. The former foregrounds individual cognition, while the latter social knowledge.

However on closer inspection, there are notable points of intersection between the two programs. If we look back into the history of social psychology we find that they have common intellectual origins and were inspired by similar concerns. More recently, the concept of representation has appeared in attitudinal research (cf. Eagly & Chaiken, 1993), just as the attitude has a place in the social representations approach (cf. Moscovici, 1976a). Since the concepts of attitude and representation are clearly related as general categories, there may be common ground for a new research agenda.

To anticipate the conclusion of this chapter, the ambiguous figure in Figure 16.1 acts as a metaphor for the individual and the social context in social psychology. The figure invites changes in perspective and to do so is to understand its totality. In recent years, however, social psychology has moved to an almost exclusive focus on one perspective, that of the individual. While this research has made many notable advances, a more complete social psychology would seek to complement the focus on individual psychological processes with the related focus on the social context, the role of social regulations, communication, and culture in the determination of attitudes.

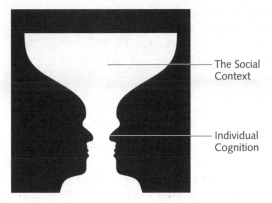

Figure 16.1   The dual perspectives of social psychology.

This chapter, drawing on the work of many others, is a modest attempt to point in the direction of clarifying some theoretical issues and methodological developments at the intersection of both programs that might point towards the specification of a new program of research.

The Attitudinal Research Program

"The definition of the attitude in terms of people's evaluations of entities is consensual in psychology and the social sciences" (Eagly & Chaiken, 1993, p. 270). Lying behind this state of affairs is a second consensus that mental states such as attitudes are the triggers of action. Cognitive determinism is the foundation of research on attitude structure, attitude change, and on the relations between attitudes and behavior. If the attitude was not a putative antecedent of behavior, it is doubtful whether the program of research on the attitude would have been quite so extensive. The "ideal case" is the political opinion poll. With appropriate sampling and question wording, verbal responses locating attitude objects (political parties or candidates) on an evaluative dimension of judgment (approve/disapprove) are as good a predictor of voting and election results as can be found. On this assumption attitudes achieved and have maintained a central position in social psychology and in many fields of applied social psychology for more than half a century.

The history of the attitude program, and one might say of social psychology more generally, can be characterized as a secular shift towards increasing individualization of phenomena, and to greater quantification in research. For the early theorists the attitude was conceived as the individual counterpart of social values and embedded in group relations (Thomas & Znaniecki, 1918) or as social sentiments (Asch, 1952). But this dual focus on the individual and the social has been lost in favor of an almost exclusive concentration on individual cognitive processes (for a discussion see Farr, 1996; Graumann, 1986). While the resulting conceptualizations of the attitude assumed that their origins were social in nature and acquired through experience, with some notable exceptions, the social was implicit and relegated to the unseen background. In the foreground of theoretical developments and empirical research was the individual cognitive system, extracted from the social context.

The movement towards the attitude as a primarily individual process took root in the 1920s and 1930s. At this time there were a number of significant developments resulting from innovations in attitude scaling and measurement. The advent of attitude scales allowed researchers to move away from qualitative and ethnographic studies to quantitative comparisons between individuals and groups over space and time. These developments brought a welcome "scientific perspective" to social psychology, enabling the subdiscipline to compare itself favorably with the dominant experimental tradition. It is interesting, however, as explained by Jaspars and Fraser (1984), that the construction of Guttman and Thurstone scales is implicitly based on a presumption of shared representations of the attitude object in question. But the rather time-consuming procedures of collecting a range of items from different contexts and the use of judges for item analysis, was soon replaced by the Likert scale with its more efficient methodological individualism (Farr, 1993).

Although Sherif (1936) and Sherif and Sherif (1956) demonstrated that norms, attitudes, and behaviors were socially constructed, and Lewin (1952) located attitudes in a social context, linking attitude change to group norms, this seminal research was categorized as group dynamics and its crucial significance for attitude theory neglected. In the 1950s and 1960s the attitude program moved on to models of cognitive structure with the organizing principle of individual consistency. In this period the foundations of contemporary experimental social psychology were laid. The laboratory experiment and analysis of variance procedures came to be *the* methodology of social psychology. Phenomena that did not lend themselves to this style of research were almost defined out of scope. In pursuit of the fundamental elements of the attitude and the processes underlying attitude change, the nature of the attitudinal object in empirical studies was increasingly treated as an irrelevance.

The directive role of attitudes in action was challenged by some anomalous findings (La Piere, 1934; DeFleur & Westie, 1963), but these were not regarded as significant threats to the program. But later, Wicker's meta-review of a wide range of studies indicating generally low correlations between attitudes and behaviors provided a more worrying challenge (Wicker, 1969). As a result attitude research went out of fashion and social psychology, regrouping under the umbrella of Heider's naïve psychology (Heider, 1958), turned its attention towards attribution theory and its derivatives.

However, Fishbein and Ajzen (1975), drawing on rational choice and expectancy value models, reinvigorated the attitude program with the theory of reasoned action. Where there was an explicit choice to be made, for example voting or consumer behavior, the model, which included a form of social determination in the formation of behavioral intentions, performed well. Essentially it is a model of the sovereign individual whose preferences (attitudes) are either supported or constrained by the perception of what "significant others" think he or she should do. Critical tests and developments of this model of attitude saw the introduction of increasingly more complex statistical procedures, and the addition of other antecedents of the behavioral intention such as past behavior (Bentler & Speckart, 1979) and perceived behavioral control (Ajzen, 1988). The social normative beliefs have been of minimal interest and it is perhaps only in the work of Charng, Piliavin, and Callero (1988), working in the symbolic interactionist tradition, that a serious consideration of the social, in terms of self-identity, has been introduced into the theory.

Taken as a whole, the contemporary program essentially concerns attitude structure and judgmental processes, drawing on cognitive psychological models of associative networks, memory mechanisms, schemas, and scripts. It seems as though, following the migration of cognitive psychologists towards neuropsychological processes, many social psychologists decided to take up residence in the vacated ground of individual cognition. That said, it is encouraging to see in a series of forward looking papers commissioned by the *European Journal of Social Psychology* under the umbrella "Agenda 2000," that the social is being rediscovered, see for example Schwarz (2000).

The majority of attitudinal research has been based on cross-sectional experimental studies in laboratories using scalar measures of the evaluative component of the attitude. The standard analysis of variance designs of the 1960s and 1970s have been supplemented with multiple regression, causal modeling and other multivariate techniques. Other approaches such as field studies, time series analyses, the use of representative samples, or studies of particular population subgroups, and in particular qualitative methods to understand attitudes in their wider context have not featured significantly in the program. The paradigmatic specification of the appropriate concepts and methods has sidelined any interest in the social and developmental aspects of attitudes. This is not to deny the value of cognitive approaches to the attitude, but rather to point out that individual cognition is only one perspective on the ambiguous figure.

The Social Representations Program

The theory of social representations has been criticized for assuming a sociological perspective, hence it is not proper social psychology. Admittedly the theory draws on Durkheim (1996, first published 1898) and has parallels in the work of the sociologists Berger and Luckman (1967) and Blumer (1969). But, it offers a novel and distinctive social psychological perspective. For example, Durkheim's notion of collective representations – religious and mythical imperatives – is too static to account for contemporary societies characterized by a diversity of social segments, a flood of developments in science and technology, the explosion of the mass media, and the secular decline in the influence of monolithic institutions and doctrines. It is with the understanding of people in this modern world that the theory of social representations was conceived.

Essentially the theory assumes that social phenomena do not occur as something that is outside the individual, but rather within a dynamic process of interaction and communication. Thus the social is not merely a backdrop against which individual processes are foregrounded. The social, whether society, culture, or group, and the individual are not conceived as opposed universes. On the contrary, while the social shapes the contents of individual minds, so is the social a product of communication and interaction between individual minds. The "thinking society" typified by interpersonal and mediated communication is the arena where reality is constructed and negotiated.

Within the program of research on social representations two related but somewhat distinct traditions can be identified. On the one hand, there is a tradition focusing on the production of knowledge, and on the other hand, there is a second tradition focusing on the structure of knowledge. In both these traditions knowledge can be taken as synonymous with "common sense."

The production of knowledge

The production of knowledge is an active and social process of making sense of reality, a reality in contemporary times that is frequently confronted by the shock, or at least the challenge, of the new. To understand the processes whereby the new is understood (re-presented), the theory of social representations relies on a form of contractual realism. Faced with a reality of sort, a community engages in discussion until it finds a negotiated solution. As an illustration, consider some work that we have been doing with a number of colleagues in Europe on biotechnology in the public sphere. This concerns the reception of the new developments in the life sciences that have resulted from recombinant DNA technology (Gaskell et al., 1997; Durant, Bauer, & Gaskell, 1998). At one level there is the primary objectification of biotechnology as it is described in scientific journals, seen in the activities of researchers in laboratories, and in the new applications and products of modern biotechnology.

But for us as social psychologists the interest is in the processes by which the public makes sense of, or makes a reality of this technology, what we call the secondary objectification. Biotechnology, described in the mass media in utopian and dystopian visions, is of such significance that it simply cannot be ignored. The human genome project has been likened by scientists to the quest for the Holy Grail, the opening of the book of life. With genes described as determining diseases, individual characteristics, and social behaviors, the genetic map is the new scientific astrology. Applications such as the cloning of animals, genetic testing, cross-species gene transfers, genetically modified foods, and the patenting of life forms have projected this esoteric science into the public sphere. Because it challenges many "taken for granteds" about the natural order, people feel concerned, even threatened by this new science.

Confronted by this challenge, how do the public respond when biotechnology is unfamiliar and for the most part incomprehensible? Few sit on a philosopher's stone to contemplate the matter in splendid isolation. The majority rely on media reporting and conversations with their network of family and associates. Biotechnology becomes a reality through images, metaphors, and ideas taken from films and media reporting, myths like Frankenstein and Faust, recent events such as the crisis over mad cow disease, and beliefs about the contribution of science to progress, etc. The familiarization of biotechnology takes place through the complementary processes of anchoring and objectification (Moscovici, 1976a). Anchoring is a process of naming and classifying, the unknown is fitted into existing structures of knowledge. In this process the object is transformed and becomes a category of conversation, for example cloning anchors nucleic transfer techniques, and GM food anchors novel foods produced by genetic manipulation. Objectification gives a tangible form to the abstract idea, for example "Dolly the sheep" objectifies cloning, and for some opponents "Frankenfoods" objectifies GM foods. A re-presentation of biotechnology is not a final outcome but rather it is a process that is essentially socially generated and sustained. This process does not occur in a homogeneous society, but in a multitude of social groupings with different lifeworlds. Different social groups consume media with different agendas, they call upon different knowledge bases, have particular concerns and enthusiasms, and as a result cultivate different representations. Hence, we observe a number of realities of biotechnology in the public sphere, from the enthusiastic support of business milieu to the opposition of the environmental milieu. Just as the primary objectification of biotechnology as a science has changed over time, so is there an evolution in the secondary objectifications. This is seen in the ways in which it is represented in different ways by different groups at different times.

Of course people can and do express attitudinal positions regarding applications of biotechnology. For example, some are more enthusiastic than others about new genetically modified foods. But, what is striking when we talk to people in indepth interviews and in focus groups is that they do not merely focus on attitudes in the sense of evaluative judgments. They want to tell us about what biotechnology means to them, how they understand the new technology in relation to other scientific developments and historical events, what it means in terms of moral and ethical issues, and how such developments in science may affect them and their children. Although people do have attitudes towards biotechnology, it is what processes and resources lie behind these attitudes that is our prime concern. In other words, our objective is to describe and account for the multiple and changing representations of the "reality" of biotechnology amongst the public. Furthermore, we assume that these representations of biotechnology may play an important role in the development of the technology itself. They constitute a sociopolitical environment that may act to facilitate or constrain the emerging reality of the technology. In this sense we conceive of biotechnology as a dynamic system in various environments, in which public opinion or attitudes are neither cause nor effect, but constitutive of the system.

In the broader program of research on social representations there are notable studies concerning, for example, the reception of psychoanalytic ideas in France (Moscovici, 1976a) and in India (Wagner, Duveen, Themel, & Verma, 1999), of public spaces in Brazil (Jovchelovitch, 1995), and what it means to live with the mentally ill (Jodelet, 1991). In all of these studies there is an interest in the contents of common sense, as well as the processes by which it is generated. A social representation without content and communication is an oxymoron. It is only where the issue is of relevance to the group concerned that one finds social representations, for amongst other functions they express the group's response to a challenge to common sense, the taken for granted.

A key feature of Moscovici's study concerns the social determination of the contents of the mind. He shows that normative control and communication are organizing principles lying behind the "common sense" of a particular group. The study concerns the ways in which three distinct subcultures of French society in the 1950s responded to the challenge of psychoanalytic ideas, and cultivated different representations of this new "science." The study is based on interviews, social survey data, and media analysis with the objective of understanding the relations between characteristics of social systems, communication processes, and cognitive functioning. Moscovici shows that in the communist party, a group with a high level of social control predicated on a world-view of conflict, the communication strategy is that of propaganda. This seeks to enforce a stereotypical rejection of psychoanalysis as an instrument of Western imperialism. By contrast, the Catholic hierarchy adopts the strategy of propagation with the aim of accommodating certain aspects of psychoanalysis, the symbolic and spiritual, into the existing religious dogma. Here, in a well-organized but not hegemonic group, the communication seeks to influence attitudes. Finally, in the newspapers catering for the somewhat amorphous urban elite, the journalists diffuse information from specialist sources to their readership, with the intention of merely informing opinions.

Each communication strategy corresponds to a particular expression of the social representation, in terms of content, organization, and intended effects on behavior. For Moscovici, the attitude is conceived as a structure of evaluative judgments related to particular group norms which lead to communications directed towards different forms of persuasion. Hence, attitudes may be seen as one of a number of possible functions of a social representation.

Moscovici's notion that representations are embedded in social relationships and communicative practices is also seen in the work of Doise (1990) and De Giacomo (1980) where Tajfel's social identity theory provides concepts to analyze the group dimension (see Doise, Chapter 7, this volume; Brewer, Chapter 22, this volume). It was this ambition to integrate the social and the cognitive that prompted us to use social representations as the framework for our research on the reception of modern biotechnology, rather than an attitudinal or risk perception approach. Reflecting on our research we recently outlined a formulation of a program of research on social representations (Bauer & Gaskell, 1999). At the heart of the analysis is a specification of the basic unit of analysis for the emergence of representation. This is the Subject–Object–Project–Subject relation, SOPS, a triangle of mediation with a time dimension. The minimal social system involved in representation is a dialogical triad: two persons, (subject 1 and subject 2) who are concerned with an object (O). The triangle of mediation (S–O–S) is the basic communication unit for the elaboration of meaning. Meaning is not an individual or private affair, but always implies the "other," concrete or imagined. While individually cognized, both in form and content of cognition, the presence of the other is always implicated, based on communication in the past, present and future.

To this basic triangle a time dimension, both past and future, must be added to capture the implied or espoused project (P) linking the two subjects. In this way the meaning of an object is an emergent property related to a past and future time horizon. The basic system is now (S–O–P–S), and can be imagined as a "toblerone," an elongated triangle (the shape of the famous Swiss chocolate). At any point in time a representation is a triangular slice through the toblerone, the apexes standing for subject 1, subject 2 and the object O, associated by the joint project of the two subjects.

The meaning of an object, take for example psychoanalysis or biotechnology, changes and evolves with the differentiation of social groups. Over time, various triangles of mediation coexist and form a social system. Depending on the project of the group, social representations may serve a variety of functions including ideological, identity, mythical, stereotypical, or attitudinal.

From this discussion we formulate a number of implications for research on social representations. These include multilevel analysis covering mediated and interpersonal communication, the use of natural groupings (social networks), the analysis of communication systems within groups, the study of the content, structure, and functions of representation and the use of longitudinal research designs. These implications constitute an "ideal type" model, a paradigm for research addressing concepts, key distinctions, and methodological choices.

Structural approaches to representations

Within the program of social representations a parallel approach concerns the structural features of representations (Abric, 1993; Flament, 1994a). While those concerned with the production of knowledge are more interested in the evolution and functions of the "taken for granted," within the structural approach the objective is to understand the structure of the "taken for granted" and how it is adapted to action contexts. Abric (1989, Chapter 4, this volume) outlines a two-fold structuring of the representation, the central system or the core, and the peripheral system, the interface with reality. A social representation is organized around a core that determines its meaning and structure. The core is determined by historical, sociological, and ideological conditions. It is a defining characteristic of a group, and is consensual, coherent, and stable.

Our research on biotechnology provides an illustration of the central core and the periphery (Allum, 1998). The data were qualitative in nature, the transcripts of five focus group discussions, and responses to an open-ended question included in a representative sample survey of British adults, "what comes to mind when you think about modern biotechnology in a broad sense, that is including genetic engineering?" These were analyzed using the ALCESTE program which determines word distribution patterns in a text corpus. From a contingency table of word associations, correspondence analysis provides what may be cautiously interpreted as the structure of representations. Following the content of the topic guide used in the focus groups, three applications of biotechnology featured prominently in the mapping of the representation: GM foods, reproductive technologies, and the breeding of transgenic animals to provide organs for human transplants (so-called xenotransplantation).

However, the results suggest that representations of biotechnology are at an early stage of maturity as there is a relative paucity of metaphors and concrete objectifications observed in the data. The exception is GM food which is anchored (discussed) in the familiar consumer contexts of shopping and choices about healthy food. But other elements of the representation are only vaguely anchored in concrete contexts. Xeno-transplantation, for example, is seen as a type of grizzly science fiction, and reproductive issues anchored in ideas of "the master race," "eugenics," and "designer babies." Without much exposure to biotechnology in practice, it would seem that the anchors are drawn from historical events and popular culture. But perhaps the most striking finding is that all three components of the representation are "anchored" in an ethical and moral framework, which appears to be shared by both supporters and opponents. The themes of "playing god" and "tampering with nature" are repeatedly explored and appear to be the way in which people are able discuss their anxieties about these new developments in science and technology. Hence, in Britain in 1997, at a time when few had much familiarity with biotechnology, the challenge is met through a core representation based on the familiar polarity of good and evil.

Similarities between the Structure of Social Representations and Attitudes

There are many parallels between social cognition and the structural approach to social representations. This is not surprising as in large measure both share a common inheritance in Gestalt psychology. The notion of structures organized around a core and periphery, what McGuire terms the "basal-peripheral analysis" is gestalt in origin and made an influential contribution to the broader cognitive revolution in social psychology. Consider the classic works by Asch (1946) on social perception and Heider (1958) on causal attribution. This central and peripheral distinction was a central part of Asch's research on trait inferences. Like the core elements in social representations, the source traits exercise a determining influence on the meaning of the peripheral traits attributed to a person. Heider's account of attributional phenomena proposes a "causal nexus of the environment" to explain the tendency to attribute a causal relations to the events taking place in the environment from units comprising a set of relations among elements. The causal nexus is linked to "dispositional properties," the unchanging structures and processes that allow people to understand social phenomena.

The idea that some attitudes are more stable than others, and therefore more resistant to change, has been a focus of research since Hovland's Yale Communications Program. The distinction between durable and changing elements may be explicitly recognized as a structural property (e.g., core and periphery) or implicitly acknowledged in notions such as attitude strength.

More recently structural models of cognition using organizing principles such as scripts or schema, again a product of the Gestalt perspective, lead to the idea of attitudes and representations as a structure in memory. An increase in the frequency of activation of a given concept increases its accessibility in memory and makes the concept more readily available. And with greater availability so is there greater strength of association between the particular concept and the object, and greater consistency between the structural configuration and action. (See Fazio, 1990 for an attitudinal perspective; Flament, 1994a; Rouquette, 1994; Abric, 1989 for the parallel representational perspective.)

Finally, in the writings of Rokeach (1970) on belief systems we find parallels to both traditions of social representations discussed in this chapter. For Rokeach a belief system is characterized by a central – peripheral dimension with the central beliefs being consensual, resistant to change, and having widespread repercussions for other beliefs. Rokeach writes about three varieties of beliefs. Firstly, there are the primitive beliefs defined as the taken for granteds of life, which owe their consensual status to universal social support. Secondly, with segmented social support are the nonprimitive beliefs, linked to authority figures and reference groups, and carrying expectations of differences of opinion and controversy. Thirdly, there are what he called the peripheral beliefs, derived from other forms of belief to serve various social functions. Interestingly in this formulation we see the core and periphery distinction of the structural theorists, the social determination of different forms of belief, and with the nonprimitive beliefs a specification close to social representations.

Turning to the peripheral elements in the structural model of social representations there are once again parallels with attitudinal research. The notion that the peripheral elements are flexible and adapted to the particular circumstances is also seen in Cialdini, Levy, Herman, and Evenbeck's (1976) concept of "elastic shifts" which function to maximize situational outcomes. Here strategic shifting around an attitudinal position occurs in different settings, rather than real changes in attitudes. This might be seen as an example of Hovland, Janis, and Kelley's (1953) latitude of acceptance concept, or of context effects in survey research (Gaskell, Wright, & O'Muircheartaigh, 1995).

So we have a number of examples of intersections between the concepts of the attitude and the social representation. In the next section some implications for social psychology are developed.

Attitudes and Social Representations: Scope for a Common Program

The broad area that stands out for collaborative efforts is the analysis of the development, structure and functions of attitudes and social representations. This, I would argue, should be predicated on the assumption that both the social context and individual cognitive processes must play a part in theorizing, empirical research, and explanation.

In this endeavor the relatively neglected nature of the social is perhaps a key question for discussion. First, consider the structural theorists of social representations with their emphasis on the core elements of the representation. Is it not too monolithic to conceive of the core of belief systems as necessarily consensual? Surely, as seen in the work of Moscovici, Rokeach, and Doise there is a relation between group characteristics, forms of communication, and the structure and function of representations. On account of particular group characteristics, some representations are consensual and in all probability serve ideological functions. But few groups have the strong normative regulation, or elaborated ideology of the communist milieu that Moscovici analyzed. As we are finding in our study of biotechnology in the wider public, the dynamics of the social are the dynamics of differences, of overlapping and sometimes competing representations of an object. With the social groupings we are researching, perhaps with characteristics more typical of the urban–liberal and the Catholic milieus, we find what can best be seen as a number of emerging cores, as the science and its applications move into the domain of common sense.

It is the understanding of differing receptions of the "new" within any one society, and the evolution and functions of such different realities, that poses the challenge. Because communication is controversial and distinguished by debate and argument, our models must accommodate dissent and opposition within the framework of collective activity. What is shared is that which makes communication possible, in terms of agreement and disagreement. In other words, it makes it possible to understand opposing views. If we think of the "social" not in the straitjacket of consensus but also in terms of sharing, we can explore differences in the representations of an object. To share is to have a part of the whole, but not necessarily to have the same part as everyone else. This is the distinction made by Harré (1984) when he talks of distributed versus collective representations. In the former all people carry the same representation, while in the latter, all carry part of the representation, but it is only realized socially. This collective form of the social is conceptually and empirically far more plausible amongst the mass of people with multiple identities and in groups without strong normative controls. If representations were distributed, then an interview with a single representative of a group would be sufficient to capture the viewpoint of the whole group. It conjures up a static society in which conversations would be almost redundant. The reality is competing representations, communication and conflict, and social change. These concerns about the use of the terms social, core, collective, and consensus as synonymous equally applies to empirical demonstrations of the existence of a social representation based on multivariate statistics or the counting of heads (see Rose et al., 1995 for a discussion).

It is still possible to maintain the idea of a consensual core, but only if the consensual refers not to agreement about the specific contents of representations, but rather to an agreement about the broader frame of discourse (c.f. Gamson & Modigliani, 1989). That is an agreement on what issues are relevant and can be discussed, rather than the position on these issues.

For the attitudinal theorists the issue is almost the counterpoint of the problem facing structural theorists of social representations. How can the attitudinal approach free itself from the straitjacket of researching the sovereign individual whose cognitive system operates in a social vacuum? This is perhaps not as difficult as might be imagined. Most cognitive social psychologists probably agree with Bartlett's assertion that schema are the products of an active process of construction and reconstruction (Bartlett, 1967, first published 1932) or, as Neisser puts it, "perception and cognition are usually not just operations in the head, but transactions with the world" (Neisser, 1976, p. 11). But, while accepting the notion of the construction of mental events, there is little interest in the ways in which such construction occurs outside the head.

Perhaps one way of escaping the strait jacket would be to ask whether the attitude, as currently conceived, is an over-inclusive category. Should social psychology continue to asume that there is one model of the attitude that can capture all manifestations of the phenomenon? There is sufficient research on the "behavior" of attitudes to support the idea that the concept should be reformulated into a range of phenomena. For example, there are likely to be interesting theoretical implications related to differences between non-attitudes (Converse, 1970), distal beliefs (Abelson, 1986), action related scripts and attitudes (Abelson, 1976 and Fazio, 1990) and other concepts such as identities, stereotypes, and ideology. Such a decomposition drawing on theoretical ideas and empirical findings could lead to the specification of "ideal types" with different characteristics in terms of their origins, structure, stability, functions, and extent of social determination. This endeavor would call for a return to the integration of research in social cognition and group processes. And finally to complete the circle, a candidate term for the superordinate category of these "ideal types" could be the "representation."

Such a commitment would carry some methodological implications. To study the social dimensions of attitudes it is essential to select objects of study that have relevance and meaning for the actors involved. The attitude program has relied too often on trivial objects of study and on the single method of the Likert type seven point scale as if its construct validity was a given. In researching the social dimension we need to think beyond the traditional small group study using complete strangers. Most communication that matters takes place between people who are part of a social network or milieu brought together by a common project.

It is notable that research designs, methods, and respondents used in the social representations tradition are varied. While some of the methods are common to attitudinal studies, others, such as the use of word associations, of individual and group interviews, of texts from various sources (e.g., the media) and studies of natural rather than ad hoc groups, offer new opportunities for the empirical analysis of the "thinking society" at work. Recognizing the value of a broader range of methods, including qualitative inquiry, would add greatly to research on attitudes.

Quantification is not the be all and end all of social scientific research. Too much emphasis on quantification as seen in the structural approach to representations and in the attitude program can be problematic. The risk is that of operationalism, where the concept comes to be defined by its methodology and takes on a determining role in theorizing (Gigerenzer, 1991). It will take more than operations and statistics to clarify the nature of attitudes and of the core and peripheral elements of representations.

In conclusion, I hope that there is scope for a constructive debate about the conditions of production, and on the structure, functions, and transformation of attitudes, and other forms of representation. Such a collaboration is likely to lead to the specification of a variety of questions from individual cognition to communicative processes in different social, subcultural, and cultural contexts. It would push social psychology to bring into focus both perspectives of the ambiguous figure with which I introduced this chapter. No doubt it will be a considerable challenge, but it is one that could reinvigorate social psychology in the twenty-first century, and bring with it more prominence for the discipline in society.

17

Social Cognition, Social Representations, and the Dilemmas of Social Theory Construction

Arie W. Kruglanski

Social Representations and Social Cognition Research Programs

As social psychologists our aim is to formulate general theories capable of explaining significant social phenomena in the world at large. Social representation and social cognition researchers went about this objective in disparate ways. It is not that the two approaches exhibited totally diverse perspectives on human social behavior. Gaskell (Chapter 16) notes several similarities between the attitudes and social representations research programs. Such similarities are not surprising. Representations, as the very name implies, are cognitive even if shared by entire groups of people. So are of course attitudes, beliefs, knowledge structures, categories, stereotypes, or lay theories studied by social cognition researchers. Structural issues (like the distinction between central and peripheral representations and its relation to susceptibility to change, or that between categorization/anchorage and exemplification/objectification) are topics of great interest to both social cognition (cf. Petty & Krosnick, 1995; Smith & Zarate, 1992) and social representation workers (Abric, 1993).

Nor is the notion that human knowledge is socially constructed, a mainstay of the social representation position, incompatible with much social cognition research that stresses the themes of "social reality" (Festinger, 1954) or "shared reality" (Hardin & Higgins, 1996), the anchorage of attitudes in group norms (Lewin,

1947) or the importance of group consensus to the maintenance of one's epistemic stability (Kruglanski, 1989; Kruglanski & Webster, 1991; 1996). Indeed, both research programs contain strong commitments to both cognitive and social elements, albeit they emphasize them to different degrees: in the representations program the "social" is often the figure and the "cognitive" the ground, whereas in the social cognition program these "figure-ground" relations are inversed. These matters of relative emphasis are not trivial, however, and they have led the social representations and social cognition camps in strikingly different research directions.

Social cognition research has focused on phenomena occurring "within the head" of isolated individuals. Whereas social contents (e.g., of various ethnic stereotypes) have often figured in social cognition experiments, they were generally tangential to the true research purpose which was to discover the general principles that govern how persons perceive, remember and think about socially-relevant stimuli. By contrast, socially-relevant contents have typically constituted a corner stone of social representations research. How specific groups of people think about psychoanalysis, biotechnology, public spaces, or madness, for example, was at the center of research attention; it was of interest in its own right rather than serving as an illustration of some abstract, decontextualized principles.

I agree with much of the critique leveled by social representations researchers in regard to the social cognition paradigm. Though our research and theorizing have often been very rigorous and sophisticated, they for the most part concerned phenomena occurring *within individuals* and were divorced from those occurring *between individuals, within groups,* and *between groups.* Secondly, the social cognition research project has been thoroughly academic in orientation and divorced from real-life social issues occurring in the world at large. As a consequence, social-cognition researchers may have had lamentably little voice in the general social science dialogue about larger social issues (cf. Kruglanski, 1999).

Of these two failings, the first may be on its way to amendment. The purely individualistic emphasis is increasingly supplemented by application of social cognitive principles in the social realm (see Levine, Resnick, & Higgins, 1993). My own research program on the need for cognitive closure has been of that nature (for reviews see, e.g., Kruglanski & Webster, 1996; Webster & Kruglanski, 1998) in demonstrating that a motivational factor that impacts how the individual forms impressions, judgments, or attributions has fundamental consequences for classic social psychological phenomena at the interpersonal, group, and intergroup levels of analysis. It is noteworthy, however, that even though some social cognition theories are applicable to various social phenomena, they do not typically incorporate social-context variables as its basic constructs. There is a good reason for it.

The Mixing of Levels of Analysis

An abstract theory formulated at a given level of analysis is *instantiated* at lower analytical levels. Care should be exercised, however, not to intermix levels of analysis, that is, not to incorporate into a theory stated at a given level of analysis its specific instances stated at a lower analytic level. These notions may be illustrated by reference to the excellent research program by Lorenzi-Cioldi (Chapter 15) on taking social context into account when explaining the construction of self-representations.

Lorenzi-Cioldi demonstrates that whether one's group occupies a dominant position or a subordinate position in society determines: (a) the extent to which the societal norm comes to match the characteristics of the group. Specifically, the societal norm matches characteristics of the dominant group to a greater extent than it does those of the subordinate group; furthermore, (b) members of the subordinate group self-represent in terms of their group membership to a greater extent than do members of the dominant group. Whereas members of the subordinate group view themselves as an aggregate of interchangeable persons, members of a dominant group see themselves as a collection of individuals. Correspondingly, the salience of their group membership is greater for the subordinate than for the dominant group.

Based on these findings it is argued that a full understanding of mental representations needs to take the social context into account, and to include in the theory the molar level of analysis adopted by social representation theorists. Failure to do so might reflect what Schweder and Sullivan (1990, pp. 407–408) have called "the inclination to rush from the discovery of some local context specific and meaning saturated regularity (discovered in the lab) to the representation of it as a fundamental law or basic process." I too am very much against a "rush" to fundamental principles or premature closures, and so were Kurt Lewin and Ernst Cassirer who admonished us not to confuse local or *phenotypic* accounts for general or *genotypic* ones that are the desiderata. But the question is what here is phenotypic and what genotypic?

Take the finding that the salience of group membership is lower for the dominant group than for the subordinate group. Why might it be so? Several potential explanations come to mind. Perhaps people adapt to a superior status more than to an inferior social status? Perhaps superior status represents a *match to a standard* of social desirability, or a fulfilled social goal, whereas inferior (subordinate) status represents a mismatch or an unfulfilled goal. Based on the work of Lewin and Zeigarnik, a fulfilled goal or a match to a standard should be less memorable than an unfulfilled goal or a mismatch and this may account for the differential saliency of the group membership for dominant or subordinate group members.

A different though a somewhat related explanation is that membership in a subordinate group is a negative feature of one's self-representation, i.e., a "blemish," and negative features are known to be more salient and hence better remembered than positive features like membership in a dominant group. Thirdly, because membership in a subordinate, low prestige group may be *problematic* for individuals, they may attempt to cope with it, perhaps through efforts to suppress the negative membership. Ironically, as we know from Wegner's (1994) work, repression may often rebound and flood our mind with just the troubling thoughts one attempted to repress, in this case one's subordinate or inferior social status.

These possibilities could certainly be explored in subsequent research. But what they share in common is that they approach the difference between dominant versus subordinate groups from an individual, or intrapersonal perspective. The intrapersonal variables they invoke include in this case the individual's matched or unmatched standards, her or his attempts at the suppression of unpleasant thoughts, or the general saliency for the individual of negative versus positive features.

To reiterate, a psychological theory can be instantiated in multiple (lower-level) ways that should not as such be incorporated into the theory. Say we discover that group membership is more salient for persons in subordinate groups than for members in dominant groups *because* mismatches are more salient than matches. That is, one way of instantiating, or operationally defining differential saliency, is by comparing dominant with subordinate group membership. But clearly there are many other determinants of saliency beside the dominant/subordinate status of a social group. For example, saliency may depend on numerosity, and Hamilton and Gifford (1976) have argued that, therefore, minorities are more salient than majorities, negative behaviors are more salient than positive behaviors, unexpected behaviors may be more salient than positive behaviors, vocal conduct may be more salient than silent conduct, etc.

Because there are so many potential ways of operationally defining saliency, there is no point in incorporating them all into the theory. Rather than being concise and parsimonious as a good scientific theory should be, our theory may become quite unwieldy and sprawling. Now, I am not suggesting that the interesting distinction between dominant versus subordinate groups discovered by Lorenzi-Cioldi is *necessarily* explicable by reference to general intraindividual processes. What I am suggesting is that it is worth exploring whether it might not be so explained. Premature incorporation of a given social context variable into a theory of mental representations might lure us precisely into the *phenotype trap* that Schweder and Sullivan (1990), Lewin (1951), and Cassirer (1923) so wisely admonished us against, namely assuming that what you *see* (empirically) is what you *get* (theoretically).

A similar problem relates to Martha Augustinos's critique of social cognition research on categorization. Augoustinos argues that social categorization is hardly the product of individual cognitive activity alone, but also the product of collective and ideological processes. She points out compellingly that the symbolic and ideological nature of stereotypes has been relatively neglected in the categorization research program and that there is much more to social categories than one might gather by scanning the recent social cognition literature. Thus, categories need not be "threadbare" but occasionally they may "elaborate an impoverished social reality." Categories can play a central role in "system justification" as the work of Jost and Banaji (1994) has demonstrated. Categories, moreover, can be ephemeral, unstable, and constructed ad hoc to accomplish various social actions (such as persuasions, blamings, denials, refutations, accusations) during a discursive episode.

Augoustinos concludes with a plea for an integrative theory of categorization. I take this to mean that stereotyping theory should include all the numerous insights she mentions, for instance that stereotyping can serve ideological, system-justifying, discursive, explanatory, or elaborative functions. But again we should be careful lest we overly complicate things by mixing apples and oranges that is, theoretical constructs and their instantiations. Take the notion that stereotyping can serve ideological, or system justifying interests. At the general intraindividual level this may mean that the construction of social categories is affected by motivation. The motivation to uphold a stable social reality, the motivation to advance one's long term interests, or the transient contextually based objectives of cajoling, persuading, etc.

But should all those various motivations be part of the theory of categorization? Not if their effects could be conceptualized in the same general terms. For instance, if one could argue on a general level that social constructions (such as social categories) are influenced by motivation so that their contents or structure are fashioned to fulfill the individual's various needs, one would not need to incorporate into the theory the countless needs that could be involved, e.g., the "system justification," "class interests," "outgroup derogation," "identity formation," or the plethora of other possible needs because their impact on the construction of social categories would be the same, generally speaking.

In short, the attempt by social cognition theorists to develop cognitive-level theories and apply them to social phenomena is justifiable from the philosophy of science perspective. Injecting the social context into cognitive theorizing might not work if it involves the intermixing of analytic levels by incorporating into formulations stated at a given level of analysis, special instances of their theoretical constructs stated at a different (and lower) level. This is not to say that the cognitive approach is the only or the best theoretical perspective on social psychological phenomena. But it is a feasible approach to investigating such phenomena as the history of our discipline (from Kurt Lewin onward) attests. Other approaches are certainly possible including the cultural, biological, or genetic perspectives on human sociality (for reviews see Higgins & Kruglanski, 1996). In all cases, however, the uniformity of the analytic level should be observed else the theoretical statements we concoct become confusing and unwieldy.

Whereas the social cognition program has recently begun applying the cognitive principles to explain various social phenomena, it has not attempted to alter its purely academic perspective and it has remained aloof in regard to societal issues at large. By contrast, the social representations movement has been thoroughly immersed in specific social topics and issues. Though this could have been an advantage, it could constitute a problem as well. The issue is one of a compelling justification for the research endeavor, that might be lacking in some cases of content-bound social representations work.

The Justification Issue in Social Representations Research

As noted earlier, the overarching objective of social psychological research, its "regulating ideal" as Popper might have put it, is to construct well-articulated theories that provide novel insights into major social psychological problems. Viewed from that perspective, a social psychological research effort should "pass muster" on two criteria: (a) is the theory at issue articulated well-enough; and (b) are the problems being addressed truly major or significant. Social cognition research emphasized the first criterion while paying hardly any attention to the second. We have many elegant models in the field that have still to be applied to significant social problems in the world out there. By contrast, a possible criticism of some (though by no means all) social representation research is that it largely disregarded theory testing and, moreover, it did not sufficiently justify its selection of the representational contents it investigated. Gaskell (Chapter 16, this volume) notes that "A social representation without content . . . is an oxymoron." But there are infinite contents out there and unless a given content is of particular importance in some sense (e.g., it figures importantly in a current societal debate) there seems little reason to choose it for a descriptive study. The problem is compounded by the fact that social representations may vary widely across time and space. As Gaskell puts it (Chapter 16, this volume) "contemporary societies (are) characterized by a diversity of social segments, a flood of developments in science and technology . . . and the secular decline in the influence of monolithic institutions and doctrines." Accordingly, the social representations of most topics should be extremely diversified across communities and within the same community across time. And it is, therefore, legitimate to ask why it is important to study say, the representation of biotechnologies in Europe in the 1990s, the representation of psychoanalysis, or of childhood, in France in the 1970s, of public spaces in Brazil in the 1990s, or of mental illness in Italy in the 1980s. Because of the transiency and diversity of social representations, the local significance of each has to be justified with care. It is my impression that such justification effort has been lacking to some extent in content-bound social representations research.

The Forest – Trees Issue in Social Representations Research

Gaskell notes that social representations research emphasized contents as well as process. But, again, my reading of the literature (e.g., Belelli, 1987) attests that the emphasis on contents often takes the upper hand and overrides the explication of process in abstract or general terms. In other words, the process of change or the formulation of representations is often depicted in terms of the specific contents being addressed, rather than in terms of transcendental principles that apply to the case at hand. This carries the danger of fragmentation, and the redundant discovery of seemingly multiple process-notions that aren't but diverse specific manifestations of the same principles. Admittedly, Moscovici's (1976a) original formulation did identify important process principles (anchorage, objectivization diffusion, propagation, and propaganda) but these do not always play an important explanatory role in social representation research of the descriptive, content-bound, type. This poses the danger of redundancy, rediscovery of the same "wheel," cast differently in every instance of social representations research, in short, a multiplicity of "trees" that hide the underlying forest.

Conclusion

Social cognition and social representation researchers share the same objective: Developing powerful ideas that apply to significant social problems. Social cognition has taken the intraindividual approach to the issue. Its failing has not been that it has not incorporated social context variables into its theoretical edifices but that it has failed to bring them to bear on important social problems. The social representations paradigm, however, has overemphasized social contents without sufficient attention to their unique significance both in terms of the societal "here and now" and in terms of their illumination of transcendental social psychological principles. Perhaps the encounter, critique, and contrast afforded by this volume will set us all on the way to developing the kind of social psychology "worthy of its name" that Gaskell calls for.

18

Social and Societal Pragmatism

Susan T. Fiske

The social representation of the discussant has, as its core, a person who talks with insufficient preparation; the social representation of the commentator is not much improvement. (I will endeavor to do better here.) Both discussant and commentator have, as peripheral features, three variants: (a) "Let me tell you what is wrong with these papers, and why they are not as good as you thought" – a kind of public journal review; (b) "Let me tell you what is right with these papers, and why they are better than you thought" – a kind of public letter of reference; and (c) "Let's ignore the papers, and talk about my research" – a kind of public narcissism. All three variants aim to make the commentator appear competent, but they do not do much for likeability. Nevertheless, this commentary will pursue all three variants of the peripheral features, although not fitting the central feature, instead having fully digested these excellent contributions.

The chapters by Professors Augoustinos, Gaskell, and Lorenzi-Cioldi offer three cogent analyses urging détente, constructive engagement, between the forces of social cognition and the forces of social representation. Indeed, my own work sympathizes with this idea, in urging that "thinking is for doing" (Fiske, 1993b, paraphrasing James, 1981, first published 1890). Much of social cognition work, including my own, takes an implicitly pragmatic stance, viewing social perceivers as adapting to different situations. If individual social perception functions for social adaptation, it does not operate only on a principle of least effort (the pure cognitive miser). Nor does social perception operate on a principle of sheer accuracy as a goal (the naive scientist). Social perceivers attempt good-enough accuracy, given their purposes in the context of a particular social interaction (the motivated tactician) (Fiske & Taylor, 1994).

Only a small step separates interpersonal social pragmatism from societal and ideological pragmatism. The interpersonal functions emerge from social cognition research, and the societal functions emerge from social representation research. Social representations researchers argue that socially shared understandings of unfamiliar phenomena operate to ease discourse, reduce threat, solidify the ingroup, and justify the groups' goals.

Indeed, the two levels of analysis – individual pragmatism and societal pragmatism – connect. Because other people constitute the most relevant evolutionary niche (Caporael, 1997), individuals' core social motivations adapt them to group life (Stevens & Fiske, 1995). The core motive to belong to a group and get along with the ingroup (e.g., Baumeister & Leary, 1995) fits with a variety of other social motives, among them creating a shared understanding. Social representations constitute exactly such shared understandings that allow the individual to function in the group and the group to function in society. Stereotypes, for example, function as shared social understanding (Fiske, 2000) that justify the status quo social hierarchy (Fiske, 1993a; Glick & Fiske, in press; Jost & Banaji, 1994; Sidanius & Pratto, 1999). The three chapters each illustrate principles of both social and societal pragmatism.

Augoustinos

Long an advocate of linkages between social cognition and social representation, Martha Augoustinos specifies why, when, and what categories are used. This chapter nicely links category use to societal issues, focusing on a case study, representing Aborigines. The chapter argues that social cognition research treats common social categories (age, race, gender) as nonproblematic, as givens. Perhaps due to such challenges, social cognition researchers have indeed been examining the societal bases of racial categorization (Banks & Eberhardt, 1998) and essentialistic theories of stereotypes (e.g., Yzerbyt, Rocher, & Schadron, 1997).

Augoustinos also argues that social representations function to make strange objects familiar, which (at a societal level) closely fits social cognitive descriptions of schemas' functions (Fiske & Taylor, 1994). In social cognitive terms, some categories become automatic, not because they are biologically given, but because they are socially pragmatic for groups and for society. People individually acquire cultural stereotypes through repeated exposure, making them automatic (Devine, 1989).

The case of socially representing Aborigines reflects paternalistic prejudice turned contemptuous, when formerly acquiescent subordinates become threatening (Fiske, Xu, Cuddy, & Glick, 1999; Fiske, Glick, Cuddy, & Xu, 2000; Glick & Fiske, in press). Old cultural stereotypes change to new cultural stereotypes, when relations between groups change. Stereotypes reflect status and interdependence relations between groups, justifying extant hierarchies. Such strategic use of stereotypes in communication reflects a long-standing perspective of social representation theory, but also a growing social cognitive approach to communication (Ruscher, Hammer, & Hammer, 1996).

In short, a range of American and European researchers are going beyond the narrow view of the cognitive miser, to the more flexible view of a motivated tactician, who sometimes uses shortcuts and sometimes engages in effort, always responsive to social forces. Taking us to the societal level, Augoustinos reminds us that the motivated tactician operates with self-protective and self-enhancing societal justifications (e.g., Jost & Major, in press).

Lorenzi-Cioldi

Social forces give rise to mental representations. In particular, group dominance determines who is represented as an individual and who as a group member. Dominants are independent, autonomous persons, whereas subordinates such as Aborigines are collective, category-based group members. Dominants are heterogeneous individuals who may come in aggregates, but subordinates are homogeneous groups. Thus, oppressed groups partake of their category more than dominant groups do. Women have gender more than men do; blacks have race more than whites do (Fiske, 1998). This asymmetry serves a societal function, namely justifying the subordination of the lower group, whose members all allegedly possess stereotypic attributes and deserve their status. Fabio Lorenzi-Cioldi suggests that subordinates are represented in terms of abstract prototypes, whereas dominants are represented as exemplars, which allows more variability for exceptional individuals or special personalities.

Subordinates are not only powerless, but also deviant; they depart from the cultural default. The American cultural default person is male, white, heterosexual, middle class, of moderate age. Subordinate groups are female, or colored, or homosexual, or poor, or elderly. Because subordinate status is so often confounded with deviation from the cultural ideal, one might assume they are identical, but perhaps deviance and subordination are not equivalent. Perhaps not only subordinate groups, who lack status and power, but any group who departs from the cultural default is perceived in collective terms (Fiske et al., 1999, 2001). For example, some high-status groups may not be dominant culturally. Thus, in the U.S., both Jews and Asians are viewed as successful, competent, and high status, but not as culturally dominant; they also are interpreted in collective terms. Feminists, career women, and black professionals similarly are perceived to be high status, but they are hardly culturally dominant. They do not set the cultural norms. Some high-status groups are treated as collectives because they are not culturally dominant. Perhaps it is any nondefault, "marked" groups who are seen as collectives, not only subordinate group members.

Pragmatically, it would make sense for social representations to form around subgroups that deviate from the cultural norm. Deviations require an explanation. To defend the norm threatened by deviation, society must justify the position of the subordinates on the one hand. The oppressed who cooperate in their position (traditional women, disabled people) are nice, but not competent or else they would be moving up in status. The oppressed who exploit their lower position (people on welfare, gypsies) are not nice and not competent. In either case, they are homogeneous lumps, which helps consolidate their position.

On the other hand, the high-status deviants require a different kind of explanation. Why are these groups doing so much better than society's default? Rich people have individual stories that fascinate us, but as a group, stereotypes apply to them too: greedy, cold, driven, competent in their pursuits. So, too, in the U.S., at least, Jews and Asians. Stereotypes of the competent but inhuman high-status groups serve to justify their (unfair and costly) advantage. The pragmatic social representation justifies the culturally dominant view of how competence and warmth combine, highlighting the risks of deviation by lack or excess. The social representation of the outgroups, low and high, explains the relative positions of groups and stabilizes them by prescribing norms.

Gaskell

George Gaskell does for attitudes what Augoustinos and Lorenzi-Cioldi do for stereotypes. He argues that both attitudes and social representations create sense-making, for example in making common sense of biotechnology, but do so at different levels of analysis, individual and societal. My reading of the attitudes literature is that it does make a place for the interpersonal functions of attitudes, not just the individual functions. For example, attitudes serve a social adjustive function as well as an object-appraisal function (Eagly & Chaiken, 1998). From the individual to the interpersonal does not constitute a mere quibble, for the interpersonal links attitudes to society.

Both attitudes and social representations, at their distinct levels of analysis, certainly take up a knowledge function. According to a social representations view, attitudes explain how the new is understood (re-presented), with the role of anchoring and classifying. This is equivalent to categorizing, at the individual attitude level. Attitudes serve an object appraisal function (good for me, bad for me), a sense-making category at the most basic level.

Nevertheless, the novel role for social representations in attitudes research is to emphasize the relationship of attitudes to one's own meaning, own societal context, own dilemmas, and own family. People defend the community's integrity by communicating these attitudes, much as they do by communicating stereotypes, as noted earlier. The useful distinctions among diffusion, propagation, and propaganda illustrate graduated defenses across national (and nationalistic) groups.

In the case of attitudes, the core is normative (in sense of ideal?), but the periphery is action oriented, functional in that sense. Of course, the core serves a function as well, but the periphery may be more concrete and applicable to specific circumstances.

Let's Talk about Me

Augoustinos and Gaskell both note the emphasis on process to the exclusion of content in stereotyping and attitudes respectively. I had come to the same conclusion, as we began to study the content of ambivalent stereotypes. We (Fiske et al., 1999, 2001) have differentiated two ambivalent stereotypes: (a) envious stereotypes directed toward the high-status, threatening, competent but cold outgroups (the rich); (b) paternalistic stereotypes directed toward the low-status, unthreatening, incompetent but warm outgroups (traditional women); as well as two unambivalent stereotypes: (c) contemptuous stereotypes directed toward low-status, exploitative outgroups (welfare recipients); and (d) admiring stereotypes directed toward the ingroup or its closest allies, who are allowed to be both warm and competent. These four social representations perpetuate and justify the way things are. Indeed, we could call them social representations without shame, for we ask respondents for the cultural consensus on the various groups' images. As such, they share the societal level of analysis so well represented in the chapters brought together here. Maybe, then, the social representation of the commentator moves from the narcissistic referee, to a member of the larger ingroup.

Part V

Social Representation and
Social Identification

19

Representations, Identities, Resistance

Gerard Duveen

From the perspective of social representations, social identity appears as a function of representations themselves. In elaborating this view, this chapter draws primarily on research on the development of social gender identities to argue the following points: (a) identity is as much concerned with the process of being identified as with making identifications; (b) identities can be construed as points or positions within the symbolic field of a culture, in other words, identities are constructed externally and not simply elaborated internally; (c) representations always imply a process of identity formation in which identities are internalized and which results in the emergence of social actors or agents; (d) identities provide ways of organizing meanings so as to sustain a sense of stability; (e) an identity is essentially an asymmetry in a relationship which constrains what can be communicated through it; and (f) we need to consider the possible varieties of forms of social identity.

Introduction

For almost as long as there has been social psychology the question of identity has been construed as the answer to the question "Who am I?" And the answer has generally been that "I am who the Other says I am." We can look back to William James as the *locus classicus* of this sense of identity in his famous dictum that "A man has as many social selves as there are individuals who recognize him" (1981, p. 281, first published 1890). James, as is well known, construed the Self as a duality of the I – the Self as a knowing subject – and the Me – the Self as it is known. Following James, this perspective was further elaborated in Cooley's notion of the "looking-glass self," and particularly in G. H. Mead's conception of the Self as a dialogue between the I and the Me, between the I which reacts to the attitudes of others and the Me which is the sum of the attitudes of others which have been internalized. (An important exception to the tradition of James, Cooley and Mead is Jean-Paul Sartre (1974), for whom the answer to this question is not that I am who the other says I am, but rather I am what I make of what the other says I am.)

While these classical authors wrote almost exclusively about the self, more recent writers have tended to focus on the concept of social identity conceived, in Tajfel's terms, as "that part of an individual's self-concept which derives from his knowledge of his membership of a social group (or groups) together with the value and emotional significance attached to that membership" (1981, p.255). In this conception, Tajfel is careful to leave a space within the self which is not accounted for by any social identification, although he has little to say about what this space might be. And although this conception has continued to animate work in contemporary Social Identity Theory, there have also been some dissident voices. Jean-Claude Deschamps (1982), for instance, sketches a perspective in which social identity is conceived as a function of relations of power between groups where access to a sense of self as a bounded and autonomous individual is seen as the expression of a specific form of symbolic capital. On this view self becomes a function of the constructions of identity, rather than identity being a subset of the self. However, it is not my intention in this paper to try and unravel any consistent pattern in the relations between self and identity, in part because the issues being addressed in this area of social psychology continue to be considered by different authors under the rubric of "self" or "identity." When Oyserman and Markus (1998), for example, discuss the self as social representation, they are recognizably referring to the same phenomena which Barbara Lloyd and I discussed as social identity (Duveen & Lloyd, 1986). There may be good – or bad – reasons for preferring one term to the other, either for some substantive purpose or in relation to the way these terms have figured in the discourse of social psychology. But we should not lose sight of the phenomenon under discussion, namely the ways in which individuals or persons or agents come to have a sense of who they are through a recognition of their position within the symbolic space of their culture.

Although in more recent years the question of identity has been more usually framed as a discussion of social identity rather than directly in terms of the self, nevertheless, the question "Who am I?" has remained central to this discussion. At the same time it has also been noticeable that there has been relatively less attention to the nature of the answers given to this question in terms of the *content* of the categories through which identities are defined. Henri Tajfel was a notable exception, who, while interested in formulating general propositions about the sources and consequences of social identity, was also deeply concerned with the nature of these categorizations. What it meant to be defined as a Jew in Europe in the 1930s, or as Black in Britain in the 1960s and 1970s were enduring questions for him. And although there have been some other examples of work which has tried to address similar questions – Breakwell (1979) on women for example – this strand has been a minority interest in work on social identity, and a minority which has struggled to exert any strong influence on a dominant and well-organized majority for whom social identity theory has been framed as a discussion of the processes through which identity is sustained or manipulated rather than on the content of those identities.

A lack of concern with the content of identities in contemporary social psychology is also accompanied by a one–sided view of the process of identity itself. Consider, for example, the newborn child, newly arrived into a world which is already structured by the social representations of the communities into which they arrive. The circulation of representations ensures that the child is born into a world in which meanings already exist, and which have, in some way or another, already prepared the way for the child. Even before they are born, at times even before they are conceived, children are already the objects of the hopes, fears, aspirations, and anxieties of the people who will become its parents. The child may be wanted or unwanted, parents may wish for a boy or a girl, and so on. Once the child is born, the parents' representations which underlie their construction of the child as a social object also influence and regulate the ways in which they interact with the child. Representations of gender, and of the process of development itself, structure the relationships which emerge through the interaction between parents and children. As the child develops, they also begin to internalize the identities which have been extended to them, and in their turn they develop into social actors capable of taking their place as competent and functioning members of their community. Before they are capable of independent activity in the field of gender (or any other social field) children are the objects of the representations of others. A child is always a construction before it is a reality, but a construction of others, and through this construction its parents and others extend to it a social identity, they locate it in a social space. The situation of the child expresses something fundamental about the nature of identity, namely that identity is as much about the process of being identified as it is about the process of identification.

My first concern in this chapter is to illustrate how approaching identity from the perspective of social representations can take us back to a concern with the content of identities. This concern has grown out of an interest in the development of social representations, particularly in relation to gender (cf. Lloyd & Duveen, 1990, 1992). And it is no accident that questions of the relations between representations and identities are posed so clearly from a developmental perspective focused on the process of children's emergence as social actors, that is, as active participants in a symbolic community.

The Development of Social Gender Identities

Becoming an actor in the field of gender

Like all good developmental narratives, this one begins with the newborn baby, who, with its instinctual reactions and emerging schemes, remains without any sense of self as either agent or identity. But for others around the child – principally parents, siblings, and so on – this newborn infant is not a neutral object, but one which is invested with the characteristics of a social identity. For the other, the baby is already a little boy or a little girl, and by extending a social identity to the child the other incorporates the child into a representational system which both gives the child a social location as well as regulates the action of the other towards the child. In this sense the child is first of all an object in the representational world of others, who anchor this new and unfamiliar being in a particular classification and give them a particular name, and who objectify their representations through the ways in which they interact with the child.

For the newborn infant one of the key constitutive acts of the other is the assignment of the child to a sex group. In a famous study Rubin, Provenzano, and Luria (1974) asked the parents of newborn children to describe their babies. Even when there were no differences in birth weight, birth length, or *apgar* scores, these descriptions varied systematically as a function of the biological characteristics of children's external genitalia. At this point in their lives these children had literally done nothing, and yet their very physical form served as signifiers for *others* to project a gender identity on to them. As we have shown elsewhere (Lloyd & Duveen 1990, 1992; Duveen 1994), this extended social identity is progressively internalized by children who, by the age of four, are already capable of establishing themselves as independent actors in the field of gender. It may be helpful here to trace out some of the key moments in this development.

In the first 18 months of children's lives their gender identity is regulated by the actions of others. Observations of women who were themselves the mothers of young children playing with six-month old infants illustrate some of the ways in which this occurs. In these studies (Smith & Lloyd, 1978; Smith, 1982) the women had not previously met the babies they were asked to play with, and the children were presented to them dressed and named stereotypically as either girls or boys. In fact half the time these children were cross-dressed and cross-named. Regardless of the biological sex of the child, the first toy offered to them for play was usually one which carried a gender marking consistent with the child's apparent gender. Thus a child presented as a girl was usually offered a doll, while a child presented as a boy was more likely to be offered a hammer. Even more striking were these women's reactions to these infants' gross motor activity. Such activity is not itself an indicator of gender, being a feature of the behavioral repertoire of both girls and boys. However, when this activity was produced by a child dressed and named as a boy the women offered both verbal and motor encouragement, stimulating further activity. The same behavior produced by a child dressed and named as a girl was viewed by the women as a sign of distress, to which they responded by soothing and calming the child.

From these studies it is apparent that for young infants toys and other objects of material culture do not carry any clear gender signification. It is the actions of *others*[1] which recognizes the marking of objects and connects these significations with the signifying aspects of the child's presence in a coherent representational praxis. With the emergence of the semiotic function at the end of the sensorimotor period, children themselves begin to take on a more active role in controlling and regulating their expression of gender.

The emergence of children as independent actors in the field of gender can be seen in observational studies of children playing in pairs with familiar peers of the same age (these studies are reviewed in Lloyd & Duveen, 1989, 1990). In one of these studies boys and girls aged three to four years were each observed twice, once playing with a girl and once playing with a boy. All of these observations took place in a room furnished with a variety of toys with known gender markings as either feminine (e.g., dolls, saucepans, shopping bags) or masculine (e.g., guns, trucks, briefcases).[2] Each time a child picked up a toy, therefore, their choice could be identified as being either congruent with their own gender, or incongruent with their own gender. Analyses of these toy choices showed a strong and asymmetrical pattern. Boys made far more congruent than incongruent toy choices, whereas girls tended to choose more evenly between both congruent and incongruent toys. This asymmetry could also be clearly seen in the length of time children played with different gender marked toys.

The asymmetry between boys and girls evident in their play with gender marked toys contrasted sharply with these children's performance on a range of cognitive and linguistic tasks, in which they were asked to sort pictures of people and toys according to gender, or to identify appropriate gender marked words. Although children's knowledge of these different codes for gender marking increased as they developed, few differences were found between girls and boys. The differences observed between girls and boys in their use of toys, therefore, could not be attributed to any difference in their knowledge of how these objects were marked for gender. Rather, it seems that even at this young age children are using their knowledge to construct different identities. For the boys in these studies, the material culture of toys seems not just to carry particular significations of gender, but also to provide an arena in which they need to express a clearly differentiated identity. The girls, by contrast, while not oblivious to the gender marking of toys, do not use this material culture as a resource for expressing a differentiated identity.

In this early acquisition of gender identities one can see clearly how their thoughts and actions become structured in terms of the representations of the communities in which they are growing up. Their identities are not simply internal elaborations of meanings, but the reconstruction of externally constructed patterns of meanings. Further, one can also see in these studies something of the complexity of the process of internalization. Children, as we have argued (Duveen & Lloyd, 1986; Lloyd & Duveen, 1990, 1992), are not simply internalizing social representations, but, as they do so they are also constructing particular identity positions in relation to these representations.

Representations in pretend play

The emergence of the semiotic function is marked by the appearance of a wide range of representational activities, and in a recent contribution Hans Furth (1996) has argued that the emergence of these activities also marks the emergence of the child as an active participant in the collective world. His claim, as he puts it, is that "these mental constructions have an inherently societal character, such that the *mental object itself is a societal object*" (1996, p. 26, original emphasis). On this basis he also suggests an endogenous origin for human society, for which the clearest evidence is to be seen in the pretend play of young children. Pretend play begins to emerge in young children with the emergence of the semiotic function itself, and by the fourth and fifth years it is established as a social and collective form of activity in which children not only evoke and recreate aspects of the world they inhabit, but also a forum in which their understanding of this world can be given structure and organization. Furth himself analyzes some examples of the construction of what he calls the "societal frame" in young children's play, as have other authors such as Corsaro's (1990) account of Italian kindergarten children's recreation of a banking system. The following example, however, returns to the theme of gender, and is taken from our own research with children in the first year of formal schooling (in England this means with five year olds).

This example, transcribed from video records of children during free play in the classroom of an ordinary infants school (Lloyd & Duveen, 1992), illustrates children's belief that physical/sexual contact between sex group members needs to be validated through marriage. Oscar is chased for some time by the girls but once he is kissed by Christine, perhaps somewhat to his surprise, he proclaims (turn 16) that he is going to marry her. Children create a simple world in which physical contact between sex group members is construed as sexual and involves marriage. In this world actions have direct and predictable consequences.

1. Edith: . . . and Lulu kiss, uhm, Oscar. Go on.
2. Christine: I'm not playing now.
3. Edith: Go away, then

4. Lulu:	No, you kiss Oscar and I kiss Darren.
5. Edith:	I know. Look. You (Joan) kiss him Darren.
6. Lulu:	And I'll kiss Oscar.
7. Edith:	Joan kiss Oscar.
8. Edith:	Joan kiss Darren, and Oscar kiss . . .you!
9. Joan:	(Starts for Darren, who runs) Hey!
10. Edith:	Come here. (Grabs Lulu and moves her towards Oscar, not unwillingly) No, kiss! Kiss her on the lips. Kiss her on the lips. Come on!
11. Lulu:	No way!
12. Edith:	Go on. Kiss her. Kiss her.
13. Christine:	(Makes a dash for Oscar) I kissed him.
14. Oscar:	I kissed HER!
15. Edith:	Oooh!
16. Oscar:	(Points at Christine) I'm going to marry her.
17. Edith:	(With Lulu, no longer struggling, very close) Kiss her.
18. Oscar:	I'm going to marry her.
19. Sally:	(Also closing in on Oscar)
20. Oscar:	All right (But which one should he kiss?)
21. Sally:	Kiss me. (They kiss)
22.	(All laugh. Oscar throws himself back on sofa)

Central to the social representations of gender in this extract is a reproductive meta-phor that offers an image of gender in terms of the bipolar opposition of the mascu-line and feminine. This is an image which children appear to have acquired very early in their lives and which persists into adulthood. (De Rosa, 1987, also notes that the iconic aspects of social representations of madness are acquired early in life.) In discussing the process of objectification Moscovici refers to the *figurative nucleus* of a social representation, "an image structure that reproduces a conceptual struc-ture in a visible manner" (Moscovici, 1981). The most graphic examples of iconic aspects of social representations of gender in our work concern children's evocation of sexuality in their play, where sexuality is evoked precisely as the union of bipolar opposites, and once established is celebrated through the rituals of marriage and domestic life. Indeed for these children there is a syncretic fusion of sexual relations, the institution of marriage, and the complementarity of gender roles in domestic life. The structure of a bipolar opposition is the connecting thread between these different elements, each of which implicates the others, so that when one element is evoked in play it can lead to the evocation of the others.

The figurative nucleus of bipolar opposites also supports a conceptualization of social life in terms of two complementary but exclusive categories. This conceptual structure influences how children interpret the world around them, while their participation in collective life provides a scaffolding which confers further legiti-macy on this conceptual structure. In sexuality, or more precisely heterosexuality, difference is both asserted because it depends on the presence of bipolar opposites, and also overcome at the same time through the union of these opposites. Sexuality, therefore, can take on a privileged status for young children because it offers the clearest resolution to the problem of difference. As I argued earlier, the image of bipolar opposition connects sexuality with marriage and domestic life, and in their play children's engagement with this theme expresses and celebrates a certain understanding of the world. In this understanding sex and gender are reduced to a single dimension, and it is the difference between the categories of masculine and feminine which are emphasized, while differences within each of these categories are obscured.

Variations in social identities

A primary function of social representations is the construction of social objects that provide a stable pattern of meanings for social actors. As in Piaget's analysis, this conception emphasizes the correlative relationship between the construction of the object and the construction of a sense of self. In other words, the construction of an object is one aspect of a developmental process that also extends to the formation of identities. Thus in addition to the construction of the object as a stabilizing function in the process of social representation, we also need to consider the identity function of representations. Piaget, of course, conducted his analysis at the level of epistemological relations between subject and object, a level of abstraction which assumes a homogeneity in the forms of subjects and objects which are constructed (cf. Duveen, 1994, 1997). But in the social world, such homogeneity cannot be taken for granted; rather, the social world is more frequently marked by heterogeneity, difference, and hierarchy. Different social groups construct different understandings as they establish a stable view of the world and their place within it. As this suggests, there is a close relationship between stability and identity as functional aspects of social representations.

An identity is first of all a way of making sense of the world, a way of organizing meanings that provides a sense of stability. In the preceding section I reviewed some aspects of the early development of gender identities, emphasizing the transition from extended identities as children are incorporated into the social world through the actions of others, to internalized identities as children become independent actors in the field of gender. In this research identities are considered as characteristics of gender groups, but further research revealed a need to consider variations in identities within gender groups and as a consequence of differentiated patterns of social organization.

In this study (Lloyd & Duveen, 1992) we followed children through their first year of compulsory schooling (which in England means the year in which children become five), using firstly ethnographic techniques to describe the structure of gender organization in the classroom, and then more structured observational techniques. The pattern of gender organization varied from classroom to classroom. Both the school as an institution and the teacher as key actor influenced the formation of a local gender culture in each classroom, so that at times the same items of material culture could take on different gender meanings in different classrooms. When this study was undertaken there was much public discussion about the influence of gender in education, and various initiatives set in motion by Local Education Authorities which aimed to provide equal opportunities for girls and boys in school. Within the schools this sometimes produced conflict and discussion among teachers and between teachers and headteachers, a division of opinion which could loosely be characterized as contrasting views of "sex differences" as natural, with views of "gender differences" as open to social influences. Such conflicts were an important source for the variations we observed in local gender cultures in different classrooms.

The second theme that this study highlighted was the importance of investigating variations among girls and among boys. While it was possible to see some general patterns in the ways girls and boys behaved – for example in their choice of whom to play with, or in the way they used the material culture of the classroom, including both toys and other objects as well as different spaces – considerable variations within sex groups were also observed. Thus, while in general patterns of association among children showed a tendency toward gender segregation, with boys choosing to play with other boys and girls with girls, we also observed significant variations in these patterns, especially among the girls. For example, some girls formed themselves into very tightly knit little groups of two or three who rarely interacted with any other children in the classroom, girls or boys. Other girls showed a general tendency to associate primarily with girls, while a third group also included some of the boys among their play partners. These different styles of associating with their peers can be seen as the expression of different forms of feminine identity, and indeed, when we used information about children's pattern of peer association as an index of gender identity we found some consistent effects linking different forms of identity to children's pattern of using both objects and space in the classroom.

By the end of their first year of schooling, children were able to express differentiated and varied gender identities in their classroom practice. However, the same sophistication was not nearly so clearly expressed in children's reflective knowledge of the codes for marking gender in the classroom. Again, as in the earlier studies, we devised a series of judgment tasks to explore children's knowledge of gender marking, using as stimuli the kinds of materials familiar from the classroom. In only some isolated examples did children's performance on these tasks relate to the peer-association index of gender identity. More generally, children's responses could be divided according to the demands of the task. When children were asked only about their knowledge of gender marking, girls and boys displayed a similar level of competence. However, when children were also able to express a preference their responses were divided on the basis of their membership in a sex group.

No doubt these results reflect something of the developmental process involved as children move from practical activity to reflexive awareness. But some of the difficulty is also related to the content of the representations themselves, to the meanings that gender holds for these children. Our ethnographic observations suggested that children are often the most conservative elements in the gender culture of the classroom. As we saw in the analysis of children's pretend play in the classroom, their representations of gender are structured around a figurative nucleus of a bipolar opposition, a structure that suggests some reasons for children's conservatism about gender in the classroom. As an image, a bipolar opposition offers a degree of clarity and simplicity which is also consistent with children's limited capacity for any cognitive elaborations which might require greater sophistication. Children's resistance to any influence of an egalitarian voice in representations of gender is also a resistance to losing this clear and sharp image of the world. Thus the image of bipolar opposition crystallizes for the child a state of understanding which also fuses the form of knowledge (its categorical structure) with the content of knowledge (the separation between things masculine and things feminine). All things masculine tend to cohere together and to separate from things feminine. As we noted in our ethnography, separation along these lines can come to characterize the pattern of interaction in the classroom, and once established in this way the dynamic interplay of activity and understanding is capable of sustaining such moments over extended periods of time.

Yet as well as representing difference the image of gender as a bipolar opposition also represents hierarchy, for the difference between the genders is also a relation of power. Notwithstanding the extent to which this image is saturated with notions of hierarchy and power, so long as the *difference* between the bipolar opposites can be resolved, the *hierarchy* can be obscured. The union of bipolar opposites in sexuality, or the complementarity of marriage and domestic roles, presents an image in which the aspect of hierarchy is masked. Yet the masculine and the feminine are not equals, and the shadow which this inequality casts can be observed in the disputes which break out over access to resources, and in the psychological patterns of overvaluing same gender group and devaluing the opposite gender. For the girls, of course, the reproduction of the hierarchy of gender also brings with it the devaluation of their own gender. It is perhaps not surprising that it is among girls that we have seen evidence of a break with the hegemony of a strict bipolar opposition. From this point of view the girls' refusal to attribute as feminine any socially undesirable behaviors in one of our interview measures can be seen as one such indication. In our ethnography we also recorded a number of episodes of girls challenging this image, usually by competing with boys for masculine marked resources. In comparison to the dominance of an image of gender as a bipolar opposition, such examples are marginal to the general run of life in the reception class. Yet they serve to illustrate that even among the children gender is not an entirely uncontested terrain, even here relations of power can generate resistance. Indeed, in so far as any identity is as much a system of exclusion as of inclusion, identity formation always implies the prospect of points of resistance.

Identities and Resistance

Thus as well as enabling individuals to sustain a stable sense of themselves and the world they inhabit, identities also project individuals into a social world marked by a complex set of relationships between social groups. The idea of identifications as a form of positioning of the self in relation to representations also needs to take account of the complex dynamics which may be involved. Wherever representations are internalized they are linked to a process of identity formation, which can sometimes take surprising forms. For example, we do not usually think of children's internalization of representations of mathematics as being linked to specific social identities, but this can indeed be the case. When the form of mathematics which children internalize is linked to their identity as the member of a marginalized social group, this can lead to a disruptive relationship in their schooling, and it is only when we see the consequences of difficulties and failures in school that the sense in which representations of mathematics also express a social identity becomes apparent (de Abreu, 1993, 1995). If the relationship between representation and identity is usually opaque in the field of mathematics, it can nevertheless become clear in some contexts. The pervasiveness of variations and differences associated with gender ensure that the relationship between representations and identities is clear across a very wide range of contexts. That this should be so is due to the significance of gender as a dimension of power in the social world.

In recent years identity in social psychology has become more of a formula than a concept – an operating variable in the calculus of experimental designs. This is not the fault – or the inheritance – of Henri Tajfel (1981a) who originally proposed what has become known as social identity theory. Tajfel himself always strove to make identity a concept that could bear the weight of the presence of the individual in the social world, a complex, problematic and sometimes contradictory presence. In all Tajfel's work we can see the struggle to connect forms of social psychological thought and explanation to the complexities of social life and social experience, and without the weight and concrete struggle for this presence his work would have been quite different. In too much of the work around the theme of social identity since Tajfel's death there is little sign of this struggle continuing. The forms of the theory initiated by Tajfel have persisted and even been extended, but too often they have been empty forms so that identity has become a vacuous notion, a transparent glass case enclosing nothing.

Yet Tajfel's work itself cannot be said to have been successful in its struggle. By focusing on processes with the hope that content would take care of itself in the concrete particularity of specific cases, his work opened up the possibilities which John Turner (1987) and others have developed. Identity is a process – of course it is, and no doubt the consequences of categorization can be seen in the processes of identity. But to initiate the discussion of identity in the motivational drive to acquire a positive self-concept is to start from the wrong place. Before it becomes thematized as a struggle for the individual, an identity is first a social location, a space made available within the representational structures of the social world. It is this which gives categorizations their power, not categorizations which determine identities. The fundamental problem with social identity theory is that it offers a theory of the consequences of categorization, but is mute on the question of why individuals should categorize themselves in particular ways. Why is it that young children come to categorize themselves in terms of gender? The answer might seem to be extraordinarily obvious – gender is one of the central dimensions of power in our societies, and as such is articulated in a representational field which not merely surrounds the child from the moment of their birth, but can even predate their conception in the hopes, wishes, fears, and anxieties of their parents. But if we follow social identity theory we find there is no means for grasping this priority of representations over identities. To paraphrase a famous dictum of Sartre's we can say that *representations precede identities*. And just as in Sartre's analysis, essence is a projective work of experience, so we can say that identities take shape through the engagement of the individual in the world of representations.

In fact even the term "individual" is problematic in this discussion. The person who takes on an identity is himself or herself a product of a representational system. As Mauss (1985), Geertz (1993b, first published 1973), Shweder (1991), and others have shown, the category of the person is a cultural construction, a point which actually reinforces the argument that representations precede identities. To be sure there is a dialectic of representations and identities in the life of individuals and groups. As Lucien Goldmann (1976) saw so penetratingly, the identities which emerge in the course of development constrain the representations which individuals or groups might accept. In his terms the limiting case was one where the conditions for the acceptance of a new representation entailed the dissolution of an existing identity – which means change for the individual, or disbandonment, schism, or reorganization for the group. Identity, then, is not some thing, like a particular attitude or belief, it is the force or power which attaches a person or a group to an attitude or a belief, in a word, to a representation.

Goldmann's argument is important since it links identity to communication, to what it is possible to communicate in a relationship, and what is incommunicable, or where communication itself can lead to change and reorganization. The stability of particular forms of identity is therefore also linked to the stability of the network of social influences which sustain a particular representation. As the balance of influence processes change, so too does the predominant representation, and consequently the patterns of identity which are a function of that representation (cf. Duveen, 1998). We can then consider identity as an asymmetry in a relationship which constrains what can be communicated through it – both in the sense of what it becomes possible to communicate and in the sense of what becomes incommunicable (and potentially a point of resistance), or communicable only on condition of a reworking of that identity.

Resistance, then, is the point where an identity refuses to accept what is proposed by a communicative act, that is, it refuses to accept an attempt at influence. Points, or moments of resistance, can remain limited within the immediate contexts in which they occur. Or they can also develop into a broader social response, and escape from the limiting horizons of particular exchanges and become linked to a coordinated and constructive attempt at influencing the pattern of social thought. Resistance which occurs first in the microgenetic evocation of social representations (cf. Duveen and Lloyd, 1990), can lead both to ontogenetic transformations (where identities themselves are restructured) and to sociogenetic change (where resistance becomes first a resistance to a change in identity, and then linked to an effort to influence the wider social world to recognize that identity).

Conclusion – Varieties of Social Identities

I began this discussion by referring to William James's notion of the multiplicity of social selves, and I want to conclude by returning to this theme from the perspective I have outlined in which identity is considered a function of social representations. But, as Barbara Lloyd and I (Duveen & Lloyd, 1990) have suggested, we can distinguish between different types of social identity, or more precisely between different types of relation between representations and identities. On the one hand, there are social representations which impose an imperative obligation on individuals to adopt a particular identity, that is circumstances where there is an "external obligation which derives from the ways in which others identify an individual in terms of particular social categories" (Duveen & Lloyd, 1990, p. 7). This is the case with the gender identities I have been discussing. On the other hand, however, the influence of social representations is exercised through a contractual obligation rather than an imperative one, so that an individual voluntarily joining a social group contracts to take on a particular social identity.

This distinction between imperative and contractual obligations as forms of identity may not exhaust all the possibilities, but it serves to introduce a discussion of differences and variety in forms of identity. Indeed, as Deaux, amongst others, has recently emphasized, a focus on the contents of identities leads to a consideration of variations in the form of identities and the different consequences which may follow for thought, feeling and action (Reid & Deaux, 1996; Deaux, Reid, Mizrahi, & Ethier, 1995). The implication here is that we need to extend the analysis of the relationship of representations and identities to provide a frame for understanding varieties of social identities, a theme which would also enlarge the scope of the discussion of social identity in contemporary social psychology.

Notes

This paper was originally presented at the conference in New York in October 1998, and I am grateful to the British Academy for their support for my participation in this conference through the award of an Overseas Conference Grant. I should also like to thank Kay Deaux and Gina Philogène for their helpful editorial comments. Soon after the completion of this chapter I learned of the death of Hans Furth in November 1999. He was my first doctoral supervisor and I benefited not only from his unparalleled grasp of Piaget's genetic epistemology but also from the example of his intellectual rigour and integrity. I would like to dedicate this chapter to his memory.

1   In these studies the others were always women who were themselves mothers, a choice dictated by the contingencies of organizing laboratory studies rather than any theoretical presupposition. There is no reason to suppose that such effects are peculiar to women rather than men, nor to adults rather than older children.

2   The gender marking of these toys had been established by asking a sample of adults to select toys which were appropriate for either a girl or a boy.

20

Social Representational Constraints upon Identity Processes

Glynis M Breakwell

This chapter attempts to address a fundamental question: how does the identity of the individual relate to social representational processes? How might individual identity dynamics influence the development of social representations and how might social representations influence the creation and maintenance of identity? In order to propose any answers, it will be necessary first to examine the relationship between social representations and what will be called here "personal representations." A personal representation is used to refer to the manifestation of a social representation at the level of the individual. Social representations are deemed social because they are generated in social interaction, they are shared by a number of individuals, they refer to social phenomena, they are manifested in social artifacts (for example, norms, rituals, or literature) and they serve social functions for the communities or groups that evolve them. They have an existence independent of their presence in any one individual's cognitions. However, while their existence is not solely or exclusively dependent upon being present in the thoughts, feelings or actions of an individual, nevertheless they may be expressed in individual cognitions, emotions and behavior. To the extent that a social representation is present in an individual's cognitions, emotions or behavior, it exists as a personal representation.

The social representational world is complex and dynamic. Moscovici (1976a, first published 1961), in moving away from Durkheim's notion of collective representation, emphasized the multiplicity of social representations that exist in modern societies and their capacity for change. In doing so, he highlights, and others (Jodelet, 1991) have also subsequently stated, that social representation can be regarded both as a product and as a process. Social representation the process, through interindividual and intergroup communication involving anchoring and objectification, generates social representation the product. It would seem reasonable to assume that, in this complex world of different and changing social representations, any one individual would rarely have access to all of the social representations that are operating and might not have access in its entirety even to a single social representation. Individuals will have different roles in the social process of construction, elaboration, and sharing of the representation. Essentially, this is to suggest that each individual is uniquely positioned in relation to the process of social representation. Later it will be argued that it is possible to model how the individual relates to the process of social representation by reference to identity dynamics. Initially, however, the ways in which the individual may relate to social representations as products are explored.

The interesting problem lies in explaining why some components of a particular social representation are incorporated into a personal representation and others are not. The individual's relationship to any social representation can be described along a number of dimensions:

1   Awareness: individuals will differ in their awareness of the social representation; some individuals will simply not know that there is a social representation in existence, others will know only part of its scope, and yet others will be fully aware of its structure and content. For instance, awareness of the available social representations of Einstein's special theory of relativity will differ across people. Awareness is likely to be determined, in part, by previous personal experience which, in turn, will be controlled to some extent by membership of different groups or communities. But awareness will also be determined by the significance of the target for representation. If the target changes in significance due to some change of social or physical circumstances, awareness of existing social representations will alter. For example, with reports of scientific estimates of the growth of the hole in the Earth's ozone layer and the consequent global warming, the significance of social representations previously generated by environmentalist activists was heightened.

2   Understanding: individuals will differ in the extent to which they actually understand the social representations of which they are aware. There is ample evidence that individuals are capable of reproducing a dominant social representation even though they cannot explain how or why its elements fit together and, if challenged, they cannot justify it. For instance, in the late 1990s many people were aware of the social representation of the Millennium Bug (or Year Two Thousand Problem). This entailed the predicted collapse of systems dependent upon computers as midnight December 31, 1999 chimed in the new century because these computers were not programed to recognize dates after that day. The social representation was interesting because it was elaborated to include what one must do to protect oneself from the effects of the collapse

(e.g., avoid air journeys at that time, take out plenty of cash in advance because the banking systems would cease to function, etc.). While many people could detail these elements of the social representation, equally many did not know what all of this meant.

3   Acceptance: individuals will differ in the extent to which they believe or accept a social representation even if they are fully aware of it. Typically, people can say: this is what is generally believed but, nevertheless, this is what I believe. For instance, I might know that other people believe the world is round but I believe it is pear-shaped and the rivers run out of the stalk. Similarly, I might say that I know that the majority of people believe that microwave ovens are safe and useful but personally I have a theory that they are dangerous and liable to fry your eyes because they leak waves that no one can detect. People can know (in the sense of being able to reproduce at will) not only contradictory social representations of the same target but also be able to identify at the same time a separate representation of it which is their own. This personal representation may be unique only in the specifics and may share many of the common features of the social representation but it has been intentionally personalized. The extent to which the personal representation echoes the social representation reflects in part the degree to which the latter is accepted. The importance of being able to personalize the social representation so that it appears individualized should not be ignored. While seeking identification and community membership at one level, people also simultaneously seek distinctiveness and differentiation. The personalizing of social representations is part of that process of establishing and protecting an identity.

4   Assimilation: the individual does not accept (to whatever extent it is accepted) the social representation in some clinically detached way. It will be assimilated to preexistent systems of personal representation (developed originally on idiosyncratic cognitive biases and capacities). This substratum of already extant personal representations will differ across individuals and the ultimate shape of the new personal representation will be influenced by it differentially for each individual. Just as social processes ensure that the new social representation is anchored in prior social representations, at the individual level cognitive and emotional processes ensure that it is anchored in prior personal representations. In fact, there must be an intimate connection between the social processes of anchoring and objectification and their parallel individual processes. The social communication which ensures that novel events and ideas are interpreted in terms of existing systems of meaning is generated by individuals using prior knowledge mediated through cognitive and conative networks. The social exchange can produce understandings which no single participant to the interaction might be able to create but at some level even these emergent representations are limited in some ways by the capacities of the individuals involved to anchor and objectify.

5   Salience: the salience of a social representation will differ across people and for the same person across time and contexts. The salience of the social representation, for instance, may increase if the group or community which generates it is important to the individual. Similarly, it may increase if the social representation becomes relevant to the individual's ongoing activity. At the level of the community, if the target for social representation is nonsalient it is likely that the social representation will be difficult to elicit, simple, undifferentiated and relatively unconnected with other components of the community's belief system. For instance, Hassan (1986) did a study of the social representations held of female circumcision by British, Rural Sudanese and Urban Sudanese. She found that the British had a rudimentary social representation of female circumcision but one which was consensually held; in the Sudan (where the practice is widespread) there were very complex social representations which attributed religious and social significance to the procedure and, importantly, there were a number of variations in the social representation each associated with different parts of the community (urban versus rural; male versus female). At the level of the individual, the salience of the social representation will be likely to influence how accurately and completely personal representation mirrors it. There is, however, no empirical evidence on this yet.

It is notable that some of the dimensions which shape the personal representation are potentially nonvolitional (for example, awareness and understanding), others are volitional (for example, acceptance). However, this distinction may be rightly regarded as arbitrary. Even those which appear volitional are largely predisposed by prior social experiences and constrained by identity requirements as will be illustrated later.

Types of Social Representation and the Scope for Personal Representation

The underlying premise in what has been said here so far is that there is a role for the individual in shaping the development of the social representation. In fact, the process whereby the social representation is generated and sustained is a continuing exchange between personal representation and social influence mediated through communities. However, the nature of and scope for individual impact upon the social representational process depends in some ways upon the type of social representation concerned and upon the structure of the social representation itself.

Moscovici (1988) identified three types of social representation:

1   Hegemonic representation: these are shared by all members of a highly struc-
    tured group without them having been produced by the group; they are uni-
    form and coercive.
2   Emancipated representations: these are the outgrowth of the circulation of knowl-
    edge and ideas belonging to subgroups that are in more or less close contact –
    each subgroup creates and shares its own version.
3   Polemical representations: these are generated in the course of social conflict or
    controversy, and society as a whole does not share them, they are determined
    by antagonistic relations between its members and intended to be mutually
    exclusive.

Whether these are actually different types of social representation or just different
inevitable phases in the overall life span of a social representation can be debated.
There has been little empirical work that has pursued whether the tripartite classification is viable. Nevertheless, it is clear from this that individuals and communities
in some cases will choose between social representations and use them creatively
for their own purposes. The three types of social representation Moscovici proposes offer differing degrees of freedom for the individual to construct a personal
representation. The hegemonic representation supposes little individual variation.
The emancipated representation supposes individual variation based upon differential exposure within group contexts. The polemical representation supposes individual variation based upon the prevailing conditions of intergroup conflict. Of
course, it is the scope for personalizing representations which emerges when emancipated or polemical representations prevail about a target that is one of the necessary conditions for innovation and change. This assertion is not meant to trivialize
or ignore the real differentials between individuals in their power to maintain or to
proselytize their personal representations. One of the things which this perspective
emphasizes is that personal representations will be perpetually under pressure to
change from the social representations which surround them. Individuals who are
powerful (through position, expertise, or other route) are more likely to be able to
retain their own personal representations and to be able to influence the development of social representations. The role of the individual in mediating emancipated
and polemical representations needs to be examined empirically.

The nature of personal representations will also be affected by the structure of
the social representation. Abric (1994c) has argued that social representations comprise a central core (an indispensable combination of basic underlying components
linked in a specific constellation and tied systematically to a set of values and norms
associated with the group espousing the social representation) and the peripheric
elements (the way the representation is articulated in concrete terms depending
upon context). Abric argues that the core is resistant to change but that the peripheric
elements are responsive to changing context. By adapting, the peripheric elements

can protect the core from having to change. Following Abric might lead one to conclude that individuals will be different from each other in the personal representations that they construct not in the core but in the peripheric elements. Empirically, problems in differentiating core from periphery make testing this hypothesis difficult. It is, however, worth pursuing. To do so, would, of course, demand an operational definition of peripheric elements which did not depend upon the extent to which they are consensually included in the representation. Moliner and Tafani (1997) have made an interesting start in this direction by examining how far components of a social representation can be ordered in terms of an evaluative dimension.

Identity Processes and Social Representation Processes

For some time some researchers have been trying to model the relationship between identity processes and social representational processes (Breakwell, 1993). The central argument is that identity dynamics will determine the individual's relation to the social representation as a product and to social representation as a process. It is also argued that social representations are prime determiners of the substance of identities. Before going further here with this discussion, it may be worth outlining some assumptions that will underlie the remainder of the chapter. In an arena of theory which is evolving and where clear definition of concepts has been requested, it would seem sensible to briefly outline the model of identity that will be used here. The model is that of Identity Process Theory (IPT) (Breakwell, 1986, 1994).

IPT proposes that the structure of identity is a dynamic social product of the interaction of the capacities for memory, consciousness, and organized construal (that are characteristic of the biological organism) with the physical and societal structures and influence processes which constitute the social context. Identity resides in psychological processes but is manifested through thought, action, and affect. It can therefore be described at two levels, in terms of its structure and in terms of its processes. People are normally self-aware: actively monitoring the status of their identity. The levels of self-monitoring may differ across the life span and it is considered possible that they may vary across different cultures. IPT makes no a priori assumptions of developmental or cultural universalism concerning self-monitoring. Further empirical studies are needed on the question.

The structure of identity can be described along two planes: the content dimension and the value dimension. The content dimension consists of the characteristics which define identity: the properties which, taken as a constellation, mark the individual as unique. It encompasses both those characteristics previously considered the domain of social identity (group memberships, roles, social category labels, etc.) and of personal identity (values, attitudes, cognitive style, etc.). The distinction between social and personal identity is abandoned in this model. Seen across the biography, social identity is seen to become personal identity: the dichotomy is purely a temporal artifact. Of course, the content dimension is organized. The organization can be characterized in terms of (a) the degree of centrality, (b) the hierarchical arrangements of elements, and (c) the relative salience of components. The organization is not, however, static and is responsive to changes in inputs and demands from the social context besides purposive reconstruction initiated by the individual. Each element in the content dimension has a positive or negative value/affect appended to it; taken together these values constitute the value/affective dimension of identity. The value/affective dimension of identity is constantly subject to revision: the value of each element is open to reappraisal as a consequence of changes in social value systems and modifications in the individual's position in relation to such social value systems.

The structure of identity is postulated to be regulated by the dynamic processes of accommodation/assimilation and evaluation which are deemed to be universal psychological processes. Assimilation and accommodation are components of the same process. Assimilation refers to the absorption of new components into the identity structure; accommodation refers to the adjustment that occurs in the existing structure in order to find a place for new elements. Accommodation–assimilation can be conceptualized as a memory system and subject to biases in retention and recall. These biases are said to be predictable since identity change is guided by certain "identity principles." The process of evaluation entails the allocation of meaning and value/affect to identity contents, new and old. The two processes interact to determine the changing content and value of identity over time; with changing patterns of assimilation requiring changes in evaluation and vice versa.

The processes of identity are guided in their operation by principles that define desirable states for the structure of identity. The actual end states considered desirable, and consequently the guidance principles, are temporally and culturally specific. In Western industrialized cultures the current prime guidance principles identified are: continuity, distinctiveness, self-efficacy, and self-esteem. These four principles vary in their relative and absolute salience over time and across situations. There is evidence that their salience also varies developmentally across the life span. Identity is created within a particular social context within a specific historical period. The social context can be schematically represented along two dimensions concerning, in turn, structure and process. Structurally, the social context is comprised of interpersonal networks, group and social-category memberships, and intergroup relationships. The content of identity is assimilated from these structures which generate roles to be adopted and beliefs or values to be accepted. The second dimension consists of social influence processes that conspire to create the multifaceted ideological milieu for identity. Social influence processes (education, rhetoric, propaganda, polemic, persuasion, etc.) establish systems of value and beliefs, reified in social representations, social norms, and social attributions, which specify an arena in which both the content and value of individual identities are constructed.

IPT does not suggest that identity is totally determined by its social context. There are contradictions and conflicts within the ideological milieu, generated by intergroup power struggles, which permit the individual some freedom of choice in formulating the identity structure. Changes in identity are therefore normally purposive. The person has agency in creating identity. Furthermore, the limitations of the cognitive information processing system (primarily those associated with memory) themselves impose some constraints upon identity development. At the most basic level, for instance, the inability to retrieve self-relevant material from memory may restrict identity modification even if such change would apparently be inevitable given the individual's social position and experiences.

Changes in the structure or processes of the social context will call forth changes in identity varying in extent according to: (a) their personal relevance; (b) the immediacy of involvement in them; (c) the amount of change demanded; and (d) how negative the change is deemed to be. Movement of the individual from one position in the social matrix to another will bring pressure to bear for a change in identity since this is likely to introduce a changed pattern of social influences and restrictions. A threat to identity occurs when the processes of assimilation/accommodation are unable, for some reason, to comply with the principles of continuity, distinctiveness, self-efficacy, and self-esteem. Threats are aversive and the individual will seek to reinstitute the principled operation of the identity processes. For a threat to evoke action, it must gain access to consciousness. It is therefore possible to distinguish between occupying a threatening position and experiencing threat. If coping strategies are effective, occupancy of a threatening position may lose its power to threaten.

Any activity, in thought or deed, which has as its goal the removal or modification of a threat to identity can be regarded as a coping strategy. Coping strategies can be pitched at a number of different levels: the intrapsychic, interpersonal and group/intergroup. The nature of these coping strategies are outlined in detail elsewhere (Breakwell, 1986). Essentially, the choice of coping strategy is determined by an interaction between the type of threat involved, the salient parameters of the social context, the prior identity structure, and the cognitive and emotional capacities available to the individual.

The IPT approach to identity emphasizes the vital role of social representational processes in shaping identity but also suggests that identity processes may be significant in determining the evolution of social representations (Breakwell & Canter, 1993). In developing this argument it is important to remember that we are not merely referring to social identity (that part of identity derived from group memberships) but to the total constellation of characteristics which comprise the whole identity (including those which might be considered psychological attributes, for example personality traits or cognitive capacities, that is, aspects of the person which are long-lived and, though differentially manifest across situations, relate to behavior in a systematic manner). Traits (whether cognitive or emotional) and social identities from the viewpoint of the entire biography of the individual are not discrete and separate. Traits can become a part of self-categorization. For example, having the trait of shyness can lead to self-definition as part of some conceptual grouping of shy people; it may even lead to seeking out the company of other shy people and, thereby, to group membership. Traits certainly lead to classifications imposed by other people. For instance, the shy person is identified as such and whole domains of social behavior are no longer expected of her. In contrast, group membership may call forth or intensify certain traits: membership of a political party of the Right might actually nurture conservativeness.

All aspects of identity (not just those derived from group memberships) are very important determinants of the individual's participation in the production, transformation, and use of social representations. Both group memberships and personality traits affect exposure to social representations and their acceptance and use. Membership will first affect exposure to particular aspects of a social representation, as well as to the target of the representation itself. Groups ensure that members are informed about, or engaged with, social representations which are central to group objectives and definition (Chombart de Lauwe, 1984; Emler & Dickinson, 1985). Outgroups ensure that members are presented with other aspects of social representations which may be rather less in keeping with the ingroup's interests. Memberships will affect individual acceptance (or rejection) of the social representation. They do this sometimes by establishing the extent of the credibility of the source of the social representation, or at other times by explicit commentaries on the representation. Memberships will affect the extent to which the social representation is used. Definition of "use" in this context is difficult but would include: the frequency with which the social representation is reproduced (that is, communicated to others) and addressed (that is, used as a point of reference in making decisions, assimilating new information, and evaluating a situation).

Meanwhile, there are two ways in which traits relate to social representation processes. Firstly, traits as psychological or cognitive states shape the individual's exposure to, acceptance of, and use of a social representation. Moscovici argues that social representations are a product of interindividual communication/interaction and many traits would recognizably influence the course of such interaction. To go back to the shy person, shyness could prevent participation in many areas of communication necessary either to acquire or to influence a social representation. There are other examples. The trait of curiosity has a self-evident relationship to gaining exposure to a variety of social representations. In our research on the public images of science and scientists, we have shown that curiosity is also related to a general proclivity to accept and use, as well as access, novel ideas (Breakwell & Beardsell,

1992). Secondly, traits in so far as they can be self-conscious self-definitions also shape readiness to expose oneself to, accept, or use a social representation. At this level, traits are self-categorizations and it could be argued that they are also social identities. However, they still need to be treated as different from those social identities that are derived from group memberships. This is particularly relevant since identities derived from memberships will be subject to group-determined pressures towards particular types of social representation which are absent (at least initially) where self-ascribed traits are concerned.

Some Empirical Illustrations: The Representations of Hazards

At the Social Psychology European Research Institute in Surrey, UK, we have examined how far individual variations in identity characteristics will explain use and acceptance of social representations. We have particularly explored how IPT might predict differential patterns of exposure to, acceptance of and use of social representations. As indicated above, IPT postulates that individuals seek to generate a structure for their identity which is characterized by self-esteem, continuity, distinctiveness, and self-efficacy. It suggests that if they find that esteem, continuity, distinctiveness, or efficacy are threatened, individuals will use a variety of strategies to protect or regain them. We now have an extensive series of studies which illustrate that individuals in the same social category will accept and use (i.e., reproduce or act in accordance with) a particular social representation to differing degrees depending upon its potential impact upon their identity esteem, continuity, distinctiveness, and efficacy.

For instance, individuals will reject social representations of their local environment as being polluted (despite objective evidence that it is) if attachment to that place features as an important aspect of their personal sense of distinctiveness (Bonauito, Breakwell, & Cano, 1996). This study involved estimates of risk in relation to the levels of beach pollution (locally and nationally) in six English coastal resorts. Three hundred and forty four 16-year-olds were sampled, all lived in towns where beaches had been officially declared either clean or polluted by the European Union. If beaches are declared clean by the European Union they are given what is called a blue flag. Having this accolade has a significant impact on the marketability of the town for tourism. The sample were asked to indicate how far they were attached to their locality (place identification) and their nationalist sentiments were also assessed. They were further asked to index the extent of the pollution of which they were aware on their local beaches. Finally, they were asked to rate the level of beach pollution locally and the level of beach pollution nationally. Essentially, the data showed that over and above the impact of the rating of pollution which was given by the European Union, local attachment to the place and nationalism predicted representations of the extent of pollution locally and nationally. The requirements of place identity are associated with a rejection of the representation of the risk of pollution in the area that is generated formally by European Union legislation. Given the generally negative feelings of the British people towards the European Union, it should hardly be surprising that nationalism was associated with a rejection of the European Union's evaluation of the British environment. More surprisingly, both attachment to the locale and nationalism were associated with a reduction in the perceived "objective evidence" of beach pollutants and both had a direct impact upon the perceived level of local beach pollution. This study illustrated that processes of identification limit willingness to accept social representations of hazards. It suggests that they tend to construct personal representations that are consonant with the identity requirements – in this case those aspects of identity dependent upon affiliation to place.

This first example of the role of identity dynamics in acceptance of a social representation had a strong intergroup component, the second example does not. This involves what might be called an emancipated social representations of risk and again there is evidence that identity processes will predict the representation that is espoused. This study involved more than two thousand 9 to12-year-olds in the UK (Thrush, Fife-Schaw, & Breakwell, 1997). In a longitudinal study over three years, children were asked, on three occasions separated by a year, a series of questions about what they thought to be the risks associated with smoking (these included questions concerning the health risks associated with smoking as well as the social stigma and disadvantages associated with smoking today). We used cluster analysis to establish whether there were subgroups in the sample that held differentiable social representations of the risks of smoking. The cluster analysis yielded two clear clusters of children. The first cluster adhered to a representation of the risks of smoking which was extremely negative (that is to say they perceived smoking as highly socially undesirable and high in health risks). The other cluster regarded smoking as less risky (having less social stigma attached to it, and being associated with lower health risks). There were clearly two social representations of smoking and of the risks associated with smoking that these children could potentially use: the "official" high risk one and an alternative benign one. We found that children who reproduced the benign alternative were more likely to have parents and friends who were smokers and who they believed accepted the alternative social representation. Essentially, we showed that children with "significant others" who they believed to accept the alternative, use it themselves. Identification processes are predisposing the use of certain social representations. In this case, the social representation of smoking which is chosen is clearly predicted on the basis of identification with family and friends who they believe to also accept that social representation of smoking.

Our studies would suggest that polemical social representations of risk are most significantly mediated by identity processes. Many environmental hazards generate polemical social representations of risk, created by agencies or groups in conflict. Under these circumstances the social representations of risks the individual chooses will be highly influenced by identity requirements. An example comes from a study of how a community responded to a potentially hazardous waste-incinerator being sited locally (Twigger-Ross & Breakwell, 1999). The company wishing to introduce the development wanted to do so in an area which was already highly industrialized and where they had a well-established chemical processing complex. The introduction of this new waste incinerator was opposed by various environmental groups including Greenpeace and Friends of the Earth. We studied the people in this community throughout the lengthy process of gaining legal planning consent for the new incinerator. In a survey of 2000 local residents, we indexed the extent to which individuals perceived that there would be a risk arising from the development of the new waste incinerator, their trust in the governmental regulation of such risks, the image which they held of the company, and their concern for the environment and their acceptance of "Green" beliefs. Residents varied in their representation of the risk. The representation that they reproduced depended upon the extent to which they identified with environmentalist groups but also upon the extent to which they identified with the company as a trusted and traditional employer in the area.

Essentially, in each of these studies we found that individuals reject social representations that might threaten important aspects of their identity. However, it is probably too simplistic to use the term "rejection" when examining how identity constraints motivate the way a social representation is treated. What often happens is that the social representation is subtly modified in personal use. For instance, it can be slightly reanchored or there is a minor tweak to the objectification (often through use of different exemplars). Yet, in effect, individuals who are actively engaged in identity maintenance and development are also perforce engaged in social representation creation and change. Of course, whether or not their renovation of the social representation gains common acceptance or use is a function of the processes outlined in the theory of social representations itself. The significant point that all our studies have shown is that there is never total consensus upon a social representation. All our research illustrates variety among individuals despite elements of agreement and consensus. Empirical studies emphasize divergence amidst universalism. Moreover, the divergence is not random. It is lawful and, in part, predictable in terms of IPT expectations concerning the desire to achieve and maintain esteem, efficacy, distinctiveness, and continuity for identity.

Of course, it might be argued that these are not new assertions. For many years social psychologists have been illustrating that self-concept biases affect attitude, value, and belief structures and their propensity for change. The significance of asserting the role of identity for the development of social representations theory is perhaps more novel since the significance of the individual is largely minimized in it. Empirical work in this area may also represent one way in which the divide between social representations theory and mainstream variants of social cognition and social influence theories in social psychology may be bridged. The most evident problem with resorting to the type of empirical work described above to substantiate theoretical arguments within the social representations approach is that other researchers may not accept that what has been studied is actually a social representation. To the extent that it is shown to be subject to individual variation in expression that is related to identity dynamics, it can be said not to be a social representation at all. Unless definitive operational criteria are established against which the existence of a social representation can be assessed, all one can say to such criticisms is that the evidence should be allowed to accumulate which describes the varying relationships between the properties of individual identities and the shape of personal representations.

Social Representational Constraints on Identity Development

This all suggests that identity processes are salient in social representation use and possibly in their development. However, social representations are equally salient in identity development. IPT proposes that identity is a social construct. Pervasive social representations are an instrument that defines identity elements and provides them with significance and meaning. Most importantly social representations attribute identity elements with value (good or bad). Social representations also have a significant role to play in establishing what strategies of identity protection and development can be used when individual is faced with a threat.

One of our studies illustrates these relationships. This concerns the situation of social workers who are assaulted by their clients. There has been a reasonably strong and consensual social representation within the social work profession that provides a theory of why and how a social worker gets attacked. This social representation includes a clear image of the type of social worker who runs into trouble: inexperienced, authoritarian, with poor social work skills, female, working in field settings which are "dangerous" (Rowett, 1986). This social representation includes an explanation which accounts for the nature of the interaction which generates violence. It states that the social worker who is attacked fails to use certain basic principles of good practice in their approach to the client. Now the fact that there is considerable evidence to show that this "theory" is wrong in most respects is irrelevant. Despite considerable attempts to dislodge it through training within the profession, this social representation which offers a coherent explanation of client violence is still pervasive. In such a context, the implications for a social worker of being a victim of an assault are serious. Rowett worked with social workers to explore their reactions following assault. Total rejection of the social representation is rare – even when their personal experiences clearly do not match the theory. Self-evaluations (particularly of efficacy) do change negatively (but markedly less for those who even partially reject the social representation).

IPT says they will try to maintain efficacy, esteem, continuity, and distinctiveness. This social representation of the attacked social worker is a direct attack on both efficacy and esteem. Rowett showed that the social workers who coped best following an attack were those who focused upon continuity and distinctiveness. In terms of distinctiveness, typically they claimed that unlike others who are attacked they did not panic (and this also has overtones of claims of efficacy). They also make arguments concerning continuity. They place the event in context – context of their whole career – and show that previously they have not been the victim of attack and that they have not changed. This is also a means of distancing themselves from the identity implications of the social representation of the assaulted. But some appear to completely accept the social representation. They apply it wholesale to themselves, often deciding to leave the profession.

There is an interesting feature of this type of social representation and its effect upon identity. The social representation includes elements which constrain what coping strategies will be effective when dealing with the threat to identity that it poses. This social representation denies the validity of certain strategies for coping. It says that social workers who are assaulted will engage in denial, will refuse to acknowledge their own part in generating the attack. By including this element the social representation protects against its own dismissal.

It would be possible to describe other studies which illustrate the power of social representations to circumscribe identity development and change (Flick, 1998). These social representations are operating as more than simple stereotypes. They provide elaborate theories that explain and predict behavior patterns, which justify decisions and contribute value to characteristics. Identities are built in this social representational milieu. Such social representations establish the range of possible identities. However, if the earlier arguments concerning the capacity of the individual to customize the social representation in generating a personal representation are valid, then identities while constrained by social representations are not determined by them. Individuals are not the passive recipients of the impressions of social representations. Often they work with them. Mainly, they do not simply reject them in some defensive way – even if they deny their validity. They accept them as part of the social reality in which they must operate. Even as they realize that they are changed inexorably by them, they recognize too that they can influence the nature of these changes.

21

E-motional Memory and the Identity System: Its Interplay with Representations of the Social World

Marisa Zavalloni

Psychosocial identity lies at the boundary between the individual Self and the social Self. It can be seen as a reservoir of experiential memories and of affectively charged representations that guide, often unconsciously, our discourse on Self, Alter, and society. As memory content, it emerges in a continuous transaction between a person and the sociocultural environment. It then lives in the mind as a transactional mechanism, resonating with what seems important and valuable in the world. In this chapter I will present a general model to account for its structural and dynamic aspect.

I introduced the term ego-ecology two decades ago (Zavalloni, 1980; Zavalloni, 1983; Zavalloni & Louis-Guérin, 1984) to describe a transactional perspective for the study of psychosocial identity and an approach that focuses on what is activated in the mind/brain, consciously and unconsciously, when people think and speak about the social world. Today, this perspective is echoed in the idea of the embodied mind, which is being studied by second-generation cognitive science (Varela, Thompson, & Rosch, 1991; Lakoff & Johnson, 1999).

To present and illustrate the ego-ecological perspective, I will describe how it took form through the interweaving of various influences. Erikson (1968) with his view of identity as an elusive combination of individual and of social characteristics and as an internal environment helped to set the stage. Moscovici' s (1976a, first published 1961) theory of social representations (SR) as a complex combination of linguistic, affective, and cognitive dimensions was the second determining influence. Finally, there was the encounter with the emerging field of cognitive science.

Step by step over the years, a model of the identity system – which is still open, still evolving – has materialized. By retracing its genealogy I will display its working characteristics in the order in which they emerged during the different stages of the research.

Erikson: Identity as an Internal Environment

Erikson is credited with the introduction of identity as an object of research in psychology. The circumstances of his life, those of a European psychoanalyst who emigrated to America at a time when cultural theories and an interdisciplinary *Zeitgeist* flourished there, may have made identity a compelling issue. The concept of identity offered an ideal platform for transforming the Freudian individual, a system of instincts and drives, into a complex mixture of social and psychological forces.

Yet, after writing about this issue for twenty years, Erikson (1968) still felt incapable of adequately defining this term. He noted that: "the more one writes about the subject, the more the word becomes a term for something as unfathomable as it is all pervasive. One can only explore it by establishing its indispensability in various contexts" (p. 9). As he mused about this elusive entity, he suggested that identity could be seen as an internal environment. He borrowed from the ethologists the idea of the *Umwelt* to denote not merely the environment which surrounds you, but which is also in you. He did not specify the nature of the internal environment nor a method for exploring it. This he saw as a task for the future, but he envisioned a new field in which a "psychoanalysis sophisticated enough to include the environment" would combine with a "social psychology psychoanalytically sophisticated" (p. 24).

This prediction did not materialize as such. However, two unforeseen developments made the idea of an internal environment a conceivable starting point for research on identity. The first was the introduction of social representations theory, the second the emergence of cognitive science.

Moscovici: Anchoring and Objectification

From the beginning, one could see a compatibility between Erickson's idea of identity as an internal environment and social representations theory (Moscovici, 1976a, first published 1961). The idea of social representations, in sharp contrast with other concepts of social psychology such as attitudes and beliefs, addresses the inner working of the mind as it endeavors to make sense of the world (Moscovici,

1968). Representations of the social world are certainly elements of the internal environment and therefore of identity, and at the same time these representations as elements of culture and ideology live as elements of the external environment. The ego-ecological perspective was designed to explore this transaction between the inner and the outer.

Moscovici (1976a, first published 1961) in his influential work introduced two concepts that have a bearing on this issue. Anchoring refers to the impact of preexisting mental content on the creation and transformation of social representations; objectification shows how an abstract concept is translated into a concrete entity. These concepts, which contribute to the understanding of common sense knowledge, anticipate the concerns of what has become known as cognitive science. I expected that these mechanisms would come into play in the creation and functioning of that part of the internal environment that includes one's identity.

To explore the conditions under which anchoring and objectification operate in the representations of social objects that are linked to the identity system required, as a phenomenologist would say, the suspending or bracketing of all that has been said about these representations in terms of stereotypes, categories, or, more recently, prototypes. The problem was to determine the nature of the link between social representations and that part of the internal environment that comprises the identity system. To solve it, on the empirical side, led to the development of the Multistage Social Identity Inquirer (MSII). This instrument is designed, using ingroup representations as a starting point, to reveal some universal characteristics of memory and of mental functioning while engaging in a dialogue with a person on central issues in her life. The analytical focus is on the natural content of the mind, that is to say on words, emotions, and thoughts, which coalesce to, become the identity system. It reflects mental mechanisms that have guided us to conceive a particular, content oriented, memory system that we have called e-motional memory (Zavalloni & Louis-Guérin, 1984).

Identity as a Natural System of Representations, Discourse, and Memories

The MSII was developed stage by stage from the results that were obtained in a given stage but also by assimilating new trends in the field of psychology. Thus, Stage I reflects the nomothetic (statistical) approach that was common at the time. The results revealed the basic shortcoming of this method, which is an exclusive reliance on what could be called first order data, that is, words or variables without context (Zavalloni, 1971). Stage II was designed to remedy part of this problem, but it was Stage III that fully explored the issue of words context with the power of an idiographic methodology. The shift to an idiographic approach was facilitated by the emergence of cognitive science, and it led to the development of ego-ecology (Zavalloni, 1980, 1983). The term ego-ecology was introduced to describe an approach that would focus on the transaction between an ego (identity as an internal environment and a memory system) and its environment (the sociocultural space). The results of Stage III could be translated into a model of identity as a system of language, affect and representations that reflects a particular form of mental functioning in a given cultural and historical setting. This model addresses some of the issues raised by second-generation cognitive science, such as the work of the unconscious, the embodiment of the mind, and the transactions between culture and the person. It also uncovers the nature of the link between social groups and the Self. The model is naturalistic because it is based on words, arguments, and experiential memories specific to each respondent.

To outline the principal elements of the identity system as an affective cognitive complex, I will retrace the steps by which it was created. To illustrate each step I will use excerpts from a protocol that is part of an ongoing study on the relation between identity and creativity being conducted with a sample of well-known writers and thinkers. The illustrative protocol is that of the philosopher Mary Daly.

MSII Stage I. Representations of Social Groups: Egomorphism and Binary Opposition

In my first attempt (Zavalloni, 1971) to understand the relation between identity and the representations of the social world, I relied on free descriptions of several ingroups (what comes to mind when you think about . . .). To lead the respondents to adopt different perspectives in relation to the same ingroups, each ingroup was at first presented as WE (we the . . .), then this same ingroup was presented as THEY (they the . . .). Once the responses were obtained, the respondents were asked whether the words produced to describe the ingroups would also apply to themselves as persons (egomorphic) or not (allomorphic), and whether these words were positive or negative.

The results obtained from a sample of 120 respondents indicated that ingroup representations in the condition WE were most of the time self-ascribed (egomorphic) and positive. In the condition THEY the same ingroup representations were most often negative and not self-ascribed as a kind of binary opposition. For instance, Jenny, a 22-year-old woman, described WE Jews as: "intelligent, open minded, have a good sense of humor we can laugh about ourselves, not at all religious, liberal, often radical." This same respondent described THEY the Jews as: "often narrow minded, intensely preoccupied with being Jewish, self-righteous, often loud, ostentatious, all their friends are Jews, they truly look down on people." Only a minority of respondents failed to make a distinction between the two conditions (WE and THEY).[1]

These results suggested the existence of a recoding mechanism by which the focus on the ingroup as an abstract concept would activate, automatically and unconsciously, a subgroup group closer to the respondent in the WE condition and a disliked subgroup (binary opposition) in the THEY condition.

MSII Stage II: Recoding and the Emergence of Background Thinking

Ingroup recoding could be seen as the particular form that anchoring and objectification display in relation to identity. It reveals the existence of an automatic subconscious mental activity at the periphery of consciousness that I called background thinking. Background thinking refers to all that is activated, automatically and subconsciously at the periphery of consciousness when words are produced. Even though scattered references to background thinking exist in the literature, psychologists do not seem to have appreciated its significance; consequently it has not been studied systematically. Our research has led us to uncover the structural and dynamic elements that were hidden in this phenomenon and its role in person/ environment transactions. Recoding was found to be one of the elements of background thinking.

Stage II of the MSII was designed to display the content of recoding by adding a new question: when you described WE (or THEY the) . . ., who did you see? The subgroups did in fact appear. For instance, going back to the previous example, the respondent stated that when answering WE Jews are: "I was thinking of those Jews who are more or less dissociated from Jewish institutions. The group is conscious of its ethnicity but is not the temple-going, self-conscious Jewish group." When answering THEY the Jews she was thinking about were "those still associated with the synagogue." In this process, all the respondents were able to name the hidden referent of the representations they had produced. Once we know these referents, the representations that are produced acquire a kind of relative realism that escapes the observer when these background elements remain hidden. What traditional psychology would have dismissed as stereotypes appear to be the result of complex subconscious automatic memory processes that lead to the core of the identity system. Let us now turn to Stage I and II of Mary Daly's protocol.

MZ:	If you think of philosophers in terms of WE, what comes up to mind?
MD:	Adventurous, courageous, geniuses, passionate, intuitive, and logical. *(Egomorphic descriptions)*
MZ:	And now if you think of philosophers in terms of THEY, what comes to mind?
MD:	Dry, narrow minded, boring, lifeless. *(Allomorphic descriptions)*
MZ:	When you described WE philosophers who did you see?

MD: I was thinking of myself. I cannot say Nietzsche, I cannot say Virginia Woolf . . . they all disappoint me somewhat.

MZ: And when you described THEY the philosophers who did you see?

MD: The post moderns, Derrida, Lacan.

The Elemental Identity Space

The Elemental Identity Space was the first general structure to emerge from the MSII. This space is shaped by the intersection of the two axis: the axis Self – NonSelf and the axis POSITIVE – NEGATIVE as illustrated in the chart showing Mary Daly's statements. In this example, only two subspaces (Self + and NonSelf –) are filled. The elemental identity space began to display the existence of an organic connection between representations of social groups and the identity system.

The words or representations produced in quadrant A activate as background thinking, referents and subgroups that are important to the respondent (group recoding). Quadrant B contains words indicating personal shortcomings or external threats. Quadrant C activates what is perceived as an unattainable ideal or the desirable, and quadrant D is the subspace of the negative NonSelf. This latter quadrant often echoes words that activate in the background, subgroups and referents that are disliked or hated and the expression of counter values. Persons that elicit pity sometimes appear here. Not all quadrants are necessarily filled. In Mary Daly's protocol, for example, quadrants B (negative Self) and C (positive NonSelf) are not used in relation to the group philosophers but may be activated in relation to other groups.

A SELF+ Adventurous, courageous geniuses, passionate intuitive, logical	C NONSELF+
B SELF –	D NONSELF – Dry, narrow-minded, boring, lifeless

The elemental identity space reveals how a sharing of attributes between the group and the Self creates a social link, a link by which the social and the personal world are set in a continuous transactional relation. The elemental identity space also indicates the importance of NonSelf elements in the identity system. They emerge as the implicit referents of egomorphic representations (quadrant A and B) but also as the expression of what is disliked and hated in the world (quadrant D). NonSelf sometimes appears as an idealized figure (quadrant C). It should be clear by now that to limit identity to the concept of the Self is a fundamental error. Stage I and II of the MSII can be easily quantified and used to compare groups in relation to the elemental identity space. (For work along these lines, see Tselikas, 1986; Chauchat & Durand-Delvigne, 1999).

Over the years, the model of the identity system has acquired different elements that the content of each quadrant has revealed in its particularity and that is being explored in stage III of MSII. In this chapter I will focus on the structure and dynamic of quadrant A. But first I will briefly review the context in which these ideas took shape.

The idiographic shift

When identity is conceived of as an internal environment, we necessarily refer to some kind of memory. In the early seventies, the emergence of cognitive science produced a new *Zeitgeist* in psychology that made the study of this kind of memory content scientifically plausible. There was a renewed interest in the work of Bartlett (1967, first published 1932) who relied on verbal protocols. Also, Piaget's clinical method[2] for the study of thinking processes in children relied on verbal protocols, and it inspired the method of thinking aloud developed by Newell and Simon (1972) for the study of problem solving. It was their groundbreaking work that guided us toward a particular way of approaching memory and mental processes in the identity domain: *psychocontextual analysis*, which is now Stage III of the MSII.

Representing the first generation of cognitive science, Newell and Simon studied problem solving among adults through verbal protocols and then simulated problem solving by developing computer programs. At another level they offered much more. They promoted a radically new way of doing psychology that was based on a general idiographic[3] epistemology. Adopting the style of a manifesto, they argued that the nomothetic tradition with its hypothetical constructs, variables, and the reliance on statistics was an evolved phase of psychology. If the goal of psychology was to understand cognitive processes, they claimed, it was necessary to study individuals one at a time while performing a particular task and to gather as much data as possible to identify the information that he or she possesses and the accompanying processes.

By creating models of human information processes applicable to a single individual performing a particular task, they reversed the position of experimental psychology which conceives of the individual as a simple intersection in a statistically defined population: "This aspect of the theory, highly visible against the contrasting background of experimental psychology, is really just a consequence of viewing the human as a complex mechanism (of whatever kind) whose parts and connections can ultimately be deciphered. This point of view is accepted in most sciences outside psychology without question or comment" (Newell & Simon, 1972, p. 10).

Even today, in social psychology the usual argument is that the idiographic approach may provide a deep understanding of a single case but that general laws can be uncovered only by the nomothetic (statistical) approach. In contrast, Newell and Simon, and Piaget before them, argued that when processes are concerned, general principles would emerge by the accumulation of individual data, as protocols are gathered one at time. Then it may be possible to determine what, in terms of processes, is common to all or to some and finally to sort out all the sources of differences. This is in fact a pretty obvious proposition since a cognitive process represents a sequence of events linked within the individual as a single system – a proposition not even worth mentioning were it not for what has happened to cognitive science as adopted by social psychologists. In the field of developmental psychology Valsiner (1997) has recently argued along similar lines and claimed universality in systemically analyzed single cases

The idiographic epistemology is a crucial ingredient of the ego-ecological project, which was designed to uncover the links between representations and the identity system. To understand how this project took form requires situating the ego-ecological perspective in relation to other conceptual and methodological developments that have emerged to pursue similar goals.

Social cognition: on the wrong track

In mainstream social psychology, the impact of cognitive science was immediate, superficial and probably restrictive. It led to the emergence of a new area of research that became known as social cognition (Carrol & Payne, 1976). What characterizes the area of social cognition is the simultaneous adoption of the metaphor of the human as an information processing system and a total allegiance to strict nomothetic orthodoxy based on variables and statistical manipulations.

If this choice could be seen as a kind of epistemological incoherence, it is because the proponents of social cognition did not refute Newell and Simon's arguments. On the contrary, they claimed to have adopted them, while continuing to practice the old ways of doing psychology. Under these conditions, the failure of their project seemed highly predictable. Newell (1990) himself reflected on this issue in his last work. Pondering the social dimension of thought, he muses on how cognitive science could have helped create a model of the social persona that could have been utilized as a component of social psychology. What is called social cognition, he observes, has tried for fifteen years to follow the model of cognitive science but the initial promise has not been realized. Its backers have found it liberating to adopt terms such as encoding, or to refer to processes such as storage and retrieval. Yet by continuing to utilize the traditional paradigm of social psychology, they have produced a model of humanity that is a shadow of what it could have been. Newell concludes by saying that the research generated by the field of social cognition "has failed to extract very much of use from cognitive mechanisms and has remained with the standard methodological paradigm of social psychology, which is a form of comparative statistics. Independent variables are defined *sui generis*, dependent variables are defined ad hoc, and the studies attempt to establish how the dependent variables differ given differences in the independent ones" (1990, p. 492).

An additional demonstration of the irrelevance of social cognition research to cognitive science is the absence of any reference to this area of research when cognitive science is criticized for failing to account for the social and affective dimensions. This criticism of first-generation cognitive science and of the computational model of the mind associated with it draws attention to the failure of computer programs to simulate what happens in the social areas where reasoning must be gauged in the context of a world vision, of a belief system, and of personal desires in an effectively charged situation. These problems were identified from the beginning. For instance, Newell (1973) deplored the inability of computer simulation to account for the interplay between affect and cognition. Gardner (1985) saw the future of cognitive science in an effort to explain how culture is mapped onto the brain. These issues have been central to the ego-ecological project from the start.

The elusive search for culture, meaning, and affect

Well after the ego-ecological approach came into being, attempts were made by some researchers to address similar issues. An eclectic group reassembled under the banner of cultural psychology, all sharing an interest in reactivating the study of the role of culture in human affairs. Shewder (1991) described cultural psychology as a branch of the interpretive science. Cole (1997) in a recent and influential book sees cultural psychology as a once and future discipline. Following Wundt's lead it will become a second psychology concerned with the unity of the mind and culture. In practice the focus of the author is on the study of cognitive performance in different cultural settings. It is Bruner (1991) who on the surface comes closer to the ego-ecological project by adopting a perspective that he names "contextual transactionalism," by which he means the study of the interaction between a person and her environment. According to Bruner, human actions, mental events or the Self need to be situated, which is to be seen as continuous with a cultural world – any psychological act can be seen as an emergent property of inter-relationships. This position coincides with the ego-ecological standpoint. Both positions also argue that in a transactional context, not only the traditional conceptual apparatus of psychology, but also the computer model of cognitive science is of little use. The difference between the two positions surfaces in their epistemological and methodological choices. Bruner's solution for implementing his transactional perspective has been to borrow concepts and methods from anthropology, history, linguistics, and literary criticism; ours is to conceive a specific transactional psychology.

Bruner (1991) argues that in order to understand the nature and the origin of the Self, an interpretive effort is required, akin to that used by historians or anthropologists trying to understand a period or a people. The Self thus becomes a "story teller," and its narrative provides the basis for understanding its transactional and cultural nature. Yet, I would argue that cultural psychology is no more logically bound to the interpretive stance and to the study of language and narrative per se than to the hypothetical constructs of the nomothetic tradition. Even the best analysis of a narrative or an anthropological description will not answer the crucial question that has triggered the cultural and transactional "revolution": what happens when a person as a body/brain/mind encounters other people or a cultural event? A linguistic or hermeneutic analysis of narratives will not reveal the process by which the body/mind/brain participates in a communal cultural creation. In relying on narratology (in particular on the work of Ricoeur, 1981), Bruner is thus led to characterize a person's narrative by its sequentiality, its factual "indifference," its unique way of managing departures from the canonical and by the nature of its dramatic qualities (Bruner, 1991).

The psychological dimension of a narrative that is linked to representations of the social world stems from mental activity of another order associated with memory processes, affect and experience. All of this is addressed by the ego-ecological project that could be seen as a form of experimental phenomenology in which the interpretive stance is replaced by a guided exchange between the observer and the subjects. The goal is to display the contextual meaning of social representations (what will be described below as e-motional memory). The result will be a complex elemental unit, which we will call the affective representational circuit (ARC). It includes a multidimensional narrative that reveals the mechanism by which an embodied mind transacts with the sociocultural environment. The results permit us to envision for psychology, not an unthinking surrender to literary criticism, to linguistics, or to anthropology, but rather a future of "transactional cooperation" with these disciplines using, as a starting point, social representations theory.[4]

From social representations to identity

The goals of social representations research are multifaceted. What Jodelet (1989) proposes comes close to the ego-ecological project: "Social representations need to be studied by articulating affective, mental and social elements and in integrating next to cognition, language and communication, the social relations that affect representations and the material and social reality upon which they intervene" (p. 41). To explore social representations in their link to historically situated identities seems to subsume much of this program. The empirical issue could be framed by the question: What is activated in the mind when people think about social groups and why? In cognitive terms the problem space is one of memory processes that are still unrecognized in psychology. The philosopher Searle (1992) wrote: "We think of memory as a storehouse of propositions and images, as a kind of big library or filing cabinet of representations. But we should think of memory rather as a *mechanism* for generating current performance, including conscious thought and actions, based on past experience" (p. 187). The author does not say how a memory content can become a mechanism. However, his idea fits the model of identity as a memory system that has emerged from psychocontextual analysis (MSII Stage III).

MSII Stage III: Psychocontextual Analysis and the Emergence of E-motional Memory

Earlier, when discussing the mechanism of group recoding, I introduced the notion of background thinking as mental content subconsciously activated at the periphery of consciousness when words or representations describing aspects of the social world are produced. Stage III is an idiographic approach that we call psychocontextual analysis. It is designed to further display this mental content to uncover memory processes that connect social representations and the identity system (e-motional memory). As a procedure, psychocontextual analysis can be described as a guided exchange between the researcher and a participant that often requires minimal probing: What do you mean by . . . (word) . . . And when it applies to you? Since when do you think of yourself as . . .? How important is . . . to you? Each probe is designed to disclose the unique experiences and mental environments that have a bearing on the production of words, that is, representation. At the same time it reveals certain universal structural forms that make it possible to construct a model of the functioning of the identity system as e-motional memory.

The content of the different quadrants of the elemental identity space (see Figure 21.1) has its own contextual structural form.[5] Quadrant A (eumorphic space) is the principal purveyor of structural identity elements characterized by a positive energy. These include: collective memories, identity prototypes, experiential memories, values, attitudes and preferences, desires and motivation, and an expressive orientation, by which I mean a kind of standpoint from which each person addresses the world. Each probe generates a narrative, that implicitly or explicitly, recalls traditional hypothetical constructs in psychology, such as self-concept, attitudes, and motivation. However, what is important is that we are led to realize that these elements, instead of representing hypothetical entities that lead to autonomous psychological domains, are constitutive of a single psychological unit. They all converge and work in unison with a particular concrete word, sometimes occupying a foreground position and sometimes working in the background. In contrast, mainstream psychology has worked as if many words or rather variables were

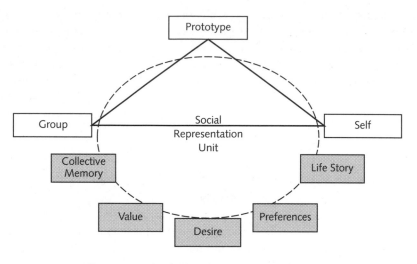

ARC represents the display of the context of SR generated
to describe the group (Background Thinking)

Figure 21.1 The affective representational circuit (ARC): A dynamic unit.

circling around an *autonomous* construct such as values, motivation, attitudes, or whatever. As a result it was difficult if not impossible to understand what kind of relations existed between these constructs. The endless questions of how attitudes are related to behavior, feelings to cognition and so on, suddenly are solved by the display of a living system and its structural elements. It is also important to mention the extralinguistic factors that accompany the narrative generated by a word representation. The expressions of feelings, desire, enthusiasm, and admiration are verbalizations of bodily arousal, of an energy, that can then be literally observed as a particular animation that the speaker displays when elaborating on the various contexts of an identity word. The resulting model of the basic unit of the identity system is the affective representational circuit (ARC) (see Fig. 21.1).

To illustrate the functioning of ARC, I will go back to Mary Daly's protocol and present the psychocontextual analysis of the word *adventurous*, the first word produced to describe We philosophers

Word meaning:

MZ: What do you mean by adventurous?
MD: To be adventurous is what it means to be alive. . .it has to do with the work you have to do, with encounters with some exciting people and spirits and animals.

Self-meaning:

MZ: And when it applies to you as a person?

MD: I am adventurous, not in the conventional sense, but in the sense of wanting to journey into the heart of the matter. I have had experience of moving into different dimensions, of traveling across time and space. . . .

Life story:

MZ: When did you first think of yourself as adventurous?

(a) *Synergistic encounter[6] and identity prototype*:

MD: I was four and a half years old and I fell in love with Carole who was five and a half. She was my hero; until she moved away one year later and I lost all contact with her. She was adventurous, breaking the furniture, scratching them. My mother who had strict rules did not want her in the house anymore. Her mother would read us advanced books. I remember a purple, exciting book. I would listen to that. Some years later I remember reading: *The Call of the Wild*. It is about a dog that was stolen, and that escapes into the wild North; he survives, and lives with the wolfs. I remember the dog howling to the deep sky. It was a mystical experience, a spiritual travel.

In this protocol, the appearance of the word adventurous is linked to an external source, as a desirable quality of an admired person. From its initial connection, the word adventurous is associated with breaking household rules by a daring ALTER. This word acquires over time other meanings and follows a spiritual and existential trajectory. It should eventually be analyzed in its connection with other words used to describe WE philosophers, such as courageous, genius, logical, intuitive. Each identity word possesses its own trajectory, while contributing to the meaning of the other words. As we will see, the original meaning of adventurous – "breaking the rules" – will reappear in a subsequent exchange. Several identity dimensions emerge in Mary Daly's narrative without any probing.

(b) *Motivation and life goals*

MD: I wanted to be a writer, my family was not educated but they gave me shining books. Not ordinary books, they were shining, colored. I just knew that they were my world, my reality. The starting point of wanting to become a philosopher was in my adolescence. . . . I went walking and a clover blossom spoke to me: I am. It provided an intuition of being and this intuition led me to write a doctoral dissertation whose title was *The Intuition of Being in Jacques Maritan*. When I was young I attended a working-class school, therefore I could not study philosophy, it did not exist there. To do that, finally, I had to cross the ocean, to Friburg; it was a tremendous risk. I was truly an adventurer. Although I had no money I managed to travel throughout Europe and my mind exploded.

The additional dimensions comprising the affective representational circuit, motivation, preferences, values, expressive orientation, emerge without further probing in the autobiographical narrative. The word adventurous appears as a psychological cell in action. As a transdimensional entity it cuts across several psychological dimensions, motivation, values, and attitudes. As a transtemporal entity it operates as a marker of important events throughout life. In its transactional trajectory, *adventurous* sparks in *daring*, remarkable books while creating a cultural figure of women and of feminists.

From identity words to cultural creation

MD: To be adventurous is what *Pure Lust* is about: desires, the opening on the sky . . . I invented the word *be-dazzling*, it is in the *Wickedary*, and it refers to the be-dazzling adventurous voyager, it creates and carries energy to overcome the foreground with the brilliance of the background. The relation between be-dazzling and adventurous is very close. Adventure sometimes means travel, sometimes nature, sometimes a connection with another person, or an aesthetic feeling. Sometimes it is the light, the spirit, the energy; this is be-dazzling. All this multiplicity of meaning allows you to overturn everything and it is linked to taking risks; it breaks the taboo against the dullness. All this was not very strong when I wrote *The Church and the Second Sex*. I became conscious of it when I was writing *Gyn/Ecology*. When I broke the taboos and threw down some oppressing coverings I found happiness. Happiness is activity, as Aristotle said, you seek to know and for that I use the metaphor of the voyager. Words are like carriers bringing the reader metaphorically over the hedge. The primary struggle is to be-dazzling and not let the foreground color it. This means to be in touch with ourselves and with creativity, constantly risking because it is the most important thing.

This excerpt documents the oscillation of an identity word from the inner to the outer and vice versa, and the weaving of new but related words such as be-dazzling. As a result new cultural figures emerge on the sociocultural space.

Creating the new from the old: enter the pirate

Identity words and their representational contexts, as living cells of the mind, do not remain static. During their trajectory through time, they absorb new elements and respond creatively to new contexts. What emerges not only modifies the present, but also the past, by reactivating forgotten experiences. In the excerpt that follows, obtained three years after the first, Mary Daly explains how a new figure, the pirate, has acquired an important role in her forthcoming autobiography: *Outercourse: the logbook of a radical feminist* (1993).

Self-meaning:

MD: It is related to the word adventurous, I had to be a pirate to steal the idea of the pirate so that the very concept of piracy is an act of piracy. Pirate as a feminine image, is close, across time, to witches, and crones. It represents an outlaw who steals back the identity of the pirate.

Life story:

MD: During childhood I loved the book *Treasure Island*. Before that, I remember a woman who was peddling books and who came to our house. My mother wanted to buy for me some books about the sea that had ships on the cover. The woman snapped back: "What an idea to buy this for a little girl." So my mother bought for me, instead, something about a little engine . . . I felt that something has been taken from me. I also used to take a boat up and down the Hudson River when I was a little kid. I used to have a captain hat to sail in this boat. The city is an island, Ireland is an island.

Synergistic encounter:

MD: A few years ago I was in Ireland on a boat with some friends, wearing some kind of head-covering, they said: "If there are pirates, you certainly are one." This amused me; then I thought about the idea of the subliminal sea [an important theme in *Outercourse*], and of a woman pirate: Granuaile (Grace O'Mally) from County Claire; she lived in the sixteenth century and was a contemporary of Queen Elizabeth I. The Queen received her at the royal palace.

Identity prototype:

MD: The pirate is an outlaw and, and this makes me think of Carole. As I wrote in the first chapter of *Outercourse,* Carole was my hero, she broke all the rules . . . [see above]; this is what a pirate does. I, also, remember reading *Treasure Island.*

I noted that this book was absent in the first protocol, and she commented: "before I could recapture the image of the pirate, I could not identify with those described in *Treasure Island* who were unlikeable, very cruel pirates." This indicates how memories of the past change as a function of the present. This should not lead to discarding autobiographical memories as unreliable, but rather to exploring their evolution according to the changing circumstances of one's life. In this example the exchange about the pirate reactivates (resonance effect) the word adventurous with all its emotional power, a condition for its assimilation into the ARC as a prototype or exemplar of this identity-word. Simultaneously, it triggers a conceptual creation: the subliminal sea. An idea that is developed in *Outercourse*. The metaphor of the pirate also extends the meaning of breaking the rules.

Cultural creation:

> MD: I have the feeling that in my books I have plundered the treasures that have been stolen from women and that I am bringing these back to them. Several women to whom I have spoken about the pirate told me how important and powerful this figure was for them.

In this new protocol, adventurous acquires a more combative meaning as compared to the earlier one, and recaptures the dimension of "breaking the rules" which was the original memory associated with Carole and that could be related to life circumstances. These excerpts show how the identity system constantly reconfigures past, present, and future, while maintaining its basic sameness. Continuity and change in the context of identity are not antonymic. Bruner's Self as a storyteller is echoed in this narrative but there are added structural and dynamic elements that direct the researcher toward specific psychological mechanisms.

The word adventurous unfolds along the structural path of what we have described as the affective representational circuit (ARC) as a kind of hypertext's link that navigates around all dimensions that comprise ARC: ingroup representation, biographical elements, the expression of values, motivation, and an expressive orientation that leads to philosophical creations that subvert the cultural landscape. This narrative also includes extralinguistic elements that belong to the affective order, translated by an animated voice, the expression of interest and of feelings. All this together demonstrates how by using as a starting point an ingroup word representation we can "exchange" with core elements of the identity system.[7]

Meeting second-generation cognitive science

The identification of ARC bring us close to the concern of second-generation cognitive scientists who have replaced the computational view of the mind with the idea of the "embodied" mind, by which they refer to the neural structures of the brain and the importance of the cognitive unconscious in human thought. The most developed research area in this new field is the analysis of metaphorical thinking and its role in everyday understanding and in philosophical thought (Lakoff & Johnson, 1999). Another interesting direction is the introduction by Mandelbilt and Zachar (1998) of the notion of dynamic unit that offers a new conception of unit in cognitive science and how this unit functions by blending different cognitive dimensions. The mental activity by which a word representation, via ARC, also blends different psychological dimensions fits precisely the idea of the dynamic unit. ARC also represents an empirical finding that directs us toward a reversal of the analytical tradition of mainstream psychology. Motivation, self-concepts, attitudes, and values, which have been constructed in psychology as separate domains of research, now appear as structural invariants of the context of particular words. Contexts are reactivated simultaneously either in the foreground or as background thought whenever a word representation is spontaneously produced. A word representation can thus be seen as a linking agent between several psychological dimensions and between different domains of experience. As a result, some psychological theories will have to be revised. For instance our data suggest that ingroup preferences derive from the fact that the WE creates a representation of a given group from all that we value and desire. It is this mental construction and not a deep-seated motive to increase one's self-esteem, as proposed by Tajfel (1978), that creates a more desirable form (gestalt) for a group constitutive of our identity. We can now attempt to understand the role of affect in the creation and expansion of identity as an internal environment.

Memory as mechanism: the resonance effect

The excerpts from Mary Daly's protocol not only illustrate the transdimensionality, transtemporality, and transactionality of word representations but also the process by which memory content is created and functions as a mechanism that I have called the *resonance effect* (Zavalloni, 1981, 1990). Resonance is a popular term in everyday discourse. Despite this popularity, the phenomena that it represents have not been studied. Lazarus (1991) noted that more attention should be paid to "unarticulated processes" like resonance, to fully understand how emotions are generated. For him resonance refers to "an amorphous or ineffable sense of connection between what is in us and something in the outer world" (p. 154). In the present context, the resonance effect refers to the reactivation, as background thinking, of the compressed context of identity words (intrapsychic resonance). This implies that in every act of thinking is engaged a psychic totality that reaches beyond the particular context wherein the act occurs. When an identity word enters the field of consciousness, the representational network associated with it vibrates, amplified, as it were, by the experience, the imagination, and the emotions that form the sedimented layers of meaning of the identity word.

I argue that the range of emotions that accompany a word representation and their various contexts reflects the conditions by which this mental content is memorized. We have described the identity system as e-motional memory (Zavalloni &

Louis-Guérin, 1984). Now, the notion of the resonance effect provides the key to understanding how this system grows and operates as a form of thought in transaction with the world. Let us to go back to the idea of a synergistic encounter, when an event or some events arouses some degree of affect: for instance, in Mary Daly's protocol, to the memory of Carole breaking the household rules. I believe that the ensuing feeling of "admiration" is the experience of a neuronal, chemical, or electrical event, whatever state of the brain allows this feature to become an element of long-term memory. Whenever, in the future, an element compatible with this memory is encountered, a resonance will be triggered that recaptures the original content and the emotion associated with it. As a result, the neuronal condition of "memory readiness" will also be reinstated. In its elemental simplicity, the resonance effect will provide the dynamic, the energy by which the identity system, as e-motional memory, will be created in its transaction with the world.

The data suggest another important function of the resonance effect in the continuation of the identity system as e-motional memory. As an automatic, subconscious, reactivation of memory content as background thinking, the resonance effect produces the necessary rehearsal by which any kind of memory (Norman, 1972) is kept alive.

MSII Stage IV

The last stage for the unfolding of the identity system represents a cooperative endeavor between the researcher and its subject. Its purpose is to generate a number of what we called sociomotivational nuclei (Zavalloni & Louis-Guérin, 1984). This is done by asking the respondent to identify different relations that he or she can detect between the different representations. These relations can be described as contiguity, implication, incompatibility, and opposition. I briefly note the relation in Mary Daly's narrative between the identity word adventurer (Case A) and lifeless, boring, dry (negative NonSelf – Case D).

> MD: If I pay attention to them I would block my creative energy. It is always distracting, not worth discussing. Is what stops adventure, is what stops sparking, spooking, is just a slow downing of energy, is evil. During my public speaking there are women that are very excited. They say that I say what they have always thought but nobody had said it before. There is a tremendous enthusiasm among some and then there are the others. I do not pay attention to them, the great blobs that control academia.

What materializes in this opposition is a vital relation of contrasting emotions and of cultural struggle. The philosopher emerges as a cultural engine that in transaction with the world drives to change it. This narrative demonstrates the relation between the various elements of the identity space. The contextual meaning of lifeless, boring, dry, lead directly in the dysmorphic space of Case C (negative state of the Self). The contrasting emotional states related to the content of Cases and A, D, and C are clearly observable in the voice of the narrator. This example supports the idea of a specific identity energy linked to the creation of social representations and of the Self. It also demonstrates the role of extralinguistic features in human discourse and the unfolding of the mechanisms that we have described in their structural and dynamic aspects.

The discourse that is generated through the MSII may have far reaching implications for developing links between social psychology and clinical research, but also with cognitive science, anthropology, and sociology. The respondent can apprehend his or her identity as a complex network that is not ordinarily accessible to consciousness in its entirety. From this standpoint, issues that are relevant to different disciplines can be addressed, while maintaining the core representations at the center of the analysis.

The result is a model of the relations between social representations and identity that may provide the missing link toward the integration of cognitive science and psychology as a whole, including the understanding of cultural creation but also integration of the clinical domain. This model addresses the modalities of person/culture transactions as they relate to particular exchanges with people who had a determining influence on one's life. This leads us to a reversal of perspective in the research, bringing concrete word representations from the periphery to the center of research, without losing sight of the fundamental objective of psychology, which is to understand the general principles of psychic functioning. The vastly increased capabilities of the interactive computer can be harnessed to handle the vast amount of relevant data from the neighboring sciences to recreate the naturalistic conditions to fully understand humans as transactional agents. It will require a collective effort that perhaps some researchers will be tempted to undertake.

Notes

This research was made possible by a grant from the CRSH.

1   The conditions under which WE and THEY are nonoperative are described in Zavalloni and Louis-Guérin (1984).

2   Before, as Newell and Simon (1972) note, Piaget's work was hardly familiar to American psychologists and there was "no way at the time for bringing that work, even when known, into any kind of relevant conceptual relations to mainstream American behaviorism" (p. 875).

3   Piaget used to say that his clinical method did not reflect any antipathy toward statistics but that simply reflected the nature of his research problem. For a recent treatment of verbal data along these lines, see Ericcson & Simon (1993).

4   Another break with both traditional psychology and first-generation cognitive science is to be found in the postmodern form of social constructionism advocated by Gergen (1994). According to this view, language as it emerges during social interactions is the only reality. Gergen denies not only the existence of extralinguistic factors, but of the mind as well. It is hard to believe that language, thus conceived as floating in the social space without anchoring in memory or in the brain, is really all that is there.

5   For a detailed description see Zavalloni and Louis-Guérin, 1984.

6   The synergistic encounter (Zavalloni, 1986) refers to the initial state when a psychological element becomes part of the e-motional memory and then functions as a transactional mechanism blending different psychological dimensions. The state of emotional energy that results could be the condition required if the new theme is to be launched into the identity orbit. It also designates a biographical moment of heightened emotional experience.

7   To eliminate the possibility that the structural dimensions of ARC could have been induced by the method itself, I turned my attentions to literary texts and I analyzed Satre's identity word genius (Zavalloni, 1986) and more recently Nietzsche's identity words: wicked and evil (Zavalloni, 1998). In both cases I was able to prove that these words would reappear in all the contexts constitutive of ARC.

22

Social Identities and Social Representations: A Question of Priority?

Marilynn B. Brewer

In their chapters in this volume, Breakwell and Duveen both make reference to the three types of social representation identified by Moscovici (1988) – *hegemonic* (uniform representations shared by all members of a single highly structured group), *emancipated* (representations that are the outgrowth of shared knowledge within subgroups), and *polemical* (representations that are generated by social conflict and antagonistic relations). Of these three forms, the notion of "social identity" certainly qualifies as an emancipated representation. Social identity is a concept that has been invented and reinvented across the social and behavioral science disciplines to provide a critical link between the psychology of the individual and the structure and function of social groups. Although the term is used widely throughout the social sciences, its meaning and associative structure vary dramatically across intellectual schools and research groups. Clearly this is a case where shared meaning is vested in subgroups, each with its own version of the concept and its core elements. Because of this, any discussion of the relationship between social representations and social identities becomes a case illustration of the very topic of discussion.

From the three chapters in this section of the volume, I have extracted three different working definitions of the social identity construct. Implicit in Zavalloni's use of the term psychosocial identity is a deeply personal, subjective meaning system – an internal representation that includes representations of the social world but is relatively unconstrained by shared representations or collective understandings. From this perspective, social identities are *projections* of the subjective and personal to the "we," rather than the assimilation of external influences into the self. By contrast, the chapters by Breakwell and Duveen are more concerned with the processes by which social representations – as meaning systems existing external to the individual – become *introjected* or incorporated into personal identities.

For both Breakwell and Duveen, the concepts of personal identity and social identity are essentially merged as the joint product of individual and social processes. The theme in both chapters is the relationship between social representations and social identity as mutual exchange, an integrated system in which both shape each other through processes of assimilation and accommodation. In Breakwell's analysis, social identity is that part of the content of personal identity derived from social representations and the group memberships that give rise to them. As the product of identification with groups, this definition comes closest to that represented by the early social identity theory of Tajfel (1981a). In Duveen's analysis, social identities reflect the internalization of expectations and representations associated with the individual's position or location in society and its symbolic culture. This perspective comes closest to the concept of social identity as represented in the symbolic interactionist tradition of U.S. sociology (e.g., Stryker, 1980, 1987).

To these three representations, I would like to add yet a fourth conceptualization of the meaning of social identity – one that comes closer to that reflected in self-categorization theory (Turner, Hogg, Oakes, Reicher, &Wetherell, 1987) and my own optimal distinctiveness theory of social identity (Brewer, 1991). This is the idea of a group or collective identity that is an *extension* of the self-concept to *include* others who share a common group membership. Whereas person-based social identities reflect the extent to which a group or category membership is represented as an integral part of an individual's self-concept, group identities refer to the perception of self as an integral or interchangeable part of a larger group or social unit. Thus, these two meanings of social identity are essentially inverses of each other, reversing the nature of the part-whole relation. Group-based social identity is best captured by Turner's self-categorization theory, in which social identity is defined as a "depersonalized" sense of self entailing "a shift towards the perception of self as an interchangeable exemplar of some social category and away from the perception of self as a unique person . . ." (Turner et al., 1987, p. 50). This is the essence of what Thoits and Virshup (1997) refer to as collective or "we" identities, identification of the self *with* the group as a whole.

Group identification influences the self concept in two ways. First, when a group identity is engaged, the construal of self extends beyond the individual person to a more inclusive social unit. The boundaries between self and other group members are eclipsed by the greater salience of the boundaries between ingroup (us) and outgroups (them). The fortunes and misfortunes of the group as a whole are incorporated into the self and responded to as personal outcomes. Second, the attributes and behaviors of the individual self are assimilated to the representation of the group as a whole, enhancing those features that make the group distinctive from other social categories and at the same time enhancing uniformity and cohesion within the group (cf. Turner, 1991; Turner et al., 1987, Chapter 5).

This conceptualization of social identity shifts the focus of attention somewhat from "what" to "who" – from *content* of representations to *composition* of the social community that gives rise to those representations. In this latter conceptualization, the essence of a social identity lies in the shared rules of inclusion and exclusion that determine the boundary between who is "us" and who is not us. This boundary, in turn, places limits on the processes of interaction, communication, and social influence from which social representations arise. In the remainder of this discussion I hope to illustrate how this shift of perspective can enrich our understanding of the nature of the mutual relationship between social identity and social representations.

From Social Identities to Social Representations and Back Again

In the analyses by Breakwell and Duveen, the relationship between social representations and social identity is discussed primarily in terms of how social representations influence or become incorporated in the content of individual identity. To be sure, both recognize that individuals play an active role in this process of assimilation, resisting or modifying social representations in accord with their own identity needs and structure. As Breakwell (Chapter 20, this volume) puts it, "aspects of identity . . . are very important determinants of the individual's participation in the production, transformation, and use of social representations." Still, the analysis begins with social representations as meaning systems that already exist "out there" (i.e., external to the individual) and then are incorporated into the individual's own subjective meaning system, perhaps with subtle modification to suit the person's own identity needs. Group memberships (the source of social identities) influence this process by first determining which social representations an individual is exposed to, and then by affecting the extent to which the social representation is accepted and used. In fact, Duveen explicitly advocates the priority of social representations, claiming that representations precede identities. This analysis begs the important question of how social representations are formed in the first place.

Breakwell explicitly mentions that identity processes may play a role in the production, creation, and change of social representations but does not treat this as a *group* process. Group memberships are assumed to function in the same way as other individual traits to "shape the individual's exposure to, acceptance of, and use of a social representation" (Chapter 20, this volume). This treatment seems to me to underestimate the role of group identification in the *creation and production* of social representations as group products. Interestingly, Breakwell's list of identity needs (self-esteem, continuity, distinctiveness, and self-efficacy) does not include the need for belonging despite the central role that this motive plays in social psychology, even in the context of Western cultures (e.g., Brewer, 1991, 1997; Baumeister & Leary, 1995; Staub, 1999). By neglecting the individual's need to achieve and maintain connectedness to social groups, Breakwell is overlooking an important way in which identity processes determine the evolution of social representations and shape their content.

In his chapter in this volume, Moscovici reiterates his view of the "central problem" of social psychology in general and social representation theory in particular – the question of what binds people together in a social group and makes them act together in a collective manner. By one account, social representations are the "glue" of social life. Shared meanings define social groups and make coordinated collective action possible. Social representations not only provide the content of the meaning systems that characterize a social group but also play a role in defining and maintaining the boundaries of social collectives – group boundaries exist where shared meaning breaks down or is nonexistent. In this view, social representations are, indeed, prior to social identities; groups and group identities expand and contract, change and evolve as a function of the processes that give rise to shared meanings.

As with any complex system, however, there is a chicken-and-egg problem with this account. If social representations make social groups possible, then what makes social representations possible? Another view of this relationship is that shared meaning systems evolve because individuals seek membership in bounded social groups – i.e., that social representations derive from group formation processes rather than vice versa. This alternative view rests on the recognition that both social identities and social representations arise from motivational as well as cognitive processes.

The chapters by Breakwell and Duveen acknowledge that individual needs and motives play a significant role in the acceptance and use of social representations. But the influence of motivational factors in the evolution of social representations runs much deeper than this. Shared understandings don't just "happen" as a consequence of exposure to the content of verbal and nonverbal communications from others. Social representations don't necessarily arise spontaneously from any social interaction. Shared meaning is an *achievement* based on an active, effortful process of exchange and mutual influence. Because effort is implicated, the process depends on motivation – the desire to understand the other's meaning, to see the world as the other sees it, and to allow the other's view to influence one's own. Without such motivation, individuals or groups can talk "at" each other with no emergent shared representations at all.

So what motivates an individual to become engaged in a mutual meaning-making process and with whom? I have already alluded to the critical importance of the need to belong as a factor in group identification and the emergence of social identities. The need to avoid isolation, the fear of exclusion, and the desire to be included in some larger social unit all drive the individual to seek and maintain connections with others in the context of relatively large social groups. But the need for inclusion is not unsatiable; at some point the desire to belong comes in conflict with an equally important opposing need for differentiation and distinctiveness. The end result is a dynamic equilibrium achieved through identification with distinct, bounded social collectives (Brewer, 1991). Although the capacity for interpersonal connectedness is continuous, social relationships are in actuality structured into discrete social units – the categorical boundaries that differentiate "us" from "them." The same processes that give rise to intergroup boundaries also place boundaries on the engagement of social motives toward mutual cooperation, exchange, and influence that are required for the emergence of social representations.

Ingroup identities imply mutual obligations on the part of group members (Brewer, 1997). Social identification entails an obligation to know and subscribe to the common symbols and norms that differentiate the ingroup from others – in short, to be an expert on the group culture and shared meaning system. It also entails an obligation to influence and be influenced by others within the group until shared meaning is achieved on any issue that impinges on the group's identity. But the obligation stops at the group boundary. Even if intergroup social interaction is high, ingroup – outgroup boundaries create a discontinuity of mutual social influence and emergent social representations.

This analysis of the role of social identification in the creation and maintenance of social representations is consistent with a self-categorization perspective on group formation and social influence (Turner, 1985, 1991; Haslam, Turner, Oakes, McGarty, & Reynolds, 1998). According to this perspective, social consensus is not an automatic outcome of exposure to information from others but requires *active coordination* of individuals' perceptions and behavior in an effort to reach agreement. Shared group membership serves to regulate cognitive activity not only by providing a common perspective on social reality but also by providing a basis for mutual influence (Haslam et al., 1998). A common social identity motivates individuals to engage in a process of reaching agreement through persuasion, negotiation, and argument (Reicher, Hopkins, & Condor, 1997). Consistent with my earlier point about the "who" of group identity:

> the nature of collective action will flow from the definition of social categories; the extent of who forms part of the collective and who the collective acts against will relate to the boundaries of ingroup and outgroup: the direction which the collective takes will relate to the content of group identity and ability to gain influence over the collective will relate to who is prototypical. (Reicher et al., 1997, p. 110)

According to self-categorization theory, consensus is achieved through social interaction only to the extent that the interaction is premised upon a shared social identity relevant to the issue at hand. Reaching agreement and common understanding requires effort and openness, including exchanging information, identifying shared beliefs, specifying frames of reference, articulating background knowledge, clarifying points of disagreement, and monitoring the effectiveness of communication attempts. Psychological group membership (social identification), rather than social pressure or information per se, is the basis for the formation of shared meaning. From this perspective, social representations are a collective accomplishment realized in the context of specific ingroup – outgroup categorizations – the expression of a social identification process that mobilizes and motivates group meaning formation and mutual influence.

In this view, then, social identities are prior to social representations. Before the requisite processes of social representation formation can be engaged, individuals must have a sense of common identity that motivates coordinated behavior and defines who is open to influence from whom. Rather than social representations providing the glue for the formation and maintenance of social groups, the existence of bounded social groups provides the conditions that give rise to social representations.

These alternative accounts of the interrelationship between social identity and social representations are, of course, not mutually exclusive. Which has priority depends on where one breaks into the reciprocal causal system. To explain the emergence of new social representations certainly requires the prior existence of some definable social community with shared concerns, opportunity for interaction, and motivation to reach agreement or common understanding of an issue. Alternatively, social communities exist only to the extent that there are shared representations of what constitutes that social group. Social representations provide the content on which the assumption of shared identity can be based. Hence, the question of priority of social identity over social representation or vice versa is just as unanswerable (and just as meaningless) as the proverbial chicken and egg conundrum.

A Case at Hand

In many respects, the CUNY Conference on Social Representations constituted a living experiment on the interrelationship of social identities and social representations. On the one hand, the composition of the group of invited participants and the explicit purposes of the conference brought together representatives of distinctly different intellectual traditions, each with its own collective understanding of concepts such as social construction, identity, and social categorization that were of common interest and concern. The question for many of us at the outset was whether we were engaged in a common enterprise from complementary or competing perspectives, or perhaps engaged in entirely different enterprises with no real point of contact at all. No doubt the conference organizers were aware that they were creating a situation rife with potential for emergence of polemical social representations.

On the other hand, participation in the conference entailed something of a commitment to a common social identity as a community of scholars of social psychology. Over the course of the two days, the consequences of that commitment to achieve some measure of common understanding were evident in efforts to identify shared background knowledge, translate terms across different meaning systems, cross-reference ideas, and engage in continuous discussion. In the process, I think it became evident to all of us that the emergence of shared representations is the product of motivated effort in which shared group membership played an important role.

23

Meaning and Making: Some Comments on Content and Process

Kay Deaux

The three authors in this section address what for me, and I presume for many social psychologists, is one of the fundamental questions of our discipline: what is the relationship between the individual and the social system? How can we best represent the ways in which the larger system of social and cultural beliefs are incorporated by a specific group or individual? How can we move from a highly individualistic conception of the person to one that recognizes social context as the medium in which individual beliefs and actions are established and enacted, while at the same time allowing for individual variation in internalization and expression? These are the questions that these authors address, bringing social representation theory and various models of social identification to a joint encounter. In doing so, they offer us some important alternatives to the decontextualized models of social psychology that assume universality while ignoring even the most immediate conditions that shape observed behavior.

As is evident, the three authors do not share a single vision, nor do their analyses begin at a common starting point. For Duveen, the analysis begins with social representations, as he argues that "identity is first a social location, a space made available within the representational structures of the social world" (Chapter 19, this volume). For Breakwell, individual identity processes appear to take precedence, as reflected in her statement that "identity dynamics will determine the individual's relation to the social representation" (Chapter 20, this volume). Zavalloni positions herself somewhat between these two, analyzing a psychosocial identity that is described as lying between the individual and the social self.

These different positionings speak to the complexity of the issues at hand. They also, through their distinctive paths of argumentation, direct us to different aspects of the social identity – social representation relationship. In my comments here, I want to consider two very general issues inherent in this relationship – first, content and second, process. With regard to content, we want to ask about the meanings or the material with which identities and representations are constituted. To what extent does the meaning of a social identity, as defined from the perspective of the individual, reflect or map onto the shared cultural representations? With regard to process, we need to explore the ways in which social identities are made or constructed, from the raw material of personal experience and socially shared beliefs. What do the authors tell us about the manner in which social identities and social representations develop, merge, and change?

On Content

As Duveen notes in his introductory section, consideration of the content of social identities has been a minor strand in the research emanating from Tajfel's theory. In general, adherents of social identity theory have been far more interested in analyzing the ways in which social identity influences and is influenced by specific forms of intergroup encounters. Certainly the widespread adoption of the minimal group paradigm, in which one's social identity is arbitrarily defined as being a perceiver of blue or green dots or even an X versus an O, did little to foster interest in content. Somewhat more recognition of content is given by those who work in the framework of self-categorization theory (Oakes, Haslam, & Turner, 1994; Turner, Hogg, Oakes, Reicher, & Wetherell, 1987). Here the notion of self-stereotyping, for example, speaks to the culturally shared definitions of a category, addressing the question of when individuals will describe themselves in terms of the stereotyped attributes of their category. At the same time, content itself is never the central concern in this theory, serving rather to illustrate the highlighted theoretical processes. Thus the interest that the present authors show in questions of meaning, each with a different emphasis, is a welcome and valuable contribution to the debate.

In charting the elemental identity space within her ego-ecology model, Zavalloni concentrates on the words that a respondent uses to characterize a particular self-relevant category, dimensionalizing these words by their relevance to self (self versus nonself) and their evaluation (positive versus negative). In depicting the way that philosopher Mary Daly characterizes the "we's" and the "they's" within philosophy, she offers a set of positive traits related to self and a set of negative traits related to other philosophers. (The intergroup distinction here appears to be unambiguous, in that no positive traits are assigned to others and no negative traits are assigned to self.) Although attention to the meaning at the level of the individual case is intensive in Zavalloni's model, she gives less attention to the ways in which these individual (and probably idiosyncratic) meanings reflect or are shaped by the larger social context. Thus, although critical of ways in which social psychology has (mis)used the models of cognitive science, and certainly giving more attention to issues of culture, language, and affect as they are evidenced in the meaning system of her chosen respondent, Zavalloni is consistent with many other social psychologists in taking the individual perspective as point of origin.

Duveen, in contrast, starts from the cultural representations, in this instance focusing on the social representations of gender. As Duveen notes, beliefs about what it means to be a boy versus a girl are deeply entrenched, and parents act on these beliefs as soon as, and in some cases even before, a child is born (in cases where parents know or believe they know the sex of the child in advance of birth). As children develop, they quickly apprehend the cultural scripts for sexuality, parental role relationships, and other gender-scripted domains, and their behaviors reflect those understandings. Central to this representation of gender is a perceived bipolarity of masculine and feminine, which as other authors have shown, is central to the gender belief system (Kite & Deaux, 1987) and is acquired in the process of socialization and development (Biernat, 1991). Also important in Duveen's discussion is the emphasis on gender representations as an expression of societal hierarchies. Thus the meaning system associated with gender is not a catalogue of value-neutral beliefs, but rather describes a system of power relationships between the sexes that also becomes part of the incorporated identity structure.

Duveen's work on gender provides one example of the ways in which the content of social representations, and in turn of social identities, are critical to the expression of beliefs and behaviors. Such a concern with meaning is evidenced in other types of identity analysis as well. Perhaps the best example is the work of investigators exploring the shape of African American identity within the United States (Cross, 1991; Cross & Fhagen-Smith, 2000; Sellers, Smith, Shelton, Rowley, & Chavous, 1998). In these analyses, content is a central concern as investigators consider the wide range of meanings associated with that ethnic/racial identity, including ideological and political beliefs as well as the more conventional traits and attributes.

Breakwell, in describing her empirical work on social identity and social representations, raises the question of variable representations of the same target object. In her study of the perceived risks of smoking, she found two distinct clusters of children, whose representations of smoking differed sharply. These children in turn were parts of different social networks, in each case one that shared the child's own representation of smoking. These results underline the importance of going beyond the category label in the analysis of both social identity and social representation to assess the meanings that reside within. It is at this level of meaning that the variations between subcommunities, which Jovchelovitch (Chapter 11, this volume) and others describe, become so critical.

The analysis of meaning clearly calls for a greater diversification of methods than many social psychologists currently use, a point that Philogène (Chapter 3, this volume) makes as well. As Duveen's analysis of children's play talk shows, issues of content can be approached effectively through more qualitative methods, including discourse analysis and interviews. Social psychologists have not, as a rule, embraced these more qualitative approaches to data, preferring instead to deal with more easily controlled quantitative indices (though as we noted earlier, the times they are a changing!). At the same time, concern with content does not necessarily privilege qualitative approaches. As Doise and his colleagues have shown (Doise, Clémence, & Lorenzi-Cioldi, 1993), numerous quantitative methods are also available for the analysis of social representations. It is certainly valid to suggest that the experimental method alone will not move us sufficiently far toward an understanding of content as it is constructed and lived. But both qualitative and quantitative methods can and do easily exist outside the realm of the experimental laboratory, and both can move us forward in our understanding of the content and meaning of social identities.

On Process

Although questions of process can be analytically distinct from issues of content, the message that we learn from the work represented in these chapters is that such a division is unwise. Indeed, social representations are defined as *both* product and process, and it is that dual focus that gives the model such cogency. While inextricable from issues of content, the processes by which social identities are shaped by and reflective of the social representations of a culture can be highlighted in their own right. Such an analysis is clearly central to the agenda of these three authors.

Breakwell begins with the assumption, which I hold as well, that the meaning of a social identity for each individual has shared as well as idiosyncratic elements. Thus the social representation of gender may provide a consensual set of beliefs, accepted as stereotype by the majority of people in a culture, while the individual's own identification as man or woman may include only some of those elements. (Spence, in her 1985 analysis of masculinity and femininity, makes a similar point about variations in self-defining gender attributes as a result of differential experience.) This position is, it might be noted, in contrast to the position of self-categorization theory, wherein the sharing of a social category implies a psychological interchangeability of people who possess the same attributes (Oakes, Haslam, & Turner, 1994).

If one assumes some individual variation in the self-ascribed meaning of a social identity, it is then necessary to develop an account of how those differences might emerge. Breakwell makes an important contribution here, suggesting five ways in which individual variation might develop. These five points of divergence are (a) one's awareness of the social representation, (b) one's understanding of the representation, (c) the willingness of the person to accept the representation as an aspect of self-definition, (d) the ability to anchor the representation in one's pre-existing system of personal representation, and (e) the salience of the representation for the individual. Stipulation of these possibilities is a crucial first step. A next step would be to more fully articulate the conditions that create, for example, greater awareness or increased willingness to accept the representation.

This domain of variation and choice initially seems quite different from the picture that Duveen paints of a gender representation system being present at birth and almost automatically taken on by the developing child, in keeping with the representations and influences of the communities in which the child is immersed. Yet Duveen, too, in introducing the concept of resistance, considers the possibility that individuals may refuse to accept the influence of the larger social network. As one example, he points to differences between boys and girls in their acceptance of gender hierarchy, with girls reacting against the gender devaluation that the prevalent hierarchy entails. Although the specific conditions that facilitate resistance and the processes by which the individual restructures an identity are not detailed by Duveen, he does provide a window through which these questions can be considered. (For Zavalloni, individual construction seems to be the major issue, as the shared meanings of a category are ignored in favor of idiosyncratic meaning systems.)

I suspect there are a couple of issues that need to be sorted out here that would help in understanding the SR—SI process. One of these is the distinction between what Duveen calls imperative versus contractual obligations, similar to what sociologists have termed ascribed versus achieved statuses. In the former case, the social identity is almost automatically assumed, typically because there are visible means of categorization and because the categories are in widespread use within the culture. Gender, race, and age are such categories. In contrast, contractual or achieved categories are chosen by the person, to a greater or lesser extent. Further, as Brewer notes in her commentary, the category itself may be constructed *de novo* by the group, in which case the social representations are being created rather than taken from a pre-existing representational network. These differences in the preeminence and history of the social category need to be considered in the analysis of the social representation process.

Another issue, perhaps an extension of Breakwell's acceptance criteria, concerns the motivations that people have for accepting representational elements into their self-definition. To some extent, I suggest that people choose both their categories of social identification as well as the meanings and content of those categories based on their functional utility. In other words, people consider, though perhaps not always consciously, what a category or meaning will do for them, that is, what functions it will serve (Deaux, Reid, Mizrahi, & Cotting, 1999). Taking this approach, we have found that different groups serve different functions for their members. Some processes, such as ingroup cooperation, are important for sports teams (lacrosse players in our research) as well as religious groups (e.g., Mormons). Intergroup comparison is a key issue in some social identity groups; self-understanding is a goal for others. It seems quite likely that people are thus taking on certain social identifications, and the meanings associated with them, so as to satisfy certain motives or to achieve certain states. Such functionally driven choices would also, I suspect, shape the pattern of meaning that an individual would draw from the prevailing social representations about that group, choosing those elements that were most supportive of the functions one wanted to satisfy.

This idea of functional utilities shares some aspects with Breakwell's theory of identity process, in which she proposes that people generate their identity structures in such a way as to achieve self-esteem, continuity, distinctiveness, and self-efficacy. Breakwell's motivational analysis, however, concentrates wholly on individual concerns. The Deaux et al. analysis (1999), in contrast, considers motives related to interpersonal, intragroup, and intergroup functioning as well, thus making it easier to link to the communicative processes involved in social representations.

This analysis of individual motives for claiming a social identity may offer some insight into the identity process. Yet, we must avoid shifting the causal weight back primarily to the individual. The analysis of social identity vis à vis social representations is important precisely because it forces us to consider context and culture as integral to the process. Notions of positioning (see Doise, 1986; Elejabarrieta, 1994) are helpful here, in reminding us that individuals position themselves in a group, while at the same time groups are themselves positioned within the prevailing cultural space. Further, as Elejabarrieta (1994) notes, groups do not standardize social representations but rather provide a dynamic context in which social positions are expressed. It is these dynamics, enacted through communication and negotiation, that make the relationship between social identity and social representation so compelling. At the same time, it requires a complexity of conceptual analysis that continues to challenge both our methods and our theories as we confront the basic question for social psychologists of the relationship between individuals and social systems.

24

Epilogue

Kay Deaux and Gina Philogène

At this point, we might ask how well the bridges, as envisioned early on in this project, have developed. Will social representation theory take hold in U.S. soil, as it has in many other countries, and provide a new framework for analyzing social psychological phenomena? Or, approaching the bridge from the other end, will familiarity with work on social representations allow investigators whose work is shaped by the dominant paradigms in the United States to bring their tools to bear on the further development of social representation theory? The answers to these questions are obviously not ours to provide. Each reader will form his or her own conclusion about the potential cross-fertilization that the chapters in this volume may suggest.

It is also important to note, in thinking about the metaphorical bridge, that the lands on either side of the bridge are not so totally distinct from one another nor homogeneous within themselves. As noted earlier in the Introduction to the volume, social psychology takes many forms wherever it is practiced. That point should be even clearer now. Within the group of investigators working in the tradition of social representation theory, as represented in this volume, there are wide variations in style and method, as well as in theoretical emphases within the general representation framework. Similarly, authors of the commentaries are not unified in their positions either.

Certainly many points of common ground emerge on a reading of this text. Concerns with the structure of attitudes and cognitions, for example, are evident in many different chapters. Although representatives of the social representation position are more committed to understanding these structures as they are socially shared than is characteristic of much contemporary work in social cognition, few social psychologists would deny the significance of historical and cultural factors. Similarly, conceptions of social identification inevitably deal with some concept of shared attributes and group-based construction, whatever the broader theoretical framework from which they emerge.

Nonetheless, there are certainly differences in perspective or emphasis that can be observed. The level of theorizing tends to be somewhat different. As Doise (1993a) has noted, social representation theory is "a general theory about a metasystem" (p. 157) that serves to "orientate the research effort" (p. 161). As such, it can be complemented by more detailed analyses of processes that, while consistent with the orienting framework, may be consistent with other theories as well. Predominant theories in social psychology tend to be of a more specialized, middle-range level of analysis, placing somewhat greater restrictions on the scope of phenomena that they are designed to account for.

At the same time, social representation work is often more concerned with the particular case than are some other social psychological theories. In common with other models that emphasize unique historical conditions and specific cultural contexts, social representation theory requires the investigator to take the particular into account before assuming universality. Work done within the social representation framework is also inherently more social, in some respects. Processes such as communication and group consensus are central to the enterprise. In contrast, the recent history of social psychology in the United States is one of encouraging other fields, such as communications and organizational behavior, to claim the territory that these less-individualistic phenomena represent.

As we assess the present and look to the future, however, we see both evidence of compatibility and the promise of even greater rapprochement between various strands of social psychological theorizing. We continue to believe that social psychology is an important discipline, uniquely positioned in the social and behavioral sciences to make the synthesis between the individual and the social system, to analyze basic processes while taking cultural context into account. More likely than sociology to consider the agentic contribution of individuals and more aware of historical and cultural influences than traditional cognitive psychology, a social psychological perspective is essential. Rapprochement does not mean homogenization, however. Rather, the idea is to tackle the diversity through the mutual exchange of ideas, discovering where the strengths and weaknesses of theories lie and where their synthesis can move us forward.

Social representation is one, though certainly not the only, theoretical framework that calls on us to take a broad view of social processes and events and to keep true to a vision of a *social* psychology. What it does, perhaps better than some other theories, however, is to incorporate ideas of change. One of the striking characteristics of modern society is the changing nature of social realities. Given the accelerating rate of change in many societies, it is important for our theories to offer some framework for analyzing the processes of change. How does change come about? How do we internalize transformations? What are the constraints and limits on change? For questions such as these, it is essential that we widen our lens, beyond the individual to the cultures in which we participate and by which we are shaped. Here we are asking not only for a psychology that is truly social, but one that is dynamic as well, able to deal with shifting patterns as well as stable processes.

In conclusion, this volume should be seen as an argument for the plurality of social psychological approaches. Our hope is that it will contribute to continued dialogue, debate, and cross-fertilization among those who approach our field from different theoretical and methodological stances. Such discussions, we believe, will both test the possibilities and extend the limits of social psychology for the future.

References

Abelson, R. P. (1976). Script processing in attitude formation and decision making. In J. S. Carrol & J. W. Payne (Eds.), *Cognition and Social Behavior* (pp. 35–45). Hillsdale, NJ: Lawrence Erlbaum.

Abelson, R. P. (1986). Attitudes are like possessions. *Journal for the Theory of Social Behavior*, *16*, 223–250.

Abric, J.-C. (1976). *Jeux, Conflits et Représentations Sociales*. These d'Etat, Aix-en-Provence, Universite de Provence.

Abric, J.-C. (1984). A theoretical and experimental approach to the study of social representations in a situation of interaction. In R. Farr & S. Moscovici (Eds.), *Social Representations* (pp. 169–184). Cambridge: Cambridge University Press.

Abric, J.-C. (1987). *Cooperation, Competition et Représentations Sociales*. Cousset: Del Val, Switzerland.

Abric, J.-C. (1989). L'étude experimentale des représentations sociales. In D. Jodelet (Ed.), *Les Représentations Sociales*. (pp. 187–203). Paris: Presses Universitaires de France.

Abric, J.-C. (1993). Central system, peripheral system: Their functions and roles in the dynamics of social representations. *Papers of Social Representations*, *2* (2), 75–78.

Abric, J.-C. (1994a). Les représentations sociales: Aspects théoriques. In J-C. Abric (Ed.), *Pratiques Sociales et Représentations* (pp. 11–35). Paris: Presses Universitaires de France.

Abric, J.-C. (1994b). L'organisation interne des représentations sociales: Système central et système périphérique. In C. Guimelli (Ed.), *Structures et Transformations des Représentations Sociales* (pp. 73–84). Neuchâtel: Delachaux et Niestlé.

Abric, J.-C. (Ed.) (1994c). *Pratiques Sociales et Représentations*. Paris: Presses Universitaires de France.

Abric, J.-C. (1998). L'étude des représentations sociales de la banque en France: Une nouvelle approche méthodologique. In V. Rigas (ed.). *Social Representations and Contemporary Social Problems* (pp. 2–10). Athens: Elliniki Grammata.

Agi, M. (1980). *De l'Idée d'Universalité comme Fondatrice du Concept des Droits de l'Homme: d'Après la Vie et l'Oeuvre de René Cassin*. Antibes: Editions Alp'Azur.

References

Ajzen, I. (1988). *Attitudes, Personality and Behaviour*. Cambridge: Oxford University Press.

Allen, N.J., Pickering, W .S. F., & Miller, W. W. (1989). *On Durkheim's Elementary Forms of Religious Life*. London and New York: Routledge and Kegan Paul.

Allport, G. W. (1954). *The Nature of Prejudice*. Reading, MA: Addison-Wesley.

Allum, N. C. (1998). A social representational approach to the comparison of three text corpora using ALCESTE. Unpublished doctoral dissertation, Methodology Institute: London School of Economics, London.

Alomes, S., & Jones, C. (1991). *Australian Nationalism: A Documentary History*. North Ryde: NSW, Collins, Angus, & Robertson.

Apfelbaum, E. (1979). Relations of domination and movements for liberation: An analysis of power between groups. In S. Worchel & W. Austin (Eds.), *The Social Psychology of Intergroup Relations* (pp. 188–204). Chicago: Nelson-Hall.

Arendt, H. (1958). *The Human Condition*. Chicago: University of Chicago Press.

Ariés, P. (1960). *L'Enfant et la Vie Familiale sous L'Ancien Régime*. Paris: Plon.

Asch, S. E. (1946). Forming impressions of personality. *Journal of Abnormal and Social Psychology, 41*, 258–290.

Asch, S. E. (l952). *Social Psychology*. New York: Prentice Hall.

Augoustinos, M. (1991). Consensual representations of the social structure in different age groups. *British Journal of Social Psychology, 30*, 193–205.

Augoustinos, M., & Innes, J. M. (1990). Towards an integration of social representations and social schema theory. *British Journal of Social Psychology, 29*, 213–231.

Augoustinos, M., Tuffin, K., & Rapley, M. (1999). Genocide or a "failure to gel?" Racism, history, and nationalism in Australian talk. *Discourse & Society, 10*, 351–378.

Augoustinos, M., & Walker, I. (1995). *Social Cognition. An Integrated Introduction*. London: Sage.

Bache, R.M. (1895). Reaction time with reference to race. *Psychological Review, 2*, 475–486.

Bachelard, M. (1997). *The Great Land Grab*. Melbourne: Hyland House Publishing.

Bangerter, A., & Lehmann, K. (1997). Serial reproduction as a method for studying social representations. *Papers on Social Representations, 6*, 141–154.

Banks, R. R., & Eberhardt, J. L. (1998). Social psychological processes and the legal bases of racial categorization. In J. L. Eberhardt & S. T. Fiske (Eds.), *Confronting Racism: The Problem and the Response* (pp. 54–75). Thousand Oaks, CA: Sage.

Banton, M. (1988). *Racial Consciousness*. London: Longman.

Bargh, J. A. (1994). The four horsemen of automaticity: Awareness, intention, efficiency, and control in social cognition. In R. S. Wyer, Jr, & T. K. Srull (Eds.), *Handbook of Social Cognition* (Vol. 1) (pp. 1–40). Hillsdale, NJ: Erlbaum.

Bargh, J. A., Chen, M., & Burrows, L. (1996). Automaticity of social behavior: Direct effects of trait construct and stereotype activation on action. *Journal of Personality and Social Psychology, 71*, 230–244.

Barthes, R. (1964). Rhétorique de l'image, *Communicatins 4*; trad. It. (1985) La retorica dell'immagine, in *L'Ovvio e l'Ottuso*, Torino, Einaudi.

Bartlett, F. C., (1967). *Remembering*. Cambridge: Cambridge University Press.

Bateson, G. (1954). Une théorie du jeu et du fantasme. In G. Bateson (1977), *Vers une Ecologie de l'esprit, Tome I* (pp. 209–224). Paris: Seuil.

Bateson, G. (1979). *Mind and Nature: A Necessary Unity*. New York: Dutton.

Bauer, M. W., & Gaskell, G. (1999). Towards a paradigm for research on social representations. *Journal for the Theory of Social Behaviour, 29* (2), 163–186.

Bauman, Z. (1982). *Memories of Class. The Pre-history and After-life of Class*. London: Routledge & Kegan Paul.

Baumeister, R. F., & Leary, M. R. (1995). The need to belong: Desire for interpersonal attachments as a fundamental human motivation. *Psychological Bulletin, 117,* 497–529.

Beck, U., Giddens, A., & Lash, S. (1994). *Reflexive Modernization: Politics, Tradition and Aesthetics in the Modern Social Order*. Cambridge: Polity Press.

Bell, D. (1992). *Faces at the Bottom of the Well: The Permanence of Racism*. New York: Basic Books.

Bem, S. L. (1981). Gender-schema theory: A cognitive account of sex-typing. *Psychological Review, 88,* 354–364.

Bem, S. L. (1982). Gender-schema theory and self-schema theory compared. *Journal of Personality and Social Psychology, 43,* 1192–1194.

Bem, S. L. (1993). *The Lenses of Gender. Transforming the Debate on Sexual Inequality*. New Haven & London: Yale University Press.

Bentler, P. M., & Speckart, G. (1979). Models of attitude—behaviour relations. *Psychological Review, 86,* 452–464.

Berger, P. L., & Luckmann, R. (1967). *The Social Construction of Reality*. Harmondsworth: Penguin.

Bhabha, H. K. (1994). *The Location of Culture*. London: Routledge.

Biernat, M. (1991). Gender stereotypes and the relationship between masculinity and femininity: A developmental analysis. *Journal of Personality and Social Psychology, 61,* 351–365.

Billig, M. (1988). Social representations, objectification and anchoring: A rhetorical analysis. *Social Behavior, 3,* 1–16.

Billig, M. (1991). *Ideology and Opinions*. London: Sage.

Billig, M. (1996). *Arguing and Thinking: A Rhetorical Approach to Social Psychology* (2nd ed.). Cambridge: Cambridge University Press.

Blonsky, M. (1994, February 25). About advertising. Mixing peril and apparel. *New York Newsday*, pp. 56–58.

Blumenfeld-Kosinski, R. (1990). *Not of Women Born: Representations of Caesarean Birth in Medieval and Renaissance Culture*. Ithaca: Cornell University Press.

Blumer, H. (1969). *Symbolic Interactionism: Perspectives and Method*. Englewood Cliffs: Prentice Hall.

Bonaiuto, M., Breakwell, G. M., & Cano, I. (1996). Identity processes and environmental threat: The effects of nationalism and local identity upon perception of beach pollution. *Journal of Community & Applied Social Psychology, 6,* 157–175.

Bourdieu, P., & de Saint-Martin, M. (1978). Le patronat. *Actes de la Recherche en Sciences Sociales, 20–21,* 3–82.

Breakwell, G. M. (1979). Women: Group and identity? *Women's Studies International Quarterly, 2,* 9–17.

Breakwell, G. M. (1986). *Coping with Threatened Identities*. London: Methuen.

Breakwell, G. M. (1993). Integrating paradigms, methodological implications. In G. M.

Breakwell & D. V. Canter (Eds.), *Empirical Approaches to Social Representations* (pp. 180–201). Oxford: Oxford University Press.

Breakwell, G. M. (1994). The echo of power: A framework for social psychological research [The Myers Lecture]. *The Psychologist, 7* (2), 65–72.

Breakwell, G. M., & Beardsell, S. (1992). Gender, parental and peer influences upon science attitudes and activities. *Public Understanding of Science, 1* (2), 183–197.

Breakwell, G. M., & Canter, D. (Eds.). (1993). *Empirical Approaches to Social Representations.* Oxford: Oxford University Press.

Brewer, M. B. (1991). The social self: On being the same and different at the same time. *Personality and Social Psychology Bulletin, 17,* 475–482.

Brewer, M. B. (1997). On the social origins of human nature. In C. McGarty & S. A. Haslam (Eds.), *The Message of Social Psychology* (pp. 54–62). Oxford: Blackwell Publishers.

Broverman, I. K., Vogel, S. R., Broverman, D. M., Clarkson, F. E., & Rozenkrantz, P. S. (1972). Sex-role stereotypes: A current appraisal. *Journal of Social Issues, 28,* 59–78.

Bruner, J. (1991). *Acts of Mind* . Cambridge, MA: Harvard University Press.

Calhoun, C. (Ed.). (1992). *Habermas and the Public Sphere.* Cambridge, MA: MIT Press.

Camporesi, P. (1995). *Juice of Life: The Symbolic and Magic Significance of Blood.* New York: Continuum.

Canguilhem, G. (1991). *The Normal and the Pathological.* New York: Zone Books.

Canter, D. V., & Monteiro, C. (1993). The lattice of polemic social representations: A comparison of the social representations of occupations in favelas, public housing, and middle-class neighborhoods of Brazil. In G. M. Breakwell & D. V. Canter (Eds.), *Empirical Approaches to Social Representations* (pp. 223–247). Oxford: Oxford University Press.

Caporael, L. R. (1997). The evolution of truly social cognition: The core configurations model. *Personality and Social Psychology Review, 1,* 276–298.

Carroll, J. S., & Payne, J. W. (1976). *Cognition and Social Behavior.* Hillsdale, NJ: Erlbaum.

Charng, H., Piliavin, J. A., & Callero, P. L. (1988). Role identity and reasoned action in the prediction of repeated behaviour. *Social Psychology Quarterly, 51* (4), 303–317.

Charuty, G. (1991). La maîtrise chrétienne de la démesure. In P. Chambat (Ed.), *Modes de Consommation, Mesure et Démesure* (pp. 163–171). Paris: Editions Descartes, coll. Université d'été, 1991.

Cassin, R. (1951). *La Déclaration Universelle et la Mise en Oeuvre des Droits de l'Homme.* Paris: Librairie du Recueil Sirey.

Cassirer, E. (1923) *Substance and Function.* Chicago: Open Court.

Chauchat, H., & Durand-Delvigne (1999). *De L'identité Du Sujet au Lien Social.* Paris: Presses Universitaires de France.

Chombart de Lauwe (1984). Changes of the representations of the child in the course of social transmission. In R. Farr & S. Moscovici (Eds.), *Social Representations.* Cambridge: Cambridge University Press.

Chomsky, N. (1975). *Reflections on Language.* New York: Pantheon Books.

Churchland, P. M. (1992). *Matter and Consciousness.* Cambridge, MA: MIT Press.

Cialdini, R. B., Levy, A., Herman, C. P., & Evenbeck, S. (1976). Elastic shifts of opinion: Determinants of direction and durability. *Journal of Personality and Social Psychology, 34,* 663–672.

Clémence, A. (1998). Le travail dans la pensée quotidienne. In M. Hunyadi & M. Manz (Eds.), *Le Travail Refiguré*. Genève: Georg.

Clémence, A., Doise, W., & Lorenzi-Cioldi, F. (1994). Prises de position et principes organisateurs des représentations sociales. In C.Guimelli (Ed.), *Structures et Transformations des Représentations Sociales* (pp. 119–152). Neuchâtel: Delachaux et Niestlé.

Clémence, A., & Doise, W. (1995). La représentation sociale de la justice: Une approche des droits dans la pensée ordinaire. *L'Année Sociologique*, *45*, 371–400.

Clémence, A., Doise, W., de Rosa, A. S., & Gonzalez, L. (1995). La représentation sociale des droits de l'homme: Une recherche internationale sur l'étendue et les limites de l'universalité. *Journal International de Psychologie*, *30*, 181–212.

Clémence, A., Egloff, M., Gardiol, N., & Gobet, P. (1994). *Solidarités Sociales en Suisse*. Lausanne: Réalités sociales.

Cole, M. 1997 *Cultural Psychology*. Cambridge : Harvard University Press.

Converse, P. E. (1970). Attitudes and non-attitudes: Continuation of a dialogue. In E. R. Tuffe (Ed.), *The Quantitative Analysis of Social Problems* (pp. 168–189). Reading, MA: Addison-Wesley.

Corsaro, W. (1990) The underlife of the nursery school: Young children's social representations of adult rules. In G. Duveen & B. Lloyd (Eds.), *Social Representations and the Development of Knowledge*. Cambridge: Cambridge University Press.

Crespi, F. (1996). *Manuale di Sociologia della Cultura*. Bari: Laterza.

Crocker, J., Major, B., & Steele, C. (1998). Social stigma. In D. T. Gilbert, S. T. Fiske, & G. Lindzey (Eds.), *The Handbook of Social Psychology* (Vol. 2) (pp. 504–553). New York: Oxford University Press.

Cross, W. E., Jr. (1991). *Shades of Black*. Philadelphia: Temple University Press.

Cross, W. E., Jr., & Fhagen-Smith, P. (2000). Patterns of African American identity development: A life span perspective. In B. Jackson & C. Wijeyesinghe (Eds.), *New Perspectives on Racial Identity Development*. New York: New York University Press.

Dahrendorf, R. (1964). The education of an elite: Law faculties and the German upper class. In P. Lazarsfeld & T. H. Marshall (Eds.), *Transactions of the Fifth World Congress of Sociology* (pp. 259–274). Louvain, Belgium: ISA.

Danziger, K. (1997). The varieties of social construction. *Theory and Psychology*, *7*, 399–416.

Dauzat, A. (1956). *Les Noms de Personnes: Origine et Evolution* (4th ed.). Paris: Librairie Delgrave.

de Abreu, G. (1993). *The Relationship between Home and School Mathematics in a Farming Community in Rural Brazil*. Unpublished doctoral dissertation, Cambridge University .

de Abreu, G. (1995). Understanding how children experience the relationship between home and school mathematics. *Mind, Culture and Activity*, *2*, 119–142.

Deaux, K., Reid, A., Mizrahi, K., & Ethier, K. (1995). Parameters of social identity. *Journal of Personality and Social Psychology*, *68*, 280–291.

Deaux, K., Reid, A., Mizrahi, K., & Cotting, D. (1999). Connecting the person to the social: The functions of social identification. In T. R. Tyler, R. M. Kramer, & O. P. John (Eds.), *The Psychology of the Social Self* (pp. 91–113). Mahway, NJ: Erlbaum.

DeFleur, M. L., & Westie, F. R. (1963). Attitudes as a scientific concept. *Social Forces*, *42*, 17–31.

De Giacomo, J. P. (1980). Intergroup alliances and rejections within a social movement. *European Journal of Social Psychology*, *76* (1), 138–140.

References

DeMott, B. (1990). *The Imperial Middle: Why Americans Can't Think Straight about Class.* New York: William Morrow.

Denzin, N. K., & Lincoln, Y. S. (2000). *Handbook of Qualitative Research* (2nd ed.). Thousand Oaks, CA: Sage Publications.

de Rosa, A. S. (1987). The social representations of mental illness in children and adults. In S. Moscovici & W. Doise (Eds.), *Current Issues in Social Psychology* (Vol. 2). Cambridge: Cambridge University Press.

de Rosa, A. S. (1988a). How to sell pullovers by provoking discussion on social issues. The role of the advertising for activating and diffusing controversial social representations. In V. Rirgas (Ed.) *S. R. and Contemporary Social Problems* (pp. 228–277). Athens: Ellinika Grammata.

de Rosa, A. S. (1988b). Sur l'usage des associations libres dans l'étude des représentations sociales de la maladie mentale. *Connexions, 51,* 27–50.

de Rosa, A. S., & Smith, A. (1997). Strategie comunicative da minoranza attiva nello scenario dei pubblicitari: il caso Benetton-Toscani. *Micro & Macromarketing, 1,* 99–126.

de Rosa, A. S., & Losito, G. (1996). E' bianca o nera ? Interpretazioni conflittuali e atteggiamenti contrastanti nei confronti della comunicazione pubblicitaria "ambigua" di Benetton. *Rassegna di Psicologia, 2,* (13), 75–115.

de Rosa A.S., Sinigaglia P., Abric J.C. (1996) *The Application of Two Projective Techniques to the Study of Advertising: The Associative Network and the Associative Card.* Paper presented during "Controversial social representations 'of' and 'around' advertising: how to sell pullovers by provoking discussion on social issues." Symposium organised at the at the 11th General Meeting of the E.A.E.S.P. (July 13th-18th, Gmunden, Austria).

de Rosa, A. S., & Smith, A. (1998a). Représentations sociales polémiques et styles d'influence minoritaire, la communication publicitaire de Benetton. *Bulletin de Psychologie, 51 436* (4), 399–416.

de Rosa, A. S., & Smith, A. (1998b). Retorica pubblicitaria e rappresentazioni sociali. La comunicazione Benetton come caso esemplificativo. *Ikon, Ricerche sulla Comunicazione Pubblicitaria, 37,* 173–208.

Deschamps, J.-C. (1982). Social identity and relations of power between groups. In H. Tajfel (Ed.), *Social Identity and Intergroup Relations* (pp. 85–98). Cambridge: Cambridge University Press.

Deschamps, J.-C., Lorenzi-Cioldi, F., & Meyer, G. (1982). *L'Échec Scolaire.* Lausanne: Favre.

Deutsch, M. (1985). *Distributive Justice.* New Haven: Yale University Press.

Devine, P. G. (1989). Stereotypes and prejudice: Their automatic and controlled components. *Journal of Personality and Social Psychology, 56,* 5–18.

Diaz-Veizades, J., Widaman, K. F., Little, T. D., & Gibbs, K. W. (1995). The measurement and structure of human rights attitudes. *Journal of Social Psychology, 135,* 313–328.

Doise, W. (1984). Levels of analysis in the experimental study of intergroup relations. In S. Moscovici & R. Farr (Eds.), *Social Representations* (pp. 255–268). Cambridge, MA: Cambridge University Press.

Doise, W. (1985). Les représentations sociales: Définition d'un concept. In W. Doise & A. Palmonari (Eds.) (1986), *L'Étude des Représentations Sociales. Textes de base en Psychologie* (pp. 81–94). Neuchâtel, Paris: Delachaux et Niestlé.

Doise, W. (1986). *Levels of Explanation in Social Psychology.* Cambridge: Cambridge University Press.

Doise, W. (1989). Attitudes et représentations sociales. In D. Jodelet (Ed.), *Les Représentations Sociales* (pp. 221–238). Paris: Presses Universitaires de France.

Doise, W. (1990). Social beliefs and intergroup relations: The relevance of some sociological perspectives. In C. Fraser & G. Gaskell (Eds.), *The Social Psychology of Widespread Beliefs.* Oxford: Clarendon.

Doise, W. (1992). L'ancrage dans les études sur les représentations sociales. *Bulletin de Psychologie, 45,* 189–95.

Doise, W. (1993a) Debating social representations. In G. M. Breakwell & D. V. Canter (Eds.), *Empirical Approaches to Social Representations* (pp. 157–170). Oxford: Clarendon.

Doise, W. (1993b). *Logiques Sociales dans le Raisonnement.* Neuchâtel: Delachaux & Niestlé.

Doise, W., Clémence, A., & Lorenzi-Cioldi, F. (1993). *The Quantitative Analysis of Social Representations.* London: Harvester Wheatsheaf.

Doise, W., & Herrera, M. (1994). Déclaration universelle et représentations sociales des droits de l'homme: Une étude à Genève. *Revue Internationale de Psychologie Sociale, 7,* 87–107.

Doise, W., Spini, D., & Clémence, A. (1999). Human rights studied as social representations in a cross-national context. *European Journal of Social Psychology, 29,* 1–29.

Doise, W., Staerklé, C., Clémence, A., & Savory, F. (1998). Human rights and Genevan youth: A developmental study of social representations. *The Swiss Journal of Psychology, 57,* 86–100.

Doms, M. (1983). The minority influence effect: an alternative approach. In W. Doise & S. Moscovici (Eds.) *Current Issues in European Social Psychology* (vol. 1) (1–32). Cambridge: Cambridge University Press.

Douglas, M. (1966) *Purity and Danger: An Analysis of Concepts of Pollution and Taboo.* London: Routledge and Kegan Paul.

Dovidio, J., & Gaertner, S. L. (1986). *Prejudice, Discrimination, and Racism.* Orlando, FL: Academic Press.

Duhem, P. (1903). *L'Invention de la Mécanique.* Paris: Chevalier et Rivière.

Durant, J., Bauer, M. W., & Gaskell, G. (Eds.). (1998). *Biotechnology in the Public Sphere: A European Source Book.* London: Science Museum.

Durkheim, E. (1983). *Pragmatism and Sociology.* Cambridge: Cambridge University Press.

Durkheim, E. (1996). Représentations individuelles et représentations collectives. In *Sociologie et Philosophie.* Paris: Presses Universitaires de France.

Durkheim, E. (1998). *The Elementary Forms of the Religious Life.* London: Routledge.

Durkheim, E., & Mauss, M. (1963). *Primitive Classification.* Chicago: Chicago University Press. (edited with an introduction by Rodney Needhan).

Duveen, G. (1994). Crianças enquanto atores sociais: As representações sociais em desenvolvimento. In S. Jovchelovtich & P. Guareschi (Eds.), *Textos em Representações Sociais.* Petropolis, Brazil: Vozes.

Duveen, G. (1997). Psychological development as a social process. In L. Smith, J. Dockrell, & P. Tomlinson (Eds.), *Piaget, Vygotsky and Beyond.* London: Routledge.

Duveen, G. (1998). The psychosocial production of knowledge: Social representations and psychologic. *Culture and Psychology, 4,* 455–472.

Duveen, G. (2000). Introduction: The power of ideas. In G. Duveen (Ed.), *Social Representations: Studies in Social Psychology. Serge Moscovici*. Cambridge, England: Polity Press.

Duveen, G., & Lloyd, B. (1986). The significance of social identities. *British Journal of Social Psychology, 25*, 219–230.

Duveen, G., & Lloyd, B. (1990). Introduction. In G. Duveen & B. Lloyd (Eds.), *Social Representations and the Development of Knowledge*. Cambridge: Cambridge University Press.

Eagly, A. H. (1987). *Sex Differences in Social Behavior: A Social-role Interpretation*. Hillsdale, NJ: Lawrence Erlbaum.

Eagly, A.H., & Chaiken, S. (1993). *The Psychology of Attitude Change*. Fort Worth, TX: Harcourt, Brace, Jovanovich.

Eagly, A. H., & Chaiken, S. (1998). Attitude structure and function. In D. T. Gilbert, S. T. Fiske, & G. Lindzey (Eds.), *The Handbook of Social Psychology* (4th ed., Vol. 1) (pp. 269–322). New York: McGraw-Hill.

Eagly, A. H., & Mladnic, A. (1989). Gender stereotypes and attitudes toward women and men. *Personality and Social Psychology Bulletin, 15*, 543–558.

Eco, U. (1976). *A Theory of Semiotics*. Bloomington, Indiana: Indiana University Press.

Eco, U. (1987). *Travels in Hyperreality: Essays*. London: Picador.

Eco, U. (1990). *The Limits of Interpretation*. Bloomington: Indiana University Press.

Edwards, D. (1991). Categories are for talking: On the cognitive and discursive bases of categorization. *Theory and Psychology, 1*, 515–42.

Edwards, D., & Potter, J. (1992). *Discursive Psychology*. London: Sage.

Elejabarrieta, F. (1994). Social positioning: A way to link social representations and social identity. *Social Science Information, 33*, 241–253.

Eley, G. (1992). Nations, publics and political cultures: Placing Habermas in the nineteenth century. In C. Calhoun (Ed.), *Habermas and the Public Sphere* (pp. 289–339). Cambridge: MIT Press.

Emler, N., & Dickinson, J. (1985). Children's representation of economic inequalities: The effects of social class. *British Journal of Developmental Psychology, 3*, 191–198.

Ericsson, K. A., & Simon, H. A. (1993). *Protocol Analysis: Verbal Reports as Data*. Cambridge, MA: MIT Press.

Erikson, E. (1968). *Adolescence, Youth and Crisis*. New York: W. W. Norton & Company.

Essed, P. (1991). *Understanding Everyday Racism*. London: Sage.

Evans-Pritchard, E. (1981). *A History of Anthropological Thought*. New York: Basic Books.

Farge, A., (1992). *Dire et Mal Dire. L'Opinion Publique au 17e Siécle*. Paris: Seuil.

Farr, R. M. (1987). Social representations: A French tradition of research. *Journal for the Theory of Social Behaviour, 17*, 343–370.

Farr, R. M. (1993). Common sense, science and social representations. *Public Understanding of Science, 2*, 189–204

Farr, R. M. (1993). Theory and method in the study of social representations. In G. M. Breakwell & D. V. Canter (Eds.), *Empirical Approaches to Social Representations* (pp. 15–38). Oxford: Clarendon.

Farr, R. M. (1995). Representation of health, illness and handicap in the mass media of communication: A theoretical overview. In I. Marková & R. Farr (Eds.), *Representations of Health, Illness and Handicap* (pp. 3–30). Chur: Harwood Academic Publishers.

Farr, R. M. (1996). *The Roots of Modern Social Psychology*. Oxford: Blackwell.

Farr, R. M., & Moscovici, S. (Eds.) (1984). *Social Representations*. Cambridge: Cambridge University Press.

Fazio, R. H. (1990). Multiple processes by which attitudes guide behaviour: The MODE model as an integrative framework. In M. Zanna (Ed.), *Advances in Experimental Social Psychology*, *23*, 75–109. San Diego: Academic Press.

Ferguson, G. O. (1916). The psychology of the Negro: An experimental study. In *Archives of Psychology* (Vol. 36). New York: Science Press.

Festinger, L. (1954). A theory of social comparison processes. *Human Relations*, *7*, 117–140.

Firbas J. (1992). *Functional Sentence Perspective in Written and Spoken Communication*. Cambridge: Cambridge University Press

Fischler, C. (1990). *L'Homnivore*. Paris: Odile Jacob.

Fishbein, M., & Ajzen, I. (1975). *Belief, Attitude, Intention and Behaviour*. London: Addison Wesley.

Fiske, A. P., Kitayama, S., Markus, H. R., & Nisbett, R. E. (1998). The cultural matrix of social psychology. In D. T. Gilbert, S. T. Fiske, & G. Lindzey (Eds.), *Handbook of Social Psychology* (Vol. 2) (4th ed.) (pp. 915–981). Boston: McGraw Hill.

Fiske, S. T. (1992). Thinking is for doing: Portraits of social cognition from Daguerreotype to laserphoto. *Journal of Personality and Social Psychology*, *63*, 877–889.

Fiske, S. T. (1993a). Controlling other people: The impact of power on stereotyping. *American Psychologist*, *48*, 621–628.

Fiske, S. T. (1993b). Social cognition and social perception. In M. R. Rosenzweig & L. W. Porter (Eds.), *Annual Review of Psychology* (Vol. 44) (pp. 155–194). Palo Alto, CA: Annual Reviews Inc.

Fiske, S. T. (1998). Stereotyping, prejudice, and discrimination. In D. T. Gilbert, S. T. Fiske, & G. Lindzey, (Eds.) *The Handbook of Social Psychology* (Vol. 1) (4th ed.) (pp. 357–411). New York: McGraw-Hill.

Fiske, S. T. (2000). Stereotyping, prejudice, and discrimination at the seam between the centuries: Evolution, culture, mind, and brain. *European Journal of Social Psychology*, *30*, 229–322.

Fiske, S. T., Glick, P., Cuddy, A., & Xu, J. (2001). A model of (often ambivalent) Stereotype content, based on social structure: Groups' status and competition predict their competence and warmth. Manuscript under review, Princeton University.

Fiske, S. T., & Taylor, S. E. (1994). *Social Cognition* (3rd ed.). New York: McGraw Hill.

Fiske, S. T., Xu, J., Cuddy, A. J. C., & Glick, P. S. (1999). (Dis)respect versus (dis)liking: Status and interdependence predict ambivalent stereotypes of competence and warmth. *Journal of Social Issues*, *55*, 473–491.

Fjæstad, B., Olsson, S., Olofsson, A., & v. Bergmann-Winberg, M.-L. (1998). Sweden. In J. Durant, M. W. Bauer & G. Gaskell (Eds.), *Biotechnology in the Public Sphere* (pp.130–143). London: Science Museum.

Flament, C. (1982). Du biais d'équilibre structural à la représentation du groupe. In J.-P. Codol and J.-P. Leyens (Eds.). *Cognitive Analysis of Social Behavior*. Martinus Nijhoff: The Hague (Netherlands), 151–168.

Flament, C. (1994a). Aspects périphériques des représentations sociales. In C. Guimelli (Ed.),

Structures et Transformations des Représentations Sociales (pp. 85–118). Neuchâtel: Delachaux et Niestlé.

Flament, C. (1994b). Le plaisir et la rémunération dans la représentation sociale du travail. *Cahiers Internatinaux de Psychologie Sociale*, *23*, 61–69.

Flament, C. (1994c). Structure, dynamique et transformation des représentations sociales. In J.-C. Abric (Ed.), *Pratiques Sociales et Représentations* (pp. 37–57). Paris: Presses Universitaires de France.

Flament, C., Abric, J.-C., & Doise, W. (1998). Recherches expérimentales sur les représentations sociales. In J.-L. Beauvois & R.-V. Joule (eds.) *Vingt Ans de Recherche en Psychologie Sociale*. Grenoble: PUG.

Fleck, L. (1936). The problem of epistemology. In R. S. Cohen & T. Schnelle (Eds.) (1986), *Cognition and Fact, Materials on Ludwig Fleck*. Boston Studies in the Philosophy of Science, vol. 87. Dordrecht, Holland: Reidel.

Flick, U. (1995). Social representations. In J. Smith, R. Harré & L. Langenbore (Eds.), *Rethinking Psychology*. London: Sage.

Flick, U. (1998). *The Psychology of the Social*. Cambridge, MA: Cambridge University Press.

Fodor, J. A. (1992). *A Theory of Content*. Cambridge, MA: MIT Press.

Folkes, V. S., & Kiesler, T. (1991). Social cognition: Consumers' inferences about the self and others. In S. Robertson & H. H. Kassarjian (Eds.), *Handbook of Consumer Behavior*. Englewood Cliffs, NJ: Prentice-Hall.

Fraser, N. (1990). Rethinking the public sphere: A contribution to the critique of actually existing democracy. *Social Text*, *25*, 56–80.

Freud, S. (1921). Psychologie des masses et analyse du moi. *Oeuvres Complètes*. *Volume XVI* (pp. 1–84). Paris: Presses Universitaires de France.

Furth, H. G. (1996). *Desire for Society: Children's Knowledge as Social Imagination*. New York: Plenum Press.

Gamson, W. A., & Modigliani, A. (1989). Media discourse and public opinion on nuclear power: A constructivist approach. *American Journal of Sociology*, *95*, 1–37.

Gardner, H. (1985). *The Mind's New Science*. New York: Basic Books.

Gaskell, G., Bauer, M., & Durant, J. et al. (1997, June 26). Europe ambivalent on biotechnology. *Nature*, *387*, 845–847.

Gaskell, G., Wright, D., & O'Muircheartaigh, C. (1995). Context effects in the measurement of attitudes: A comparison of the consistency and framing explanations. *British Journal of Social Psychology*, *34*, 383–393.

Geertz, C. (1993a). *Local Knowledge*. London: Fontana Press.

Geertz, C. (1993b). *The Interpretation of Cultures*. London: Fontana Books.

Gellner, E. (1992). *Reason and Culture*. Oxford: Blackwell Publishers.

Gerard, H. B., & Orive, R. (1987). The dynamics of opinion formation. In L. Berkowitz (Ed.), *Advances in Experimental Social Psychology* (Vol. 20) (pp. 171–201). San Diego: Academic Press.

Gerard, H. B., & Wagner, W. (1981). *Opinion importance, co-orientation and social comparison*. Unpublished manuscript, University of California, Los Angeles.

Gergen, K. J. (1994). *Realities and Relationships*. Cambridge, MA: Harvard University Press.

Gervais, M. C., & Jovchelovitch, S. (1998). Health and identity: The case of the Chinese community in England. *Social Science Information, 37* (4), 709–729.

Gibson, J. J. (1986). *The Ecological Approach to Visual Perception.* Hillsdale, NJ: Lawrence Erlbaum Associates.

Giddens, A. (1971). *Capitalism and Modern Social Theory: An Analysis of the Writings of Marx, Durkheim and Max Weber.* Cambridge: Cambridge University Press.

Giddens, A. (1978). *Durkheim.* London: Fontana Books.

Gigerenzer, G. (1991). From tools to heuristics: A heuristic of discovery in cognitive psychology. *Psychological Review, 98,* 254–267.

Gilbert, G. M. (1951). Stereotype persistence and change among college students. *Journal of Abnormal and Social Psychology, 46,* 245–254.

Gilligan, C. (1982). *In a Different Voice.* Cambridge, MA: Harvard University Press.

Glass, R. (1964). Insiders-outsiders: The position of minorities. In P. Lazarsfeld & T. H. Marshall (Eds.), *Transactions of the Fifth World Congress of Sociology* (pp. 141–156). Louvain: ISA.

Glick, P., & Fiske, S. T. (in press). Ambivalent stereotypes as legitimizing ideologies: Differentiating paternalistic and envious prejudice. In J. T. Jost & B. Major (Eds.), *The Psychology of Legitimacy: Ideology, Justice, and Intergroup Relations.* Cambridge: Cambridge University Press.

Goldmann, L. (1976). *Cultural Creation in Modern Society.* Saint Louis: Telos Press.

Goody, J. (1977). *The Domestication of the Savage Mind.* Cambridge: Cambridge University Press.

Gould, S. J. (1980). *The Panda's Thumb: More Reflections in Natural History.* New York: Norton

Graumann, C. F. (1986). The individuation of the social and the desocialisation of the individual: Floyd Allport's contribution to social psychology. In C. F. Graumann & S. Moscovici (Eds.), *Changing Conceptions of Crowd Mind and Behavior* (pp. 97–116). New York: Springer-Verlag.

Graumann, C. F. (1996). The Origins of the EAESP: Social Psychology in Europe. In B. Rime (Ed.) EAESP Profile: A Guide to the European Association of Experimental Social Psychology. Munster, Germany.

Greenwald, A. G., & Banaji, M. R. (1995). Implicit social cognition: Attitudes, self-esteem, and stereotypes. *Psychological Review, 102,* 4–27.

Greenwald, A. G., McGhee, D. E., & Schwartz, J. L. K. (1998). Measuring individual differences in implicit cognition: The implicit association test. *Journal of Personality and Social Psychology, 74,* 1464–1480.

Greenwood, J. D. (Ed.) (1990). *The Future of Folk Psychology.* Cambridge: Cambridge University Press.

Greimas, A. J. (1970). *Du Sens.* Paris: Seuil. Trad. It. (1974). *Del senso.* Milano: Bompiani.

Grice, P. (1989). *Studies in the Way of Words.* Cambridge, MA: Harvard University Press.

Griffith, D. R. (1984). *La Pensée Animale.* trad. Fr.: Paris, Denoël, 1988.

Griffitt, W., & Veitch, R. (1974). Pre-acquaintance, attitude similarity and attraction revisited: Ten days in a fallout shelter. *Sociometry, 37,* 163–173.

Grize, J. B., Vergès, P., & Silem, A. (1987). *Salariés Face aux Nouvelles Technologies.* Paris: CNRS.

Guillaumin, C. (1992). *Sexe, Race et Pratique du Pouvoir*. Paris: Côté-Femmes.

Guimelli, C. (1994). Transformation des représentations sociales, pratiques nouvelles et schèmes cognitifs de base. In C. Guimelli (Ed.), *Structures et Transformations des Représentations Sociales* (pp. 171–198). Neuchâtel: Delachaux et Niestlé.

Guimelli, C. (1998). Differentiation between the central core elements of social representations. *Swiss Journal of Psychology, 57* (4), 209–224.

Guiot, J. M. (1977). Attribution and identity construction: Some comments. *American Sociological Review, 42*, 692–704.

Gunji, T. (1982). *Towards a Computational Theory of Pragmatics*. Indian University Linguistics Club (mimeograph).

Habermas, J. (1973). Wahrheitstheorien [Theories of truth]. In H. Fahrenbach (Ed.), *Wirklichkeit und Reflexion* [Reality and Reflection]. Pfullingen, Germany: Neske Verlag.

Habermas, J. (1989). *The Structural Transformation of the Public Sphere: An Inquiry into a Category of Bourgeois Society*. Cambridge: Polity Press.

Habermas, J. (1991). *The Theory of Communicative Action: Reason and the Rationalization of Society*. Cambridge: Polity Press.

Habermas, J. (1992). Further reflections on the public sphere. In C. Calhoun (Ed.), *Habermas and the Public Sphere* (pp. 421–461). Cambridge, MA: MIT Press.

Hacking, J. (1989). *Representing and Intervening*. Cambridge: Cambridge University Press.

Hamilton, D. L., & Gifford, R. K. (1976). Illusory correlation in interpersonal perception: A cognitive basis for stereotypic judgments. *Journal of Experimental Social Psychology, 12*, 392–407.

Hamilton, D. L., & Sherman, J. W. (1994). Stereotypes. In R. S. Wyer Jr. & T. K. Srull (Eds.), *Handbook of Social Cognition* (Vol. 2) (pp. 1–68). Hillsdale, NJ: Lawrence Erlbaum.

Hamilton, D. L., Stroessner, S. J., & Driscoll, D. M. (1994). Social cognition and the study of stereotypes. In P. G. Devine, D. L. Hamilton, & T. M. Ostrom (Eds.), *Social Cognition: Contributions to Classic Issues in Social Psychology* (pp. 291–321). New York: Springer.

Hamilton, M. C. (1991). Masculine bias in the attribution of personhood: people = male and male = people. *Psychology of Women Quarterly, 15*, 393–402.

Hardin, C., & Higgins, E. T. (1996). Shared reality: How social verification makes the subjective objective. In R. M. Sorrentino & E. T. Higgins (Eds.), *Handbook of Motivation and Cognition: Foundations of Social Behavior* (Vol. 3) (pp. 28–84). New York: Guilford.

Harding, S. (1986). *The Science Question in Feminism*. Ithaca: Cornell University Press.

Harman, G. (1986). *Change in View*. Cambridge, MA: MIT Press.

Harré, R. (1984). Some reflections on the concept of social representation. *Social Research, 51*, 927–938.

Haslam, S. A. (1997). Stereotyping and social influence: Foundations of stereotype consensus. In R. Spears, P. J. Oakes, N. Ellemers, & S. A. Haslam (Eds.), *The Social Psychology of Stereotyping and Group Life* (pp. 119–143). Cambridge, MA: Blackwell Publishers.

Haslam, S. A., Turner, J. C. , Oakes, P. J., McGarty, C., & Reynolds, K. (1998). The group as a basis for emergent stereotype consensus. In W. Stroebe & M. Hewstone (Eds.), *European Review of Social Psychology* (Vol. 8) (pp. 203–239). Chichester, UK: Wiley.

Hassan, A. (1986). *Social Representations of Female Circumcision*. Unpublished master's thesis, University of Surrey.

Heelas, P., Lash, S., & Morris, P. (Eds.). (1996). *Detraditionalization: Critical Reflections on Authority and Identity*. Oxford: Blackwell Publishers.

Heider, F. (1958). *The Psychology of Interpersonal Relations*. New York: Wiley

Heine, S. J., & Lehman, D. R. (1997). Culture, dissonance, and self-affirmation. *Personality and Social Psychology Bulletin, 23*, 389–400.

Heisenberg, W. (1975). *Across the Frontiers*. New York: Harper.

Herzlich, C. (1972). La représentation sociale. In S. Moscovici (Ed.), *Introduction à la Psychologie Sociale, Tome 1* (pp. 303–325). Paris: Larousse.

Herzlich, C. (1973). *Health and Illness: A Social Psychological Analysis*. London: Academic Press.

Higgins, E. T., & Bargh, J. A. (1987). Social cognition and social perception. *Annual Review of Psychology, 38*, 369–425.

Higgins, E. T., & Kruglanski, A. W. (Eds.) (1996). *Social Psychology: A Handbook of Basic Principles*. New York: Guilford.

Hollis, N., & Lukes, S. (1982). *Nationality and Relativism*. Cambridge, MA: MIT Press.

Holtz, R. and Miller, N. (1985). Assumed similarity and opinion certainty. *Journal of Personality and Social Psychology, 48*, 890–898.

Holub, R. (1991). *Jürgen Habermas: Critic in the Public Sphere*. London: Routledge.

Horton, R., & Finnegan R. (Eds.) (1986). *Modes of Thought*. London: Faber & Faber.

Hovland, C. I., Janis, I. L., & Kelley, H. H. (1953). *Communication and Persuasion*. New Haven: Yale University Press.

Hraba, J., Hagendoorn, L., & Hagendoorn, R. (1989). The ethnic hierarchy in The Netherlands: Social distance and social representation. *British Journal of Social Psychology, 28*, 57–69.

Humana, C. (1992). *World Human Rights Guide* (3rd ed.). New York : Oxford University Press.

Humphrey, J. P. (1984). *Human Rights and the United Nations: A Great Adventure*. New York: Dobbs Ferry.

Hurting, M.-C., & Pichevin, M.-F. (1990). Salience of the sex category system in person perception: Contextual variations. *Sex Roles, 22*, 369–395

Hutchins, E. (1995). *Cognition in the Wild*. Cambridge, MA: MIT Press.

Ignatow, G., & Jost, J. T. (2000). *"Idea Hamsters" on the "Bleeding Edge": Metaphors of Life and Death in Silicon Valley*. Unpublished manuscript, Stanford University, LA.

Isambert, F. A. (1982). Inégalités culturelles et différenciation religieuse. In J. Kellerhals & C. Lalive d'Epinay (Eds.), *Inégalités – Différences*. Bern: Lang.

Iyengar, S. S., & Lepper, M. (1999). Rethinking the value of choice: A cultural perspective on intrinsic motivation. *Journal of Personality and Social Psychology, 76*, 349–366.

Jackman, M. R., & Senters, M. S. (1980). Images of social groups: Categorical or qualified? *Public Opinion Quarterly, 44*, 341–361.

James, W. (1978). *Pragmatism and the Meaning of Truth*. Cambridge, MA: Harvard University Press.

James, W. (1981). *The Principles of Psychology*. Cambridge, MA: Harvard University Press.

Jaspars, J., & Fraser, C. (1984). Attitudes and social representations. In R. M. Farr and S. Moscovici, (Eds.), *Social Representations* (pp. 101–123). Cambridge: Cambridge University Press.

References

Jelsøe, E., Lassen, J., Mortensen, A. T., Frederiksen, H., & Wambui Kamara, M. (1998). Denmark. In J. Durant, M. W. Bauer & G. Gaskell (Eds.), *Biotechnology in the Public Sphere* (pp. 29–42), London: Science Museum.

Jodelet, D. (1984). Représentation sociale: phénomènes, concept et théorie. In S. Moscovici (Ed.), *Psychologie Sociale* (pp. 357–378). Paris: Presses Universitaires de France.

Jodelet, D. (1989) (Ed.). *Les Représentations Sociales*. Paris: Presses Universitaires de France.

Jodelet, D. (1991). *Madness and Social Representations*. London: Harvester Wheatsheaf.

Jodelet, D. (1993). Indigenous psychologies and social representations of the body and self. In U. Kim & J. W. Berry (Eds.), *Indigenous Psychologies. Research and Experience in Cultural Context*. Newbury Park, London: Sage.

Jodelet, D. (Ed.). (1997). *Les Représentations Sociales*. Paris: Presses Universitaires de France.

Jost, J. T. (1995). Negative illusions: Conceptual clarification and psychological evidence concerning false consciousness. *Political Psychology, 16*, 397–424.

Jost, J. T., & Banaji, M. R. (1994). The role of stereotyping in system-justification and the production of false-consciousness. *British Journal of Social Psychology, 33*, 1–27.

Jost, J. T., Burgess, D., & Mosso, C. (In press). Crises of legitimation among self, group, and system: A theoretical integration. In J. T. Jost & B. Major (Eds.), *The Psychology of Legitimacy: Emerging Perspectives on Ideology, Justice, and Intergroup Relations*. New York: Cambridge University Press.

Jost, J. T., & Major, B. (Eds.) (In press). *The Psychology of Legitimacy: Emerging Perspectives on Ideology, Justice, and Intergroup Relations*. New York: Cambridge University Press.

Jovchelovitch, S. (1995). Social representations in and of the public sphere: Towards a theoretical articulation. *Journal for the Theory of Social Behaviour, 25* (1), 81–102.

Jovchelovitch, S. (1996). In defence of representations. *Journal for the Theory Social Behaviour, 26* (2), 121–135.

Jovchelovitch, S. (1997). Peripheral communities and the transformation of social representations: Queries on power and recognition. *Social Psychological Review, 1* (1), 16–26.

Jovchelovitch, S. (1998a). Emancipation and domination in social representations of public life. *Interamerican Journal of Psychology, 32* (2), 169–189.

Jovchelovitch, S. (1998b). *Hybridity in Social Knowledge: Belief, Representation and Identity among the Chinese Community in England*. Paper presented at the IV International Conference on Social Representations, Mexico.

Jovchelovitch, S. (1998c). Re(des)cobrindo o Outro: Para um entendimento da alteridade na teoria das representações sociais. In A. Arruda (Ed.) *Representando a Alteridade* (pp. 69–82). Petrópolis, Rio de Janeiro: Vozes.

Jovchelovitch, S. (2000). *Representações Sociais e Esfera Pública: Um Estudo Sobre a Construção Simbólica dos Espaços Públicos no Brasil*. Petrópolis, Rio de Janeiro: Vozes.

Jovchelovitch, S., & Gervais, M. C. (1999). Social representations of health and illness: The case of the Chinese community in England. *Journal of Community & Applied Social Psychology, 9*, 247–260.

Joyner, C. (1989). Creolization. In C. R. Wilson & W. Ferris (Eds.), *Encyclopedia of Southern Culture*. Chapel Hill, NC: University of North Carolina Press.

Judd, C. M., & Park, B. (1993). Definition and assessment of accuracy in social stereotypes. *Psychological Review, 100*, 109–128.

Kahneman, D., Slovic, P., & Tversky, A. (Eds.) (1982). *Judgment under Uncertainty: Heuristics and Biases.* Cambridge: Cambridge University Press.

Karlsson, J.C. (1995). The concept of work on the rack: Critiques and suggestions. *Research in the Sociology of Work*, 5, 1–14.

Kashima, Y. (2000). Recovering Bartlett's social psychology of cultural dynamics. *European Journal of Social Psychology*, 30, 383–403.

Kashima, Y., Yamagushi, S., Kim, U., Choi, S.-C., Gelfand, M., & Yuki, M. (1995). Culture, gender, and self: A perspective from individualism-collectivism research. *Journal of Personality and Social Psychology*, 69, 925–937.

Katz, D., & Braly, K. (1933). Racial stereotypes of one hundred college students. *Journal of Abnormal and Social Psychology*, 28, 280–290.

Katz, I., & Hass, R. G. (1988). Racial ambivalence and American value conflict: Correlational and priming studies of dual cognitive structures. *Journal of Personality and Social Psychology*, 55, 893–905.

Kelley, H. (1992). Common sense psychology and scientific psychology. *Annual Review of Psychology*, 43, 1–23.

Kenny, D. A., & La Voie, L. (1985). Separating individual and group effects. *Journal of Personality and Social Psychology*, 48, 339–348.

Kihlstrom J. F., & Cantor, N. (1984). Mental representations of the self. In L. Berkowitz (Ed.), *Advances in Experimental Social Psychology*, 17, 1–47. New York: Academic Press.

Kinder, D. R., & Sears, D. O. (1981). Prejudice and politics: Symbolic racism versus racial threats to the good life. *Journal of Personality and Social Psychology*, 40, 414–431.

King, M. L., Jr. (1964). *Why We Can't Wait.* New York: Signet Books.

Kirchler, E., & de Rosa, A. S. (1996). Wirkungsanalyse von Werbebotschaften mittels Assoziationsgeflecht. Spontane Reaktionen auf und überlegte Beschreibung von Benetton-Werbebildern. *Jahrbuch der Absatz und Verbrauchsforschung*, 1, 67–89.

Kite, M. E., & Deaux, K. (1987). Gender belief systems: Homosexuality and the implicit inversion theory. *Psychology of Women Quarterly*, 11, 83–96.

Kohlberg, L. (1981). *Essays in Moral Development. Vol. I: The Philosophy of Moral Development.* New York: Harper & Row.

Kohlberg, L. (1983). *Essays in Moral Development. Vol. II: The Psychology of Moral Development.* New York: Harper & Row.

Köhler, W. (1917). *L'Intelligence des Singes Supérieurs.* Paris: Presses Universitaires de France, Les classiques de la psychologie, Centre de Promotion de la Lecture, 1973.

Kotler, P., Clark, J. B., & Scott, W. G. (1997). *Marketing, Management: Casi.* Turin: Prentice-Hall.

Koyré, A. (1936). La sociologie française contemporaine. *Zeitschrift für Sozialforschung*, 5, 210–264.

Kripke, S. (1972). *Naming and Necessity.* Oxford: Oxford University Press.

Kripke, S. (1980). *Naming and Necessity* (2nd ed.). Oxford: Oxford University Press.

Kruglanski, A. W. (1989). *Lay Epistemics and Human Knowledge: Cognitive and Motivational Bases.* New York: Plenum.

Kruglanski, A. W. (1999, October). That "vision thing": The state of theory in social and personality psychology at the edge of the new millenium. Paper presented in N. Kerr

References

(Chair). *Theory Development and Testing in Social Psychology.* St. Louis, Missouri.

Kruglanski, A. W., & Webster, D. M. (1991). Group members reaction to opinion deviates and conformists at varying degrees of proximity to decision deadline and environmental noise. *Journal of Personality and Social Psychology, 61,* 215–225.

Kruglanski, A. W., & Webster, D. M. (1996). Motivated closing of the mind: "Seizing" and "freezing." *Psychological Review, 103,* 163–183.

Lahlou, S. (1996a). La modélisation de représentations sociales à partir de l'analyse d'un corpus de définitions. In E. Martin (Ed.). *Informatique Textuelle* (pp. 55–98). Coll. Etudes de Sémantique Lexicale. Institut National de la Langue Française. Paris: Didier Erudition.

Lahlou, S. (1996b). The propagation of social representations. *Journal for the Theory of Social Behaviour, 26* (2), 157–175.

Lahlou, S. (1998). *Penser Manger. Alimentation et Représentations Sociales.* Paris: Presses Universitaires de France.

Lakatos, I., & Musgrave, A. (1970). *Criticism and the Growth of Knowledge.* Cambridge: Cambridge University Press.

Lakoff, G. (1987). *Women, Fire and Dangerous Things: What Categories Reveal about the Mind.* Chicago: University of Chicago Press.

Lakoff, G., & Johnson, M. (1999). *Philosophy in the Flesh.* New York: Basic Books.

Landes, J. (1988). *Women and the Public Sphere in the Age of the French Revolution.* Ithaca: Cornell University Press.

Landi, P., & Pollini, L. (1993). *Cosa c'Entra l'Aids con i Maglioni?* Milan: Arnoldo Mondadori Editore.

LaPiere, R. T. (1934). Attitudes versus actions. *Social Forces,13,* 230–237.

Lauren, P. G. (1999). *The Evolution of International Human Rights. Visions Seen.* Philadelphia: University of Pennsylvania Press.

Laurens, S., & Masson, E. (1996). Critique du sens commun et changement social; Le rôle des minorités. *Cahiers Internationaux de Psychologie, 32,* 13–32.

Lazarus, R. S. (1991). *Emotion and Adaptation.* New York: Oxford University Press.

Lebart, L., Morineau, A., & Bécue, M. (1989). *SPAD-T. Système Portable pour l'Analyse des Données Textuelles, Mauel de l'Utilisateur.* Paris: Cisia.

LeCouteur, A., Rapley, M., & Augoustinos, M. (in press). "This very difficult debate about Wik": Stake, voice and the management of category memberships in race politics. *British Journal of Social Psychology.*

Lee, Y.-T., & Ottati, V. (1993). Determinants of in-group and out-group perceptions of heterogeneity. *Journal of Cross-Cultural Psychology, 24,* 298–328.

Legrenzi, P. (1993). Se puo imparare a ragionare. *Il Mulino, XLII,* 656–665.

Lerner, M. J. (1977). The justice motive: Some hypotheses as to its origins and forms. *Journal of Personality, 45,* 1–52.

Leung, K., & Bond, M. H. (1989). On the empirical identification of dimensions for cross-cultural comparisons. *Journal of Cross-Cultural Psychology, 20* (2), 133–151.

Levine, J. M., Resnick, L., & Higgins, E. T. (1993). Social cognition in groups. *Annual Review of Psychology, 44,* 585–612.

Lévi-Strauss, C. (1966). *The Savage Mind.* London: Weidenfeld & Nicholson.

Lévy-Bruhl, L. (1923). *Primitive Mentality.* London: George Allen & Unwin.

Lévy-Bruhl, L. (1985). *How Natives Think.* Princeton: Princeton University Press.

Lewin, K. (1943). Forces behind food habits and methods of change. *Bulletin of the National Research Council, 108,* 35–65.

Lewin, K. (1947). Group decision and social change. In T. M. Newcomb & E. L. Hartley (Eds.), *Readings in Social Psychology* (pp. 330–344). New York: Henry Holt & Co.

Lewin, K. (1951). *Field Theory in Social Science.* New York: Harper Brothers.

Lewin, K. (1952). Behaviour and development as a function of the total situation. *Field Theory in Social Science* (pp. 238–304). London: Tavistock Publications,

Leyens, J-P., Yzerbyt, V., & Schadron, G. (1994). *Stereotypes and Social Cognition.* London: Sage.

Linville, P. W., & Fischer, G. W. (1993). Exemplar and abstraction models of perceived group variability and stereotypicality. *Social Cognition, 11,* 92–125.

Linville, P., & Jones, E. E. (1980). Polarized appraisals of out-group members. *Journal of Personality and Social Psychology, 38,* 689–703.

Lloyd, B., & Duveen, G. (1989). The reconstruction of social knowledge in the transition from sensorimotor to conceptual activity: The gender system. In A. Gellatly, J. Sloboda & D. Rogers (Eds.), *Cognition and Social Worlds.* Oxford: Oxford University Press.

Lloyd, B., & Duveen, G. (1990). A semiotic analysis of the development of social representations of gender. In G. Duveen & B. Lloyd (Eds.), *Social Representations and the Development of Knowledge.* Cambridge: Cambridge University Press.

Lloyd, B., & Duveen, G. (1992). *Gender Identities and Education.* London: Harvester Wheatsheaf.

Lorenzi-Cioldi, F. (1988). *Individus Dominants et Groupes Dominés* [Dominant individuals and dominated groups]. Grenoble: Presses Univesitaires.

Lorenzi-Cioldi, F. (1991). Self-enhancement and self-stereotyping in gender groups. *European Journal of Social Psychology, 21,* 403–417.

Lorenzi-Cioldi, F. (1993). They all look alike, but so do we, sometimes . . . Perceptions of ingroup and out-group homogeneity as a function of gender and context. *British Journal of Social Psychology, 32,* 111–124.

Lorenzi-Cioldi, F. (1994). *Les Androgynes* [The androgynes]. Paris: Presses Universitaires de France.

Lorenzi-Cioldi, F. (1995). The self in collection and aggregate groups. In I. Lubeck, R. van Hezewijk, G. Petherson, & C. W. Tolman (Eds.), *Trends and Issues in Theoretical Psychology* (pp. 46–52). New York: Springer.

Lorenzi-Cioldi, F. (1997). *Questions de Méthodologie en Sciences Sociales* [Methodology of social sciences]. Paris: Delachaux and Niestlé.

Lorenzi-Cioldi, F. (1998). Group status and perceptions of homogeneity. *European Review of Social Psychology, 9,* 31–75.

Lorenzi-Cioldi, F., & Dafflon, A.-C. (1998). Norme individuelle et norme collective, I: Représentations du genre dans un société individualiste. *Swiss Journal of Psychology, 57,* 124–137.

Lorenzi-Cioldi, F., & Doise, W. (1990). Levels of analysis and social identity. In D. Abrams & M. Hogg (Eds.), *Social Identity Theory* (pp. 71–88). New York: Harvester.

Lorenzi-Cioldi, F., Eagly, A. H., & Stewart, T. (1995). Homogeneity of gender groups in memory. *Journal of Experimental Social Psychology, 31,* 193–217.

Lorenzi-Cioldi, F., & Joye, D. (1988). Répresentations de catégories soci-professionnelles: Aspects méthodolgiques. *Bulletin de Psychologie, 40,* 377–390.

Lorenzi-Cioldi, F., & Meyer, G. (1984). *Semblables ou Différents?* International Labor Office: Geneva.

Maass, A., & Clark, R. D. (1984). Hidden impact of minorities: Fifteen years of minority influence research. *Psychological Bulletin, 95,* 428–450.

Macrae, C. N., Milne, A. B., & Bodenhausen, G. V. (1994). Stereotypes as energy saving devices: A peek inside the cognitive toolbox. *Journal of Personality and Social Psychology, 66,* 37–47.

Mandelbilt, N., & Zachar, O. (1998). The notion of dynamic unit: Conceptual development in cognitive science. *Cognitive Science, 22,* 229–268

Maranda, P. (1990). *DiscaAn: Users Manual.* Quebec: Nadeau Caron Informatique.

Markus, H. R., Crane, M., Bernstein, S., & Siladi, M. (1982). Self-schemas and gender. *Journal of Personality and Social Psychology, 42,* 38–50.

Markus, H. R., & Kitayama, S. (1991). Culture and the self: Implications for cognition, emotion, and motivation. *Psychological Review, 98,* 224–253.

Markus, H. R., Kitayama, S., & Heiman, R. J. (1996). Culture and "basic" psychological principles. In E. T. Higgins & A. W. Kruglanski (Eds.), *Social Psychology: Handbook of Basic Principles.* New York: Guilford.

Markus, H. R., Mullally, P. R., & Kitayama, S. (1997). Selfways: Diversity in modes of cultural participation. In U. Neisser & D. Jopling (Eds.), *The Conceptual Self in Context* (pp. 13–61). Cambridge: Cambridge University Press.

Markus, H. R., & Oyserman, D. (1998). Gender and thought: The role of the self-concept. In M. Crawford & M. Gentry (Eds.), *Gender and Thought.* New York: Springer.

Marková, I., & Wilkie, P. (1987). Representations, concepts and social change: The phenomenon of AIDS. *Journal for the Theory of Social Behaviour, 17,* 389–410.

Marouda-Chatjoulis, A., Stathopoulou, A., & Sakellaris, G. (1998). Greece. In J. Durant, M. W. Bauer & G. Gaskell (Eds.), *Biotechnology in the Public Sphere* (pp. 77–88). London: Science Museum.

Maslow, A. H. (1943). A theory of human motivation, *Psychological Review, 50,* 370–396.

Mathesius, V. (1939). On the information-bearing structure of the sentence. In S. Kuno (Ed.) (1975). *Harvard Studies in Syntax and Semnatics* (pp. 467–480). Cambridge, MA: Harvard University Press.

Mauss, M. (1969). *Essais de Sociologie.* Paris: Editions de Minuit.

Mauss, M. (1985). A category of the human mind: The notion of person; the notion of self. In M. Carrithers, S. Collins & S. Lukes (Eds.), *The Category of the Person.* Cambridge: Cambridge University Press.

McGuire, W. J. (1984). Search for the self: Going beyond self-esteem and the reactive self. In R. A. Zucker, J. Aronoff, & A. I. Rabin (Eds.), *Personality and the Prediction of Behavior* (pp. 73–120). New York: Academic Press.

McGuire, W. J. (1986). The vicissitudes of attitudes and similar representations in twentieth century psychology. *European Journal of Social Psychology, 16* (2), 89–130.

McGuire, W. J. (1989). A perspectivist approach to the strategic planning of programmatic scientific research. In B. Gholson, W. R. Shadish, Jr., R. A. Niemeyer, & A. C. Houts

(Eds.), *The Psychology of Science: Contributions to Metascience* (pp. 214–245). New York: Cambridge University Press.

McGuire, W. J., McGuire, C. V., Child, P., & Fujioka, T. (1978). Salience of ethnicity in the spontaneous self-concept as a function of one's ethnic distinctiveness in the social environment. *Journal of Personality and Social Psychology, 36,* 511–520.

McLeod, J., Pan, Z., & Rusinski, D. (1995). Levels of analysis in public opinion research. In T. L. Glasser & C. T. Salmon (Eds.), *Public Opinion and Communication of Consent.* New York: Guilford.

Meeus, W. H. J., & Raaijmakers, Q. A. W. (1987). Administrative obedience as a social phenomenon. In: W. Doise & S. Moscovici (Eds.), *Current Issues in European Social Psychology* (Vol. 2) (pp. 183–230). Cambridge : Cambridge University Press.

Midden, C., Hamstra, A., Gutteling, J., & Smink, C. (1998). The Netherlands. In J. Durant, M. W. Bauer & G. Gaskell (Eds.), *Biotechnology in the Public Sphere* (pp. 103–117). London: Science Museum.

Milgram, S. (1974). *Obedience to Authority.* New York : Harper & Row.

Millett, D. (1981). Defining the "dominant group." *Canadian Ethnic Studies, 13,* 64–80.

Minski, M. (1986). *The Society of Mind.* New York: Simon & Schuster.

Moghaddam, F., & Vuksanovic, V. (1990). Attitudes and behavior towards human rights across different contexts: The role of right-wing authoritarianism, political ideology and religiosity. *International Journal of Psychology, 25,* 455–474.

Moliner, P. (1992). *La Représentation Sociale comme Grille de Lecture.* Aix-en-Provence: Presses Universitaires de Provence.

Moliner, P. (1995) A two-dimensional model of social representations. *European Journal of Social Psychology, 25,* 27–40.

Moliner, P. (1996) *Images et Représentations Sociales.* Grenoble: PUG.

Moliner, P., & Tafani, E. (1997). Attitudes and social representations: A theoretical and experimental approach. *European Journal of Social Psychology, 27,* 687–702.

Moscovici, S. (1963). Attitudes and opinions. *Annual Review of Psychology 14,* 231–260.

Moscovici, S. (1969). Preface. In C. Herzlich. *Sante et Maladie.* Paris: Mouton.

Moscovici, S. (1971). Introduction. In C. Faucheux & S. Moscovici, *Psychologie Sociale Théorique et Expérimentale.* Paris : EHESS, Mouton, coll. Les textes sociologiques, 8. 1971.

Moscovici, S. (1974). Quelle unité: avec la nature ou contre ? In E. Morin, & M. Piattelli-Palmarini (Eds.), *L'Unité de l'Homme. Pour une Anthropologie Fondamentale. Tome III* (pp. 286–319). Paris: Seuil, coll. Points.

Moscovici, S. (1976a). *La Psychanalyse son Image et son Public* (2nd ed.). Paris: Presses Universitaires de France.

Moscovici, S. (1976b). *Social Influence and Social Change.* London: Academic Press.

Moscovici, S. (1980). Toward a theory of conversion behavior. In L. Berkowitz (Ed.), *Advances in Experimental Social Behavior* (Vol. 13) (pp. 209–239). New York: Academic Press.

Moscovici, S. (1981). On social representations. In J. P. Forgas (Ed.), *Social Cognition: Perspectives on Everyday Understanding* (pp. 181–209). London: Academic Press.

Moscovici, S. (1982). The coming era of representations. In: J. P. Codol & J. P. Leyens (Eds.), *Cognitive Approaches to Social Behavior* (pp. 115–150). La Haye: M. Nijhoff.

References

Moscovici, S. (1984a). Le domaine de la psychologie sociale. In S. Moscovici (Ed.), *Psychologie Sociale* (pp. 5–24). Paris: Presses Universitaires de France.

Moscovici, S. (1984b). The phenomenon of social representations. In M. Farr & S. Moscovici (Eds.), *Social Representations* (pp. 3–69). Paris/Cambridge: Maison des Sciences de l'Homme and Cambridge University Press.

Moscovici, S. (1985). Comment on Potter and Litton. *British Journal of Social Psychology, 24,* 91–92.

Moscovici, S. (1988). Notes toward a description of social representations. *European Journal of Social Psychology, 18,* 211–250.

Moscovici, S. (1989). Des représentations collectives aux représentations sociales: Éléments pour une histoire. In D. Jodelet (Ed.), *Les Représentations Sociales* (pp.62–86). Paris: Presses Universitaires de France.

Moscovici, S. (1993). *The Invention of Society.* Cambridge: Polity Press.

Moscovici, S. (1994). La mentalité prélogique des primitifs et la mentalité prélogique des civilisés. In S. Moscovici (Ed.), *Psychologie Sociale des Relations à Autrui.* Paris: Nathan.

Moscovici, S. (1998). Social consciousness and its history. *Culture and Psychology, 4* (3), 411–429.

Moscovici, S. (2000). What's in the name? In M. Chaib & B. Orfali (Eds.), *Social Representations and Communicative Processes.* Jonkoping: Jonkoping University Press.

Moscovici, S., & Galam, G. (1994). Towards a theory of collective phenomena II, Conformity and power. *European Journal of Social Psychology, 24,* 481–495.

Moscovici, S., & Hewstone, M. (1983). Social representations and social explanation: From the "naive" to the "amateur" scientist. In M. Hewstone (Ed.). *Attribution Theory.* Oxford: Blackwell Publishers.

Moscovici, S., & Mugny, G. (Eds.) (1985). *Perspective on Minority Influence.* Cambridge, MA: Cambridge University Press.

Moscovici, S., & Mugny, G. (1987). *Psychologie de la Convertion.* Cousset: Delval.

Moscovici, S., & Vignaux, G. (1994). Le concept de themata. In Guimelli, C. (Ed.). *Structure et Transformation des Représentations Sociales.* Paris: Delachaux & Niestlé.

Mucchi Faina, A. (1987). Mouvement sociale et conversion. In S. Moscovici & G. Mugny (Eds.), *Psychologie de la Conversion.* Cousset: Delval.

Mucchi Faina, A. (1995). Processi di influenza, gruppi sociali e innovazione. In B. Zani (Ed.), *Le Dimensioni della Psicologia Sociale.* Roma: La Nuova Italia Scientifica.

Mucchi Faina, A., Maass, A., & Volpato, C. (1991). Social influence: The case of originality. *European Journal of Social Psychology, 21,* 183–97.

Mugny, G. (1991). *The Social Psychology of Minority Influence.* Paris: Maison des sciences de l' Homme.

Mullen, B. (1991). Group composition, salience, and cognitive representations: The phenomenology of being in a group. *Journal of Experimental Social Psychology, 27,* 293–323.

Nardin, G. (Ed.) (1987). *La Benetton. Strategia e Struttura di un'Impresa di Successo.* Roma: Edizioni Lavoro.

Needham, R., (1972). *Belief, Language and Experience.* Oxford: Blackwell Publishers.

Neisser, U. (1976). *Cognition and Reality.* San Fransisco: W. H. Freeman.

Nemeth, C. (1986). Differential contributions of majority and minority influence. *Psychological Review, 93*, 1–10.

Newell, A. (1973). You can't play 20 questions with nature and win. In W. G. Chase (Ed.), *Visual Information Processing*. New York: Academic Press.

Newell, A. (1990). *Unified Theories of Cognition*. Cambridge, MA: Harvard University Press.

Newell A. J., & Simon, H. (1972). *Human Problems Solving*. Englewood Cliffs, NJ: Prentice-Hall.

Nisbett, R.E., & Ross, L. D. (1980). *Human Inference: Strategies and Shortcomings of Social Judgment*. Englewood Cliffs, NJ: Prentice-Hall.

Nisbett, R.& Wilson, T. (1977). Telling more than we can know. *Psychological Review, 84*, 231–259.

Norman, D. (1972). *Memory and Attention*. New York: Wiley.

Oakes, P. J., Haslam, S. A., & Turner, J. C. (1994). *Stereotyping and Social Reality*. Oxford, UK: Blackwell Publishers.

Offe, C. (1985), Le travail comme catégorie sociologique. *Les Temps Modernes, 41*, 2058–2094.

Ortega y Gasset, J. (1967). *The Origin of Philosophy*. New York: W. W. Norton & Co.

Oyserman, D., & Markus, H. (1998). The self as social representation. In U. Flick (Ed.), *The Psychology of the Social*. Cambridge: Cambridge University Press.

Palmonari, A., & Pombeni, M. L. (1984). Psychologists vs. psychologists: An outlook on a professional orientation. In G. M. Stephenson & J. H. Davis (Eds.), *Progress in Applied Social Psychology*, (Vol. 2). Chichester: John Wiley & Sons.

Papastamou, S., & Mugny, G. (1985). Rigidity and minority influence: The influence of the social in social influences. In S. Moscovici, G. Mugny & E. Van Avermaet (Eds.), *Perspectives on Minority Influence*. Cambridge: Cambridge University Press.

Papineau, D. (1990). Truth and teleology. In D. Knowles (Ed.), *Explanation and its Limits* (pp. 21–44). Cambridge: Cambridge University Press.

Park, B., & Hastie, R. (1987). Perception of variability in category development: Instance versus abstraction-based stereotypes. *Journal of Personality and Social Psychology, 53*, 621–635.

Park, B., Judd, C. M., & Ryan, C. S. (1991). Social categorization and the representation of variability information. In W. Stroebe & M. Hewstone (Eds.), *European Review of Social Psychology, 2*, 211–245. Chichester, England: Wiley.

Parsons, A. (1969). *Belief, Magic and Anomie*. New York: The Free Press.

Pavlov, I. P. (1927). *Conditioned Reflexes: An Investigation of the Physiological Activity of the Cerebral Cortex*. London: Oxford University Press.

Percheron, A., Chiche, J., & Muxel-Douaire, A. (1988). *Le Droit à 20 Ans*. Paris: Institut de Formation Continue du Barreau de Paris - Fondation "Droit 2000."

Petrillo, G., & Lionetto, S. (1996). Spot anti-Aids e rappresentazioni sociali. *Ikon, 32*, 289–320.

Petty, R. E., & Krosnick, J. A. (Eds.) (1995). *Attitude Strength: Antecedents and Consequences*. Mahwah, NJ: Lawrence Erlbaum.

Philogène, G. (1994). African American as a new social representation. *Journal for the Theory of Social Behavior, 24* (2), 89–109.

References ———————————————————————————

Philogène, G. (1999). *From Black to African American: A New Social Representation.* Westport, CT: Greenwood-Praeger.

Piaget, J. (1932). *The Moral Judgment of the Child.* London: Routledge and Kegan Paul.

Piaget, J. (1954). *The Construction of Reality in the Child.* New York: Basic Books.

Piaget, J. (1965). *Etudes Sociologiques.* Geneva: Droz.

Pichevin, M.-F., & Hurtig, M.-C. (1996). Describing men, describing women: Sex membership salience and numerical distinctiveness. *European Journal of Social Psychology, 26,* 513–522.

Pinker, S. (1997). *How the Mind Works.* New York: W.W. Norton and Co.

Pitkin, H. F. (1967). *The Concept of Representation.* Berkeley: University of California Press.

Potter, J., & Wetherell, M. (1987). *Discourse and Social Psychology: Beyond Attitudes and Behavior.* London: Sage.

Pratesi, L. (1999). Art and advertising: Who's afraid of contamination? In Oliviero Toscani (Ed.). *Visual Art in United Colors of Benetton Communication, Leonardo Arte* (pp. 15–21). Venezia: Elemenond Editori Associati.

Purkhardt, S. C. (1995). *Transforming Social Representations.* London: Routledge.

Putnam, H. (1975), The meaning of 'meaning'. In K. Gunderson (Ed.), *Language, Mind and Knowledge. Minnesota Studies in the Philosophy of Science* (Vol. 7). Minneapolis, MN: University of Minnesota Press.

Putnam. H. (1983). *Realism and Reason.* Philosophical Papers (Vol. 3). Cambridge: Cambridge University Press.

Rasinski, K. A. (1987). What's fair is fair – or is it? Value differences underlying public views about social justice. *Journal of Personality and Social Psychology, 53,* 201–211.

Rateau, P. (1995). Le noyau central des représentations sociales comme système hiérachise. Une étude sur la représentation du groupe. Cahiers Internationaux de Psychologie Sociale, 26, 29–52.

Reicher, S., & Hopkins, N. (1996a). Seeking influence through characterising self-categories: An analysis of anti-abortionist rhetoric. *British Journal of Social Psychology, 35,* 297–311.

Reicher, S., & Hopkins, N. (1996b). Self-category constructions in political rhetoric: An analysis of Thatcher's and Kinnock's speeches concerning the British miners' strike (1984–5). *European Journal of Social Psychology, 26,* 353–371.

Reicher, S. D., Hopkins, N., & Condor, S. (1997). Stereotype construction as a strategy of influence. In R. Spears, P. Oakes, N. Ellemers, & S. A. Haslam (Eds.), *The Social Psychology of Stereotyping and Group Life* (pp. 94–118). Oxford: Blackwell Publishers.

Reinert, M. (1986). Classification descendante hiérarchique: une méthode pour le traitement des tableaux logiques de grandes dimensions, *Data Analysis and Informatics* (pp. 23–28). Amsterdam: Elsevier.

Reinert, M. (1993). Les "mondes lexicaux" et leur "logique" à travers l'analyse statistique d'un corpus de récits de cauchemars. *Langage et Société, 66,* 5–39.

Renteln, A. D. (1990). *International Human Rights: Universalism versus Relativism.* London : Sage Publications.

Ricoeur, P. (1981). *Hermeneutics and the Human Sciences.* Cambridge: Cambridge University Press.

Ridgeway, C. L., & Diekema, D. (1992). Are gender differences status differences? In C. L. Ridgeway (Ed.), *Gender, Interaction, and Inequality* (pp. 157–180). New York: Springer.

Righetti, P. (1993). *La Gazza ladra. Per una Visione Sociosemeiotica della Pubblicità*. Milano: Lupetti & Co.

Rokeach, M. (1970). *Beliefs, Attitudes and Values: A Theory of Organization and Change*. San Fransisco: Jossey-Bass.

Rosch, B.& Lloyd, B. (1978). *Stigmatization, Cognition and Categorization*. Hillsdale, NJ: Lawrence Erlbaum.

Rosch, E. (1975). Cognitive reference points. *Cognitive Psychology, 7*, 532–547.

Rosch, E. (1978). Principles of categorization. In E. Rosch & B. B. Lloyd (Eds.), *Cognition and Categorization* (pp. 27–48). Hillsdale, NJ: Erlbaum.

Rosch, E., Mervis, C., Gray, W., Johnson, D., & Boyes-Braem, P. (1976). Basic objects in natural categories. *Cognitive Psychology, 8*, 382–439.

Rose, D., Efraim, D., Gevais, M. C., Joffe, H., Jovchelovitch, D., & Morant, N. (1995). Questioning consensus in social representations theory. *Papers on Social Representations, 4* (2), 1–9.

Rouquette, M.-L. (1994). Une classe de modèles pour l'analyse des relations entre cognèmes. In C. Guimelli (Ed.), *Structures et Transformations des Représentations Sociales* (pp. 153–170). Neuchâtel: Delachaux et Niestlé.

Rowett, C. (1986). *Violence in Social Work*. (Institute of Criminology Monograph). United Kingdom: University of Cambridge.

Rozin, P. (1982). Human food selection: The interaction of biology, culture and individual experience. In L. M. Barker (Ed.), *The Psychobiology of Human Food Selection* (pp. 225–254). Westport, CT: AVI Publishing Company.

Rozin, P. (1990). Social and moral aspects of food and eating. In I. Rock (Ed.), *The Legacy of Solomon Asch: Essays in Cognition and Social Psychology* (pp. 97–110). Hillsdale, NJ: Lawrence Erlbaum.

Rozin, P., Haidt, J., & McCauley, C. R. (1993). Disgust. In M. Lewis & J. M. Haviland (Eds.), *Handbook of Emotions* (pp. 575–594). New York: Guilford Press.

Rozin, P., Millman, L., & Nemeroff, C. (1989). Operation of the laws of sympathetic magic in disgust and other domains. *Journal of Personality and Social Psychology, 50*, 703–712.

Rubin, J. Z., Provenzano, F. J., & Luria, Z. (1974). The eye of the beholder: Parents' views on the sex of newborns. *American Journal of Orthopsychiatry, 44*, 512–519.

Ruscher, J. B., Hammer, E. Y., & Hammer, E. D. (1996). Forming shared impressions through conversation: An adaptation of the continuum model. *Personality and Social Psychology Bulletin, 22*, 705–720.

Sacks, H. (1992). *Lectures on Conversation, Volumes 1 and 2*. G. Jefferson (Ed.), Oxford: Blackwell Publishers.

Said, E. (1993). *Culture and Imperialism*. London: Vintage.

Said, E. (1995). *Orientalism: Western Conceptions of the Orient*. London: Penguin.

Salmaso, P., & Pombeni, A. (1986). Le concept de travail. In W. Doise & A. Palmonari (Eds.), *L'Étude des Représentations Sociales*. Neuchâtel : Delachaux & Niestlé.

Sampson, E. E. (1977). Psychology and the American ideal. *Journal of Personality and Social Psychology, 35*, 767–782.

Sartre, J.-P. (1974). *Between Existentialism and Marxism*. London: New Left Books.

Schutz, A. (1944). The Stranger: An essay on social psychology. *American Journal of Sociology*, *49*, 500–507.

Searle, J. (1992). *The Rediscovery of the Mind*. Cambridge, MA: MIT Press.

Searle, J. R. (1995). *The Construction of Social Reality*. New York: Free Press.

Seifert, F., & Wagner, W. (1998). Medienaktivität zur Gentechnik in Österreich – eine Längsschnittanalyse [Media activity on gene-technology in Austria – a longitudinal analysis]. *SWS-Rundschau*, *38*, 249–264.

Sellers, R. M., Smith, M. A., Shelton, J. N., Rowley, S. A. J., & Chavous, T. M. (1998). Multidimensional model of racial identity: A reconceptualization of African American racial identity. *Personality and Social Psychology Review*, *2*, 18–39.

Semprini, A. (1994a). Benetton: dalla missione all' azione. *Micro & Macro Marketing*, *2*, 157–173.

Semprini, A (1994b). *Marche e Mondi Possibili*. Milano: Franco Angeli.

Semprini, A. (1996). *Analyser la Communication. Comment Analyser les Images, les Médias, la Publicité*. Paris: L'Harmattan (tr. It. *Analizzare la Comunicazione. Come Analizzare le Immagini, i Media, la Pubblicità*. Milano: F. Angeli, 1997).

Shaver, P. R. (2000, May). *Attachment, Aging, and Interpersonal Relationships*. Invited presentation at the Conference on Aging and Relationships, sponsored by the National Institute on Aging; held at the Department of Psychology, UC Berkeley.

Shaw, E. (1979). Agenda-setting and mass communication theory. *Intenational Journal for Mass Communication Studies*, *2* (25), 96–105.

Sherif, M. (1936). *The Psychology of Social Norms*. New York: Harper and Brothers.

Shweder, R. A. (1991). *Thinking Through Cultures: Expeditions in Cultural Psychology*. Cambridge, MA: Harvard University Press.

Shweder, R. A., & Sullivan, M. A. (1990). The semiotic subject of cultural psychology. In L. A. Pervin (Ed.), *Handbook of Personality: Theory and Research*. New York: Guilford.

Sidanius, J., & Pratto, F. (1999). *Social Dominance: An Intergroup Theory of Social Hierarchy and Oppression*. Cambridge: Cambridge University Press.

Simon, A. (1969). *The Sciences of the Artificial*. Cambridge, MA: MIT Press.

Smith, C. (1982). *Mothers' Attitudes and Behaviour with Babies and the Development of Sex-typed Play*. Unpublished doctoral dissertation, University of Sussex.

Smith, C., & Lloyd, B. (1978). Maternal behavior and perceived sex of infant: Revisted. *Child Development*, *49*, 1263–1265.

Smith, E. R. (1998). Mental representations and memory. In D. T. Gilbert, S. T. Fiske, & G. Lindzey (Eds.), *The Handbook of Social Psychology* (Vol. 1) (pp. 391–445). New York: Oxford University Press.

Smith, E. R., & Zárate, M. A. (1990). Exemplar and prototype use in social categorization. *Social Cognition*, *8*, 243–262.

Smith, E. R., & Zárate, M. A. (1992). Exemplar-based model of social judgment. *Psychological Review*, *99*, 3–21.

Smith, T. W. (1992). Changing racial labels: From "Colored" to "Negro" to "Black" to "African American." *Public Opinion Quarterly*, *56*, 496–514.

Sommer, C. M. (1998). Social representations and media communication. In U. Flick (Ed.)

(1998). *The Psychology of the Social*. Cambridge, MA: Cambridge University Press.

Spence, J. T. (1985). Gender identity and implications for concepts of masculinity and femininity. In T. B. Sondregger (Ed.), *Nebraska Symposium on Motivation: Vol. 32. Psychology and Gender* (pp. 59–96). Lincoln: University of Nebraska Press.

Sperber, D. (1990). The epidemiology of beliefs. In C. Fraser & G. Gaskell (Eds.), *The Social Psychological Study of Widespread Beliefs* (pp. 25–44). Oxford: Clarendon Press.

Sperber, D., & Wilson, D. (1986). *Relevance*. Cambridge, MA: Harvard University Press.

Staerklé, C., Clémence, A., & Doise, W. (1998). Representation of human rights across different national contexts: The role of democratic and non-democratic populations and governments. *European Journal of Social Psychology, 28,* 207–226.

Stainton Rogers, R., & Kitzinger, C. (1995). A decalogue of human rights: What happens when you let the people speak. *Social Science Information, 34,* 87–106.

Stangor, C., & Jost, J. T. (1997). Commentary: Individual, group and system levels of analysis and their relevance for stereotyping and intergroup relations. In R. Spears, P. J. Oakes, N. Ellemers & S. A. Haslam (Eds). *The Social Psychology of Stereotyping and Group Life.* Oxford: Blackwell Publishers.

Stangor, C., & Lange J. E. (1994). Mental representations of social groups: Advances in understanding stereotypes and stereotyping. In M. P. Zanna (Ed.), *Advances in Experimental Social Psychology* (Vol. 26) (pp. 357–416). San Diego, CA: Academic Press.

Staub, E. (1999). The roots of evil: Social conditions, culture, personality and basic human needs. *Personality and Social Psychology Review, 3,* 179–192.

Steele, C. M., & Aronson, J. (1995). Stereotype threat and intellectual test performance of African Americans. *Journal of Personality and Social Psychology, 69,* 797–811.

Stein, G. (1962). *Selected Writings.* New York: Vintage Books.

Stephenson, G. M., Brandstätter, H., & Wagner, W. (1983). An experimental study of social performance and delay on the testimonial validity of story recall. *European Journal of Social Psychology, 13,* 175–191.

Stevens, L. E., & Fiske, S. T. (1995). Motivation and cognition in social life: A social survival perspective, *Social Cognition, 13,* 189–214.

Stich, S., (1991). *The Fragmentation of Reason.* Cambridge, MA: MIT Press.

Stoetzel, J. (1963). *La Psychologie Sociale.* Paris: Flammarion.

Stryker, S. (1980). *Symbolic Interactionism: A Social Structural Version.* Menlo Park, CA: Benjamin Cummings.

Stryker, S. (1987). Identity theory: Developments and extensions. In K. Yardley & T. Honess (Eds.), *Self and Identity* (pp. 89–104). New York: Wiley.

Stryker, S. (1989). The two social psychologies: Additional thoughts. *Social Forces, 68,* 45–54.

Tafani, E. (1997). *Structure des Représentations Sociales et Attitudes.* Thèse de doctorat, Université de Provence, Aix-en-Provence, France.

Tafani, E. (2001). Attitudes, engagement et dynamique des representations sociales: Etudes experimentales. *Revue Internationale de Psychologie Sociale,* vol. 14 (1).

Tajfel, H. (1981a). *Human Groups and Social Categories: Studies in Social Psychology.* Cambridge: Cambridge University Press.

Tajfel, H. (1981b). Social stereotypes and social groups. In J. C. Turner & H. Giles (Eds.), *Intergroup Behavior* (pp. 144–167). Oxford: Blackwell Publishers.

References

Terkel, S. (1992). *Race: How Blacks and Whites Think and Feel about the American Obsession.* New York: New Press.

Thagard, P., & Nisbett, R.E.(1983). Rationality and charity. *Philosophy of Science, 50,* 250–267.

Thibaut, J. W. (1950). An experimental study of the cohesiveness of underprivileged groups. *Human Relations, 3,* 251–278.

Thoits, P. A., & Virshup, L. V. (1997). Me's and we's: Forms and functions of social identities. In R. Ashmore & L. Jussim (Eds.), *Self and Identity: Fundamental Issues* (Vol. 1) (pp. 106–133). New York: Oxford University Press.

Thomas, W. T., & Znaniecki, F. (1918). *The Polish Peasant in Europe and America.* Boston: Gorham Press.

Thompson, J. (1995). *The Media and Modernity: A Social Theory of the Media.* Cambridge: Polity Press.

Thrush, D., Fife-Schaw, C., & Breakwell, G. M. (1997).Young people's representations of others' views of smoking: Is there a link with smoking behavior? *Journal of Adolescence, 20,* 57–70.

Todorov, T. (1992). *The Conquest of America: The Question of the Other.* New York: Harper Perennial.

Toscani, O. (1995). *Ciao Mamma.* Milano: Mondadori.

Triandis, H. C. (1994). Theoretical and methodological approaches to the study of collectivism and individualism. In U. Kim, H. C. Triandis, G. Kagitcibasi, S.-C. Choi, & G. Yoon (Eds.), *Individualism and Collectivism* (pp. 41–51). London: Sage.

Tselikas, E. (1986). *Minderheit und Soziale Identitat.* Konigstein: Verlag Anton Hain.

Turner, J. C. (1985). Social categorization and the self-concept: A social cognitive theory of group behavior. In E. Lawler (Ed.), *Advances in Group Processes* (Vol. 2) (pp. 77–122). Greenwich, CT: JAI Press.

Turner, J. C. (1991). *Social Influence.* Buckingham, UK: Open University Press.

Turner, J. C., Hogg, M. A., Oakes, P. J., Reicher, S. D., & Wetherell, M. (1987). *Rediscovering the Social Group: A Self-categorization Theory.* Oxford: Blackwell Publishers.

Twigger-Ross, C., & Breakwell, G. M. (1999, April). Risk Communication Symposium. BPS Annual Conference, Belfast.

Uexküll, J. von (1934). Mondes animaux et monde humain. Suivi de *Théorie de la Signification.* Paris: Médiations, Gonthier, 1965.

United Nations Development Programme (1996). *Human Development Report.* New York : United Nations Development Programme.

Valsiner, J. (1997). *Culture and the Development of Children's Action.* New York: Wiley

Varela, F. J., Thompson, E., & Rosch, E. (1991). *The Embodied Mind: Cognitive Science and Human Experience.* Cambridge, MA: MIT Press.

Veil, H. (1869). *L'Ordre des Mots.* Paris: Librairie A. Franck.

Vergès, P. (1992). L'évocation de l'argent: une méthode pour la définition du noyau central d'une représentation. *Bulletin de Psychologie, XLV, 405,* 203–209.

Vergès, P. (1994). Approche de noyau central: propriétés quantitatives et structurales. In Ch. Guimelli (ed.), *Structures et Transformations des Représentations Sociales* (pp. 233–49). Neuchatel: Delachaux et Niestlé.

Vygotsky, L. S. (1962). *Thought and Language.* Cambridge, MA: MIT Press.

Vygotsky, L. S. (1978). *Mind in Society: The Development of the Higher Psychological Processes*. Cambridge, MA: Harvard University Press.

Vygotsky, L. S. (1994). Tool and symbol in child development. In R. Van der Veer & J. Valsiner (Eds.), *The Vygotsky Reader*. Oxford: Blackwell Publishers.

Wagner, W. (1988). Social representations and beyond: Brute facts, symbolic coping and domesticated worlds. *Culture and Psychology, 4*, 297–329.

Wagner, W. (1996). Queries about social representations and construction. *Journal for the Theory of Social Behaviour, 26* (2), 95–120.

Wagner, W. (1998). Social representations and beyond: Brute facts, symbolic coping and domesticated worlds. *Culture and Psychology, 4*, 297–329.

Wagner, W., Duveen, G, Themel, M., & Verma, J. (1999). The modernization of tradition: Thinking about madness in Patna, India. *Culture and Psychology, 5* (4), 413–445.

Wagner, W., Elejabarrieta, F., & Lahnsteiner, I. (1995). How the sperm dominates the ovum: Objectification by metaphor in the social representation of conception. *European Journal of Social Psychology, 25*, 671–688.

Wagner, W., Kronberger, N., Allum, N., de Cheveigné, S., Gaskell, G., Heinßen, M., Midden, C., Odegaard, M., Olsson, S., Rizzo, B., Rusanen, T., & Stathopoulou, A. (1998a). Images of biotechnology and nature. In J. Durant, G. Gaskell & M. Bauer (Eds.), *Biotechnology in the Public Sphere*. London: Science Museum.

Wagner, W., Torgersen, H., Seifert, F., Grabner, P., & Lehner, S. (1998b). Austria. In J. Durant, M. W. Bauer & G. Gaskell (Eds.), *Biotechnology in the Public Sphere* (pp. 15–28). London: Science Museum.

Wagner, W., Valencia, J., & Elejabarrieta, F. (1996). Relevance, discourse and the "hot" stable core of social representation – A structural analysis of word associations. *British Journal of Social Psychology, 35*, 331–351.

Walzer, M. (1990). What does it mean to be an "American"? *Social Research, 57* (3), 591–614.

Ward, R. (1958). *The Australian Legend*. Melbourne: Oxford University Press.

Weber, M. (1925). Grundriss der Sozialökonomik. Reprinted (5th ed.) in 1972 as *Wirtschaft und Gesellschaft*. Tübingen, Germany: J. Winckelmann.

Webster, D. M., & Kruglanski, A.W. (1998). Cognitive and social consequences of the need for cognitive closure. *European Review of Social Psychology, 8*, 133–173.

Wegner, D. M. (1994). *White Bears and Other Unwanted Thoughts: Suppression, Obsession, and the Psychology of Mental Control*. New York: Guilford.

Weick, K. E. (1979). Cognitive processes in organizations. In B. Staw (Ed.), *Research in Organizational Behavior: Vol.1*. Greenwich, CT: JAI Press.

West, C. (1994). *Race Matters*. New York: Vintage Books.

Wetherell, M., & Potter, J. (1992). *Mapping the Language of Racism: Discourse and the Legitimation of Exploitation*. London: Harvester Wheatsheaf.

Wicker, A. W. (1969). Attitudes versus actions. *Journal of Social Issues, 25*, 41–78.

Wilson, B. (1970). *Rationality*. Oxford: Blackwell Publishers.

Wittenbrink, B., Judd, C. M., & Park, B. (1997). Evidence for racial prejudice at the implicit level and its relationship with questionnaire measures. *Journal of Personality and Social Psychology, 72*, 262–274.

References

Wittgenstein, L. (1958). *Philosophical Investigations.* Oxford: Blackwell.

Yagi, T. (1993). *Global Vision.* Tokyo: Robundo Publishing Inc.

"Yellowfellas rort" system. (1998, July 27). *The Advertiser.*

Young, R. J. C. (1995) *Colonial Desire: Hybridity in Theory, Culture and Race.* New York: Routledge.

Yzerbyt, V. Y., Rocher, S., & Schadron, G. (1997). Stereotypes as explanations: A subjective essentialistic view of group perception. In R. Spears, P. J. Oakes, N. Ellemers, & S. A. Haslam (Eds.), *The Social Psychology of Stereotyping and Group Life* (pp. 20–50). Oxford: Blackwell Publishers.

Zavalloni, M. (1971). Social identity through focused introspection. *European Journal of Social Psychology, 1,* 235–260.

Zavalloni, M. (1980). Identité sociale et ego-écologie vers une science empirique de la subjectivité. In P. Tap (Ed.), *Identités Collectives et Changements Sociaux.* Toulouse: Privat.

Zavalloni, M. (1983). Ego-ecology: The study of the interaction between social and personal identity. In A. Jacobson-Wedding (Ed.), *Identity: Personal and Socio-cultural.* Atlantic Highlands, NJ: Humanities Press.

Zavalloni, M. (1986). The affective representational circuit as the foundation of identity. *New Ideas in Psychology, 5,* 333–349.

Zavalloni, M. (1998). Les vicissitudes des mots identitaires: Une lecture de Nietzsche. In V. Rigas (Ed.), *Social Representations and Contemporary Social Problems.* Athens: Ellenika Grammatika.

Zavalloni, M., & Louis-Guérin, C. (1984). *Identité Sociale et Conscience: Introduction à l'Ego-écologie.* Montréal: PUM.

Index

Index